International Nietzsche Studies

Nietzsche has emerged as a thinker of extraordinary importance, not only in the history of philosophy but also in many fields of contemporary inquiry. Nietzsche studies are maturing and flourishing in many parts of the world. This internationalization of inquiry with respect to his thought and significance may be expected to continue.

International Nietzsche Studies is conceived as a series of monographs and essay collections that will reflect and contribute to these developments. The series will present studies in which responsible scholarship is joined to the analysis, interpretation, and assessment of the many aspects of Nietzsche's thought that bear significantly upon matters of moment today. In many respects, Nietzsche is our contemporary with whom we do well to reckon, even when we find ourselves at odds with him. The series is intended to promote this reckoning, embracing diverse interpretive perspectives, philosophical orientations, and critical assessments.

The series is also intended to contribute to the ongoing reconsideration of the character, agenda, and prospects of philosophy itself. Nietzsche was much concerned with philosophy's past, present, and future. He sought to affect not only its understanding but also its practice. The future of philosophy is an open question today, thanks at least in part to Nietzsche's challenge to the philosophical traditions of which he was so critical. It remains to be seen—and determined—whether philosophy's future will turn out to resemble the "philosophy of the future" to which he proffered a prelude and of which he provided a preview, by both precept and practice. But this is a possibility that we do well to take seriously. International Nietzsche Studies will attempt to do so while contributing to the understanding of Nietzsche's philosophical thinking and its bearing upon contemporary inquiry.

—Richard Schacht

Nietzsche's Philosophical Context

NIETZSCHE'S PHILOSOPHICAL CONTEXT

An Intellectual Biography

Thomas H. Brobjer

University of Illinois Press

Urbana and Chicago

Library of Congress Cataloging-in-Publication Data

Brobjer, Thomas H.
Nietzsche's philosophical context : an intellectual biography /
Thomas H. Brobjer.
p. cm. — (International Nietzsche studies)
Includes bibliographical references and index.
ISBN-13: 978-0-252-03245-5 (cloth : alk. paper)
ISBN-10: 0-252-03245-4 (cloth : alk. paper)
1. Nietzsche, Friedrich Wilhelm, 1844–1900.   2. Philosophers—
Germany—Biography.   I. Title
B3316.B76   2007
193—dc2 [B]   2007035940

Contents

Preface

A large number of interpretations of Nietzsche's philosophy are published every year in the form of books and articles. But there has been a shortage of studies that show how Nietzsche worked and thought, to which questions and thinkers he responded, and by which of them he was influenced. A few such studies have been published, mainly in German, but they all deal with specific questions, thinkers, or books. Studies of the context of Nietzsche's philosophy, and especially of his reading, are essential for a correct understanding of his thinking and to avoid anachronistic interpretations. Nietzsche did not think in a vacuum. The present study aims to fill this gap by summarizing many years of work on his library and about his reading generally and by collecting all we know about the philosophical influences on him. He certainly read much more than he led us to believe, and this reading often constituted the starting point for, or counterpoint to, much of his own thinking and writing.

This study contains much previously unpublished information about Nietzsche's reading and library, including a great deal about the annotations he made in his books. It is the first extensive study of his reading, uncovering which books he read, carefully examining the evidence for when he read them, and attempting to say something about how he responded to that reading. This study contains much new information about books he read, acquired from many hundreds of previously undeciphered and unpublished book bills (from the Goethe-Schiller Archive in Weimar) and other sources. The sources of and stimuli for many of his philosophical concepts, such as will to power, Übermensch (overman), eternal recurrence, perspectivism, and nihilism are discussed in relation to the texts he read. Furthermore, through the examination of the books Nietzsche read and their content, I have been able to show, for example, that he had a reasonably extensive knowledge of figures of whom it previously has been assumed he had none—such as Søren Kierkegaard and Karl Marx—and also some knowledge of such figures as Max Stirner, Friedrich Engels, and William James. This book constitutes an intellectual biography of Nietzsche, written from the perspective of his reading of philosophical texts, and, more importantly, through its chronological presentation and discussion of Nietzsche's reading, broadens access to the philosophical context of his thinking and writing.

Note on References

Abbreviations	Titles in German and English	Year Published
AC	*Der Antichrist* (*The Antichrist*)	1895 (but written in 1888)
EH	*Ecce homo* (*Ecce Homo*)	1908 (but written in 1888)
FW	*Die fröhliche Wissenschaft* (*The Gay* [*or Joyful*] *Science*)	1882
FW V	*Die fröhliche Wissenschaft,* Book V (*The Gay Science,* Book V) (Book V and poems were added in the second edition in 1887.)	1887
GD	*Götzen-Dämmerung* (*Twilight of the Idols*)	1889 (but written in 1888)
GM	*Zur Genealogie der Moral* (*On the Genealogy of Morals*)	1887
GT	*Die Geburt der Tragödie* (*The Birth of Tragedy*)	1872
JGB	*Jenseits von Gut und Böse* (*Beyond Good and Evil*)	1886
M	*Morgenröthe* (*Dawn*)	1881
MA	*Menschliches, Allzumenschliches* (*Human, All Too Human*)	1878
NCW	*Nietzsche contra Wagner* (*Nietzsche contra Wagner*)	1895 (but compiled in 1888)

UB	*Unzeitgemäße Betrachtungen* (*Untimely Meditation*)	1873–76
UB I	*David Strauss: der Bekenner und der Schriftsteller* (*David Strauss, the Confessor and the Writer*)	1873
UB II	*Von Nutzen und Nachtheil der Historie für das Leben* (*On the Uses and Disadvantages of History for Life*)	1874
UB III	*Schopenhauer als Erzieher* (*Schopenhauer As Educator*)	1874
UB IV	*Richard Wagner in Bayreuth* (*Richard Wagner in Bayreuth*)	1876
VM	*Vermischte Meinungen und Sprüche* (*Assorted Opinions and Maxims*)	1879
W	*Der Fall Wagner* (*The Case of Wagner*)	1888
WM	*Der Wille zur Macht* (*The Will to Power*)	Compilation of Nietzsche's notes made by his sister and coworkers. Published in 1901 and 1906 and in an enlarged edition in 1911. Today these notes can be found in volumes 10–13 of KSA.
WS	*Der Wanderer und sein Schatten* (*The Wanderer and His Shadow*)	1880 (actually published in December 1879)
Za	*Also sprach Zarathustra* (*Thus Spoke Zarathustra*) (Four books; book four was published privately.)	1883–85

KSA is the conventional abbreviation for *Friedrich Nietzsche: Kritische Studienausgabe,* 15 vols., edited by G. Colli and M. Montinari (1967, 1980). Volume 14 is a commentary volume. KSB is the abbreviation for the corresponding eight volumes of Nietzsche's letters, by the same editors. These letters have not been translated into English except for a small selection by Christopher Middleton in

Selected Letters of Friedrich Nietzsche (Indianapolis: Hackett, 1969, 1996). I refer to Nietzsche's letters by recipient and date, which makes them easy to identify, as they are published in chronological order in KSB. Letters to Nietzsche have been published in the larger bound edition, KGB (*Friedrich Nietzsche: Kritische Gesamtausgabe: Briefe*).

KSA does not contain Nietzsche's writings before he became a professor at Basel in 1869. This material has been published in *Friedrich Nietzsche: Frühe Schriften,* 5 vols. (München: C. H. Beck'sche Verlag, 1933–40, reprinted 1994), abbreviated BAW (followed by volume and page numbers). These early writings are slowly being published in the bound edition KGW, section I (i.e., *Friedrich Nietzsche: Kritische Gesamtausgabe,* also initiated by G. Colli and M. Montinari). A concordance between the pages of the KSA volumes and the KGW volumes is included in KSA 15. However, since the identifying numbers (e.g., 5[171]) are the same in both versions, it is generally easy to find any KSA reference in KGW.

All translations from Nietzsche's letters and notebooks are mine, unless otherwise stated. For quotations from Nietzsche's published works, I have used Kaufmann's and Hollingdale's translations. As is customary, the references to the content of Nietzsche's published works are to sections (sometimes referred to as aphorisms) and not to page number, unless otherwise indicated. Since Nietzsche frequently uses ellipses in his texts, all omitted text in quotations is indicated by ellipses in brackets.

Acknowledgments

For good service in Nietzsche's library in Weimar over many years, I wish to thank Frau Schmidt, Frau Matteis, Frau Fox, Frau Schneider, Frau Kuhles, Frau Ellermann-Minda, Frau Schwitalla, Dr. Frank Simon-Ritz, the director of the Anna Amalia Bibliothek Dr. Michael Knoche, Dr. Jürgen Weber, Professor Ehrlich, and especially Herr Erdmann von Wilamowitz-Moellendorff. At the Goethe-Schiller Archive, Frau Dr. Roswitha Wollkopf kindly allowed me to examine Nietzsche's many book bills and other Nietzsche-related materials. Dr. Rüdiger Schmidt made several of my visits to Weimar most pleasant and helped fill them with interesting discussions.

The staff at the Staatsbibliothek in Berlin (especially Haus 2 at Potsdamer Platz) helped me find a very large number of books. I also owe gratitude to the philosophical libraries at the Freie Universität and the Humboldt Universität in Berlin as well as many other libraries, including the university library Carolina Rediviva in Uppsala.

I wish to thank Richard Schacht and Judith Rowan for suggestions and recommendations regarding questions of language and style during the long process of production of this book. The Index was prepared by Line for Line Indexing Services.

Chapter 1, "Nietzsche As Reader," is to a large extent based on an expanded version of my article "Nietzsche's Reading and Private Library, 1885–89," *Journal of the History of Ideas* 58 (1997): 663–93.

For financial support over the many years during which I have been working on problems relating to Nietzsche's reading and library, much of it in Berlin and Weimar, I owe gratitude to the Swedish Institute, the Wenner-Gren Foundation, STINT (The Swedish Foundation for International Cooperation in Research and Higher Education), and especially the Bank of Sweden Tercentenary Foundation.

Introduction

Most great philosophers are seen as figures towering above their time. In Nietzsche's case, such a view is perhaps especially pervasive, for he fostered it himself with his claims to be "untimely" and "a destiny" and with prophetic writings such as *Thus Spoke Zarathustra*. He further distanced himself from his time by his assertions that he read little, and in his books he rarely referred to minor or contemporary figures but rather "conversed" with, and criticized, the great names. This has resulted in an exaggerated view of Nietzsche's difference—and independence—from his time, and it seems to have prevented almost all serious attempts to place and understand his thinking in its true context. This tendency is further strengthened by the fact that Nietzsche is often seen as constituting a starting point (or precursor) of and major influence on many twentieth-century thinkers, writers, and traditions.

Contrary to Nietzsche's claims in *Ecce Homo* and elsewhere that he read few books and little in general, he was in fact a rather substantial reader, sometimes a voracious one. Furthermore, most of his reading, with a few exceptions such as Schopenhauer and Plato, was not of the great masters with whom he conversed or whom he attacked in his books but was instead of minor and contemporary authors and thinkers. The books by authors who are less well known today are also the ones in Nietzsche's private library that are the most heavily annotated.

Nietzsche lived a relatively isolated life. He was remarkably apolitical and passionately cultural and intellectual. The most important context of his life was his reading, but this is an aspect that has been almost completely neglected in virtually all general discussions of him and his thinking. However, a rigorous examination of the scope of his reading and its relevance is an enormous undertaking. Nietzsche's library alone contains more than a thousand titles—almost two thousand volumes—of which a large proportion show signs of having been read, and many are heavily annotated. Needless to say, he also read many other titles that are not in his personal library.

The present investigation is not an attempt to reduce Nietzsche's writings to a string of excerpts from books. Such an attempt would be doomed to failure. Instead, it should be seen as an attempt to get below the surface level of his writings, partially by attempting to determine sources to which his writings were a response, and to show that he read much more than he claimed and than has been assumed. But more fundamental is the attempt to better understand and make known the general context in which Nietzsche thought and wrote and his dependence on this context. It is only when this context is known that we can hope to understand more fully what he meant and the reasons for his attacks on other views. Often, I have only been able to point at much of this context and perhaps briefly discuss it (or list the tables of contents of some of the most relevant books). It is my hope that future studies will examine and discuss much of this reading and context in greater detail.

Nietzsche attempted from an early age to be untimely, and he made this into a supreme condition for being a good philosopher. I take this attempt seriously and believe that he carried it through more successfully than most other major philosophers. The success of this untimeliness is clearly apparent, for example, in his apolitical and antipolitical stance, and it was a major reason for his hostility to journals and newspapers. However, no matter how untimely a philosopher attempts to be, he or she will nonetheless, in many respects, unavoidably be a child of his or her time. An understanding of this timeliness is necessary not only for understanding Nietzsche from the perspective of an intellectual and cultural historian but also for a comprehension of his positions and views in the fields of ethics, epistemology, and aesthetics, and it helps us to understand the meaning of many of his ideas and metaphors.

When we look at what was written in Nietzsche's time, much of the timeliness of his thinking becomes visible. At least until the 1880s, he was an unexpectedly conventional thinker, borrowing more from other thinkers including his contemporaries, than has been recognized before now.[1] The young Nietzsche shared not only his love of antiquity and his silence about Christianity with most philosophers of his time but also his allegiance to Schopenhauer and Wagner, his concern with tragedy and pessimism, and his elevation of artistic values and perspectives. These attitudes were rather typical of thinkers during the 1860s and 1870s and are reflected in a number of books and philosophical articles of the time. Pessimism and an interest in Schopenhauer's philosophy were especially common among amateur philosophers. In fact, the early

Nietzsche was typical enough to be selected as representative of a certain type of nonacademic philosophical thinker in "Philosophy in Germany," a review of German philosophy published in *Mind* in 1877: "A prominent representative of this pessimistic strain in our literature is Prof. Friedrich Nietzsche of Basel. [...] In the writings of Nietzsche and others of the same stamp, the pessimistic mood is combined in a very peculiar way with an enthusiastic devotion to certain ideas closely related to religious mysticism. Richard Wagner and his music are ardently worshipped by this sect of pessimists."[2] Most of the reviews of Nietzsche's books published before 1889 (i.e., at a time when he himself could read them) emphasized his relation to Schopenhauer and Wagner. Furthermore, in all the more philosophically inclined books in which Nietzsche was discussed before 1889, he was classified as a relatively typical Schopenhauerian, although two of the books also considered him the most interesting one.[3]

In this book I discuss the philosophical influences on Nietzsche. He was a broad iconoclastic and cultural philosopher, and as such he often was influenced by some who cannot conventionally be regarded as philosophers: by authors and literary critics, by theologians and religious scholars, by historians and scientists, and so on. These are not discussed in the present study, which is limited to authors and works that, in a more conventional sense, can be called philosophical.[4] The philosophical books listed and discussed in this study constitute approximately one-fifth or fewer of all the books Nietzsche is known to have read.[5]

Schematically, the philosophical influences on Nietzsche can be divided into three groups: the most important ones, other lesser but nonetheless important ones, and various minor ones. The six most important philosophical influences on him—Emerson, Plato, Schopenhauer, Lange, Kant, and Rée (along with perhaps a few others)—are reasonably well known, and most of them are frequently discussed or mentioned in the secondary literature. An account of the philosophical influences on Nietzsche obviously cannot ignore them. On the other hand, among those whose writings taught him about philosophy and how to philosophize (and how not to do it), Hartmann, Dühring, Liebmann, Spir, Mill, Spencer, Teichmüller, and many others are also of great importance but much less well known. I will in this study concentrate on these important but lesser known influences on Nietzsche. After having discussed Nietzsche as reader, I will give a schematic overview in which the influences of the most important names are discussed and summarized (chapter 2). I then will return to and discuss a number of lesser-known but nonetheless important philosophical influences on him in chronological order. Occasionally, I will mention or discuss some of the less-important influences on him along the way. Many of them are relevant for particular periods in his development or for particular questions, and some of them are also likely to be more important than they have been recognized to be thus far (chapters 3–6). Books by these figures of apparently more limited importance are numerous and therefore difficult to address in a treatise of limited size.

To aid further research on the philosophical influences on Nietzsche, I provide a detailed chronological and an alphabetical listing of all of his known philosophical reading in tables at the end of the book. Some of these books may, after examination, turn out to have been much more important for his thinking than has been realized, while others may perhaps be less important. This listing is based, in addition to work in his library in Weimar over several years, on what he wrote in letters, notebooks, and, to a lesser extent, his published books; on letters to him; on secondary sources (such as Gilman's collection of descriptions and discussions of those who knew or met him);[6] and on the "Quellenforschung" published annually in *Nietzsche-Studien* that presents hidden, or unassigned, excerpts from his reading, which Nietzsche put into his notebooks and published texts.[7] I have gleaned further information from listings of the content of Nietzsche's library and the books he borrowed from libraries as well as from my examination of unpublished papers and several hundred receipts and bills for books he bought (kept in the Goethe-Schiller Archive in Weimar). Many of the authors and titles mentioned here were not previously known to have been read by Nietzsche, and only in a few cases has it been known when he read them. References to the locations where he discusses an author or text are given in table 1; therefore, these references are mostly omitted from the text itself.

I have made no attempt to exhaust the extensive secondary material about his relation to the themes and authors discussed in this book, but I have attempted to mention the most important discussions. For further bibliographical information about Nietzsche's relation to Schopenhauer, Hölderlin, and others, an extensive Nietzsche bibliography in Weimar has been published in five volumes, *Weimarer Nietzsche-Bibliographie* (2000–2003). It contains 18,465 entries and continues to be updated.[8]

This book accordingly is divided into two parts. After an introductory discussion of Nietzsche as reader, the second chapter discusses and summarizes the major philosophical influences on Nietzsche: Emerson, Plato, Schopenhauer, Lange, Kant, and Rée. A whole monograph could be written about each of these individuals, and several such monographs have, in fact, been written about Nietzsche's relations to most of them. I emphasize his known reading and knowledge of these thinkers and mention their most important influences on him, but I have limited the discussion of them to a few pages each to make room for discussions of other less-known or completely unrecognized influences on Nietzsche.

The rest of the study follows Nietzsche's development and discusses less well-known but nonetheless important influences on his thinking. Most of the time, I consider his readings over two- to three-year periods and discuss them with reference to his general development. Nietzsche's overall intellectual development is divided into four periods: young (1844–69), early (1869–75), middle (1875–82), and late (1883–88). This is the conventional division that Nietzsche himself used and for which there are many good reasons (a number of which are discussed in the text below). However, I have not allowed this division to determine the account (which is based on smaller divisions), and other divisions are possible. The argument could be made, with some justification, that in almost all essentials, Nietzsche's thinking was consistent throughout his development, with no major changes. Another more reasonable view is the claim that Nietzsche, due primarily to the influence of Schopenhauer and Wagner, had a marked prometaphysical period during 1869–75, which he broke with fairly radically during 1875–76; that *Human, All Too Human,* 3 vols. (1878–80) constituted a reaction and overreaction to his first position; and that it is with *Dawn* (1881) that we can see the emergence of his own distinct philosophical position, which he then further developed.

I have often given the table of contents of the most important books in this section in footnotes, since that will allow the reader to get a reasonable impression of the content of the texts Nietzsche read. I have also made suggestions for further research in the text and footnotes.

1

Nietzsche As Reader

Introduction

One can easily get the impression that Nietzsche, and especially the late Nietzsche, read little. He criticized reading as insufficiently life-affirming and Dionysian: "Early in the morning at the break of day, in all the freshness and dawn of one's strength, to read a *book*—I call that vicious!" (EH, "Why I Am So Clever," 8). He also criticized reading for making one reactive and forcing one to be concerned with the thoughts of others rather than with one's own: "My eyes alone put an end to all bookwormishness, in plain terms philology: I was redeemed from the 'book,' for years I read nothing—the *greatest* favor I have ever done myself!—That deepest self, as it were buried and grown silent under a constant *compulsion to listen* to other selves (—and that is what reading means!) awoke slowly, timidly, doubtfully—but at length *it spoke again*" (EH, "Human, All Too Human," 4).

This impression is strengthened by the fact that he mentioned very few contemporary and minor authors and titles in his books. He also explicitly claimed that he read little: "It does not perhaps lie in my nature to read much or many kinds of things: a reading room makes me ill. [...] Caution, even toward new books is rather part of my instinct" (EH, "Why I Am So Clever," 3).[1] Concretely, he claimed in *Ecce Homo* that he could go months between his reading of books: "I have to reckon back half a year to catch myself with a book in my hand. But what was it?—An excellent study by Victor Brochard, les Sceptiques Grecs."[2] As suggested in a quotation above—and as a major leitmotif in his letters—his bad health (especially his poor eyesight) provides another reason to assume that he read little. This is how most philosophers and historians have treated Nietzsche: as an isolated profound thinker.

However, this impression and Nietzsche's claims are to a large extent false. Nietzsche was, in fact, a rather substantial reader. This is true not only of his younger days but also of his entire life, including even his last active years before his mental collapse in January 1889.

Nietzsche's own words about his reading are not to be fully trusted. He seems to have wanted to appear more Dionysian and original than he actually was. His claim in *Ecce Homo* not to have held a book in his hand for half a year (since Brochard) was far from true, even if we interpret "catch myself with a book in my hand" as meaning that he had read all or most of the book. Nietzsche wrote *Ecce Homo* between October 15 and November 4, 1888. He did not mention Brochard's book in his letters, and therefore it is not certain when he read it. But his notebooks from the early spring contain notes from the book, and Nietzsche himself suggested that it was more than half a year earlier. During the period May to October 1888, Nietzsche was immensely active as an author and wrote *Der Fall Wagner, Götzen-Dämmerung* and *Der Antichrist.* Nonetheless, we have evidence that he read at least eight books during those months: Jacolliot, Spitteler, Stendhal, Nohl, Goncourts, Brandes, Féré, and Hehn. There is strong reason to assume that he read more than that, especially fiction, but we have no definite evidence of that.

After claiming in *Ecce Homo* that he read little, Nietzsche stated: "I take flight almost always to the same books, really a small number, those books which have *proved* themselves precisely to me."[3] He went on to identify the books: "It is really a small number of older Frenchmen to whom I return again and again," and he mentioned Montaigne, Molière, Corneille, and Racine. He then listed more recent French writers: Paul Bourget, Pierre Loti, Gyp, Meilhac, Anatole France, Jules Lemaitre, and Guy de Maupassant. He also named Stendhal and Prosper Merimée. In the next section, he mentioned Heinrich Heine, Byron's *Manfred,* and Shakespeare. This listing is not particularly informative or reliable. For example, no ancient authors are mentioned in spite of their importance to him, which can be seen by statements such as "the Graeco-Roman splendor, which was also a splendor of books […] some books for whose possession one would nowadays exchange half of some national literatures."[4] The reason for this is that Nietzsche moved the section dealing with antiquity—"What I Owe to the Ancients"—from *Ecce Homo* to *Götzen-Dämmerung.* Another reason that it is uninformative is that the listing seems mainly to refer to fiction: reading as recreation and "mere literature." More scholarly and philosophical books are missing, and Nietzsche did read a considerable number of such books, returning frequently to some of them, such as Lange, Spir, Rée, Schopenhauer, and Emerson. As a consequence, there is only a weak correlation between this list and a listing of the writers to whom Nietzsche most often, and most approvingly, referred in his published works, such as Goethe, Homer, Shakespeare, Voltaire, Sophocles, Aeschylus, Lessing, Heraclitus, Horace, Byron, Raphael, and Montaigne.[5]

Another early listing of works that had proven themselves to him, which appears in the first draft to *Ecce Homo,* is rather different and a little more informative.[6] It contained Montaigne, Stendhal, Emerson, Sterne (*Tristram Shandy*), Lichtenberg, Galiani, and Petronius. This listing too fails to mention many incontrovertible influences, such as Goethe, Homer, Schopenhauer, and Voltaire. The fact that only two names occur in both lists should make us a bit skeptical as to their reliability. In fact, an examination of Nietzsche's reading generally confirms that he often reread books, but it also shows that he read much more often—and at least to some extent more widely—than he suggested.

Nietzsche's claim in *Ecce Homo* that "for years I read nothing" and that this was "the *greatest* favor I have ever done myself" is incorrect and misleading. The period to which he was referring was primarily 1877 but also 1876. At that time he had continuous and serious health problems and was completely released from teaching at both the University of Basel and the associated gymnasium for a full academic year, from October 1876 to October 1877. It is true that he read much less then than in other years, but still much more than "nothing." In 1876 he seems to have read at least twelve books (which he discussed in letters or copied passages from),[7] bought twenty-one titles, and borrowed twenty-six titles from the university library in Basel. In 1877, it is true, he read very few books himself. (He also bought very few books and borrowed none at all from the university library, since he was away on sick leave most of the year.) However, he did read a few—Taine, Plato, Rée, Meysenbug, Deussen, Seydlitz, Lipiner, Sterne, and probably several more—and, more importantly, a very large number of books were read to him, mainly by the other members of the Sorrento group (Rée, Meysenbug, and Brenner) and at other times by Peter Gast, Seydlitz, and possibly by his sister Elisabeth.[8] We know of well over twenty titles that were read to Nietzsche that year, including works by Voltaire, Diderot, Burckhardt, Ranke, Thucydides, Herodotus, Lope de Vega, Calderon, Cervantes, Moreto, Michelet, Daudet, Ruffini, Turgenev, Charles de Rémusat, Renan, A. Herzen, and Mainländer as well as the New Testament.[9]

Unlike the picture that Nietzsche later painted of himself and of the ideal Dionysian philosopher, the young Nietzsche was from an early age serious, studious, intellectual, and bookish and a voracious reader. He took an unusual interest in books and in reading and writing at a very early age. When he was four years old, his father began teaching him to read, and Nietzsche was quiet enough that his father allowed him to sit in his study when he worked.[10] The study, partly because of the books it contained, quickly became one of the very young Nietzsche's favorite places.[11] At school, Nietzsche soon became a model pupil who was serious and well behaved and who worked hard, although his grades were not particularly good until his second year at Pforta. In his early autobiography, he described the winter of the school year 1856–57 as a period when there was "very much to learn, and I remember that I often worked till 11, 12 [midnight] (it was winter) and in spite of that also had to get up at 5 [a.m., for further work]."[12] When he was thirteen, his mother, Franziska, had to forbid him to begin reading before 5 a.m. because the lack of light so early in the morning would strain his eyes too much.[13]

The importance of books and reading for the young Nietzsche is also reflected in the central place they took in his relation to his childhood friends, Wilhelm Pinder, Gustav Krug, Paul Deussen, and Carl von Gersdorff. They not only continually recommended and lent books to one another but also discussed their acquisitions and what they intended to request for birthdays and Christmases. Nietzsche had an intimate knowledge of, and concern for, his friends' libraries. When Gersdorff took part in the war against Austria in 1866, he wrote to Nietzsche that he could inherit his books if Gersdorff did not survive the war. This habit of discussing, recommending, borrowing, lending, and giving books to his friends continued throughout Nietzsche's life, and is one of the reasons that we have the opportunity to follow his reading in more detail than is perhaps the case for any other major philosopher.

Although the young Nietzsche engaged in some active sports such as swimming, skating, and hiking, the lists of things he wanted for birthdays and Christmases consisted almost entirely of books and musical scores.

Nietzsche also enjoyed reading to, or with, his family and friends. In 1861, for example, he mentioned in a letter that he was looking forward to reading plays aloud with his mother and sister during the Christmas vacation; in 1864 he wrote that he and Paul Deussen had read a Greek drama; and in 1866 Nietzsche read Greek texts once a week with Gersdorff and read Schopenhauer every other week with Gersdorff and Mushacke. In 1867 Nietzsche was active in the Lesecirkel in the philological society in Leipzig, of which he was a founder, and later he joined the Lesecirkel in Basel for a number of years.

In 1860 Nietzsche, Pinder, and Krug founded the cultural (scholarly, literary, and musical) society Germania, which expressed an important aspect of the active and creative side of their interest in books and literature.[14] The three members of Germania had to produce and present one work (poem, musical composition, or essay) per month and send it to the others for evaluation and critique.[15] Some of Nietzsche's most important productions at this time were written for Germania, among them his earliest extant philosophical texts, "Fatum und Geschichte" and "Willensfreiheit und Fatum."

During Nietzsche's last year at Schulpforta, 1863–64, he worked very hard, especially on his final essay about the preclassical Greek poet Theognis, and repeatedly referred to the fact that he was surrounded by a large number of books. In his first year at the university, in Bonn, Nietzsche did not work as hard, but then he moved to Leipzig and again became studious and active as a young researcher in the field of classical philology. He later came to regard the year at Bonn as an almost "lost" or wasted year. In 1865 and 1866 he acquired a relatively large number of books and made plans for much more extensive acquisitions. On October 11, 1866, he wrote to Gersdorff that "for a long time now, I have daily been considering acquiring a library," and he negotiated a contract to buy a very substantial number of books, mainly by and about ancient authors, to be paid over a period of ten years.[16] In the end, he backed out of the almost-concluded deal, probably for financial reasons. His enormous reading at this time consisted mostly of classical philological works and articles but also of literature, literary criticism, and philosophy. (He had discovered, for example, Schopenhauer in 1865 and Lange in 1866.) In the second half of 1866, he also began working on an Aeschylus dictionary, which soon became a less ambitious Aeschylus index and in the end resulted instead in Nietzsche's making an index to the first twenty-four volumes of the prestigious classical philological journal *Rheinisches Museum für Philologie*. This was no small task and came to occupy Nietzsche for extended periods during the next several years until it was published in late 1871 or early 1872 (at the same time as Nietzsche's *Die Geburt der Tragödie*). The index—which was published separately and without mention of Nietzsche's name, although he had done all the work with only a little help from his sister—consists of 176 pages and indexed approximately 24,000 pages (the volumes for the period 1842–69).[17]

At this time of intensive work and reading, Nietzsche also expressed sentiments in a letter to Gersdorff on April 6, 1867, that we associate with the late Nietzsche: "The 100 books on the table before me are so many pairs of pliers which extinguish the nerve of independent thinking." Nietzsche often made such statements, but this did not prevent him from being a substantial reader.

During his time as a professor at Basel (1869–79), particularly during the first seven years, he was forced to work very hard and seems to have read even more copiously, especially in the field of classical philology and for the purpose of preparing classes.[18] During his last three years as a professor, his reading was more limited due to his ill health.

From 1879 to the end of his active life in January 1889, Nietzsche had no permanent address and a very limited income. This creates a number of practical problems for our understanding of his reading. These difficulties are probably important ingredients in the erroneous belief that the late Nietzsche read little.

When Nietzsche left Basel in 1879 he moved some of his books to his family home in Naumburg and sent a substantial number to his friend Franz Overbeck's mother-in-law, Frau Rothpletz, in Zürich. These books were later (1892) moved to Naumburg. Elisabeth Nietzsche claimed that he sold a significant number of books, especially philological ones, in 1879.[19]

Nietzsche traveled frequently during the last ten active years of his life. Traveling was difficult for him and almost without exception made him ill, and it was more difficult still with a heavy load of books. Nonetheless, during the first half of these ten years Nietzsche often brought a large number of books with him. In 1883 he took 104 kilograms of books to Sils-Maria. He left them there until the next summer, when he brought them first to Zürich and then probably to Mentone and Nice.[20]

In 1881 Nietzsche spent the winter and spring in Genoa (November 1880–May 1881). When he moved on, he left a crate or suitcase containing books and other belongings with his landlady there. He never picked it up, and its contents were therefore lost to him, although his sister was later able to retrieve some of the books.[21]

During 1885–88, Nietzsche had books stored at several different sites, including in Genoa and at his mother's home in Naumburg, as discussed above. More importantly, we know that he had a relatively large number of books in Nice. In 1885 he referred to a "Bücherkiste," chest or crate of books there; in 1887 he mentioned "a great amount of books";[22] and in 1888 he wrote that three "Bücherkisten" were being shipped from Nice to Turin and later that they had arrived.[23] The first crate referred to in Nice is likely to have been the large 104-kilogram crate. He also had at least one chest of books in Sils-Maria.[24] Apart from this, he used libraries and sent books through the post relatively frequently.

During the last ten years of his active life, Nietzsche lived on a small pension from the University of Basel and constantly worried about his expenses. In spite of this, he bought a not insignificant number of books during these years: very roughly, about one hundred books in the last four years of his active life (i.e., about one book every two weeks). Apart from reading books in libraries, buying books, and acquiring some sent to him by the authors, Nietzsche borrowed a significant number of books from friends (especially Overbeck and Gast), mostly through the mail.

Another practical consideration regarding Nietzsche's reading is the fact of his frequent illnesses. This too may be an important ingredient in the belief that he read little. His health problems included recurrent migraines, stomach ailments, and, most important in regard to his reading, weak eyesight and severe eye problems: "For the sake of reading and writing I need glasses Nr. 3.—if my three eye doctors had been correct I would have become blind years ago. There are only a very few hours every day for writing and reading; and when the weather turns dark, none."[25]

The problems with Nietzsche's eyes constitute a major theme in his letters throughout the last ten years.[26] The condition was so serious that he often referred to himself as half- or three-quarters blind, and he worried about becoming completely blind. For long periods he could not serve himself at dinner and hence had to be served. This was one reason that he preferred to eat alone so as not to be humiliated before the other hotel or boarding guests. The state of his eyes determined, to a large extent, when and where he traveled: "My three-quarters-blindness forced me to give up all my own experimentation and as fast as possible to flee to Nice, which my eyes have 'learned by heart.' Yes, truly! And it has more light than Munich! Until now, I know no area with the exception of Nice and Engadin [Sils-Maria] where I can manage to be working with the eyes a few hours daily."[27]

In spite of the problems with migraines and semiblindness, Nietzsche seems even during the worst periods to have been able to work for a couple of hours most days. Meta von Salis, who knew Nietzsche personally in the second half of the 1880s, claimed that he was an avid reader: "Nietzsche had 'le flair du livre' and read much in spite of his problem with the eyes."[28]

When Nietzsche's eye problems prevented him from reading and writing, he turned to others for help.[29] His mother, sister, and Peter Gast often read to him. Occasionally other acquaintances of Nietzsche's, such as Gersdorff, Rée, Romundt, Meta von Salis, and Resa von Schirnhofer, seem to have read to him,[30] but during the 1880s his isolation was too great for much to have been read to him by friends and family. He dreamed about having a "reading-machine" and added: "Otherwise I will remain below what I can achieve and will be unable to acquire sufficient intellectual nourishment."[31] Sometimes he hired strangers to read to him. For example, in 1885 it seems that Nietzsche employed "a German lady from Meiningen" to read and write for him for several weeks in Sils-Maria,[32] and in 1883 (and perhaps also in 1884) he had a pastor's widow, who had lived in America for many years, translate from English and read to him two hours daily.

The fact that Nietzsche read much more and was much more responsive to this reading than he purported does not mean that many of his Dionysian claims, such as "Only ideas *won* by *walking* have any value," are completely at variance with his own actual practice.[33] Although he sat at a desk or a table much more than has been assumed (shown by the size of his library, the number of books he bought and borrowed, the frequent annotations in the books, and especially the large number of quotations, excerpts, and even page references to books in his notebooks), it is also true that especially during his most important period, the 1880s, he spent much time out of doors, taking walks nearly every day and carrying a notebook in which he recorded his thoughts. When he returned home to his guesthouse he would then usually copy these notes into a different notebook, and he used some of them later in his published writings.

Nietzsche's Use of Libraries and Bookshops

In several of the young Nietzsche's autobiographical essays, he emphasized how much he valued visits to his maternal grandfather—whom, as the closest relative, the Nietzsche family visited almost every holiday—and that his favorite activity there was to use his grandfather's study and library. We know for certain that Nietzsche used his grandfather's library from the time he was eleven or twelve, but probably he had begun using it several years earlier. As a teenager and young man, Nietzsche was a frequent and intensive user of the more academic and specialized libraries in Pforta and Leipzig (and probably, to a lesser extent, also in Bonn). He also borrowed books and musical scores from the Leihbibliothek associated with the Naumburger bookshop Domrich and paid a monthly fee for the right to do so.[34]

Nietzsche used the rather extensive library in Pforta not only during his stay there during 1858–64 but also during the next few years. Occasionally he also borrowed books from his current and former teachers at Pforta.

We have no direct knowledge of Nietzsche's use of libraries in Bonn, but in 1865 he began to use libraries in Leipzig intensively, especially the university library but also the Stadtbibliothek (also referred to as the Rathsbibliothek), where in the second half of 1866 he regularly spent Monday, Wednesday, and Saturday afternoons working with handwritten manuscripts of ancient texts. His use of the university library was even more extensive. He claimed to borrow books there daily,[35] and when he was ill, on vacation, or in Naumburg for military service, he wrote of his longing for the library in Leipzig and stated more generally: "I thirst like that biblical deer for a larger town and a library."[36] Even in the 1880s, when he lived abroad and very rarely and unwillingly visited Germany, he nonetheless went to Leipzig on several occasions for the purpose of using the libraries and bookshops there.

In 1867 and 1868, Nietzsche planned to go to Paris to study and work for a year. His plans about what to study varied (although classical philology was always the most obvious alternative), and in a number of letters he referred with pleasure to the idea of working in Parisian libraries.[37] He continued to use libraries frequently in the 1870s and 1880s. Contrary to his claim that reading rooms made him ill (quoted at the beginning of this chapter), he praised Turin for its good libraries[38] and wrote to his sister: "one cannot even with ten horses draw me to a place where, if I am correctly informed, not even a good library is to be found."[39] Libraries were important for his reading, and the quality of the libraries was an important factor in deciding his travels and places of residence. Occasionally before deciding to visit a town, he even wrote to libraries to inquire if they were suitable for his purposes.[40] During his last four active years he used the libraries in Nice, Leipzig, Chur, Venice, and Turin and the Hotel Alpenrosen's library in Sils-Maria. He probably also used the library in Zürich and possibly in other towns, and he planned to visit Stuttgart for the sake of its library.

Nietzsche, like most bookworms, liked and had close contact with a number of bookshops throughout his life. Even as a very young child, he liked to visit bookshops.[41] In 1866, while studying at the university in Leipzig, he made serious plans to acquire a substantial library, but these plans fell though. Instead, he continued to buy books individually. He surely bought many of them in Leipzig, but no book bills survive from this early time. Nietzsche's first landlord in Leipzig had a secondhand bookshop (where Nietzsche discovered and bought Schopenhauer's *The Word As Will and Representation*), and later he wrote to his mother and sister that over time his abode in Leipzig would probably be filled with books. He also remained in close contact with the Domrich bookshop in Naumburg, ordered a number of books from it,[42] and used its Leihbibliothek. Furthermore, the Domrich bookshop regularly sent Nietzsche a rather large number of books to look at that they thought would be of interest to him and that they hoped he would buy (somewhat like a modern book club). When Nietzsche was away from home, he sometimes asked his sister to return such books to the bookshop.

Later, in Basel, Nietzsche continued to have close contact with several bookshops and regularly bought books. For 1875—the year when he seems to have bought the largest number of books—book bills show that he bought more than seventy-five titles, well over a hundred volumes. In the 1870s and 1880s he had continual contact, mainly by mail, with the antiquarian Alfred Lorentz in Leipzig and ordered many books from him. In the 1880s many of the books that Nietzsche bought were French, and he is likely to have bought most of them in Nice, where he spent his winters from 1883 until 1887–88 (although we lack the evidence of book bills). Still later, in 1888, he was very fond of the large trilingual bookshop Löscher in Turin. He was a frequent and good enough customer to know its manager and to make contacts through it.[43] Nietzsche frequently used other bookshops, ordered book catalogs, and asked for recommendations of new book titles.[44] He found some of the most important books in his life as random discoveries in bookshops. For example, he stumbled upon the works of Schopenhauer and Dostoyevsky in this way.

We are to a remarkably large degree able to follow the development of Nietzsche's own private library and his acquisition of books.[45] There exist two lists of the books he possessed as early as 1858 and another listing from late 1858 or early 1859, when he was only fourteen years old, written by the young Elisabeth. This latter list contains thirty titles (to which three more were added immediately afterward by Nietzsche's hand).[46] Nietzsche made a fourth list of seven titles in 1861 (or possibly 1862) under the title "Bibliothek." A fifth listing, with the title "My Books," dates from 1863 and contains about sixteen titles (and almost none of those listed in 1858, although several of these books remain in Nietzsche's library today). At this time Nietzsche was studying and living at Pforta, and his books were divided between home and Pforta. The two latter listings probably refer to his books at one of these two places. The further development of his library, the hundreds of book bills (never published), the publication dates of the books in the library, his discussions in letters and notes, and the style of his annotations all yield important information.

Reading and Annotation Habits

The young Nietzsche rarely made annotations in his books. His early manner of reading thus differed significantly from that of his later years. In particular, the later Nietzsche's habit of entering into a dialogue with the texts—expressed in underlines and marginal lines, exclamation marks, question marks, and nota benes (NBs) in the margins and, most importantly, by reactions in the margins or at the top or bottom of the pages, from single words to extended comments—are all but completely missing in the young Nietzsche's books. In general, few of the young Nietzsche's books contain any annotations at all, nor, with the exception of a very few, do they contain his name. Most of those that do contain annotations were marked up by the pupil or student Nietzsche with the intention of understanding or learning, often with translations of Greek words, and not for the sake of dialogue, discussions, or debate. The young Nietzsche was well behaved even in regard to his books.

A few of the more generally interesting works that the young Nietzsche read contain annotations. These works include Emerson (two works, very heavily annotated), Schopenhauer (few annotations), and Petöfi (small markings beside some of the poems). However, most of these annotations either certainly or probably were made at a later date. Unfortunately, Nietzsche's first copies of Emerson's *Versuche,* Schopenhauer's *Die Welt als Wille und Vorstellung,* and Lange's *Geschichte des Materialismus* have been missing from the library since before 1875. Emerson was stolen, Lange was given away, and Schopenhauer was probably also given away after Nietzsche had acquired the complete works. The annotated copies of these works in the library today are thus not Nietzsche's first copies but instead are ones he acquired later.

During the 1870s Nietzsche began to make an increasing number of annotations in his books and still more in the 1880s. An examination of the books he annotated in the 1870s and 1880s shows that he was often a highly interactive reader. Many of the annotated books contain more than ten annotations (mostly underlining and marginal lines) per page for whole chapters. Nietzsche's comments in the margins of many books show that he often entered into a sort of dialogue with the author, expressed in frequent use of such words as "yes," "no," "good," "very good," "bravo," and "why," for example. Occasionally, longer comments are found in the margins or at the bottom of a page.

Nietzsche as reader was much more tolerant and better informed than one would perhaps have guessed from knowing only his published statements. This can be seen, for example, in his reading of J. S. Mill, Lecky, and the brothers Goncourt, all of whom Nietzsche curtly dismissed in his published writings and letters. Nietzsche's several copies of books written by Mill, Lecky, and Goncourt, respectively, are heavily annotated and full of positive exclamations but contain relatively few negative words and comments.

The late Nietzsche's annotations are mostly made in lead pencil. Sometimes he used red or blue pencil. (In books that he read early, he not infrequently used brown and black ink.) Occasionally, annotations with lead and colored pencil are found in the same book and on the same pages, implying at least partial rereadings. And it seems likely that he also often reread books with a lead pencil in his hand, or with no pencil at all, making double and triple readings difficult to determine.

Nietzsche extremely rarely wrote his name or the date in his books. Mostly, but not always, his style and handwriting are recognizable in the annotations. His "NBs" are especially frequent and characteristic.

The most commonly recurring annotations, apart from marginal lines and underlinings, are (in approximate order of decreasing frequency): "NB," "!," "ja," "gut," "sehr gut," "?," "nein," "bravo," "falsch," names of persons, "warum?," and "ecco." In French books, some of the shorter comments are in French. Occasionally, but rarely, invectives such as "Esel" (ass) and "Vieh" (cow) appear. Nietzsche rarely annotated the beginning of books, possibly suggesting a sort of suspended judgment.

It should also be noted that Nietzsche read many of the books in his library that bear no annotation or other definite signs of having been read. From discussions in his letters or excerpts into notebooks, we know that he read a number of books that show no physical sign of having been read. The library also contains a number of books that he certainly did not read, some of them containing pages that had never been cut open (as was often necessary).

Unfortunately, a large number of the books in the library, including many of the annotated books—perhaps as many as a third—were bound, or re-bound, in Weimar under the direction of Nietzsche's sister. In that process the pages were trimmed so that many of the annotations, especially the longer comments, were completely or partially lost and are therefore often unintelligible.

The Importance of Reading for Nietzsche

One of the first things one notices when reading Nietzsche's works (with the exception of *Zarathustra*) is the large number of names of persons that occur throughout the books. These are much more frequent than in the works of most other philosophers. This wealth of names is a reflection of his belief that the writings of an author express his personality, and Nietzsche's interest is, generally speaking, directed much more toward the man than toward the work.[47] Therefore, few titles, but many authors, occur in his books. A second fundamental aspect of Nietzsche's philosophizing is his rejection of abstract—or pure—thinking, which turns his philosophizing into a sort of dialogue with earlier thinkers: "I too have been in the underworld, like Odysseus, and will often be there again. [...] There have been four pairs who did not refuse themselves to me. [...] With these I have had to come to terms when I have wandered long alone, from them will I accept judgment, to them will I listen when in doing so they judge one another. Whatever I say, resolve, cogitate for myself and others: upon these eight I fix my eyes and see theirs fixed upon me."[48]

The list of names changed from time to time, but Nietzsche's dialogue with great (and minor) thinkers continued.[49] The dialogues with the great thinkers are highly visible in Nietzsche's works. But equally important are the dialogues with less well-known thinkers, and these are almost completely invisible.

The task of making them visible—begun on a large scale by Montinari—is an important contribution to our understanding of Nietzsche.

Nietzsche was an unusually personal and existential philosopher who continually made use of his experiences (including the people he met and the books he read) in his philosophy. Beginning at least in 1879, when he resigned from his professorship at the University of Basel, his life became increasingly isolated. He rarely met his friends or other intellectually stimulating people. This increased the necessity and value of reading for him. His relative isolation, especially during the last ten active years of his life, also meant that much of his communication with others was done in the form of letters, many of which have been preserved. This enables us to follow his reading of books, and his response to this reading, more closely than is the case for most other major thinkers.

The general view among modern readers and philosophers seems to be that Nietzsche created his thoughts and philosophy out of himself. This is surely, to a large extent, true, but it is also true that Nietzsche's reading was much more extensive than has been believed so far, that it was of immense value for him, and that he sacrificed much for the sake of reading.

Many of both the major and the minor themes in Nietzsche's writings are profoundly influenced by his reading, even in his later, more independent, books. *Beyond Good and Evil* (1886) contains more than 107 different names of persons, most of them authors whom he had read. *On the Genealogy of Morals* (1887) is to a large extent a response to Nietzsche's reading of, and about, "English psychologists," especially including Paul Rée, anthropology, cultural history, and the history of law. (His library contains ten books within the field of law, and the majority of these he annotated.) *Twilight of the Idols* (1888), which Nietzsche called "my philosophy in a nutshell," contains two main parts. The first is a summary of Nietzsche's philosophy, and the second (with chapters titled "The 'Improvers' of Mankind," "Expeditions of an Untimely Man," and "What I Owe to the Ancients") is essentially a discussion of Nietzsche's reading. And *The Antichrist* (written in 1888) would have been a very different book had he not read Jacolliot, Strauss, Renan, Wellhausen, Tolstoi, Dostoyevsky, and many books about Buddhism, Christianity, St. Paul, and Luther as well as the Bible itself.

Nietzsche on the Art of Reading

Nietzsche had strong objections to general reading. This is perhaps most clearly expressed in the preface to *Beyond Good and Evil* where the reason for this objection is also given: "with the aid of freedom of the press and the reading of newspapers, achieve a state of affairs in which the spirit would no longer so easily feel itself to be a 'need'!" This critique of reading as making things abstract, and especially its application to the reading of newspapers and journals, is a recurrent theme in his letters and writings and is related to his claim that one should be untimely. It is, at least partially, a heritage from Schulpforta, where the reading of newspapers was discouraged or prohibited since it was regarded as preventing a deeper concern with history and antiquity. Nietzsche's fundamental objection to reading is that it makes the reader impersonal. This applies especially to scholarly reading. "The scholar, who really does nothing but 'trundle' books [...] finally loses altogether the ability to think for himself. If he does not trundle he does not think. He *replies* to a stimulus (—a thought he has read) when he thinks—finally he does nothing but react."[50] For similar reasons, he claims that "Only ideas *won by walking* have any value."[51] It is, however, a misconception to draw the conclusion from this that Nietzsche opposed all forms of reading and every form of reader (as his own writing and his desire for readers make plain).

As is so often the case with the understanding of Nietzsche, the critical or destructive side of his thinking has been emphasized much more than its constructive side. Nietzsche criticizes "bad" reading and what he called the modern reader, whom he said sought comfort or drunkenness when reading.[52] The modern reader, Nietzsche says, "takes about five words in twenty haphazardly and 'conjectures' their probable meaning,"[53] adding, "how lazily, how reluctantly, how badly he reads!"[54] But he says much about the importance and value of "good" reading. For a time he even planned and collected notes for a work on how to read.[55] Speaking about the transition from antiquity to the Middle Ages, Nietzsche expresses his regret for what existed in antiquity but then was lost: "Every prerequisite for an erudite culture, all the scientific [or scholarly] *methods* were already there, the great, the incomparable art of reading well had already been established—the prerequisite for a cultural tradition, for a uniform science."[56] Even in the relatively early *Human, All Too Human* (1878), Nietzsche wrote a section titled "The Art of Reading" in which he claims: "It was only when the art of correct reading, that is to say philology, arrived at its summit that science [scholarship] of any kind acquired continuity and constancy."[57]

What is the right reading according to Nietzsche? Right reading primarily requires not insight or a special method but rather character and training. In theory it is simple; it is in practice that it is difficult and rare. Fundamentally, it requires two qualities. First, it requires slow, careful, thoughtful reading that is able to defer judgment and decision.[58] Second, but equally important, is the almost opposite quality of the reader's personal presence, involvement, and rumination.[59] The correct synthesis of these abilities leads to good reading.

However, to this some other qualities need to be added, and Nietzsche especially emphasized courage, to dare to see the world as it is.[60] Nietzsche's recurrent praise of realism—of not falsifying the world—included the art of reading well.[61] In the preface to *Der Antichrist,* he emphasized that his readers must have intellectual integrity, courage, and reverence for themselves.[62]

A good example of the frequent failure to grasp Nietzsche's manner of thinking and working and the sort of misunderstandings that this can lead to can be found in the interpretation of the third essay of *On the Genealogy of Morals* in the English-speaking world (especially by ahistorical analytical and postmodern readings). Nietzsche claimed in the preface to the book that the whole third essay could be seen as an example of how to read him, how to interpret aphorisms.[63]

> If this book is incomprehensible to anyone and jars on his ears, the fault, it seems to me, is not necessarily mine. It is clear enough, assuming, as I do assume, that one has first read my earlier writings and has not spared some trouble in doing so: for they are, indeed, not easy to penetrate. [...] In other cases, people find difficulty with the aphoristic form: this arises from the fact that today this form is *not taken seriously enough.* An aphorism, properly stamped and molded, has not been "deciphered" when it has simply been read; rather, one has then to begin its *exegesis,* for which is required an art of exegesis. I have offered in the third essay of the present book an example of what I regard as "exegesis" in such a case—an aphorism is prefixed to this essay, the essay itself is a commentary on it. To be sure, one thing is necessary above all if one is to practice reading as an *art* in this way, something that has been unlearned most thoroughly nowadays—and therefore it will be some time before my writings are "readable"—something for which one has almost to be a cow and in any case *not* a "modern man": *rumination.*[64]

Ironically, Nietzsche's words of advice often have been completely misunderstood, and, in fact, further misled many readers to believe that one should interpret Nietzsche with extreme "freedom." Correctly understood, Nietzsche's advice is just the opposite. The reason for this misunderstanding is that many interpreters have understood the brief motto or epigraph ("Unconcerned, mocking, violent—thus wisdom wants *us:* she is a woman and always loves only a warrior") from *Thus Spoke Zarathustra* to be what Nietzsche meant by the first aphorism, and there is indeed little connection between this epigraph and the content of the third essay. Thus, the interpretation or "exegesis," it was argued, should be very, not to say extremely, "free." However, Nietzsche actually was referring to the first section of the essay, which indeed is closely linked to what follows—in fact, it is a summary of sections 2–28—and was written and added to the essay afterward.[65] Interpretation or exegesis here, far from being free and imaginative, is thus to be thoroughly based on a close reading of the text.

One special and unusual aspect of Nietzsche as reader is that he used reading not only to gain information and stimulus but also to diagnose the authors he read. He believed that individual human beings, persons or character constitute the ultimate telos, or value, not truth, actions, beliefs, or social reforms. This led him to analyze books not primarily in terms of truth, actions, and beliefs but rather in terms of character; in short, it led to an ad hominem approach.[66] It was possible to take such an approach within the framework of the text—that is, to analyze and discuss what the text actually says, whether it is consistent and without self-contradictions, and what effect it might have on character—and to some extent Nietzsche did this (often, for example, when referring to the Bible). But more frequently he chose to use the text as a symptom of the author's character and thus made a diagnosis rather than an analysis. The reason for this was his belief in the limited nature and importance of reason and consciousness as mere surface phenomena and symptoms, which ought not to constitute the end of analysis.

2

The Major Philosophical Influences on Nietzsche's Thinking

Introduction

Nietzsche was educated as a classical philologist and had a very limited philosophical education in the conventional sense. As a philosopher he was largely an autodidact. He never had a living philosophical teacher or mentor who could help him develop. He therefore developed late, and almost all of his philosophical development came in response to reading.

Contrary to common assumption, Nietzsche's education even in classical philosophy was minimal during his time at school and at the university. At Schulpforta there was almost no teaching of philosophy, and even ancient philosophy seems to have been almost completely absent from the curriculum. As a university student, he took three courses in philosophy during his first year at Bonn (of a total of the twenty-nine courses he attended between 1864 and 1867), two on Plato and one general introduction to the history of philosophy. One was given by the philologist Otto Jahn and two by the philosopher Karl Schaarschmidt, but none of them seems to have been of much importance to Nietzsche.[1]

Emerson

Nietzsche's very first important encounter with philosophy (before both Plato and Schopenhauer) was with the American philosopher and writer Ralph Waldo Emerson, who probably stimulated both Nietzsche's break with Christianity and his discovery of philosophical thinking. Although Nietzsche rarely referred to Emerson in his published writings, he continued to read and be stimulated by Emerson almost every year of his life and annotated books by him (in German translation) more heavily than perhaps any other books in his library. And in letters and notes he highly praised Emerson with such comments as "the author richest in thought this century."[2]

Nietzsche seems to have begun to read Emerson in 1861–62, for Emerson was one of six authors mentioned in a list of Nietzsche's most important reading that year.[3] More importantly, Nietzsche's earliest philosophical writings are two essays from April 1862 with the titles "Fatum und Geschichte" ("Fate and History") and "Willensfreiheit und Fatum" ("Freedom of the Will and Fate")—of six and three printed pages, respectively—both of which were strongly influenced by Emerson.[4] Both essays are surprisingly interesting and contain much that foreshadows Nietzsche's future philosophy.[5] Nietzsche wrote the subtitle "Thoughts" to the first essay "Fatum und Geschichte," and the best description of these essays is probably that they constitute Nietzsche's thoughts inspired by his reading of Emerson's essay "Fate" in *Die Führung des Lebens* (*The Conduct of Life*).

It is not known how Nietzsche discovered Emerson, but a chance discovery in a bookshop is possible, for *Die Führung des Lebens* appeared in 1862. Nietzsche continued to read Emerson's *Die Führung des Lebens* intensively in 1863 and copied extensive excerpts from it. In early 1864 he listed Emerson first among his most important reading during 1863.[6] In 1863 Nietzsche wrote excerpts from the essay "Schönheit" in *Die Führung des Lebens* and planned to write more extensive excerpts from other essays for his friends. We know that Nietzsche also had read and probably acquired Emerson's collection titled *Versuche* (*Essays*) in 1864 or earlier.[7]

Nietzsche seems to have continued to read Emerson in the ensuing years. In a letter from 1866 Nietzsche referred to and paraphrased Emerson's essay "Nature" (published in the second part of the German translation of *Essays*) and in late 1867 or early 1868 wrote a short quotation with a page reference to *Versuche* into his notebook.[8]

In 1874 Nietzsche brought *Versuche* with him to Bergün, where he spent the second half of July and the early part of August, and read it there while finishing and revising his *Schopenhauer as Educator* (1874), which contains two important references, in the first and the last sections, to Emerson.[9] On the return journey to Basel, Nietzsche's copy of *Versuche* was stolen from him, but he quickly bought a new copy, which is the heavily annotated copy in his library today.

With the possible exception of the period 1869 to 1873, Nietzsche appears to have read Emerson almost every year from 1862 until his mental collapse in 1889. This makes it likely that Emerson was the most read and reread author of all those Nietzsche read.[10] His library contained four titles in 1942 (of which two have since been lost) and an issue of the *Atlantic Monthly* with a long essay by Emerson in English.[11]

Emerson's influence on Nietzsche was enormous and can be compared to that of Schopenhauer in depth and extent. Both Emerson and Schopenhauer were important in forming Nietzsche as a philosopher and thinker, and effects of this early influence, reinforced by later reading, reverberated throughout his whole life and entire writings. However, it is difficult to determine with certainty the details of the influence. It is possible to argue that Emerson influenced Nietzsche's literary style and colored his overall thinking, including in such important matters as in his relation to religion, history, culture, morality, and the view of man and his highest tasks.[12]

Although it seems likely to me that there exist important Emersonian influences on Nietzsche in all these areas, it is difficult to separate them from other general influences, including those of Schopenhauer, Kant, antiquity, and Christianity and from other aspects of Nietzsche's own thinking. Thus, although it is important to be aware of Emerson's profound influence on Nietzsche, which colored much of his thinking, specific examples become speculative and almost impossible to confirm or rule out. However, there is ample evidence of a profound general influence:

1. The reading of Emerson's *Die Führung des Lebens* probably constituted the earliest philosophical influence on Nietzsche and as such was comparable to and prepared the way for the better-known influence of Schopenhauer.

2. The reading of Emerson profoundly influenced the content of Nietzsche's first (or earliest extant) philosophical writings, the essays "Fatum und Geschichte" and "Willensfreiheit und Fatum" that foreshadow much of Nietzsche's later philosophy.

3. Nietzsche's reading (and annotations) of Emerson began early and continued for the rest of his life. Emerson is likely to be the author he read and reread more than any other. Nietzsche's copy of *Versuche* is probably the most heavily annotated book in his library,[13] with about nine hundred places in the text where he wrote comments despite the fact that his first copy of the book— probably also heavily annotated—was stolen in 1874.

4. Nietzsche not only read and copiously annotated the works by Emerson but also made extensive excerpts from Emerson's *Versuche,* even to the point that he had a black notebook seemingly for that sole purpose.[14] With the exception of Eugen Dühring's *Der Werth des Lebens,* which Nietzsche read in 1875, he did not excerpt any other book or author to a comparable extent.

5. Although it is not obvious in the published works, Nietzsche continually praised and quoted Emerson throughout his life. The young Nietzsche read and excerpted much from Emerson. The letters in which he recommended Emerson to his friends (for example, Gersdorff) have been lost but are likely to have

been highly enthusiastic. The only evidence we still possess is Gersdorff's eager response.[15] Later, in 1874, Nietzsche referred to "the excellent Emerson,"[16] and in 1879 he referred to "Emerson, the richest American."[17] In 1881 Nietzsche was still more effusive: "Emerson. I have never felt so at home, and in my home, in a book as—I cannot praise it, it stands me too near."[18] Shortly thereafter, Nietzsche called Emerson "the author richest in thought this century."[19] In 1882 Nietzsche took a saying from Emerson as a motto for his *The Joyful Science* and placed it on the title page, and in the book he praised Emerson as one of the four greatest authors of the nineteenth century.[20] In a letter to Overbeck from 1883 Nietzsche wrote, "I experience Emerson as a *twin-soul* [*Bruder-Seele*]."[21] And in another letter, from the next year, he referred to him as "such a fantastically great being, rich in soul and spirit."[22] In 1887–88 Nietzsche strongly praised Emerson in comparison to Carlyle as "much more enlightened, adventurous, multifarious, refined than Carlyle; above all, happier. . . . Such a man as instinctively feeds on pure ambrosia and leaves alone the indigestible in things."[23] And in an early draft to Nietzsche's autobiography *Ecce Homo* (1888), in which he described his own development and reading, he wrote: "*Emerson, with his Essays, has been a good friend and someone who has cheered me up even in dark times: he possesses so much scepsis, so many 'possibilities,' that with him even virtue becomes spiritual [geistreich].*"[24]

It has been claimed, often not without good reasons, that many of Nietzsche's most important teachings—perspectivism, the will to power,[25] experimentalism, *gaya scienzia,*[26] elitism, an emphasis on cultural and existential values— were stimulated by the reading of Emerson. Perhaps most remarkable and most surprising is the claim that Nietzsche's *Thus Spoke Zarathustra,* in its general conception and in its two principal ideas—the Übermensch and the eternal recurrence—as well as in the character of Zarathustra, was profoundly and decisively inspired by Emerson. At least for the case of the figure of Zarathustra, the emphasis of Emerson as the primary source of inspiration has become the standard view. This is incorrect, but Emerson may still have been important for the conception of the work.[27]

Plato

Plato is the philosopher whom Nietzsche refers to more frequently than any other with the exception of Schopenhauer. It is often taken for granted that Plato was the first philosopher who influenced Nietzsche, but as we have seen above, that was not the case. Nietzsche's interest in Plato appears to have begun during his last year at Schulpforta (1863–64). His very first references to Plato come from that year, when he asked permission to buy and have bound the first two volumes of Plato's dialogues in Greek, edited by Hermann. This edition consists of six volumes, and all six are in Nietzsche's private library. It seems likely that he also bought the last four volumes at or near this time. In his notebook from 1863 he wrote that he planned to read the *Apology, Crito,* and *Euthyphron* (possibly in Greek) during the holidays. The *Symposium* seems soon to have become his favorite dialogue. In August 1864 Nietzsche wrote the essay "Ueber das Verhältniß der Rede des Alcibiades zu den übrigen Reden des platonischen Symposiums,"[28] and in a short autobiography, "Mein Leben," which he wrote on the occasion of leaving Pforta after six years, he stated: "I remember with the greatest pleasure the first impressions of Sophocles, Aeschylus, Plato, especially in my favorite piece, the Symposium, and then the Greek lyricists."[29]

Nietzsche's interest in philosophy, and particularly in Plato, is also confirmed by his Greek teacher at Pforta, Professor Karl Steinhart, himself an important Plato scholar who wrote many articles on Plato and edited the complete works of Plato. Steinhart had written a letter of recommendation for Nietzsche (and Paul Deussen) to Carl Schaarschmidt, a professor of philosophy at Bonn and a former student of Steinhart's at Schulpforta. In this letter Steinhart wrote: "The other, *Nietzsche,* has a profound and capable nature, enthusiastic for philosophy, in particular the Platonic, in which he already is quite initiated. [...] [H]e will with pleasure, especially under your guidance, turn to philosophy, which after all is the direction of his innermost drive."[30]

However, with the exception of the school essay mentioned above, Nietzsche hardly ever mentioned Plato, either in letters, notes, or other school essays, before or during his time at Pforta. It seems likely that his interest in, and perhaps enthusiasm for, Plato began only during the last few months at Pforta and as such was somewhat exaggerated both by Nietzsche himself in his short autobiographical sketch and by Steinhart, who sympathized with Plato and wrote the letter of recommendation to another Platonic philosopher.

At Bonn in 1865, Nietzsche attended two courses on Plato, one given by Schaarschmidt and one by Jahn.[31] These lectures—to the extent that he attended them—do not seem to have left any mark on Nietzsche's writings of the time. More generally, during his years as a university student (1864–68), he made a large number of references to Plato, but almost all of them were scholarly and oriented toward questions of classical philology and were not directed at Plato himself or his thinking.[32] Instead, Nietzsche used Plato and his writings at this time to discuss other topics (especially Theognis and Democritus).[33] The notes from his last year as a student (1868) also contain a relatively large number of lists of future plans and courses to give. Plato, among many other topics, is often mentioned in these lists. These references, however, say almost nothing about Nietzsche's view of Plato. This absence of Plato's philosophy in Nietzsche's thinking and writing at this time is perhaps surprising. Plato was, to be sure, mentioned in a letter of April 15, 1868, to Zarncke, the founder and editor of the *Literarische Centralblatt für Deutschland,* as one name on a list of ten ancient writers who "stand close to me," implying that Nietzsche would be willing to write reviews of books about them, but Plato was not emphasized.[34] Plato was also discussed in letters between Nietzsche and Deussen, who eventually wrote his dissertation on Plato. However, Nietzsche's statements in the correspondence were unenthusiastic, and he actually advised Deussen against such an undertaking.

It is not until after Nietzsche became a professor at Basel in 1869 that we find evidence of a more serious consideration of Plato, Platonic philosophy, and Platonic questions in their own right and for their own sake or, perhaps more correctly, for the sake of teaching them. Nietzsche began to teach Plato at the Pädagogium during his first term in Basel (summer 1869) and at the university during the winter term of 1871–72. The other stimulus for thinking about Plato at this time was Nietzsche's work on *The Birth of Tragedy.* At this time Nietzsche's independent views—both positive and negative—about Plato began to emerge, but the negative seem to have prevailed. In 1869 and 1870 he referred to Plato's ethical optimism and associated him with Socrates and Euripides as a theoretical man,[35] a view that he later expressed in *The Birth of Tragedy* (1872). He also referred to Plato's hostility to art at this time, a statement that he repeated a number of times in the ensuing years.[36] In early 1871 Nietzsche again blamed Socrates, Euripides, and Plato for the separation of the Apollinian and the Dionysian—that is, for the disintegration of Greek culture[37]—and then made his most spectacular statement in regard to Platonism: "My philosophy, *inverted Platonism:* the further away from true being, the more pure, beautiful, better it is. The life of appearance as goal."[38] However, Nietzsche's references to Plato after this statement were not significantly more critical than his earlier statements. His attitude seems to have remained mixed, although some of the positive statements he made may merely have been efforts to evoke the interest of his students.

In the early 1870s Nietzsche was deeply involved in reading Plato and preparing lectures about him and his thinking. He discussed and summarized all of the Platonic dialogues for his students and discussed Plato's life and thinking in detail, but mostly it was the conscientious teacher Nietzsche, not the iconoclastic philosopher, who spoke in these lectures.[39] At the university Nietzsche lectured on Plato during the winter terms of 1871–72 and 1873–74, the summer term of 1876, and finally during the winter term of 1878–79. Although he used essentially the same lecture notes, he continued to think about and read Plato during these and the ensuing years.[40] In June 1877 he read Plato's *Laws,* and in April 1878 he received and read Plato's *Apology of Socrates* (his copy of it is heavily annotated).

Interestingly, and unlike the case with Emerson, Schopenhauer, Lange, and Kant, Nietzsche showed no enthusiasm and made no value statement in regard to Plato or Platonic thinking in his early letters. The two most interesting statements before 1887 (when he began to criticize Plato more explicitly in his letters) come from letters written in 1882 and 1883, respectively. In a letter of September 16, 1882, to Lou Salomé, Nietzsche wrote: "My beloved Lou, your idea of reducing philosophical systems to the status of personal records of their authors is a veritable 'twin brain' idea. In Basel I was teaching the history of ancient philosophy in just this sense, and liked to tell my students: 'This system has been disproved and it is dead; but you cannot disprove the person behind it—the person cannot be killed.' Plato, for example." This seems to emphasize and illuminate Nietzsche's ambivalent view of Plato: his rejection of most of his philosophy but his profound respect for his character. Perhaps still more interesting, and certainly more surprising, is his statement of October 22, 1883, to Overbeck, written after having published the first book of *Thus Spoke Zarathustra* and while working on the second: "While reading Teichmüller [probably *Die wirkliche und die scheinbare Welt,* which he had borrowed from Overbeck] I am continually dumbfounded with astonishment by *how badly* I know Plato and how much Zarathustra *platonizes.*"[41]

Nietzsche, however, continued to regard Plato and Platonism as representing an opposing philosophy to his own. In 1884, for example, he wrote: "Without Platonism and Aristotelianism no Christian philosophy"[42] and "Fight against Plato and Aristotle."[43] In his last year Nietzsche summarized much of his attitude by opposing Plato to Thucydides: "*Courage* in face of reality ultimately distinguishes such natures as Thucydides and Plato: Plato is a coward in face of reality—consequently he flees into the ideal; Thucydides has *himself* under control—consequently he retains control over things."[44]

In 1887, in a letter to Paul Deussen thanking him for a birthday gift from the Academy in Athens, Nietzsche claimed to be proud to have such an enemy and opponent: "perhaps this old Plato is my true great opponent? But how proud I am to have such an opponent!"[45]

Schopenhauer

Let us return to Nietzsche's youth again. His intensive interest in philosophy began with the discovery and reading of Schopenhauer's magnum opus, *Die*

Welt als Wille und Vorstellung (*The World as Will and Representation*), in late 1865 and of Friedrich Albert Lange's *Geschichte des Materialismus* the following year. Before then Nietzsche's interest in philosophy had been limited, fueled by broad general interests, by an interest in Plato during 1863 and 1864 and the ancient Weltanschauung in general, possibly by his reading of Emerson from 1862 onward, and, most importantly, by the inner conflict caused by the strain between intellectual integrity and truth contra the demands of Christian faith.[46] His discovery of Schopenhauer changed all of that.

At the age of twenty-one Nietzsche discovered Schopenhauer's *Die Welt als Wille und Vorstellung* in a bookshop in Leipzig in October or November 1865, immediately became a Schopenhauerian, and would remain so for the next ten years.[47] Two years later Nietzsche described the discovery: "I do not know what daemon whispered to me: 'Take this book home with you.' [...] At home I threw myself into the sofa corner with the treasure I had acquired, and started to allow that energetic, sombre genius to work upon me. Here every line screamed renunciation, denial, resignation, here I saw a mirror in which I caught sight of world, of life, and of my own mind in terrifying grandeur. Here the full, disinterested, sun-like eye of art looked upon me, here I saw sickness and healing, exile and sanctuary, hell and heaven."[48] This immediate affinity to Schopenhauer is not all that surprising, for Schopenhauer's philosophy goes well with Nietzsche's cultural, musical, and aesthetic interests and values and with his liking of Plato and Emerson, with their metaphysical philosophy, their emphasis on a sort of philosophy of life, and their literary and existential manner of writing. Furthermore, it seems correct, as Nietzsche later claimed, that Schopenhauer's atheism (but still with a kinship to Christianity) further attracted Nietzsche, who had left the Christian faith shortly before.[49]

The discovery of Schopenhauer profoundly strengthened the philosophical tendency in Nietzsche's thinking. His relation to Schopenhauer in 1865–69 was one of extreme enthusiasm. Nietzsche frequently read Schopenhauer; persuaded his friends to read him (and to become Schopenhauerians); continually praised Schopenhauer in his letters, referring to him as a demigod, the greatest philosopher during the last thousand years, and so forth; and treated critics of Schopenhauer as personal enemies. Schopenhauer came to affect all of Nietzsche's thinking, and Nietzsche wished, against the advice and tendency of his teacher Ritschl, to let this philosophy affect his philological writings. Nietzsche began to write philological work on more philosophical themes, such as Democritus and Diogenes Laertius, and he planned to write a history of literature from a Schopenhauerian perspective. The discovery of Schopenhauer not only changed Nietzsche's way of thinking and pushed it in a philosophical direction but also very directly influenced his thoughts, attitude, and reading. His letters from late 1865 and 1866 show a pessimistic and life-denying Nietzsche who appeared to regard life as inescapable suffering. The majority of the nonphilological books Nietzsche read in the ensuing years were recommended to him in Schopenhauer's works, were about Schopenhauer, or were written by Schopenhauerians (compare the discussions in chapters 3 and 4 below).

Nietzsche's reading of Schopenhauer also strongly improved and influenced his interest and knowledge of general philosophy and the history of philosophy. Schopenhauer continually discussed philosophical questions and other philosophers' views throughout his works. His *Parerga und Paralipomena* (1851) contains, apart from such general comments and many philosophical essays, a chapter of more than one hundred pages with the title "Fragment zur Geschichte der Philosophie."

What Nietzsche most clearly affirmed was Schopenhauer as a person, his general Weltanschauung and his pessimism but also a number of more specific aspects of his philosophy, including his views on art, music, language and style, and pity.[50]

However, along with Nietzsche's many enthusiastic notes and comments about Schopenhauer in letters, we also find a number of connected notes, covering about ten published pages and written sometime between the autumn of 1867 and early 1868, in which Nietzsche severely criticizes Schopenhauer's philosophy. In these notes Nietzsche seems to be rejecting the whole basis of Schopenhauer's philosophy.

> On Schopenhauer.
> An attempt to explain the world using a single assumed factor.
> The thing in itself takes on one of its possible forms.
> The attempt is unsuccessful.
> Schopenhauer did not regard it as an experiment.[51]

If the discussion and analysis in these notes are Nietzsche's own (rather than being based on literature critical of Schopenhauer), it probably represents Nietzsche's first extended, detailed, and independent philosophical analysis. However, it is surprising that Nietzsche's general attitude toward Schopenhauer did not seem to change in the slightest before and after this analysis. One possible reason for this is that what Nietzsche affirmed was Schopenhauer's style and general Weltanschauung, and therefore other aspects of his thought, were of little consequence to him. Nietzsche suggested such a solution in letters to Deussen, and this is how Schlechta seems to have regarded it.[52] However, such an answer seems to me unsatisfactory, both in regard to Nietzsche's intellectual integrity and given that the break with Schopenhauer's thinking in 1875–76 had such profound consequences for Nietzsche's thinking then.

Another surprising aspect of these notes appears in Nietzsche's response to two letters from Paul Deussen (both have unfortunately been lost) in which Deussen attempted to persuade him to write an apology or critique of Schopenhauer. Nietzsche claimed to have no interest in doing so and said that it would furthermore be futile, for either one accepts the overall view of a philosopher or does not (the way one either likes the smell of a rose or does not). Nonetheless, Nietzsche wrote these rather extensive notes on the matter.[53]

The reason to believe that the critique is essentially Nietzsche's own—and it has been so regarded by all commentators to date—is that no other source (or inspiration) for the notes has been found to my knowledge. Also, Nietzsche referred to specific pages in Schopenhauer's works, which would seem unlikely if the critique were drawn from someone else's work.

On the other hand, if Nietzsche worked out the critique himself, I find it surprising that it did not affect his view and evaluation of Schopenhauer at all, whereas if he basically was summarizing other persons' critiques, this lack of affect and emotional consequences is less surprising. Further research is needed to settle this point, but until more evidence is brought forth, on the whole, we probably need to assume that the critique was done by Nietzsche himself.[54]

As stated above, Nietzsche acquired Schopenhauer's *Die Welt als Wille und Vorstellung*, 2nd ed. (1844) in the late autumn of 1865 and read it intensively. He seems thereafter to have acquired a number of other works by Schopenhauer—most likely all the major works—but almost all of his references and discussions referred to *Die Welt* and *Parerga*. None of these books are in his library today. It seems likely that Nietzsche either lost them or gave them away in or around 1875. At this time, when Nietzsche was soon to begin breaking away from Schopenhauer, he copied down a fairly large number of notes from Schopenhauer's writings (for his planned critique of classical philologists, to be titled *Wir Philologen*) specifically relating to the Greeks.[55] It seems likely that this reading and use of Schopenhauer reminded Nietzsche of his doubts about Schopenhauer's metaphysics (and philosophy generally), which he had expressed as early as 1868 and felt again while writing *Schopenhauer As Educator* in 1874.[56] During the summer of 1875, in a note titled "All sorts of plans," Nietzsche expressed his intention "to thoroughly read Dühring," a Schopenhauerian philosopher, "to see, what I have of Schopenhauer, and what not. Thereafter, read Schopenhauer yet again."[57] He followed through on his plans that summer of 1875, reading both Dühring's *Der Werth des Lebens* (1865) and Schopenhauer carefully. Nietzsche's breach with Schopenhauer becomes clearly visible shortly thereafter, in 1876.

It seems possible to follow Nietzsche's breach with Schopenhauer in much more detail than has been done so far and thus to better understand both the reasons for it and some of its consequences. By following Nietzsche's excerpts and extensive commentary to Dühring's *Der Werth des Lebens* and by examining the annotations in his copy of *Arthur Schopenhauer, Sämtliche Werke* (Leipzig, 1873–74), edited by Julius Frauenstädt in six parts (though actually in nine volumes since parts I and IV are divided into several volumes), which he bought during the summer of the same year (1875) and which are still in his library today, we are able to follow his increasing distance and criticism.[58]

Nietzsche's library contains one further book by Schopenhauer, also edited by Frauenstädt, *Aus Arthur Schopenhauer's handschriftlichen Nachlaß: Abhandlungen, Anmerkungen, Aphorismen und Fragmente* (Leipzig, 1864), 479 pages. It is not known when Nietzsche acquired this work, but it contains annotations (including exclamation marks) throughout.

Nietzsche continued to read, annotate, and make excerpts from Schopenhauer's writings almost every year, even after his break with Schopenhauer, to the very end. Nietzsche continued to have respect for Schopenhauer the person but regarded his philosophy as a counterposition to his own. For example, after his break with Schopenhauer in 1875–76, Nietzsche came to be much more skeptical toward metaphysics and toward art as the justification of life, and he completely changed his view of ethics and pity.

Most of Nietzsche's continued reading of Schopenhauer was of his two main works, *Die Welt* and *Parerga,* but he also continued to read (and even study) other texts by Schopenhauer. As one example of his frequent reading of Schopenhauer after 1876, we can look at his detailed reading of Schopenhauer's *Preisschrift über die Grundlage der Moral* (*Prize Essay on the Foundation of Morality*), which gave rise to many excerpts in his notebooks around 1884,[59] and an increased discussion of Kant after this time. There are no annotations in Nietzsche's copy of this work, which is of less than two hundred pages and contains four parts. Part two, covering about seventy-five pages, is called "Critique of Kant's foundation of ethics"[60] and is a detailed discussion and critique of Kant's ethics, including many quotations, especially his *Grundlegung der Metaphysik der Sitten* (*Foundation of the Metaphysics of Morals*).[61] This also illustrates that much of Nietzsche's understanding and discussion of Kant were done from a Schopenhauerian perspective.

Lange

In August 1866, about a year after his discovery of Schopenhauer, Nietzsche made his second major philosophical discovery in the form of Friedrich Albert Lange's

Geschichte des Materialismus und Kritik seiner Bedeutung in der Gegenwart (*History of Materialism and Critique of Its Meaning in the Present*), published in 1866. It is not known how Nietzsche discovered Lange's work. Possibly, since he read it the very year it appeared, he acquired it through his close contact with bookshops in Leipzig and Naumburg or because he saw it advertised as a new title.[62] His first reference to the work and to Lange was in a letter dating from late August 1866 in which he praised the work and recommended it to his friend Carl von Gersdorff. He had just been reading the book, which seemed to have satisfied his wish to study the history of philosophy and be able to situate Schopenhauer in it,[63] and he praised it highly in the three letters in which it is mentioned.

> Finally, Schopenhauer must be mentioned, for whom I still have every sympathy. What we possess in him was recently made quite clear to me by another work, which is excellent of its kind and very instructive: F. A. Lange's *History of Materialism and Critique of Its Meaning in the Present* (1866). Here we have an extremely enlightened Kantian and natural scientist. His conclusions are summed up in the following three propositions:
>
> 1) the world of the senses is the product of our organization.
> 2) our visible (physical) organs are, like all other parts of the phenomenal world, only images of an unknown object.
> 3) Our real organization is therefore as much unknown to us as real external things are. We continually have before us nothing but the product of both.
>
> Thus the true essence of things, the thing-in-itself, is not only unknown to us; the concept of it is neither more nor less than the final product of an antithesis which is determined by our organization, an antithesis of which we do not know whether it has any meaning outside our experience or not. Consequently, Lange thinks, one should give philosophers a free hand as long as they edify us in this sense. Art is free, also in the domain of concepts. Who would refute a phrase by Beethoven, and who would find error in Raphael's *Madonna?*
> You see, even with this severely critical standpoint our Schopenhauer stands firm; he becomes even almost more important to us. If philosophy is art, then even Haym should submit himself to Schopenhauer; if philosophy should edify, I know no more edifying philosopher than our Schopenhauer.[64]

However, these enthusiastic references are the only mentions of Lange in Nietzsche's letters, and he is never mentioned at all in the published works.[65]

Nietzsche owned and read *Geschichte des Materialismus* in 1866 and reread it and made extensive excerpts from it in early 1868. In November 1868, he lent his copy to Rohde, but Rohde probably soon returned it.[66] In the 1870s Nietzsche gave his copy to his friend Romundt.[67] Nietzsche later read and quoted from the fourth edition from 1882, and finally in 1887 he bought a copy of the edition from that year, which he also read.[68] We have no evidence that Nietzsche read the greatly expanded two-volume second edition, of which the first volume appeared in 1873 and the second in 1875 (which contains a reference to Nietzsche himself), or the third (identical) edition. The fourth edition from 1882 (reprinted in 1887) was reduced in size through the elimination of most of the numerous footnotes.

One of the most important works on Lange's philosophy was written by Max Heinze—Nietzsche's teacher (and advisor) at Pforta, later his friend, and for several years his colleague at Basel—and published in *Vierteljahrsschrift für wissenschaftliche philosophie* (1877). We have no evidence that Nietzsche read this article, but it seems likely that he may have done so. We know that he read several other works that discuss Lange's philosophy in a positive way.

Lange also wrote two important political works, *Die Arbeiterfrage* (1865) and *J. St. Mills ansichten über die soziale frage und die angebliche umwälzung der sozialwissenschaft durch Carey* (1866). Nietzsche seems to have read the former; a book bill shows that he bought it in 1875.[69]

Lange's magnum opus, *Geschichte des Materialismus,* is both a detailed history of materialism (and in part a history of philosophy) and a critique of its metaphysical side.[70] From an essentially Kantian position, he rejected all forms of metaphysics but constructed a sort of dichotomy between the physical world and mental processes. He saw mechanistic explanations as indispensable within the natural sciences but rejected their validity for mental processes. Indeed, in the final analysis, he thought all the basic concepts of physics to be the products of human thinking. This is closely related to Kant's formal idealism, and Lange was one of the founders of neo-Kantianism. However, unlike Kant, Lange had a serious interest in physiological psychology, which he thought supported his dichotomy of the material and the mental.

The first edition of the work consisted of two books (which in the second enlarged edition became two volumes). The first book consists of a history of materialism before Kant, with an emphasis on Democritus, Epicurus, Lucretius, Gassendi, Hobbes, and English and Enlightenment materialism. The second book consists of three sections. Section one discusses Kant's philosophy in some detail and then treats philosophical materialism after Kant (Feuerbach, Max Stirner, Büchner, Moleschott, and Czolbe). Section two deals with materialism and natural science, physics (Boyle, Newton, Dalton, and Fechner), cosmology, and anthropological questions (including Darwin), empirical psychology, and the limits of knowledge. The third section is titled "Ethical Materialism and Religion" and includes discussions of Mill, Überweg, Strauss, and Schiller.

The reading of Lange (and Schopenhauer) was of immense importance to Nietzsche in the second half of the 1860s and has been recognized as such.[71] Both Schopenhauer and Lange built on the philosophy of Kant, who became the next major influence on Nietzsche. One expression of Nietzsche's philosophical interests in the late 1860s is found in this claim: "Kant, Schopenhauer and this book by Lange—I do not need anything else."[72] Lange's book not only gave him an outline of the history of philosophy and a defined philosophical position but also seems to have determined several of the most important philosophical books he read the following years, such as Kant, Democritus, Überweg, and Radenhausen.[73] It also does not seem unlikely that Lange's extensive discussion and critique of Strauss influenced Nietzsche's intention to write his first *Untimely Meditation: David Strauss: Writer and Confessor* (1874) and possibly some of its content.

However, the most persuasive proof of the enormous influence Lange (and Schopenhauer) had on Nietzsche's thinking is that he became increasingly dissatisfied with philology and that its place in his mind and heart was being filled by an interest in and concern with philosophy and the natural sciences instead. This antipathy is most strongly expressed in a letter to Paul Deussen in October 1868 in which he wrote: "I regard, if I am to speak mythologically, philology as a monstrosity [Mißgeburt] born of the goddess Philosophy, begotten with an idiot or cretin."[74] Nietzsche's interest after having read Schopenhauer and Lange began to move in the direction of philosophy instead of philology, and his most extensive notes during the second part of the 1860s were about the ancient historian of Greek philosophy, Diogenes Laertius, and (directly inspired by Lange) Democritus.

This move away from philology corresponded well with Nietzsche's plans—admittedly only for a brief period of time—to write his dissertation in philosophy instead of philology. He seems to have considered two closely related titles: "The Organic after Kant" and "Teleology after Kant."[75] Both themes were inspired by his reading of Schopenhauer and Lange, both of whom dealt with these questions in some detail, and many of these notes were excerpts from Lange's book.

There is no doubt that Lange constituted a strong influence on the young Nietzsche and that Nietzsche read him intensively in 1866 and 1868. But how often did he return to the work after that? This is a question not easily answered, but in 1873 Nietzsche excerpted and paraphrased the work, suggesting a reading of it then. Thereafter, he gave away his copy of the book. Notes from 1881 and 1883 may contain paraphases from Lange, but this is not certain. (They may have come from reading of other works that mention Lange.) By 1884 or 1885 at the latest, Nietzsche turned critical of Lange. He seems to have been rereading him at that time. We have several notes that contain page references to Lange's book and quotations, and in one note he explicitly claimed to be reading Lange. Nietzsche seems to have bought the fourth edition of the book in 1887 or 1888 and to have read Lange again (as shown by the annotations throughout his copy of the book).[76]

Kant

Nietzsche's reading of Kant is an important and much-discussed issue, for, with the exception of Schopenhauer and Plato, Kant is the philosopher to whom Nietzsche referred to most often by far, and Kant constitutes the background and starting point for almost all later German philosophy, including Schopenhauer and Lange. However, unlike Schopenhauer and Plato, whom Nietzsche knew well, his firsthand knowledge of Kant appears to have been slight. An awareness of Nietzsche's knowledge of Kant is important, for much of his later critique of modern philosophy, and especially German philosophy, was directed at Kant or at least was presented through his critique of Kant. Furthermore, Nietzsche's attitude toward Kant changed more than his attitude toward probably any other philosopher. The young and early Nietzsche (i.e., until about 1876) held Kant in high esteem, while after that period he became Nietzsche's main philosophical enemy. One cannot understand the reasons for Nietzsche's esteem or critique or for his change of attitude without a reasonable knowledge of Nietzsche's reading of, and knowledge about, Kant.

The best starting point is probably Curt Paul Janz's statement in his standard biography of Nietzsche in which he claims that Nietzsche acquired his first image of Kant's works through Lange's *Geschichte des Materialismus,* which was then followed by the reading of the two-volume study of Kant by Kuno Fischer in his series *Geschichte der neuern Philosophie.* Thereafter, during the end of 1867 and early 1868, Nietzsche read Kant's *Kritik der Urteilskraft* (*Critique of Judgment*), the third critique dealing with aesthetic and teleological judgment.[77] Janz further claims that it is taken for granted in Nietzsche research that Nietzsche had never read Kant in the original, with the exception of the *Kritik der Urteilskraft.* However, he adds that Nietzsche's dialogue with Kant is so strong and so detailed that surely a more cautious formulation is to be recommended: it has not yet been possible to prove a direct reading of Kant, but it also cannot be excluded.[78] Two sources need to be added to Janz's account. Schopenhauer not only was profoundly influenced by Kant but also often discussed Kant's philosophy explicitly in some detail in his writings. This is likely to have been a major source of knowledge and interest for the young Nietzsche even before he read Lange. Among the secondary literature about Kant that Nietzsche read early, apart from Schopenhauer, Lange, and Fischer, Überweg also ought to be mentioned. In 1868 Nietzsche read and studied his three-volume *Grundriss der Geschichte der Philosophie von Thales bis auf die Gegenwart* (1863–66), which also contained an extensive running bibliography in which Kant had a prominent place.

There is no work by Kant in Nietzsche's library, and almost certainly Nietzsche never owned any work by Kant. The reason to believe that Nietzsche read Kant is his enthusiasm for Kant at this time, including planning to write his doctoral dissertation on Kantian themes and such statements as "Kant, Schopenhauer and this book by Lange—I do not need anything else."[79] Furthermore, when Nietzsche applied to be transferred from the chair of philology to that of philosophy at Basel in 1871, he wrote to the authorities at Basel and claimed that among the modern philosophers he had studied Kant and Schopenhauer with special interest.[80] This view is further strengthened by the fact that we know that several of his friends read Kant at this time. The argument against Nietzsche's reading of Kant is that we have no evidence of any such reading, with the exception of the third *Critique* in 1867–68 and some very limited reading much later.

Nietzsche's interest in Kant was at its strongest in the late 1860s. A list of intended reading under the title "Zur Teleologie" from that time contains seven titles, of which four relate to Kant: Rosenkranz's *Geschichte der Kant. Philosophie,* Fischer's *Kant,* and two works by Kant himself, *Kritik der reinen Vernunft* (*Critique of Pure Reason*) and *Kritik der Urtheilskraft* (*Critique of Judgment*). We know that Nietzsche read Fischer's book and probably Kant's *Urtheilskraft* but probably not the other two works. Another list of intended reading from the same period includes two works by Kant: *Allgemeine Naturgeschichte und Theorie des Himmels* (*General Natural History and Theory of the Heavens*) and (again) *Kritik der Urtheilskraft.*[81]

In the notes to Nietzsche's lectures in Basel in the 1870s, we see his high respect for and affirmation of Kant, and we get further possible indications of his reading of Kant by means of several long quotations. These occur, for example, at the very beginning of his lectures "Vorlesungen über lateinische Grammatik" and "Darstellung der antiken Rhetorik." However, the likelihood is that these quotations were taken from the secondary literature that Nietzsche used when preparing his lectures rather than from his own reading of Kant.

In his lecture "Encyclopädie der klassischen Philologie," first given in the summer of 1871 (and possibly repeated in 1873–74), Nietzsche recommended that philologists study philosophy and look at the big picture. He especially recommended the unity of Plato's and Kant's thinking and affirmed their idealism. The same spirit is apparent in the lecture "Einführung in das Studium der platonischen Dialogue": "The theory of ideas is something enormous, an invaluable preparation for Kantian idealism. Here is taught, with every means, including that of myths, the correct opposition between the Ding-an-sich and appearance: with which every more profound philosophy begins."[82] In his lecture "Die vorplatonischen Philosophen," given for the first time in 1869–70 or in 1872 (and repeated in 1875–76 and in 1876), Nietzsche stated that the importance of Eleatic thinking was first recognized with Kantian philosophy.[83] Later in the lecture, Nietzsche emphasized that in several important ways Kantian idealism stands opposite that of Parmenides,[84] and he went so far as to claim that "if there had been a seed of profundity in Eleatic thinking, then he [Zeno] would from it inevitably have glimpsed the Kantian problem."[85]

We have no definite evidence of Nietzsche's firsthand reading of Kant between 1869 and 1887, although his references to him in the early 1870s may suggest such reading.[86] Most importantly, we have no evidence or indication of such a reading at the time when he broke with much of his earlier thinking, including Kant's, near 1876.

Late in his active life, in 1887, Nietzsche read extensively about Kant again. During a visit to the library at Chur, Switzerland, in mid-May and early June 1887, he reread Kuno Fischer's *Geschichte der neuern Philosophie: Bd. 5: Immanuel Kant und seine Lehre* and excerpted seven pages of discussions, summaries, and quotations from this work, based on five of Kant's books.[87]

The number of references to Kant in Nietzsche's published works and notebooks reflects his importance for the late Nietzsche, with approximately 150 in the late period compared to 40 in the early and 25 in the middle periods.[88] The late Nietzsche's interest is more likely due to reading of secondary sources discussing Kant and to Nietzsche's own increasing critique of Kantian-inspired thinking than to any direct reading of Kant.[89]

There is no evidence of Nietzsche's having read Kant's best-known ethical work, *Grundlegung zur Metaphysik der Sitten,* but he closely read Schopenhauer's detailed discussion and critique of this work in 1884.[90]

In view of Kant's enormous stature, Nietzsche's reading about him must have been extensive. Probably the earliest and most important influences were Schopenhauer, Lange, Überweg, and Fischer, as mentioned above. Furthermore, Nietzsche returned to Schopenhauer and Lange often and reread their works many times throughout his life. Two of Nietzsche's early friends, Deussen and Romundt, were deeply influenced by Kant and wrote books about Kant's philosophy. Nietzsche owned four books on Kant by Romundt and one by Deussen. There are no annotations in these, but Nietzsche probably read them carefully. The first book by Romundt, his *Habilitationsschrift* at the University of Basel with the title *Die menschliche Erkenntniß und das Wesen der*

Dinge (1872), deals mainly with Kant and is, in print, dedicated to "My friend Friedrich Nietzsche."[91] Another work that Nietzsche read early is Otto Kohl's dissertation: *I. Kant's Ansicht von der Willensfreiheit* (Leipzig, 1868), in which he defends Kant's view of human free will against Schopenhauer's determinism. Many other works by Julius Bahnsen, Johan Carl Friedrich Zöllner, Afrikan Spir, Rudolf Lehmann, Otto Liebmann, Philipp Mainländer, Eduard von Hartmann, and others are likely to have been important for Nietzsche's knowledge of Kant.[92]

Schopenhauer, but also Lange and Kant, to a large extent determined Nietzsche's thinking and reading about philosophy for the ten years after 1865. For a while, during the spring of 1868, Nietzsche even considered writing his doctoral dissertation in philosophy instead of classical philology on themes inspired by Lange, Schopenhauer, and Kant. In an attempt to combine his interest in philosophy with his knowledge and ability in classical philology and inspired by Lange, Nietzsche worked on Democritus during 1867 and 1868, but did not succeed in finishing the work. Nietzsche also worked on the important historian of ancient philosophy, Diogenes Laertius, and published several philological articles on him. Unexpectedly, Nietzsche was offered a professorship in classical philology in Basel in 1869 at the age of twenty-four, even before he had decided what his doctoral dissertation was going to be about. This was an offer he could not refuse, although he accepted it with some foreboding. His plan to spend a year in Paris together with Rohde had to be abandoned. For his philosophical development, the new situation meant privation and a certain conserving effect: it would delay his breach with Schopenhauer and Kant.

Nietzsche had a strong desire when he went to Basel to be more than a philologist and to teach his students something about Schopenhauer's Weltanschauung. The first years in Basel required the inexperienced Nietzsche to spend a great deal of time preparing for his lectures and teaching, of which the great majority did not concern classical philosophy. Much of his energy and enthusiasm were also spent on Wagner, music, and general culture. Nietzsche's interest in education resulted in much reading in this field and several public lectures on the theme "the future of our educational institutions." There was not much time for philosophy in the more conventional sense, but he succeeded in further developing his knowledge of and views about Plato, the pre-Socratics, and the tragic Weltanschauung. The one modern philosopher Nietzsche managed to read extensively and attentively was the Schopenhauerian and metaphysical Eduard von Hartmann (see chapter 4 below).

When a chair in philosophy at Basel became vacant in 1871, Nietzsche made an attempt to acquire it but had too little philosophical education and too few published writings to be seriously considered. However, his own description of his philosophical interests and capacity in his letter of application is of interest to us: he claimed to have intimate knowledge of ancient philosophy (aesthetics, ethics, and the history of ancient philosophy) and within modern philosophy, especially that of Kant and Schopenhauer.[93]

For the next two or three years, Nietzsche continued along the path he had begun with the publication of several "Untimely Meditations." The three major influences on him continued to be Schopenhauer, Lange, and Kant in the philosophical realm; Wagner in the cultural realm; and Greek antiquity generally. From a broader perspective, Nietzsche's general philosophical position was not unusual, especially not among nonacademic philosophers where it can be said to have been almost a standard view (and was described as such by a reviewer of German philosophy at the time).[94]

Paul Rée

In 1875–76 Nietzsche went through an intellectual crisis that resulted in his break with his earlier metaphysically and aesthetically colored Weltanschauung and with Schopenhauer, Kant, and Wagner. Nietzsche was aware of the crisis and breach—and discussed it in letters and notes at the time—and when his next book, the aphoristic *Human, All Too Human* (1878), was published, Wagner and all of Nietzsche's other friends also clearly recognized it.[95] There were several influences upon and causes for the break. From one perspective it can be seen as a resurfacing of his position from 1868: a dissatisfaction with classical philology and a desire for more substantial knowledge (historical and in the natural sciences) and for philosophy. Also of importance was Nietzsche's own examination of his idealistic position while working on the three "Untimely Mediations" about Schopenhauer (1874), classical philology (never completed but worked on during 1875), and Wagner (written in 1875 and 1876).

At this time Nietzsche began to read books about natural science, anthropology, and political economy. The one strong philosophical influence on him was the reading of, and then the personal friendship with, Paul Rée (1849–1901), who was five years his junior. Rée was a German Jewish philosopher who had written a doctoral dissertation in Latin about Aristotle's *Ethics* (Halle, 1875).[96] He had acquired an avid interest in the moral history of mankind, and this was the subject of the four books he published in his lifetime and of what was, in his own view, his magnum opus, published shortly after his death. Rée had an abiding interest in natural science and was profoundly influenced by Darwin and Schopenhauer but also by the French moralists (La Rochefoucauld, Montaigne, Vauvenargues) and Comte. His philosophy consisted largely of a combination of naturalism, empiricism, evolutionism, positivism, and utilitarianism. Nietzsche first met him briefly in 1873 through their mutual friend Heinrich Romuldt. Nietzsche's interest increased in 1875, when he found and read Rée's first book, *Psychologische Beobachtungen* (*Psychological Observations*), published anonymously earlier that year. Nietzsche thereafter wrote him a very appreciative letter (October 1875) that marked the beginning of their friendship, which developed during the spring of 1876 and lasted for about six years. Rée joined Nietzsche in Bayreuth in August 1876 and left with him—thus very literally taking Wagner's place—and was to remain Nietzsche's closest friend, ally, and inspiration during most of Nietzsche's middle period (1876–82).

Rée's *Psychologische Beobachtungen* was written in the form of aphorisms, and in it he explicitly defended the aphoristic mode of writing. It is likely that this was the strongest direct influence on Nietzsche's decision to write aphorisms (the form he used throughout his middle period). However, the book is a fairly thin volume, and Rée's second book, *Der Ursprung der moralischen Empfindungen* (*The Origin of Moral Sensations*) (1877), had a much more profound influence on Nietzsche's thinking. Rée finished the manuscript while he lived with Nietzsche (and Malwida von Meysenbug) in Sorrento. Rée's influence on Nietzsche in these years appears to have been profound. Although Nietzsche seems to have begun to be dissatisfied with his earlier aesthetic metaphysics— with Schopenhauer and Wagner before he read and met Rée—Rée nonetheless appears to have influenced, or been a catalyst for, a much further development in the direction of positivism and utilitarianism.[97] Rée seems also to a large extent to have been responsible for having encouraged Nietzsche's interest in the new influences on his thinking at this time, such as natural science, anthropology, and the French moralists. Nietzsche's involvement in the content of *Der Ursprung der moralischen Empfindungen,* and with Rée's thinking generally, is visible not only in the style and content of *Human, All Too Human* (1878) but also in the dedication Rée wrote in the copy he gave to Nietzsche: "To the father of this book, with gratitude from its mother."[98] Nietzsche was proud that his philosophy after the publication of *Human, All Too Human* was regarded as a form of "Réealism," and he approved in writing of Rée's strongly antimetaphysical and pro-Darwinian philosophy:

> For what is the principle which one of the boldest and coldest of thinkers, the author of the book *On the Origin of the Moral Sensations,* arrived at by virtue of his incisive and penetrating analysis of human action? "Moral man," he says, "stands no closer to the intelligible (metaphysical) world than does physical man." This proposition, hardened and sharpened beneath the hammer-blow of historical knowledge, may perhaps at some future time serve as the axe which is laid at the root of the "metaphysical need" of man.[99]

It thus seems that Rée had a profound influence on the middle Nietzsche's thinking, especially on his writing in the books before *Morgenröthe* (1881). The friendship ended in late 1882 over their rivalry for Lou Salomé, but Nietzsche probably had begun to distance himself from Rée's thinking before then.

Even after the middle period, Rée continued to have a profound influence on Nietzsche. In 1885 he read Rée's *Entstehung des Gewissen* (*The Origin of Conscience*), published the same year, that applies Darwinian perspectives to a discussion of the origin of bad conscience.[100] And that work, together with several rereadings of *Der Ursprung der moralischen Empfindungen*, constituted Nietzsche's main motivation to write *Zur Genealogie der Moral* (1887) and was its primary counterposition.[101]

Even after the break in Nietzsche's intellectual development in 1875–76, he frequently read Schopenhauer and Lange, but he was using them as critical sparring partners. Of the major early influences discussed in this chapter, Emerson was the only one toward whom Nietzsche did not become critical: he continued to read Emerson frequently and with enthusiasm throughout his life.[102]

As is common, once Nietzsche had passed the age of thirty or thirty-five, we no longer see any major or profound philosophical influences on him. He continued to develop intellectually in the 1880s, but there are no positive philosophical influences comparable to Schopenhauer, Lange, or Rée. However, one important new aspect was that Nietzsche, who resigned from his professorship due to illness in the summer of 1879, learned to read French fluently between 1879 and 1883, and thereafter he was profoundly influenced by French literature and culture. The influence of French philosophy (apart from the moralists whom he read in part in German translation in the second half of the 1870s) was more limited.[103]

In 1882 Nietzsche broke with Rée for personal reasons, and after this second crisis, and with the writing of *Also Sprach Zarathustra* (1883–85), he moved into his last phase. During this time there were, of course, a number of philosophical and nonphilosophical influences on Nietzsche but no single one of paramount importance. In fact, Nietzsche's philosophical development and position during the 1880s is, on the first level, best seen as an opposition and critique of philosophical positions (especially positions he himself had earlier embraced), such as Plato's, Kant's, Schopenhauer's, and that of English philosophy. This corresponds well with Nietzsche's continual emphasis on self-overcoming. On another level, however, we will see a number of positive influences on Nietzsche's thinking, even if many of these were of a nonphilosophical nature and therefore will be mentioned only briefly below.

3

The Young Nietzsche
1844–69

As is the case for most young people, Nietzsche's first philosophical influences came from persons and sources outside of philosophy. Most important was a strong Christian influence, which made him a very pious child. The early death of his father—a Protestant pastor—when Nietzsche was only five years old may well have had the effect of intensifying his childhood faith (and perhaps his desire to emulate his father). In his first years at school he was called "the little pastor," partly due to his bearing but also because he could cite long passages from the Bible by heart.[1] At least from the time when he began at Schulpforta in 1858, the ancient Weltanschauung (and from early on especially Homer) became an additional massive influence that continued to affect him until his mental collapse in 1889.

The young Nietzsche's very first mention of philosophy (to my knowledge) was made in relation to literary influences. After having read the Romantic poet and thinker Novalis in his uncle's library in 1859, Nietzsche wrote that Novalis's "philosophical thoughts interest me," but he did not show any particular interest in Novalis later on.[2] Other early literary-philosophical influences came from the reading of Hölderlin, Goethe, and Schiller, and even Byron and Shakespeare may have played a role. However, most important for Nietzsche's philosophical development before his discovery of Schopenhauer in 1865 was his relation to Christianity. According to Nietzsche himself, his first philosophical speculation, at the age of twelve, concerned the problem of evil and the nature of God.[3] That he was piously Christian until after his confirmation in March 1861 is apparent from a number of different sources: religious poems, statements in his early autobiography, letters to family and friends, and his interest in religious music.

Between 1861 and 1865, however, Nietzsche lost his faith.[4] The most important direct philosophical influences on this development are likely to have been his reading of Ralph Waldo Emerson and of Ludwig Feuerbach's *Das Wesen der Christenthum;* possibly his reading in 1861 and 1862 of the journal *Anregungen für Kunst, Leben und Wissenschaft,* which contained many articles on materialist philosophy and on theological questions;[5] possibly H. Hettner's account of Voltaire and his critique of Christianity, which Nietzsche read and extensively excerpted in early 1863; Lessing's *Nathan der Weise* (and contemporary discussions of this work) in 1864; and David Friedrich Strauss's *Das Leben Jesu* in 1865.[6] Nietzsche's skepticism regarding Christianity is fairly obvious in writings from the spring of 1862, most clearly so in the essay *Fatum und Geschichte* and in a draft of a letter dated April 27, 1862, to Krug and Pinder.[7]

Nietzsche's skepticism was possibly further encouraged by his excerpting in early 1863 of more than thirty pages of text about Voltaire as man and philosopher (including much about Voltaire's relation to religion) from the literary historian Hettner's *Literaturgeschichte des achtzehnten Jahrhunderts: Part II: Geschichte der französischen Literatur.* In early 1865, Nietzsche read David Friedrich Strauss's *Das Leben Jesu* and the closely allied Daniel Schenkel's *Das Charakterbild Jesu,* 3rd ed. (1864),[8] which seem finally to have confirmed and reinforced Nietzsche's loss of faith in the Christian God. An important, but nonphilosophical, probable additional cause for Nietzsche's increasing skepticism toward Christianity was the teaching of historical criticism at Pforta, that is, the approach or method of regarding religious texts not as holy but as historical documents to be interpreted by means of their historical content and context.[9]

Returning to the period before 1865, we can note that the philosophical author whom Nietzsche read most was Cicero. Nietzsche continued to read him well into the 1870s and gave university courses on him, but his reading of Cicero and his philological work on him seem to have had a very limited philosophical, cultural, or general influence on him.[10] The first year in which Nietzsche began to show distinctly philosophical interests was 1862, when he was seventeen and eighteen years old. That year he read Machiavelli's *Il prinicipe* (in Italian, in his extracurricular Italian class, but possibly also in German); probably Feuerbach's *Das Wesen der Christenthum;* the journal *Anregungen für Kunst, Leben und Wissenschaft;* Rousseau's *Emil;* Schiller's *Aesthetische Erziehung;* Emerson's *Die Führung des Lebens (The Conduct of Life);* and possibly also *Versuche (Essays).* And he claims to have read and refuted materialism.[11] With the possible exception of Schiller, this was all done outside the rather extensive school curriculum.

It seems likely that the question of materialism was the first philosophical topic (religious questions excepted) on which Nietzsche took an independent view, in 1861–62. Part of this involvement was later reflected in his enthusiasm for Lange's *Geschichte des Materialismus,* in his work on Democritus (and Epicurus), and in his interest in science and physiology. The extent of Nietzsche's interest in philosophy that year can further be seen in his two essays, "Fatum und Geschichte" and "Willensfreiheit und Fatum," both of which he wrote for the three-member cultural club Germania. These essays, especially the first, contain an astonishing amount that later turned up in his philosophy.[12] Emerson's influence on these essays is apparent, as is his general influence on Nietzsche. Nietzsche began to read Emerson that year (1862) and read and reread him again almost every year until at least the mid-1880s. As we have seen above, Emerson was the first major philosophical influence on Nietzsche, followed by Plato the next year and Schopenhauer in 1865.

Nietzsche had not shown any interest in Plato before 1863, but that year Nietzsche began to read him with enthusiasm, both in German and in Greek. That year and the next, he read several of Plato's dialogues; wrote a school essay on the *Symposium* for his Greek teacher,[13] Professor Karl Steinhart (an important Plato scholar); and claimed that the *Symposium* was his favorite text by Plato and one of his favorite ancient texts.[14] During Nietzsche's first year at the university in Bonn, he attended a course on the *Symposium* by the famous philologist Otto Jahn and a general course on Plato by the philosopher Carl Schaarschmidt. However, apart from this, we see no signs of any interest in Plato in 1865 or in the ensuing years until 1869 and 1871, when he himself began to teach Plato in Basel.[15]

During Nietzsche's last year at Pforta (1864), he worked hard to prepare himself for the examination and to write his final essay about the Greek aristocratic poet Theognis. Apart from his interest in Plato, Nietzsche apparently borrowed a book by Hobbes (presumably *Leviathan*) from Pinder, but no influence from such a reading has been discovered. Later that year, Nietzsche also seems to have read and discussed Lessing's Enlightenment play *Nathan der Weise,* with its critique of religious dogmatism, and several texts about it. The next year Nietzsche read Lessing's *Laokoon: oder über die Grenzen der Malerei und Poesie,* an important work in aesthetics and the philosophy of aesthetics.

The Enlightenment thinker Gotthold Ephraim Lessing (1729–81) is one of the very few German thinkers toward whom Nietzsche had a generally positive attitude throughout his development, but he seems never to have become closely engaged with Lessing. Nietzsche possessed Lessing's collected works in five volumes (Leipzig, 1867)—lost from his library after 1942—and *Minna von Barnhelm* as a separate volume.[16] Nietzsche read the latter work at school, and in 1864 and 1865, as stated above, he read *Nathan der Weise* and *Laokoon.* He claimed in a letter of April 6, 1867, to Gersdorff that he was attempting to learn to write better German with the help of Lessing, Lichtenberg, and Schopenhauer. It is likely that this was when Nietzsche acquired Lessing's collected works. Near 1880 he probably also read Lessing's translation of two dramas and a more theoretical text about drama by Diderot.[17] Nietzsche is likely to have read further works by Lessing, but it seems unlikely that this reading influenced his thinking in any major way.[18]

During Nietzsche's time as a university student, from October 1864 to April 1869—the first year at Bonn, the rest in Leipzig, excluding a year of military service and convalescence in Naumburg—he worked hard to become a classical philologist, and the greater part of his reading and writing from this period were specialized studies in the field of classical philology. However, during this time he also read a massive book about modern philosophy, attended an introductory course on the history of philosophy, discovered Schopenhauer and Lange, and thus became consciously interested in philosophy in general and in Schopenhauerian philosophy in particular.

During the winter semester of 1864–65, Nietzsche began to acquire a broader perspective on philosophy. According to a letter dated October 31, 1864, to Hermann Kletschke, the pastor at Pforta, that Nietzsche wrote in Bonn shortly after having arrived there, it appears that he already had begun to study the history of philosophy since Kant. "The latter [my scholarly activity] I especially intend this semester to direct at the study of Hebrew, and also the history of art and the history of philosophy after Kant, which I already am studying privately with the help of a few books."[19] The philosophical work he refers to here—not previously identified—is the first general work of philosophy we know that he read, and as such it constitutes the first known evidence of Nietzsche's broadening interest in philosophy. The book he read in October 1864, and continued to read for the next half year, was Karl Fortlage's *Genetische Geschichte der Philosophie seit Kant* (Leipzig, 1852), x+488 pages.[20] Fortlage strongly emphasized Kant's importance and can be regarded as a neo-Kantian[21] but also had a strong sympathy for Fichte. The work consists of a thorough discussion of German philosophy from Kant until the middle of the nineteenth century. It begins with a 75-page account of Kant's philosophy followed by a discussion of a number of minor and major philosophers, most extensively Fichte, Schelling, and Hegel (40–60 pages each) but also Schopenhauer (pp. 407–23). The book ends with four shorter and more general chapters: "The Relation between Philosophy and Socialism" (pp. 456–76), "A Comparison of the Different Systems" (pp. 477–82), "Philosophical Habits and Methods" (pp. 482–84), and "Skeptisicm As the Only True Position of Science" (pp. 484–88).

At Bonn, Nietzsche attended (rather irregularly) a large number of courses (series of lecture and seminars), of which two or three were philosophically relevant. During the winter semester of 1864–65, he attended the classicist Otto Jahn's course "Plato's *Symposium*," and in the summer semester of 1865 Nietzsche took two courses by the philosopher Karl Schaarschmidt: "Plato's Life and Teaching" and "Outline of the History of Philosophy." The notes that Nietzsche took while attending the course on the history of philosophy, which have not yet been published, make up about half of sixty handwritten pages.[22] They cover a general introduction; Indian philosophy; Greek philosophy from the sophists to Hellenistic time; a brief account of Greek and Roman patristic writings; four pages about Spinoza; short passages about Locke, Berkeley, Hume, Condillac, Bonnet, Condorcet, Buckle, and the Scottish school of common sense; a listing of Kant's works; and a one-page summary of Schopenhauer's critique of Kant's philosophy.[23] Of special interest is the absence of German philosophy with the exception of Kant (and Schopenhauer's critique of Kant). Furthermore, these notes show that already at this early time, before his discovery of Schopenhauer, Nietzsche had come across Schopenhauer's thinking not only in the journal *Anregungen für Kunst, Leben und Wissenschaft* in 1861–62 (as mentioned above) and in Fortlage's book but also in this course. The lectures probably emphasized Kant's philosophy and only used Schopenhauer as a means of approach, since Nietzsche seems later to have been unaware of any knowledge of Schopenhauer before the discovery.[24] Nonetheless, it is not unlikely that these first encounters could have facilitated Nietzsche's acceptance of Schopenhauer when he discovered him a few months later.

Nietzsche seems to have continued to read philosophy privately after the end of the term, for in September 1865, shortly before he moved to Leipzig, he wrote to his friend Mushacke: "To coffee I take a bit of Hegelian philosophy, and if I have bad appetite then I take Straussian pills, perhaps 'die Ganzen und die Halben.'"[25] He also was soon to read, appreciate, and be profoundly influenced by Strauss's best-known work, *Das Leben Jesu* (*The Life of Jesus*). However, it was the discovery of Schopenhauer's *Die Welt als Wille und Vorstellung* (*The World As Will and Representation*) in October or November 1865 that changed Nietzsche's relation to philosophy. He immediately became a Schopenhauerian, more pessimistic and fatalistic, and eventually he even became dissatisfied with classical philology. He managed to persuade several of his friends to begin reading Schopenhauer and thereafter shared his thinking with these friends. For a time in 1866 he read Schopenhauer one evening every other week with Gersdorff and Mushacke.

Nietzsche's philosophical reading during these years can be well summarized as consisting of an extensive and intensive reading of Schopenhauer's *Die Welt als Wille und Vorstellung* and *Parerga und Paralipomena* and probably also his other works as well. Second, Nietzsche began in 1866 to read a number of books (and later also articles) about Schopenhauer, such as R. Haym's *Arthur Schopenhauer* (Berlin, 1864) and V. Kiy's *Der Pessimismus und die Ethik Schopenhauers* (Berlin, 1866), and by Schopenhauerians such as Bahnsen, Spielhagen, Radenhausen, and Hartmann (the latter first in 1869). During this period Nietzsche also read works relating to the Schopenhauerian Weltanschauung, among which can be counted Lange (who was no Schopenhauerian but whose philosophy was Kantian and rather compatible with Schopenhauer's), Seneca (whom Nietzsche claims "reminds one of Schopenhauer"),[26] and Kant. (See table 1 at the end of the book for details.)

Nietzsche bought, read, and praised Julius Bahnsen's magnum opus, *Beiträge zur Charakterologie: Mit besonderer Berücksichtigung pädagogischer Fragen* (Leipzig, 1867), two volumes (442 and 362 pages), in November 1867.[27] As a Schopenhauerian, Nietzsche regarded Bahnsen as a "philosophical friend" and planned and hoped to learn to know him personally.[28] Julius Bahnsen (1830–81) followed Schopenhauer closely but at the same time developed his philosophy in a more individual direction by emphasizing that true reality is not one general will as Schopenhauer claimed but instead was many contradicting wills that constitute human beings whose inner life therefore is always in turmoil. Nietzsche also borrowed and read Bahnsen's *Zur Philosophy der Geschichte* (1872) in 1871 and 1872 and later acquired *Der widerspruch im Wissen und Wesen der Welt* (*The Contradiction in the Knowledge and Nature of the World*) (Leipzig, 1882), two volumes. (We have no definite evidence that he read it, but it seems likely that he did.)[29]

Another Schopenhauerian work that Nietzsche bought and probably read at this time was Christian Radenhausen's massive four-volume *Isis: Der Mensch und die Welt* (*Isis: Man and the World*) (first edition anonymously published in 1863 and second edition in 1870–71).[30] In the work Radenhausen attempts to construct an overall cultural history of the world based on natural science, especially Darwinism, and Schopenhauer's philosophy and by using a historical approach. The first two volumes deal mainly with religion and ethics from a naturalistic and historical perspective, the latter two with questions relating to natural science, social life, and philosophy.

Nietzsche began to read Kant in 1867. The only work we know for certain that he read at this early stage of his life was Kant's *Kritik der Urtheilskraft* (*Critique of Judgment*). (Later he did some limited further reading of Kant.) However, as we have seen above, Nietzsche also read much about Kant by Kuno Fischer, Friedrich Ueberweg, Otto Liebmann, O. Kohl, and K. Rosenkranz in addition to the extensive discussions of Kant in Schopenhauer's texts and Lange's *Geschichte des Materialismus* (*History of Materialism*). The discovery of Schopenhauer hence not only awoke Nietzsche's philosophical interest but also determined almost all of his philosophical thinking and reading in the ensuing years.

Apart from this rather extensive Schopenhauer-related reading in 1866–68 (and some general histories of philosophy discussed below), the philosophical works that Nietzsche read for the most part pertained to his study of Diogenes Laertius and of Democritus. The one exception is that he continued to read Emerson—but even Emerson, schooled in German Romantic thinking, can easily be read as compatible with Schopenhauer.

Nietzsche seems to have made some attempts to get a better overall view of philosophy, possibly motivated by a desire to understand and compare Schopenhauer's philosophy with that of others and to compensate for his lack of formal philosophical education. For this purpose Lange's *Geschichte des Materialismus* was important, but he also bought Friedrich Ueberweg's three-volume *Grundriss der Geschichte der Philosophy von Thales bis auf die Gegenwart* (*Overview of the History of Philosophy from Thales to the Present*), which contains an extensive running annotated bibliography. Nietzsche read it attentively and copied down a large number of titles for future reading in 1867–68.[31]

The most important reading Nietzsche did about general philosophy and the history of philosophy was Karl Fortlage's *Genetische Geschichte der Philosophie seit Kant* (Leipzig, 1852) in 1864–65; Schopenhauer (whose works contain much about the history of philosophy) in 1865; Lange's *Geschichte des Materialismus*, which Nietzsche continued to read and reread many times, in 1866;[32] and Ueberweg's *Grundriss der Geschichte der Philosophy* in 1867–68. Other general accounts that Nietzsche read were Kuno Fischer's *Geschichte der neuern Philosophie* in several volumes in 1867–68, 1881, and 1887; probably also both C. A. Brandis's and E. Zeller's histories of philosophy; Roth's *Geschichte unserer abendländische Philosophie* (1858) in 1869; George Henry Lewes's *Geschichte der alten Philosophie* (1871) in 1871 (and in 1875); Überweg again in 1873; and John William Draper's *Geschichte der geistigen Entwickelung Europas* (1871) and *Geschichte der Konflikte zwischen Religion und Wissenschaft* (1875) in 1875. In 1875 and 1876 Nietzsche bought several other works, but it is not known whether he read them: R. Zimmermann's *Studien und Kritiken zur Philosophie und Aesthetik* (1870), Wilhelm Windelband's *Forschung*,[33] F. Harms's *Die Philosophie seit Kant* (1876), and Hans Vaihinger's *Hartmann, Dühring and Lange: Zur Geschichte der deutschen Philosophie im 19. Jahrhundert: Ein kritischer Essay* (1876), 235 pages. He also bought Eugen Dühring's *Kritische Geschichte der Philosophie von ihren*

Anfängen bis zur Gegenwart (1873) and *Cursus der Philosophie als streng wissenschaftlicher Weltanschauung und Lebensgestaltung* (1875) in 1875 (and read them sometime between 1875 and 1883), William Lecky's *Geschichte des Ursprungs und Einflusses der Aufklärung in Europa* (1873) and *Sittengeschichte Europas von Augustus bis auf Karl den Grossen* (1879) in 1881 and 1883, and finally E. de Roberty's *L'ancienne et la nouvelle philosophie: Essai sur les lois générales du développement de la philosophie* (Paris, 1887) in late 1887 or early 1888.

Many other works that Nietzsche read also contained chapters or sections dealing with the general history of philosophy such as Alfred Espinas' *Die tierischen Gesellschaften: Eine vergleichend-psychologische Untersuchung* (1879), Eduard von Hartmann's massive *Phänomenologie des sittlichen Bewusstseins: Prolegomena zu jeder künftigen Ethik* (1879), Hellwald's *Culturgeschichte,* and several of the works by Otto Liebmann, including *Kant und die Epigonen* (Stuttgart, 1865) and *Zur Analysis der Wirklichkeit: Eine Erörterung der Grundprobleme der Philosophie* (Strassburg, 1880).

4

The Early Nietzsche
1869–74

During Nietzsche's first three years as a professor at Basel (1869–71)—a period during which he worked hard to prepare lectures and teaching, finished the extensive index to twenty-four massive volumes of the journal *Rheinisches Museum für Philologie* (which was published at the end of 1871 as a separate volume of 167 pages),[1] and wrote *The Birth of Tragedy* (published in January 1872)—his philosophical reading did not change much from the previous years. However, there were some changes. He read much more about classical philosophy, especially Plato and about Plato. There was less time to read Schopenhauer and Schopenhauerian literature (and possibly his first enthusiasm had cooled a little), although Nietzsche began to read intensively the Schopenhauerian Eduard von Hartmann's *Philosophie des Unbewussten* (1869) and continued to read him for the next six years and again later. Finally, Nietzsche also read a great deal of literature relating to philosophical aspects of Greek tragedy in relation to his work on *Die Geburt der Tragödie*. His reading about tragedy was extensive and included a large number of philological articles in the *Rheinisches Museum für Philologie*. Apart from the articles in the *Rheinisches Museum*, two strands can be observed in this reading.[2] The first includes works dealing with different aspects of tragedy, especially its aesthetic significance. Examples include Schlegel, Müller, Alberi, Wartenburg, Schiller, Vischer, and Grote (see table 1 for full titles). The second strand relates to the more specific question of Aristotle's view of tragedy. Of course, Nietzsche read Aristotle himself. Nietzsche bought Aristotle's collected works in German in 1868; possessed several individual volumes, also in German; and is also likely to have read some texts in Greek. He also read a number of studies of the Aristotelian view of tragedy—Teichmüller, Bernay, Oncken, Spengel, Reinkens—and in 1871 he heard Rudolf Eucken (1846–1926), the newly installed professor of philosophy in Basel, speak about Aristotle's relevance in contemporary times.

Among the modern philosophers, Nietzsche's reading and relation to Gustav Teichmüller (1832–88) is especially interesting, for, as professor of philosophy in Basel, Teichmüller was Nietzsche's colleague for about two years until Teichmüller moved to the University of Dorpat in 1871 and was replaced by Eucken. Nietzsche does not seem to have had a close personal relationship with Teichmüller in Basel but did read many of his books.[3] Nietzsche had probably already heard Teichmüller speak during the philological conference in Halle in October 1867, where he gave a talk titled "Die Lehre des Aristoteles über die Unterscheidung des Epos von der Tragödie."[4] Teichmüller was a highly productive writer of philosophical books. He wrote a number of studies on Aristotle's aesthetics, several volumes on the history of concepts, and, in the 1880s, works in which his own metaphysical philosophy was more clearly expressed.[5] His philosophy shared kinship with that of Leibniz and Lotze, and he was opposed to the neo-Kantians. We know that Nietzsche read the first two volumes of Teichmüller's *Aristotelische Forschungen* in 1869 and 1870. In 1879 Overbeck sent Nietzsche Teichmüller's booklet *Ueber die Reihenfolge der Platonischen Dialoge* (1879). In 1883 Nietzshe read the third volume of his *Aristotelische Forschungen, Neue Studien: Die praktische Vernunft Aristoteles*. Most importantly, in 1883 and 1885 Nietzsche read *Die wirkliche und die scheinbare Welt: Neue Grundlegung der Metaphysik* (1882), a work that was of great importance to him. In 1883 and 1885 he also referred to two unidentified books by Teichmüller that he had borrowed from Overbeck (one was almost certainly *Die wirkliche und die scheinbare Welt*),[6] and in 1881 he read a long critical discussion and review of Teichmüller's *Darwinismus und Philosophie* in Otto Caspari's *Zusammenhang der Dinge* (1881). At least until Nietzsche read *Die wirkliche und die scheinbare Welt* in 1883 and 1885, he seems to have used Teichmüller's writings mainly as a source of information but to have had little interest in his philosophy as such, or at least Nietzsche never discussed or expressed an opinion of him as a philosopher. It seems likely that Nietzsche took the word *Bildungsphilister* ("cultural Philistine"), which he used and made current in *David Strauss, the Confessor and the Writer* (1873), from Teichmüller.[7]

Nietzsche's most important new reading in the field of philosophy (apart from ancient philosophy) during his first years as a professor was Eduard von Hartmann's *Philosophie des Unbewussten: Versuch einer Weltanschauung* (1869), which he read intensively in 1869 and 1870; again, together with other works by Hartmann, in 1873 and 1874; and probably yet again in late 1887 or 1888.[8] Nietzsche read Hartmann carefully and, with the exception of Schopenhauer and Lange, is likely to have been the philosopher who taught Nietzsche most about philosophy. In particular, many of Nietzsche's references to and discussions of pessimism relate to, and were written in response to, his reading of Hartmann. Eduard von Hartmann (1842–1906) was a Kantian and Schopenhauerian, and it was as such—thus partly in a positive spirit—that Nietzsche began reading him, even though relatively soon Nietzsche turned distinctly critical toward him.[9] Hartmann was one of the best-known and most widely read German philosophers in the 1870s and 1880s.[10] He attempted, eclectically and synthetically, to construct a complete Weltanschauung. Hartmann's philosophy, inspired by Hegel as well as by Kant and Schopenhauer, was pessimistic and metaphysical in nature. Hartmann owed debts to Schelling and Leibniz for their contributions to the discovery of the unconscious. His magnum opus was *Philosophie des Unbewussten: Versuch einer Weltanschauung* (Berlin, 1869), covering about seven hundred pages.[11] The book was later published in a large number of editions and grew to three massive volumes.

Nietzsche read the book as early as 1869 and then again in 1870 and 1873. He was still interested enough in it to buy a (second?) copy of the work in 1875. Hartmann had written and anonymously published a 240-page critique of especially the scientific or natural philosophical parts of the book in 1872 with the title *Das Unbewusste vom Standpunkt der Physiologie und Descendenztheorie: Eine kritische Beleuchtung des naturphilosophischen Theils der Philosophie des Unbewussten aus naturwissenschaftlichen Gesichtspunkten* (*The Unconscious from the Perspective of Physiology and the Theory of Evolution: A Critical Discussion of the Natural Philosophical Parts of the "Philosophy of the Unconscious from the Perspective of Natural Science"*) (Berlin, 1872). Nietzsche owned and had read this work probably in 1872 or 1873.[12] In 1875 Nietzsche bought Hartmann's *Wahrheit und Irrthum im Darwinismus* (1875) and in 1879 his *Phänomenologie des sittlichen Bewusstseins* (1879), 871 pages, and read and heavily annotated it in 1883.

Hartmann concerned himself seriously with Darwinism and is likely to have been one of Nietzsche's primary sources for information and criticism on the topic.[13] Hartmann's position in relation to Darwinism can be summarized as emphasizing that it consists of several parts, of which he accepted the theory of descent, that is, evolution (and integrated it with his philosophy), while he rejected the principle of selection for both technical and philosophical reasons. He did accept that natural selection occurred, but it was, according to him, far from sufficient to explain the force of evolution.

The first we hear about Hartmann in relation to Nietzsche is in a letter of May 4, 1869, from Romundt to Nietzsche[14] in which he discusses Hartmann for about a page and in a manner that suggests that Nietzsche and Romundt earlier had spoken of Hartmann. Romundt recommended that Nietzsche read Hartmann's essay "Über die nothwendige Umbildung der Schopenhauerschen Philosophie" in the

Philosophische Monatshefte, and it seems likely that Nietzsche read the article. We know that Nietzsche read *Die Philosophie des Unbewussten* in 1869 intensively and often—"I read him often, for he has the most beautiful knowledge"—and returned to it several times, but not without a critical attitude.[15]

This early critique seems, at least partly, to be due to the fact that Hartmann added non-Schopenhauerian tenets to his philosophy (especially Hegelian ones) and that he did not sufficiently express his gratitude to and dependence on Schopenhauer. However, Nietzsche's enthusiasm was sufficient that in 1872 he sent Hartmann a copy of his just-published *Die Geburt der Tragödie.*[16] We also know that Nietzsche returned to *Die Philosophie des Unbewussten* and read and excerpted much from it during 1873, when he was preparing his second *Unzeitgemäße Betrachtungen* with the title *Vom Nutzen und Nachteil der Historie für das Leben* (1874), which also contains many explicit and implicit references to Hartmann. Most of Nietzsche's few published references to Hartmann come from this work.[17]

In 1872 or 1873 Nietzsche read Hartmann's anonymously published *Das Unbewusste vom Standpunkt der Physiologie und Descendenztheorie: Eine kritische Beleuchtung des naturphilosophischen Teils der Philosophie des Unbewussten aus naturwissenschaftlichen Gesichtspunkten* (Berlin, 1872), perhaps without knowing that it was by Hartmann.

By 1874 Nietzsche seems to have bought and read and to have been very disappointed and dissatisfied with Hartmann's *Shakespeares Romeo und Julia.* It seems as though the reading of this work, more than anything else, finally made Nietzsche highly critical of Hartmann (even before he had broken with Schopenhauer). In a letter of June 14, 1874, to Oswald Marbach, Nietzsche wrote: "In regard to Shakespeare—do you know that disgusting pamphlet by our little fashion-philosopher E. von Hartmann against Romeo and Juliet?"[18] However, Nietzsche nonetheless continued to read Hartmann, although in 1875 he referred to "Hartmannism" as an illness that Germany suffers from and referred to Hartmann as a "*Scheindenker.*"[19]

When Hartmann's dense and massive *Phänomenologie des sittlichen Bewusstseins: Prolegomena zu jeder künftigen Ethik* (Berlin, 1879) appeared, Nietzsche immediately bought (and possibly read) it. By this time he mainly read Hartmann as a source of information and maybe also as a stimulus, for Nietzsche had lost all respect for him. In a letter from this time Nietzsche referred to this work as "Hartmann's latest outrageousness 'Prolegomena to *every* future ethics'!!"[20] It is not clear whether Nietzsche read this work in 1879. If he did read it, it seems not to have left any traces in his writings and notes. More probably he waited and read it intensively, annotated it richly, and excerpted much from it during the first half of 1883, and there is ample evidence of this reading.

In 1884 and 1885 Nietzshe continued to discuss Hartmann often, and often with strongly ad hominem statements, but he probably did not reread the *Phänomenologie des sittlichen Bewusstseins.* Nietzsche apparently intended to read another of Hartmann's books, *Vermischte Schriften,* for in a note from 1883 he made a list of nine authors or books he apparently intended to read, including this one. It is not clear if he ever read this work, but he probably did not. (He seems never to have read most of the titles listed.) In 1887 he discussed Hartmann again in more detail as part of an attempt to work through his own views on pessimism, including quoting some short passages (probably an indication that he returned to Hartmann and read here and there in his works, especially the *Die Philosophie des Unbewussten*).

In 1871 and 1872 Nietzsche borrowed and read the Schopenhauerian Julius Bahnsen's *Zur Philosophie der Geschichte: Eine kritische Besprechung des Hegel-Hartmann'schen Evolutionismus aus Schopenhauer'schen Principien* (Berlin, 1872).[21] This brought to the forefront the opposition between two different interpretations and developments of Schopenhauer's philosophy: that of Hartmann's and Bahnsen's. Unfortunately, we do not know how Nietzsche reacted and stood in regard to these two alternative versions of Schopenhauer's philosophy at this time (to which later two further ones, Dühring's and Mainländer's, were added). Only much later, in 1887, did Nietzsche briefly discuss and reject them:

> But let me ask you: Should we perhaps consider that old humming-top Bahnsen as a credit to the Germans, seeing how voluptuously he revolved his life long around his real-dialectical misery and his "personal tough luck"? Perhaps precisely this is German? (I herewith recommend his writings for the purpose for which I have used them myself, as an anti-pessimistic diet, especially on account of their *elegantiae psychologicae;* they should, I think, be effective even for the most constipated bowels and mind.) [...] Neither Bahnsen nor Mainländer, not to speak of Eduard von Hartmann, gives us any clear evidence regarding the question whether Schopenhauer's pessimism, his horrified look into a de-deified world that had become stupid, blind, mad, and questionable, his *honest* horror, was not merely an exceptional case among Germans but a *German* event.[22]

However, Nietzsche's view in the early 1870s, when he himself was a Schopenhauerian, may well have been different and much more appreciative.[23] It seems likely that he also read Bahnsen in 1882 or later since he possessed one volume of his *Der widerspruch im Wissen und Wesen der Welt* (1882), but nothing is known about such a reading from that time.

In 1872–73 Nietzsche read several works that profoundly influenced his view of language. The central tenet of his philosophy of language is a denial that there exists a close correspondence between language and reality. He argues that language, concepts, and grammar force us to think in certain ways, but there is no ground for believing that this corresponds to any reality outside of language. Nietzsche thus holds a radical skepticism toward language as an instrument for our search for truth. In his early writings Nietzsche emphasized the deceptive power of words and concepts. In the text "Ueber Wahrheit und Lüge im aussermoralischen Sinne" he wrote: "What, then, is truth? A mobile army of metaphors, metonyms and anthropomorphisms—in short, a sum of human relations, which have been enhanced, transposed and embellished poetically and rhetorically, and which after long use seem firm, canonical and obligatory to a people: truths are illusions about which one has forgotten that this is what they are [...] to be truthful means using the customary metaphors—in moral terms: the obligation to lie according to a fixed convention, to lie herd-like in a style obligatory for all."[24] In his later works, he especially emphasized the power of grammar, as shown in his critique of Descartes' *cogito ergo sum*[25] and in such statements as "I fear we are not getting rid of God because we still believe in grammar."[26]

In a different and somewhat more conventional sense, that is as an historian and philologist, Nietzsche also used language to determine values and social structures in our early history. This is especially evident in *On the Genealogy of Morals* (1887). In this use of language (somewhat unusual for a philosopher at this time), he was helped by his education as a philologist and was stimulated by his historical and philological reading, especially Leopold Schmidt's two-volume *Die Ethik der alten Griechen* (Berlin, 1882), which Nietzsche possessed, read, and annotated sparingly.

The main influences on Nietzsche's philosophy of language seem to have been Schopenhauer, Gerber, and Lichtenberg. However, possible ancient influences do not seem to have been thoroughly examined—for example, Democritus, Epicurus, Plato, and Aristotle—as well as studies of ancient views and uses of language about which he read (and taught) fairly extensively, such as F. Blass and T. Benfey.[27]

Before 1872, as a classical philologist dedicated to Schopenhauer's philosophy, Nietzsche developed a philosophy of language under the influence of Lange, Hartmann, and Kant.[28] In September 1872, Nietzsche borrowed Gustav Gerber's *Die Sprache als Kunst* (*Language As Art*) (Bromberg, 1871)[29] and used it extensively for the notes to his lectures *Darstellung der antike Rhetorik*, which he held during the winter term of 1872–73.[30] And much of the content of Gerber's book also found its way into Nietzsche's text "Ueber Wahrheit und Lüge im aussermoralischen Sinne," which he dictated to Gersdorff during the summer of 1873.[31]

Although the influence of Gerber on both of these texts is undeniable, it is also true that Nietzsche probably had arrived at some of these conclusions before he read Gerber. Nietzsche goes further than Gerber in some respects but in others disagrees with him.

Shortly after having read Gerber, Nietzsche acquired, read, and annotated Georg Christoph Lichtenberg's eight-volume *Vermischte Schriften* (Göttingen, 1867), which also came to influence Nietzsche's view of language and rhetoric (discussed below in the account for the years 1875 and 1876).

The only alien influence during this time, 1869–71, was that of Montaigne's *Essays,* which Nietzsche received as a Christmas present from the Wagners in 1870 and probably read in 1871, although his more intensive reading and appreciation of Montaigne occurred later, most notably in the later 1870s and in 1884–85.[32]

In the three years after the publication of *Die Geburt der Tragödie* and the index to the *Rheinisches Museum,* Nietzsche's philosophical reading continued on the same path as before, that is, consisting to a large extent of Schopenhauerian texts and works by and about ancient philosophers. However, there was a new emphasis on the pre-Socratics rather than on tragedy as well as an emphasis on Aristotle. His reading of Aristotle broadened beyond his view of tragedy to include the early parts of the *Metaphysics,* which he mainly read for information about the pre-Socratics; the *Politics,* which he intended to teach; and especially the *Rhetoric,* which he gave courses on and translated in part into German.

Nietzsche had a special interest in and affinity for the pre-Socratic philosophers generally. This interest almost certainly evolved from his earlier interest in tragedy and the preclassical Greek Weltanschauung and literature, especially his writing on Theognis. The first of the pre-Socratics that Nietzsche turned his attention to and studied philologically and philosophically was Democritus (most intensively during 1867 and 1868). Nietzsche was probably inspired to do so by his reading of Lange's *Geschichte des Materialismus* with its high praise of Democritus. Nietzsche never finished the article on Democritus he was working on at that time. After he became a professor in 1869, his enthusiasm primarily became focused on Heraclitus and, to a lesser extent, Empedocles.[33]

Nietzsche's interest in the pre-Socratics is shown in his never-completed companion volume to *Geburt die Tragödie,* "Die Philosophie im tragischen Zeitalter der Griechen." The pre-Socratics also figured prominently in much of his *Nachlaß* from the first half of the 1870s and, most importantly, in his notes to the lectures "Die vorplatonischen Philosophen," which he delivered three or four times between 1869–70 or 1872 and 1876.[34]

In spite of some obvious affinity and of Nietzsche's high praise of the Greek sophists in 1888—inspired by his reading of Victor Brochard's *Les sceptiques grecs* (Paris, 1887)—Nietzsche seems to have had very little interest in this group of thinkers, who are often regarded as part of the pre-Socratics.[35]

In the field of modern philosophy, Nietzsche's reading in these years became broader and included several new influences, especially Kantian and neo-Kantian ones but others as well. This is not surprising, for 1872–75 is the period when he wrote his *Unzeitgemäße Betrachtungen* on different themes.[36] In relation to these works he intensively read David Friedrich Strauss's *Der alte und der neue Glaube* (Leipzig, 1872) in 1872 and 1873 (and reread it several times thereafter) and probably also several of Strauss's other works.[37] In *Der alte und der neue Glaube* Strauss argues that we are no longer Christians and that we should accept the new worldview that modern science presents to us, built especially on nineteenth-century physics and Darwinism. Nietzsche's first *Untimely Meditation* about Strauss is his least philosophically interesting book. It is somewhat surprising that he wrote it, but Nietzsche may have been encouraged by Wagner (whom Strauss had attacked in public) and motivated by Lange's critique of him and by Strauss's attack on Schopenhauer and pessimism generally.[38] In most of the book Nietzsche concentrated on Strauss's stylistic flaws, ignoring almost completely his critique of Christianity, but Nietzsche criticized Strauss's pro-German nationalism and his "philistine optimism."

In 1873 Nietzsche read a fairly large number of works relating to the study of history and the philosophy of history—for example, Hamann, Lichtenberg, Hartmann, Hegel, Schiller, Emerson, and Hume—that influenced his writing of *Von Nutzen und Nachtheil der Historie für das Leben*. The critical view of historical scholarship and the corresponding idealistic view of history presented in this essay are not representative of Nietzsche's views after 1875–76.[39] The following year, 1874, he read Schopenhauer, Hartmann, and Carl Fuchs[40] in preparation for writing *Schopenhauer als Erzieher*.

The most distinctly new influence during these years was that of Kant and the neo-Kantians, but it should be remembered that this largely can be seen as an aspect of Nietzsche's Schopenhauerian interests and heritage. (Nietzsche hardly ever even mentioned Kant without also mentioning Schopenhauer.) Most important for the first year were the Kantians Zöllner and Spir, but Nietzsche also began to read the famous neo-Kantian Otto Liebmann and the Kantian-inspired Kuno Fischer, and Nietzsche read and spent time with his friend Heinrich Romundt (1845–1919), who had come to Basel to teach and to do his habilitation (postdoctoral research) in philosophy about Kant. Nietzsche also reread Lange who, as stated above, was another neo-Kantian.[41]

Nietzsche borrowed the first edition of Afrikan Alexandrovich Spir's (1837–90) *Denken und Wirklichkeit: Versuch einer Erneuerung der kritischen Philosophie* (Leipzig, 1873; 2nd enlarged ed., 1877) in 1873, and reading it extended his knowledge of Kant and influenced his writing both in "Die Philosophie im tragischen Zeitalter der Griechen" and "Ueber Wahrheit und Lüge im aussermoralischen Sinne." Spir appears to be one of the major philosophical influences on Nietzsche.[42] Nietzsche, for example, accepted some of Spir's critique of Kant and used it for his argument in "Die Philosophie im tragischen Zeitalter der Griechen." Later Nietzsche bought, intensively read, and was further influenced by the second edition of the work (see the discussion below for 1877).

Nietzsche read the astrophysicist Johann Friedrich Zöllner and his *Über die Natur der Kometen: Beiträge zur Geschichte und Theorie der Erkenntnis,* 2nd ed. (Leipzig, 1872), 100+523 pages, in 1872, and Nietzsche's unannotated copy is still in his library. The book consists of a strange mixture of science, moral statements, and Kantian philosophy.[43] In the book, Zöllner criticized contemporary science and the praxis of science (for example, as overemphasizing the importance of experiments) from a Kantian perspective. The book led to a scandal in the scientific community. Nietzsche, who earlier in 1872 had experienced a similar but more limited critique from his colleagues, sympathized with Zöllner. In November 1872 Nietzsche wrote enthusiastically in a letter to Rohde that "there is startlingly much *for us* in it," and he even publicly defended "der edle Name Zöllners" in his article "Neujahrswort," which was published in *Musikalisches Wochenblatt* in January 1873. Nietzsche later picked up Zöllner's critique and directed it at the humanities and especially the writing of history.[44] It has also been argued that Zöllner's concept of space influenced Nietzsche[45] and that he was also possibly influenced by Zöllner's psychological theory of nature and especially his use of the expression "unconscious conclusions."[46] Later, at least by 1884, Nietzsche came to reject Zöllner.[47]

Another important Kantian influence, stimulus, and source of information was Romundt. Nietzsche came to know him in 1866 in Leipzig, where they shared an enthusiasm for Schopenhauer. Their friendship was such that Nietzsche always had the upper hand (similar to his friendship with Paul Deussen but unlike the much more equal friendships with Gersdorff, Rohde, and Rée). They frequently associated as students for about two years in Leipzig, between 1866 and early 1869, and then for another three years in Basel, where Romundt came to do his habilitation about Kant and to teach.[48] In Basel, Romundt shared a flat with Nietzsche and Overbeck for most of three years, and the three of them often discussed philosophy and shared new readings.[49] At this time Romundt had very similar philosophical interests to Nietzsche's:

Schopenhauer, Kant, Democritus, and Empedocles. We know almost nothing about the discussions held in their home, but we know that Nietzsche read a number of Romundt's books, probably six of them: his doctoral dissertation in 1869 and his habilitation book (dedicated in print to Nietzsche) in 1872, several works about Kant and Christianity during 1881–85, and possibly others later.[50] The reading in the 1880s is likely to have been less careful and more critical—as Romundt stated in his dedication to Nietzsche in the first of them, from 1882, Nietzsche had then turned antimetaphysical, while Romundt had became increasingly metaphysical[51]—but nonetheless it would have given Nietzsche new information about Kant.

In 1874 Nietzsche's continued reading of Plato, and particularly Aristotle, is noticeable.[52]

Apart from his Schopenhauerian, Kantian, and Greek reading, Nietzsche also read Marcus Aurelius and several authors discussing aesthetics, the Austrian playwright Franz Grillparzer, Hamann, and Lotze.

In 1873 Nietzsche borrowed Hamann's *Schriften und Briefe* and read his *Sokratische Denkwurdigkeiten* with appreciation (and quoted him in "Die Philosophie im tragischen Zeitalter der Griechen," sec. 2), but at the same time Nietzsche objected to his style.[53] He also made one reference to Hamann and quoted a short sentence from him in his lectures "Darstellung der antiken Rhetorik," which he held during the summer term of 1874.[54] We have no evidence of any further reading, nor does Nietzsche refer to him again.

The ground for believing that Nietzsche might have read something by the German idealist metaphysical philosopher R. H. Lotze (1817–81) at this time is that he referred to "that terrible book by *Lotze*."[55] Shortly before that, Nietzsche mentioned Lotze as someone to attack.[56] Soon thereafter Nietzsche also criticized Lotze in several letters to his friend Carl Fuchs.[57]

Nietzsche's library contains two books by Lotze, but both of them are from later years: *Grundzüge der Metaphysik: Dictate aus den Vorlesungen* (Leipzig, 1883), 94 pages, and *Grundzüge der Ästhetik: Dictate aus den Vorlesungen* (Leipzig, 1884), 113 pages. The first book contains annotations, but they appear not to be by Nietzsche's hand. The second volume is without annotations and is only partially cut open.

5

The Middle Nietzsche
1875–82

During 1875 and 1876, Nietzsche went through an intellectual and emotional crisis and changed fundamental aspects of his Weltanschauung, including breaking with Schopenhauer, Kant, and Wagner.[1] Nietzsche then exchanged his earlier enthusiasm for metaphysics, idealism, pessimism, art, and aesthetics for a position that was skeptical and free-spirited, placed science above art, and praised the Enlightenment. It appears not to have been noticed previously that in section 272 of *Human, All Too Human,* called "Annual Rings of Individual Culture," he seems to have been describing his own intellectual development:

> Men at present begin by entering the realm of culture as children affected religiously, and these sensations are at their liveliest in perhaps their tenth year, then pass over into feebler forms (pantheism) while at the same time drawing closer to science; they put God, immortality and the like quite behind them but fall prey to the charms of a metaphysical philosophy. At last they find this, too, unbelievable; art, on the other hand, seems to promise them more and more, so that for a time metaphysics continues just to survive transformed into art or as a mood of artistic transfiguration. But the scientific sense grows more and more imperious and leads the man away to natural science and history and especially to the most rigorous methods of acquiring knowledge, while art is accorded an ever gentler and more modest significance. All this nowadays usually takes place within a man's first thirty years. It is the recapitulation of a curriculum at which mankind has been labouring for perhaps thirty thousand years.[2]

He even went so far as to write a note in 1877, intended to be included in his next book, where he rejected his earlier writings: "I want expressly to inform the readers of my earlier writings [i.e., *The Birth of Tragedy* and the *Untimely Meditations*] that I have abandoned the metaphysical-artistic views which fundamentally govern them: they are pleasant but untenable. He who speaks publicly early is usually quickly forced to publicly retract his statements."[3]

Many of his later discussions of his own thinking and development, such as in new prefaces, refer to this break and how the character of his writing and thinking changes. For example, in a note from 1883 he critically characterizes his early thinking: "Behind my *first period* grins the face of *jesuitism:* I mean the deliberate holding on to illusion and the forcible annexation of illusion as the *foundation of culture.* Or put differently: <u>Buddhism</u> and a longing into nothingness (the Schopenhauerian opposition between theory and praxis is untenable). The first danger was given to W[agner]."[4]

At this time, 1875–76, Nietzsche's reading and the influences on him also changed fundamentally. As we have seen in chapter 2 above, probably the most influential causes of this change—apart from the internal changes in Nietzsche's thinking due to his examination of his position while writing the later *Unzeitgemäße Betrachtungen* about Schopenhauer and Wagner (and the unfinished "We Classicists")—was that Nietzsche began to read, and came personally to know, the positivist- and Darwinist-inspired Paul Rée, who was generally quite influenced by British and French thinking.[5] Nietzsche read Rée's anonymously published *Psychologische Beobachtungen* (1875) with great enthusiasm in October 1875. Shortly thereafter they became friends, and they subsequently played important roles for each other's writing and thinking for the next six years or so. The changes in Nietzsche's thinking, and the psychological crisis, seem to have begun before he read Rée, but the reading and friendship with him clearly reinforced and probably radicalized the changes. Nietzsche at this time changed both the content and the style of his writing. In style, he went from writing essays to writing aphorisms. There were probably many causes for this stylistic change—for one thing, his new view of philosophy and science was more compatible with short, relatively self-contained texts than with the flourishing rhetoric of essays—but Rée, who had written his *Psychologische Beobachtungen* in the form of aphorisms and at the beginning of the book argued for the use of the aphoristic form, is likely to have been the most important cause.[6]

The other major influence at this time was French thinking largely mediated through Rée, especially the French moralists (i.e., psychologists), including La Rochefoucauld, Vauvenargues, Chamfort, Montaigne, and La Bruyère, and the Enlightenment philosophes, most notably Voltaire but also Diderot, Helvetius, and Fontenelle and probably also Rousseau in his *Confessions.*[7]

> *European books.*—When reading Montaigne, Larochefoucauld, La Bruyère, Fontenelle (especially the *Dialogues des Morts*), Vauvenargues and Chamfort we are closer to antiquity than in the case of any other group of six authors of any nation.

Through these six the *spirit of the final centuries* of the *old* era has risen again—together they constitute an important link in the great, still continuing chain of the Renaissance. Their books are above the changes of national taste and philosophical colouring which as a rule every book nowadays radiates and has to radiate if it is to become famous: they contain more *real ideas* than all the books of German philosophers put together: ideas of the kind that produces ideas and which—I am at a loss to finish the definition; it is enough that they seem to me authors who have written neither for children nor for dreamers, neither for young ladies nor for Christians, neither for Germans nor for—I am again at a loss to complete my list.—But to state a clear commendation: if they had been written in Greek the Greeks would have understood them. [...] On the other hand, what clarity and delicate precision those Frenchmen possess! Even the most acute-eared of the Greeks must have approved of this art, and one thing they would even have admired and adored, the French *wittiness* of expression: they *loved* such things very much without themselves being especially gifted in them.[8]

Voltaire became one of Nietzsche's heroes and was, from this time forward, the philosopher he praised most of all in his published writings.[9] He visited Voltaire's estate in Ferney in the spring of 1876;[10] read Voltaire with Rée and Meysenbug in Sorrento later the same year;[11] dedicated his next book *Menschliches, Allzumenschliches* (1878) to Voltaire;[12] and from then until his mental collapse consistently and strongly praised Voltaire.[13]

Consistent with this sympathy and interest in the Enlightenment, which Nietzsche had not shown before 1875, is his intensive reading during 1875 and 1876 of Lichtenberg, the German Enlightenment thinker and writer of aphorisms.[14] Georg Christoph Lichtenberg (1742–99) is one of the only two German philosophers and thinkers (the other being Lessing) toward whom Nietzsche had a positive attitude throughout his development.[15] Lichtenberg is mentioned several times by Lange, not at all by Überweg, but often and positively by Schopenhauer, which may well have influenced Nietzsche's view and also may have been the reason Nietzsche began to read Lichtenberg in the first place. The young Nietzsche's only reference to him was in a letter to Gersdorff from 1867,[16] where Nietzsche said that he was attempting to improve his German style of writing with the help of Lessing, Lichtenberg, and Schopenhauer.[17] In 1873 Nietzsche acquired and read Lichtenberg's eight-volume *Vermischte Schriften* (1867) and then continued to read them intensively, especially the first two volumes, in 1875 and 1876. Nietzsche may have returned to them and read them after that—his copy of the first volume is annotated with two different pens—but we have no certain evidence of any later reading.

Apart from influencing Nietzsche's philosophy of language as mentioned above, Lichtenberg may well have contributed an important influence to

Nietzsche's use of aphorisms instead of to essays in his middle period (although Rée was almost certainly still more influential).

A fairly large number of books in the fields of the natural and social sciences that Nietzsche bought and read in 1875 and 1876 were published in a series called Internationale wissenschaftliche Bibliothek (International Scientific Library), published simultaneously in German, French, and English. The German editions were published by the Verlag von F. A. Brockhaus in Leipzig. The first book of the series, John Tyndall's *Das Wasser in seinen Formen,* was published in 1873. Thereafter, many volumes were published in 1874 and in the ensuing years. Nietzsche's library contains the first nineteen volumes of the series (all published between 1873 and 1876) as well as volumes 22, 39, 40, and 45. Most of these books are nonphilosophical, but they include some more philosophical works—including John William Draper, *Geschichte der Conflicte zwischen Religion und Wissenschaft* (Leipzig, 1871); Herbert Spencer, *Einleitung in das Studium der Soziologie* (Leipzig, 1875); Alexander Bain, *Geist und Körper* (Leipzig, 1874); and Walter Bagehot, *Der Ursprung der Nationen: Betrachtungen über den Einfluss der natürlichen Zuchtwahl und der Vererbung auf die Bildung politischer Gemeinwesen* (Leipzig, 1874)—as well as works on the relation between biology and philosophy, for example, by Oscar Schmidt, *Descendenzlehre und Darwinismus* (Leipzig, 1873), and Léon Dumont, *Vergnügen und Schmerz: Zur Lehre von den Gefühlen* (Leipzig, 1876).

Nietzsche's ordering and reading of the books in the series Internationale wissenschaftliche Bibliothek exemplifies his new and more positivistic and scientifically oriented interests at this time, and reading them is likely to have influenced and reinforced the new direction of his philosophy.[18]

Other closely related areas of interest for Nietzsche at this time was anthropology and ethnology (probably also inspired by Rée). Among the books that Nietzsche read in these fields were J. Lubbock's *Die Entstehung der Zivilisation und der Urzustand des Menschengeschlechtes* (1875) and E. B. Taylor's *Die Anfänge der Cultur* (1873) in 1875 and possibly an unidentified work by Huntley and a rereading of Bagehot's *Der Ursprung der Nationen* in 1879. This reading was important for Nietzsche's shift away from metaphysics and aesthetics to a more historical and anthropological philosophy in the later 1870s. In the very first section of the first book he published after this change, *Human, All Too Human* (1878), he contrasted metaphysical philosophy, with its belief in opposites, to historical philosophy, "the youngest of all philosophical methods," which claimed that there were no such opposites but only gradual change.[19] In the second section he wrote: "A lack of historical sensibility is the original failing of all philosophers. [...] Everything, however, has come to be; there are *no eternal facts:* just as there are no absolute truths.—From now on therefore, *historical philosophizing* will be necessary, and along with it the virtue of modesty." At least from this time onward, the historical perspective was an important one for determining Nietzsche's views.[20]

Another new influence in 1875 was oriental philosophy, especially Indian but also Confucian thinking.[21] The main source of Nietzsche's interest in and knowledge about Indian philosophy was undoubtedly his reading of Schopenhauer, but even before his discovery of Schopenhauer, Nietzsche encountered a general overview of Indian philosophy in Schaarschmidt's philosophy course, which he attended in 1865 in Bonn. We also know that in 1870 Nietzsche borrowed C. F. Koeppen's *Die Religion des Buddha und ihre Entstehung* and read and excerpted M. Müller's *Beiträge zur vergleichenden Religionswissenschaft* and *Beiträge zur vergleichenden Mythologie und Ethologie,* which contained discussions of oriental religion and philosophy.

In January 1875 Nietzsche encouraged Paul Deussen, who had written to him disclosing his plans to work on and translate works of Indian philosophy.[22] Nietzsche referred to this as a noble task and said that he had a strong desire to read the works Deussen would make available. It is clear that Nietzsche at this stage (still under the influence of Schopenhauer and metaphysical philosophy) regarded Indian philosophy favorably, for he was critical of his friend Windisch and other philologists working with Indian texts for having little interest in and understanding of Indian philosophy. Nietzsche also mentioned a public lecture by Brockhaus that he attended a few years earlier in Leipzig titled "Overview of the Results of Indian Philology" but that to Nietzsche's disappointment contained nothing about Indian philosophy. In letters to Overbeck dated May 26, 1875, and to Rohde dated December 8, 1875, Nietzsche said he would attempt to persuade his publisher to begin a series of translations of Indian philosophy and later more specifically the Buddhist text *Tripitaka.*

During 1875 Nietzsche read and bought a number of books relating to oriental philosophy. In the early part of the year he read and excerpted from O. Böhtlingk's three-volume *Indische Sprüche* (1870–73) and borrowed M. F. Müller's *Einleitung in die vergleichende Religionswissenschaft* (1874) from the university library in Basel. Nietzsche also read F. A. Hellwald's *Culturgeschichte* (1874), which contained accounts of all the major cultures, including Eastern cultures, and bought two books about Chinese philosophy, Confucius *Ta-Hio* and *Lao-tse tao.* Nietzsche much appreciated the three-volume *Indischer Sprüche* by Wolfgang Senff, which Gersdorff had sent him as an early Christmas present, and he claimed to have borrowed and read the *Sutta Nipata* in an English translation and in it found a phrase he was most fond of: "Thus I wander, lonely as the rhinoceros."[23]

This interest in Asian philosophy in 1875 was probably more a remnant of his earlier Schopenhauerian and metaphysical thinking than suggestive of the new ways of thinking to which he was turning. This interest seems also to have reached its summit in 1875, although Nietzsche continued to read some books about Eastern philosophy later, especially works by Deussen, who sent copies of the books he wrote and translated to Nietzsche.

After 1875, Nietzsche's most important reading about Eastern philosophy (apart from Schopenhauer) was Deussen's *Die Elemente der Metaphysik* (1877) in 1877 and M. Haug's *Brahma und die Brahmanen* in 1878. In 1879 Nietzsche heard J. Wackernagel's lecture on Buddhism (and then attempted to help him have it published), and in 1880 Nietzsche read and excerpted Wackernagel's *Über den Ursprung des Brahamismus* (1879) and asked in a letter to have his work on Buddhism sent to him. In the 1880s Nietzsche read H. Oldenberg's *Buddha: Sein Leben, seine Lehre, seine Gemeinde* (Berlin, 1881), which he read, annotated, and excerpted in 1882 and 1884; Deussen's *Das System des Vedanta* (1883) in 1883, 1884, and 1886; Deussen's *Die Sutra's des Vedanta* (1887) in 1887; and L. Jacolliot's *Les législateurs religieux Manou* in 1888.[24] The reading of the latter work was the stimulus for Nietzsche's often misunderstood comments about the Laws of Manu in *Twilight of the Idols* and *The Antichrist*.[25]

Another influence at this time of transition, 1875–76, was his reading of the two Schopenhauerians Eugen Dühring (1833–1921) and Philipp Mainländer (1841–76). Dühring is the philosopher Nietzsche read the most of (with the possible exception of Plato and Schopenhauer). Dühring can reasonably be regarded as one of Nietzsche's most important philosophical influences, although already by 1875, when Nietzsche began to read Dühring, Nietzsche seems to have been more in opposition to than in agreement with him. Nietzsche knew of and spoke well of Dühring as a Schopenhauerian as early as 1868 and may have read something by him at this time, but Nietzsche only began to read Dühring extensively in 1875.[26] That year Nietzsche bought seven works by Dühring. All but two contain annotations, and thus Nietzsche certainly read them. Later, in 1884–85, he bought, read, and annotated Dühring's autobiography, *Sache, Leben und Feinde: Als Hauptwerk und Schlüssel zu seinen sämmtlichen Schriften* (1882).

Dühring was not only a philosopher but also a political economist with socialist leanings and was strongly nationalistic and antisemitic with otherwise broad interests, including natural science. In his books he attempted to give a broad summary of present knowledge and a philosophy that suited the modern world. His philosophy was, broadly speaking, positivistic, owing a debt to Schopenhauer, Feuerbach, and Comte.[27] Dühring denounced metaphysics (although he nonetheless retained many metaphysical tenets) and argued that philosophy must construct a worldview in accord with the results of natural science. Nietzsche's library contains the following eight titles by Dühring, and the majority of them contain annotations or show other signs of having been read. Seven of them he bought in June 1875.

> *Der Wert des Lebens: Eine philosophische Betrachtung* (Breslau, 1865). Bought and read in 1875. Extensively excerpted and sparingly annotated.
>
> *Cursus der Philosophie als streng wissenschaftlicher Weltanschauung und Lebensgestaltung* (Leipzig, 1875). Fairly extensively annotated. Bought in 1875. Read in 1881, 1883, and 1885 and possibly in 1875 and 1888 also.
>
> *Natürliche Dialektik: Neue logische Grundlegungen der Wissenschaft und Philosophie* (Berlin, 1865). Contains a few small indications of having been read. Bought in 1875. Not known when read.
>
> *Kritische Geschichte der Philosophie von ihren Anfängen bis zur Gegenwart,* second edition, (Berlin, 1873). Annotated. Bought in 1875. Not known when read.
>
> *Kritische Geschichte der allgemeinen Prinzipien der Mechanik* (Berlin, 1873). No annotations. Bought in 1875. Not known if and when read.
>
> *Kursus der National- und Sozialökonomie, einschliesslich der Hauptpunkte der Finanzpolitik* (Berlin, 1873). No annotations. Bought in 1875. Not known if and when read.
>
> *Kritische Geschichte der Nationalökonomie und des Sozialismus,* 2nd ed. (Berlin, 1875). Annotated. Bought in 1875. Read but not known when.
>
> *Sache, Leben und Feinde: Als Hauptwerk und Schlüssel zu seinen sämtlichen Schriften* (Karlsruhe and Leipzig, 1882). Annotated. Bought and read in 1884–85.

Nietzsche may also have read other works by Dühring. For example, Nietzsche alluded briefly (without implying that he had read it) to Dühring's *Robert Mayer, der Galilei des XIX Jahrhunderts* (1880), which was being published in 1879 by Nietzsche's own publisher, Ernst Schmeitzner,[28] and Nietzsche and Schmeitzner often discussed Dühring in their correspondence.

Of the books by Dühring that Nietzsche owned, four are specifically philosophical, but most of the others also contain philosophically relevant texts. For example, *Kritische Geschichte der Nationalökonomie und des Sozialismus,* lightly annotated by Nietzsche, contains extensive discussions and accounts of political philosophy and philosophers, including especially many radical thinkers' views, from a socialist perspective.[29]

The first work by Dühring that we know for certain that Nietzsche read was his *Der Werth des Lebens: Eine philosophische Betrachtung* (1865), viii+235 pages, which he read very thoroughly during the summer of 1875—he wrote an annotated summary of 50 printed pages from it into his notebook[30]—for the explicit purpose of reexamining his own relation to Schopenhauer. Nietzsche's copy of the book is sparingly annotated, mostly relating to places where Dühring discusses *ressentiment* and revenge.[31]

In a to-do list, which shows that his original interest in Dühring was sparked by his interest in Schopenhauer, Nietzsche wrote: "3) To study Dühring, as the attempt to sort out Schopenhauer and to see what I have in Schopenhauer, what not. Thereafter, yet again read Schopenhauer."[32] He also listed Dühring (together with Schopenhauer, Aristotle, Goethe, and Plato) under the somewhat enigmatic title "Books for 8 years," possibly implying his intention to write books about these five authors.[33]

The reading of *Der Werth des Lebens* (and possibly some other works by Dühring that Nietzsche may have read at this time) was important, for it made Nietzsche work through his own philosophical position attentively. The reading of *Der Werth des Lebens* had at least four distinctly positive influences on Nietzsche: (1) It helped him break away from Schopenhauer (although Dühring was a Schopenhauerian); (2) Nietzsche came more and more to agree with and affirm Dühring's view that philosophy is and should be scientific, an important aspect of especially the middle Nietzsche's thinking (although Nietzsche did not share Dühring's optimism); (3) Nietzsche picked up the term and concept *ressentiment* from Dühring's book[34] (Dühring discussed it fairly extensively, using the French word for resentment, and Nietzsche followed him in this, and this concept and feeling became, especially for the late Nietzsche, an important negative concept, allied with nihilism and *décadence*);[35] (4) it helped Nietzsche think about the concept of justice (and revenge). Dühring argues that justice arises from the feeling of revenge and desire for equality by the weaker, and he approves of *ressentiment*, revenge, and justice. It is possible that at this early stage Nietzsche agreed with Dühring,[36] but by the time Nietzsche wrote *On the Genealogy of Morals*, he strongly rejected this view, with explicit references to Dühring, and argued that justice has its origin among the strong and active.

Nietzsche read *Cursus der Philosophie als streng wissenschaftlicher Weltanschauung und Lebensgestaltung* (Leipzig, 1875) in 1881, 1883, and 1885 and perhaps also in 1875 and 1888. He annotated the book fairly extensively, and it was clearly one of the most important philosophical works that Nietzsche thoroughly examined and entered into dialogue with.[37] In it he encountered a somewhat idiosyncratic account of many of the fields and aspects of philosophy. It is not impossible that his reading of it in 1881 was an important stimulus for his discovery of the idea of eternal recurrence (see the discussion of this concept at the end of this chapter).

It is not known when Nietzsche read *Kritische Geschichte der Philosophie* and *Natürliche Dialektik*. It is likely to have been in or near 1875 when he bought them. The former contains a few annotations distributed throughout the book, while the latter bears no definite signs of having been read, although it contains a mark on page 60, is spotty on pages 63–76, and has one dog-ear on page 124, making it likely that Nietzsche read it.

Kritische Geschichte der Philosophie, xiii+551 pages, contains a relatively conventional history of philosophy from the pre-Socratics to the contemporary period, by means of accounts of the philosophical positions of the most important philosophers. This work is likely to have been one of the major sources for Nietzsche's knowledge of the history of philosophy and its major representatives, such as Bacon, Locke, Hobbes, Descartes, Spinoza, and Comte.

The other book, *Natürliche Dialektik,* xii+227 pages, contains a discussion of the conceptual foundations of philosophy and thinking from a Kantian perspective (which Dühring later rejected). It is not known to what extent Nietzsche read and responded to this work.

The late Nietzsche became increasingly hostile toward Dühring and frequently attacked him generally (mostly in his notebooks and letters) and for his political and social views (socialism, anarchism, and antisemitism). Many, but certainly not all, of Nietzsche's references to these phenomena had Dühring as their primary stimulus.[38]

Dühring is an example of a German nineteenth-century positivist. Other important such representatives were Laas, Avenarius and E. Mach. Nietzsche had read works by the latter two (see chapter 6 in this volume), but he did not discuss them as a group.

Another Schopenhauerian philosopher whom Nietzsche read at this late stage of his Schopenhauerian period was Philipp Mainländer, pseudonym for Philipp Batz. Mainländer presented his pessimistic philosophy in the two-volume *Philosophie der Erlösung* (Berlin, 1876–86), of which the second volume was published posthumously, and argued that sexual abstinence and suicide are the best solution for man, leading to the desired state of extinction. In contrast to most pessimists, Mainländer followed his own prescription and committed suicide in 1876. He attempted to interpret (and change) Schopenhauer's philosophy so that it became less metaphysical. Mainländer did this by claiming that instead of one metaphysical will there are many individual (and immanent) wills that continually struggle with one another. Nietzsche read the first volume of *Philosophie der Erlösung* the year it appeared.[39] He mentioned the work in May 1876, in a draft of a letter to Cosima Wagner, and in early December he wrote from Sorrento that the group there intended to begin reading it together. That they (or he) in fact read it then is confirmed by notes from the time.[40] The work is also listed on a book bill from 1876. The reading of Mainländer is likely to have worked as a stimulus for much of Nietzsche's thinking about philosophy in the late 1870s.[41] It is also likely (combined with Dühring) to have helped Nietzsche to liberate himself from Schopenhauer.[42] Mainländer is perhaps also the most likely candidate as stimulus for Nietzsche's use of the phrase "God is dead," but several other likely candidates have been suggested (see the discussion at the end of this chapter). Mainländer wrote: "God has died, and his death was the life of the world."[43] By the spring of 1883, Nietzsche read the work again and quoted and discussed it in his notes.[44]

In early 1876 Nietzsche acquired the newly published German edition of his friend Malwida von Meysenbug's three-volume *Memoiren einer Idealistin* (Stuttgart, 1876), published anonymously. Nietzsche read the book attentively (and reread it the next year and probably yet again in 1888). It touched him profoundly at a time of crisis, and he recommended it to all of his friends.[45] The reading of this book was probably of limited philosophical importance for Nietzsche but of great personal importance (since it seems to have persuaded him to remain faithful to Schopenhauer, metaphysics, and idealism and thus delayed his positivistic break), and it may have been important for Nietzsche's view of women and feminism. It is the only feminist work Nietzsche ever read in a positive spirit.[46] Apart from radical politics and feminism, Meysenbug emphasized the importance of Goethe for herself (as for Nietzsche) and frequently discussed Wagner and Schopenhauer. (Wagner had given her a copy of *Die Welt als Wille und Vorstellung*, and Schopenhauer's influence on her is very noticeable in the latter part of the work, where she exchanges her activist political attitude for a more Schopenhauerian and aesthetic one.)

Nietzsche never mentions Karl Marx or Friedrich Engels, and it is generally assumed that he had no knowledge of them and their kind of thinking and socialism. However, this is not correct. Marx is referred to in at least eleven books, by nine different authors, that Nietzsche read or possessed. In six of them he is discussed and quoted extensively, and in one of them Nietzsche has underlined Marx's name.[47] The nine authors who mention or discuss Marx, whose works we know that Nietzsche either owned or read, are Jörg, Lange, Dühring, Meysenbug, Frantz, Schäffle, Frary, Bebel, and Jacoby. Of these, the books by Lange, Dühring, Frantz, Schäffle, Bebel, and Jacoby contain extensive discussions and long quotations. Nietzsche read several of these nonphilosophical books in 1876 or shortly thereafter.

During parts of 1876, Nietzsche's illness—serious problems with migraines and with his eyes and stomach—became still worse, and he was released from teaching for a full year. Later he returned to teaching, but due to continued health problems he taught much less than before (and mostly only old courses that he had given earlier) until he resigned his professorship in early 1879. His reading and his notes from these years, 1876–79 (especially 1877), were much more limited than at any other period. Many of the texts he read were in fact read aloud to him by others, including, the members of the group in Sorrento and Peter Gast, Elisabeth, and others in Basel.[48] In Sorrento, where Nietzsche lived with Meysenbug, Rée, and the student Brenner for about half a year while convalescing, they read together a fairly large number of books. Philosophically, the most relevant were Voltaire, Mainländer, and Diderot. Still more important were the reading and discussions of drafts of *Der Ursprung der moralischen Empfindungen* (1877), which Rée was finishing at this time.[49] Apart from having read and discussed this book while it was a work in progress, Nietzsche also seems to have read the finished book in 1877, again in 1883, and possibly also in 1886. During the early readings, he was profoundly influenced by it, but at least by 1882 he had turned critical toward Rée and began to read his books with a much more critical and sometimes even hostile attitude. These later readings were important for Nietzsche's writing of *Zur Genealogie der Moral* (1887), which to a large extent is a counterpoise to Rée and his book. In 1879, Nietzsche also read drafts of early versions of Rée's next book, *Entstehung des Gewissens,* and, in 1885, the finished book. This book too constituted one of the major negative influences on Nietzsche's *Zur Genealogie der Moral,* in which the second essay of three deals with the question of the origin of bad conscience.

Afrikan Spir's two-volume *Denken und Wirklichkeit: Versuch einer Erneuerung der kritischen Philosophie* (Leipzig, 1872), an important work for Nietzsche, came out in a second revised edition in 1877. Nietzsche never mentioned Spir's name in his published writings but twice referred to, or quoted, Spir (without naming him) in *Human, All Too Human.*[50] Nonetheless, many of Nietzsche's notes and comments regarding espistemological questions were written in response to, and in opposition to, *Denken und Wirklichkeit.* Spir's book was almost certainly one of the most important philosophical sources of and stimuli on Nietzsche's thinking about questions of epistemology.

The isolated and little-known Russian metaphysical philosopher Afrikan Spir (1837–90) lived most of his adult life in Germany and then Switzerland. He was primarily influenced by Kant's *Kritik der reinen Vernunft* but also by Spinoza and the British empiricists. Spir argued that it is the task of philosophy to seek absolutely true knowledge (and thus assumed the dichotomy of a true and an apparent reality, which Nietzsche came to reject), and this could only be done, he argued, by understanding consciousness and the supreme law of thought, the principle of identity. Spir published a number of books, but his magnum opus was *Denken und Wirklichkeit.* He also published a number of articles in philosophical journals, and it seems likely that Nietzsche may have read some of them.[51]

Nietzsche acquired Spir's *Forschung nach der Gewissheit in der Erkenntniss der Wirklichkeit* (1869) sometime between 1869 and 1872, and the reading of this work may have influenced Nietzsche's writing of "Ueber Wahrheit und Lüge im aussermoralischen Sinne" (in opposition to Spir, who believed in the possibility of true knowledge).[52] In 1873 and 1874 Nietzsche borrowed the first edition of *Denken und Wirklichkeit*, which consisted of an expanded and reworked version of Spir's first book. Nietzsche read it and used it in his "Die Philosophie im tragischen Zeitalter der Griechen." The work was again thoroughly reworked into the second edition in 1877, which Nietzsche bought, read, and heavily annotated. The book became an example of Kantian metaphysics (with metaphysics taken as equivalent to the unconditional, a definition he had borrowed from Spir), and as such it constituted one of the positions Nietzsche criticized in *Human, All Too Human* as part of his critique of metaphysics and his own earlier position, from a more historical and psychological perspective.

In 1881 Nietzsche again read Spir's work intensively and especially argued against his assumption that the laws of thinking give us information about the world. Against this Nietzsche argued that these laws of thinking are highly unreliable, since they are formed by superstition, the use of language (grammar), and other primitive manners of thinking. In 1885 Nietzsche again read and excerpted Spir, this time together with two other metaphysical works, Teichmüller's *Die wirkliche und die scheinbare Welt* and Paul H. Widemann's *Erkennen und Sein* (1885).[53] Opposing all three of them, Nietzsche argued against "immediate knowledge" ("unmittelbare Gewissheiten") and severely criticized Descartes' *cogito ergo sum,* which both Spir and Teichmüller assumed to be correct and took as an axiom. Spir became Nietzsche's primary example of the whole tradition of metaphysical philosophy that he rejected, from Parmenides and Plato to Kant and Spir, which assumes being, the unconditional, pure spirit, absolute knowledge, objective values, and the *Ding an sich.*

The only other important philosophical reading during 1877, apart from Rée and Spir, was Deussen's *Die Elemente der Metaphysik* (1877), a strongly Kantian and Schopenhauerian work that also contains discussions about Indian philosophy.[54] In the letter of thanks for the book, Nietzsche clearly expressed the philosophical changes he had undergone during the previous two years: "Your book serves me strangely enough as a happy *collection of everything that* I no longer hold as true. [...] Already when I wrote my small study about Schopenhauer I no longer held on to almost any of all the dogmatic aspects."[55]

Another work that probably prompted similar observations about Nietzsche's own development is Alfons Bilharz's *Der heliozentrische Standpunkt der Weltbetrachtung: Grundlegungen zu einer wirklichen Naturphilosophie* (Stuttgart and Cotta, 1879). The philosopher and physician Bilharz (1836–1925) sent him the book in August 1879, and Nietzsche must have read it, for his copy is rather heavily annotated. He does not discuss Bilharz's book, but in a draft to the chapter in *Ecce Homo* about the *Unzeitgemäße Betrachtungen* he referred positively to Bilharz's understanding of *Schopenhauer als Erzieher* and *Richard Wagner in Bayreuth* and to Bilharz as "most scientific."[56]

In 1878 and 1879 Nietzsche continued to read Emerson (and also Schopenhauer and Plato), and he bought John Locke's *Einige Gedanken über Erziehung* (Leipzig, n.d.), but it is not known if or when he read it.[57] The one field that Nietzsche seems to have been influenced by and shown an interest in during these years was French thinking, including Ernst Renan (toward whom he later turned very hostile), Montaigne, Pascal, Helvetius and Fontanelle.[58]

By 1880 Nietzsche had recovered sufficiently from his recurrent illness to begin to read and search for further material for the new turns his philosophical thinking that had taken over the previous few years. Moreover, his resignation from the university of Basel afforded him much more time for this work. In the ensuing years Nietzsche read intensively about Christianity, morality, anthropology, law, and cultural history. Most of this reading lies outside of the theme of this study, which is limited to Nietzsche's philosophical reading, but much of it strongly influenced his cultural views and thought in general.

The influence of French thinkers increased still more in importance (and Nietzsche was beginning to be able to read them without difficulty in French). This is especially true for the fields of French literature, literary criticism, and culture, about which he read extensively, but also the field of philosophy. For example, in 1880 he read La Bruyère's *Die Charaktere*, Pascal, and E. Littré's *La science au point de vue philosophique*, 4th ed. (Paris, 1876).[59] In 1881 he read Charron's *Drei Bücher über die Weisheit*, Chamfort, and Kuno Fischer's *Geschichte der neueren Philosophie I.2: Descartes Schule, Geulinx, Malebrache, B. Spinoza* (Heidelberg, 1865). Nietzsche's reading of French philosophers will be discussed in some detail in my forthcoming study *Nietzsche's Knowledge of Philosophy: A Study and Survey of Nietzsche's Reading of and Relation to German, British, and French Philosophy.*

Another, and essentially new, influence was that of British philosophy. Through Rée and some of the books that Nietzsche read on natural science, he had acquired some knowledge of British philosophy and thinking during the second half of the 1870s, but he seems to have read very little (if any) British philosophy firsthand. During the late 1870s he had accepted positivism and some aspects of scientism, especially the importance of physiology and Darwinism, to a fairly large degree, and contrary to the general assumption, he seems to have had a generally positive attitude toward British philosophy and thinking.[60] Thus, when he began to read it in the early 1880s, he did so with positive expectations.[61] However, very quickly, through the rather intensive reading of Mill, Spencer, and to a lesser extent the Irish historian and philosopher William Hartpole Lecky, these expectations were disappointed. Nietzsche's reading of and response to these authors in 1880–82 is discussed in my study *Nietzsche' and the "English"* (2007).

Among the several books about ethics that Nietzsche read during these years was the Danish bishop and theologian Hans Lassen Martensen's *Die christliche Ethik* (1871; 2nd ed., Gotha, 1873), which he read in 1880. The work consists of three volumes and was widely read and quickly translated into several foreign languages, including German and English.

Nietzsche possessed at least the first volume, with the general title *Allgemeiner Theil*, and possibly all three volumes of this work, but his copy is no longer in his library.[62] At the end of March 1880 Nietzsche asked his mother to send the book to him in Venice.[63] He then read at least the first volume during the spring and summer of 1880. Impressions from this reading can be found in his notes from this time and in *Morgenröthe* (1881).[64] This was when he began his severe critique of morality and Christianity, and his reading of Martensen, along with several other works, gave him both motivation and ammunition for this attack.

One of the most noteworthy aspects of Nietzsche's philosophy is its existentialism and his ability to speak directly to his readers. In this respect his writings differ significantly from those of most other nineteenth-century German philosophers. The reason for the personal and existential nature of his writings is probably mainly to be found in his psychology and the intensity of his undertaking. Several stylistic influences were probably also relevant, among them Schopenhauer, Emerson, and a number of literary ones such as Goethe and Stendhal. Schopenhauer, in his critique of rationalism, probably also constituted a philosophical influence on Nietzsche's existentialism. Emerson, too, was a philosophical influence. Nietzsche's relation to Kierkegaard is also interesting in this respect. There exist many striking similarities between Nietzsche and Kierkegaard. They were both critics of rationality, idealism, and the building of philosophical systems. Instead, their approach was more existential and psychological, and they both strongly emphasized the central position of the individual, the personality, and subjectivity. There also exist, of course, important differences and oppositions between their thinking, of which the most important is the fact that Kierkegaard was a profoundly Christian religious thinker, while Nietzsche regarded Christianity and religion as his main enemy and opponent.

It has generally been assumed that Nietzsche had no knowledge of Kierkegaard. In fact, however, it seems that he had a reasonable knowledge of Kierkegaard's thinking and writing, although Nietzsche never read any full text by Kierkegaard. In Martensen, there are twenty-seven consecutive pages discussing and frequently quoting Kierkegaard as an ethical individualist. The literary critic Georg Brandes, whom Nietzsche read in the 1870s and 1880s, frequently discussed Kierkegaard in some detail in his writings, including in books we know that Nietzsche read. Furthermore, during the autumn of 1887 Nietzsche read and annotated a two-page discussion of Kierkegaard's view of "repetitions" with significant similarity to Nietzsche's eternal recurrence in Harald Höffding's *Psychologie in Umrissen auf Grundlage der Erfahrung* (Leipzig, 1887), including writing "NB" in the margin and underlining Kierkegaard's name in the text.[65] Together, these and other accounts of Kierkegaard's thinking that Nietzsche read constitute about fifty pages of text and contain about five full pages of quotations from Kierkegaard.[66] Kierkegaard is unlikely to have been a profound influence on Nietzsche, but some influence cannot be ruled out.

In late 1879 or early 1880 Nietzsche read and responded favorably to the highly humanistic thinker and philosopher Josef Popper's *Das Recht zu leben und die Pflicht zu sterben* (1878). This reading and Nietzsche's response to it— never before discussed—are particularly interesting, for here we see Nietzsche's response to a highly humanistic position and to a radical form of ethical individualism (in some ways related to that of Max Stirner's). Nietzsche then responded with appreciation, but he would later become highly critical of the sort of idealist position Popper argued for. It is likely that it was Popper's praise of Voltaire and severe critique of Christianity that particularly attracted Nietzsche.[67]

During 1880 and 1881 Nietzsche seems also to have read two important Stoic discussions of philosophy and ethics, Epictetus's short *Manual* (we have no evidence that he ever read the longer *Discourses*)[68] and Marcus Aurelius's *Meditations*,[69] and he also read some secondary literature, such as Benjamin Constant Martha's *Les Moralistes sous l'empire romains, philosophes et poètes,* which he began to read during the autumn of 1879. It was at this time, probably due to this reading, that Nietzsche had the highest opinion of Stoicism. Later he became more critical toward it and also toward Epictetus. Like most Stoics, Epictetus and Aurelius both emphasized self-determination and the importance of controlling one's own will and reason. They argued that we have to accept the external world as it is but can mold our own character. An important aspect of Epictetus's philosophy, in particular, was based on submissiveness, and the ancient writer Aulus Gellius (whom Nietzsche also read) summarized his philosophy with the words "endure" and "abstain." Stoic philosophy may have been an important influence on some aspects of Nietzsche's philosophy and views on ethics. This is especially likely for his idea of eternal recurrence and *amor fati,* both of which have a close kinship with Stoic thinking, and he discovered both ideas at about this time.[70]

Another general work of ethics that Nietzsche read and excerpted in 1880, which is likely to have been important for clarifying his views of ethics and for the beginning of his attack on contemporary morality, was J. J. Baumann's *Handbuch der Moral nebst Abriss der Rechtsphilosophie* (Leipzig, 1879). This work is briefly discussed below in connection with the will to power.[71] Of importance also is Lecky's *Sittengeschichte Europas von Augustus bis auf Karl den Grossen* (1879), which Nietzsche read and heavily annotated in 1881.[72]

Another neo-Kantian whom Nietzsche never mentioned in the published works but read intensively was Otto Liebmann (1840–1912). Nietzsche ordered two of Liebmann's most important books in August 1881: *Kant und die Epigonen* (1865) and *Zur Analysis der Wirklichkeit: Eine Erörterung der Grundprobleme der Philosophie,* 2nd ed. (Strassburg, 1880), viii+680 pages.[73] We have no definite evidence that Nietzsche read the former (and it contains no annotations), but he read the latter intensively and annotated it richly during the autumn of 1881.[74] This work is likely to be the most important neo-Kantian work Nietzsche read. It contains essays from many philosophical fields, and Nietzsche clearly read it attentively, learned from it, and engaged in a dialogue with it. During or before 1887 Nietzsche also acquired Liebmann's *Gedanken und Thatsachen: Philosophische Abhandlungen, Aphorismen und Studien: Erstes Heft: Die Arten der Nothwendigkeit—Die mechanische Naturerklärung—Idee und Entelechien* (Strassburg, 1882), v+121 pages, and read it with interest and annotated it frequently. In a note from the autumn of 1887, it is evident that the reading of this work stimulated his thinking about the will to power.[75] (Its table of contents is given with the discussion of Nietzsche's reading for the year 1887 below.) No thorough examination of Nietzsche's debt and relation to Liebmann seems to have been carried out.

Another of the most important unexamined influences on Nietzsche's philosophy is Otto Caspari's *Der Zusammenhang der Dinge: Gesammelte philosophische Aufsätze* (Breslau, 1881), which Nietzsche ordered from Schmeitzner in June 1881 and read during the autumn.[76] His copy of the book is fairly heavily annotated. It seems that Nietzsche's reading of this work, which contains many discussions of contemporary works of natural science and the philosophy of science, was the source of several of the books he later ordered and read. Nietzsche is likely to have previously read several articles written by Caspari, published in the journal *Kosmos,* and also owned two of his other works.[77] Caspari was a philosopher who frequently wrote on the themes of Darwinism, anthropology, and the philosophy of nature. The reading of this book was part of the background to *Die fröhliche Wissenschaft* (1881)[78] and may even have been one of the most important sources of inspiration of Nietzsche's idea of eternal recurrence. (See the discussion of eternal recurrence at the end of this chapter.)

Nietzsche's knowledge of and relation to Spinoza is of special interest. Nietzsche's most intensive interest in Spinoza and his philosophy occurred in the summer of 1881, at the time when he began to make the transition from his middle to his late period. This is when he made several of his most important philosophical discoveries or inventions, such as eternal recurrence and *amor fati,* and when he also developed and intensified his interest in the concept of will to power. The possibility that Spinoza's philosophy worked as a stimulus or influence on these Nietzschean concepts cannot be ruled out. Furthermore, in the secondary literature, it has been claimed that Spinoza was the most important and influential modern philosopher for Nietzsche, excepting only Schopenhauer.[79] In 1881 Nietzsche wrote an enthusiastic postcard about Spinoza and emphasized six fundamental similarities between their thinking. In it he also referred to Spinoza as a precursor, and he repeated this claim in four notes during the next three or four years. There is probably no other philosopher whom Nietzsche so explicitly considered his predecessor. Spinoza is also frequently mentioned and discussed in Nietzsche's writings—approximately one hundred times[80]—both with high praise, such as, for example, of him as a "genius of knowledge," "the purest sage," and, with severe criticism, calling his philosophy "this masquerade of a sick recluse" and labeling him as inconsistent and naive.[81] It is possible to follow Nietzsche's changing evaluation of Spinoza.

And yet, as I will show below, Nietzsche never read Spinoza![82] Nietzsche, of course, encountered a number of accounts of Spinoza's thinking. One of these, that of the philosopher and historian of philosophy Kuno Fischer's *Geschichte der neuern Philosophie* (volume 2 about Spinoza), which he read twice, is of paramount importance. Thus, any discussion of Nietzsche's views and interpretations of Spinoza cannot be based on an analysis of Nietzsche's and Spinoza's philosophy (as all studies have done so far) but needs to start from Kuno Fischer's account, which is what Nietzsche read, responded to, and based his judgments and analyses upon. To discuss Nietzsche's interpretations and misinterpretations of Spinoza in relation to Spinoza's own writings is simply irrelevant.[83] Nietzsche's implicit trust in secondary accounts is perhaps surprising, but I have elsewhere in this study pointed to a large number of other such cases, including, most importantly, those of Kant and Rousseau.

I will not make a thorough analysis of Nietzsche's and Spinoza's thinking below but will examine all the information we have as to the sources of Nietzsche's knowledge and discussions of Spinoza (and in doing so will point out a number of previously unknown and unidentified sources). I will also briefly comment on a few of the most important possible influences of Spinoza on Nietzsche.[84]

Nietzsche truly discovered Baruch Spinoza (1632–77) in the summer of 1881 when he read Kuno Fischer's account of Spinoza's thinking in *Geschichte der neuern Philosophie I.2: Descartes und seine Schule: Fortbildung der Lehre Descartes. Spinoza* (München, 1865),[85] and Nietzsche thereafter wrote an enthusiastic post-card dated July 30, 1881, to Overbeck: "I am really amazed, really delighted! I have a precursor, and what a *precursor!* I hardly knew Spinoza: what brought me to him *now* was 'the guidance of instinct.' Not only is his whole tendency like my own—to make knowledge the most *powerful passion*—but I also find myself in five main points of his doctrine; this most abnormal and lonely thinker is closest to me in *these* points precisely: he denies free will—; purpose—; the moral world order—; the nonegoistical—; evil—; of course, the differences are enormous, but they are differences more of period, culture, field of knowledge. In summa: my solitariness which, as on very high mountains, has often, often made me gasp for breath and lose blood, is now at least a solitude for two. Strange!"[86] Nietzsche continued to refer to Spinoza as a predecessor in the ensuing years. For example, in 1884 Nietzsche listed Spinoza, together with Heraclitus, Empedocles, and Goethe, as such. However, Nietzsche knew of Spinoza and his philosophy long before 1881, although his earliest reference to him seems to date from 1872–73, and it was only in and after 1881 that he began to discuss him more frequently.

Nietzsche's earliest known encounter with Spinoza's thinking was in the lectures by the philosopher Karl Schaarschmidt that he attended in Bonn during the summer semester of 1865 titled "Outline of the History of philosophy" ("Allgemeine Geschichte der Philosophie"). The notes Nietzsche took while attending the course on the history of philosophy have not yet been published but constitute about half of sixty handwritten double pages.[87] These notes include a four-page section about Spinoza, more than about anyone else.

Through the writings of Goethe, Nietzsche may well have encountered Spinoza earlier. Goethe was profoundly influenced by Spinoza and describes Spinoza's importance and effect on him in, among other places, *Dichtung und Wahrheit*. Nietzsche's first reference to Spinoza in 1872–73 (and also several of his later references) seems to refer this description by Goethe. Certainly Goethe's positive evaluation, and Spinoza's importance for Goethe, is likely to have been a major reason for Nietzsche's presumed early interest.

Nietzsche's next important source for knowledge of Spinoza, from 1865 and onward, seems to have been Schopenhauer, who frequently referred to and discussed Spinoza with both positive and critical comments.[88] Friedrich Albert Lange in his *History of Materialism* (which Nietzsche read in 1866 and several times thereafter) referred to Spinoza only briefly on four pages and is thus unlikely to have been an important source.[89] In 1868 and 1873 Nietzsche read Friedrich Überweg's three-volume *Grundriss der Geschichte der Philosophie von Thales bis auf die Gegenwart* (1863–66), which contains a fairly detailed account of Spinoza's thinking on pages 56–77 in volume three. The only annotation at all in Nietzsche's copy of the book is a marginal line on one page of this account of Spinoza's thinking.[90] Another source of information about Spinoza was Eduard von Hartmann's *Philosophie des Unbewussten* (1869), which Nietzsche read in 1869, 1870, and 1873. It contains rather frequent discussions of Spinoza.

Had Nietzsche read these works attentively, he possibly could have had a reasonable knowledge of the essence of Spinoza's thinking. However, this may not have been the case, for before 1875 his only reference to Spinoza was a general one from 1872–73, which appears to have been based on Goethe's account of his reading of Spinoza in *Dichtung und Wahrheit*.[91]

In the summer of 1875 Nietzsche was sent Spinoza's *Ethics* by the Detloff's Buchhandlung in Basel but apparently decided not to buy it and returned it.[92] During that summer Nietzsche read and excerpted E. Dühring's *Der Werth des Lebens* (1865) extensively and twice briefly mentioned Spinoza in a somewhat negative spirit (which is how the antisemitic Dühring referred to him). Nietzsche is here quoting from Dühring and not expressing his own opinion.[93]

During 1876–79 Nietzsche began to refer to Spinoza with high praise,[94] referring to him as a "genius of knowledge" and "the purest sage," and in the last section of *Assorted Opinions and Maxims,* Spinoza is one of the eight names Nietzsche mentions as figures with whom he continually conversed.[95] It is not known what gave Nietzsche the stimulus at this time to begin to praise Spinoza, but most likely he was influenced by Paul Rée, whom he came to know in 1875–76. Rée mentions and quotes Spinoza a few times in his *Der Ursprung der moralischen Empfindungen* (1877), which Nietzsche read and discussed with him before it was finished. Rée was even referred to as a "new Spinoza" by a contemporary reviewer of the book, a characterization of which Nietzsche approved.[96] We have no evidence that Nietzsche read Spinoza firsthand at this time, and it seems unlikely, since in 1881 Nietzsche claimed that he hardly knew Spinoza before that moment.

However, Nietzsche continued to encounter Spinoza's name in his reading and occasionally read more extensive accounts of his thinking. For example, in 1875 Nietzsche bought Dühring's *Kritische Geschichte der Philosophie von ihren Anfängen bis zur Gegenwart* (1873), which contains a forty-page chapter on Spinoza, and read and annotated it sometime thereafter.[97] Afrikan Spir's *Denken und Wirklichkeit: Versuch einer Erneuerung der kritischen Philosophie* (Leipzig, 1873, 1872), which Nietzsche seems to have read in 1877, 1881, and 1885, contains a few short discussions of Spinoza, but they are unlikely to have made much impression on Nietzsche.[98]

Oddly enough, after having claimed in *Assorted Opinions and Maxims* (finished in January and published in early March 1879) that he was in continual discussion with Spinoza, Nietzsche did not mention him at all during the next two years, possibly suggesting that Nietzsche's enthusiasm for Spinoza in 1878 was limited and temporary. In *Dawn* (written in the spring of 1881) there are three brief and positive—but general—references to Spinoza.[99]

Nietzsche's real discovery of, and reading about, Spinoza occurred in the summer of 1881, as shown by the postcard to Overbeck, Nietzsche's notes and excerpts from this time, and his discussions of Spinoza in *Die fröhliche Wissenschaft* (1882).[100] In a letter dated July 8, 1881, to Overbeck, Nietzsche asked him to borrow several works for him from a library or reading society in Basel, including "den Band Kuno Fischer's über Spinoza." By the end of the month, Nietzsche had received it and read enough of it to be enthusiastic.[101] During this time he also copied down a number of excerpts and thoughts from, and relating to, this reading.[102] For example, Nietzsche observed that Schopenhauer's emphasis on a metaphysical will behind the world may possibly have had its origin in Spinoza's concept of appetitus.[103] In two notes from the autumn of 1881, Nietzsche claimed Spinoza as one of his ancestors.[104] Nietzsche also read other works in 1881 in which Spinoza was mentioned, but these were less important.[105]

Somewhat surprisingly after such private praise, Nietzsche's next published book, *Die fröhliche Wissenschaft* (written during the first half of 1882), was critical of Spinoza, mildly so in two sections and somewhat more so in section 333, where he asserted that Spinoza did not understand the subconscious and instinctual nature of thinking and that thinking is not something godly and calm as Spinoza assumed.[106] It seems likely that Nietzsche's enthusiasm for Spinoza was somewhat more limited when he had finished reading the book by Fischer than it was when he wrote the postcard to Overbeck but that he still accepted that they shared some fundamental similarities and therefore continued to mention him as a predecessor.

In his notes from 1883–86, Nietzsche continued for the most part to be critical toward Spinoza. He criticized Spinoza's emphasis on self-preservation as being too passive, suggested that his *amor dei* also rendered people passive, and seemed to claim that Spinoza was motivated by resentment. At the same time, in two notes from 1884 he referred to Spinoza as a predecessor,[107] and in a letter of July 2, 1885, to Overbeck, he claimed to hold the picture of Dante and Spinoza before him and that he wanted to learn from them how to live in solitude. Nietzsche added that it was easier for them, for their thinking was, unlike his, more compatible with solitude, since they had the idea of God to comfort them.

During these years Nietzsche encountered several discussions of Spinoza in the literature he read. Most important were probably Hartmann's and Teichmüller's accounts. The first four notes from 1883 seem to be based on Nietzsche's reading of Eduard von Hartmann's *Phänomenologie des sittlichen Bewusstseins: Prolegomena zu jeder künftigen Ethik* (1879), 871 pages, which he read, excerpted, and heavily annotated in 1883.[108] Hartmann discussed Spinoza fairly extensively and frequently, mostly in a critical spirit.[109] During 1883–85, Nietzsche also read Teichmüller's *Die wirkliche und die scheinbare Welt: Neue Grundlegung der Metaphysik* (Breslau, 1882), in which Spinoza is discussed on about fifteen to twenty pages, and his name is mentioned about sixty times, even more critically than in Hartmann's account, emphasizing epistemological questions rather than ethical ones.[110] In one note from the summer or autumn of 1884, Nietzsche defended Spinoza's concept of *amor dei* and explicitly criticized Teichmüller's critique of it.[111] However, nowhere in *Die wirkliche und die scheinbare Welt* is there any discussion of *amor dei,* and it therefore seems likely that Nietzsche was referring to another of Teichmüller's books. (Teichmüller often discussed Spinoza.)

In the notes from 1885 and 1886, Nietzsche continued to show an ambivalent attitude toward Spinoza and his philosophy. Nietzsche claimed that Spinoza was more profound than Descartes but Pascal was deeper than Spinoza and that Hume and Locke, in comparison to all three of them, were superficial.[112] Nietzsche seems to have appreciated Spinoza's concept of *amor dei* (and related it to his own idea of eternal recurrence).[113] But Nietzsche also expressed more general criticism and claimed that Spinoza's philosophy was determined by his moral views (which, for Nietzsche, also was true for many others) and characterized him as a religious thinker. Only these critical views (and not the positive ones) are expressed in Nietzsche's published statements in *Beyond Good and Evil* and the fifth book of *Die fröhliche Wissenschaft.*[114]

During the spring and summer of 1887, Nietzsche reread and again extensively excerpted Kuno Fischer's volume about Spinoza in the library in Chur.[115]

At this time Nietzsche also read Harald Höffding's *Psychologie in Umrissen auf Grundlage der Erfahrung* (Leipzig, 1887) in which Spinoza is discussed or mentioned on about ten pages. Nietzsche's copy of the book is heavily annotated, and on five of the pages Nietzsche annotated what Höffding said about Spinoza.[116] There was no obvious change of attitude after this reading, but two of Nietzsche's statements and discussions of Spinoza in *On the Genealogy of Morals* are derived from it.[117] Nietzsche's later references to Spinoza are general and probably have this and earlier readings as sources.

Another possible stimulus for Nietzsche's interest in Spinoza in the last year or two before 1889 could have been Resa von Schirnhofer (1855–1948), whom Nietzsche met and socialized with in 1884 and later, and who wrote a doctoral disseration on Spinoza titled *Vergleich zwischen den Lehren Schelling's und Spinozas (Comparison between Schelling's and Spinoza's Teachings)*, vi+85 pages, which she defended on January 26, 1889. At least we know that Nietzsche showed an interest in her work and in June 1888 asked how it was progressing.[118]

It was during the end of his middle period, especially during 1881–82, that Nietzsche discovered or invented many of the new ideas and concepts that caused him to move into the third phase of his development and determined much of his later thinking. To these discoveries belong eternal recurrence, *amor fati*, Zarathustra, the will to power, the Übermensch, nihilism, *décadence*, and the "death of God."[119] All of these concepts are related to and dependent upon Nietzsche's reading of specific works. I can here only briefly point to some aspects of this dependence.

The Idea of Eternal Recurrence

Nietzsche claimed that the idea of the eternal recurrence came to him suddenly in early August 1881 while walking near Sils-Maria in Switzerland. We know that he both had read about and knew of the idea of eternal recurrence before that, but for his own version of the idea his statement is likely to be correct. What happened in August 1881 was not so much that Nietzsche discovered the idea but that he suddenly discovered its consequences and made it into his own idea.

The meaning of Nietzsche's idea of eternal recurrence can be summarized as the hypothesis that the world process is cyclical and that we therefore will relive our lives an infinite number of times in identically the same way. We would not be aware of this (and certainly not remember it), but philosophically and theologically it would mean the complete rejection of every external sense of purpose, of telos, of the universe, and of human life. The idea of eternal recurrence is thus a form of extreme nihilism, which can only be overcome by affirming the present life, not its telos.[120]

The idea of eternal recurrence is far from unique to Nietzsche. It is present in much of ancient thinking (for example, among the Pythagoreans and the Stoics). The idea is natural in societies with a more or less cyclical view of time. It is present in Buddhism and Christianity,[121] and it was discussed in many contemporary scientific and literary texts in Nietzsche's day. One example, which we know he read in 1872–73, is David Friedrich Strauss's several-page discussion of a cyclical universe.[122] Nietzsche's version of the idea, however, differs from all, or most, of these in that he gives the idea a much stronger existential orientation and connects it with the question of nihilism and with the value of life. For him, it is no mere idea or hypothesis but rather an existential test and touchstone: "My teaching says: the task is to live so that you must wish to live again."[123]

A large number of possible sources or influences on Nietzsche's view of eternal recurrence have been suggested, including Heine, Schopenhauer, Hölderlin,[124] Hume,[125] Spinoza,[126] the pre-Socratics (Pythagoras, Heraclitus, and the Stoics, all of whom Nietzsche himself associated with the idea),[127] and several others, including among contemporary thinkers A. Blanqui,[128] E. Dühring,[129] J. G. Vogt,[130] and especially O. Caspari,[131] but no definite source has been identified with certainty.

Amor Fati

Closely related to the idea of eternal recurrence is the concept of *amor fati* (love of fate), which to Nietzsche meant an affirmation of life and the world (fate) in its totality. This idea constitutes a central aspect of Nietzsche's view of tragedy, philosophy, and himself.

Nietzsche discovered and used the expression *amor fati* more or less simultaneously with his discovery of the eternal recurrence in the autumn of 1881.[132] It therefore seems likely that the stimulus to the discovery of the idea was the same as for eternal recurrence. For *amor fati* specifically, Nietzsche's reading of the Stoics, of Spinoza, and of Emerson have been suggested as plausible candidates.

Zarathustra

Nietzsche found and picked up the figure of Zarathustra as his spokesman while reading the cultural historian and anthropologist Friedrich von Hellwald's *Culturgeschichte in ihrer natürlichen Entstehung bis zur Gegenwart* (Augsburg, 1874; 2nd ed., 1875), 839 pages, as discovered by Paolo D'Iorio.[133] The importance of

Nietzsche's reading of this book appears not to have been examined in spite of the fact that it probably was of immense significance to him.

The introduction of *Also sprach Zarathustra* (and thus also of section 342 of *Die fröhliche Wissenschaft*) is almost a direct quotation from Hellwald, and this is even truer of Nietzsche's very first reference to Zarathustra: "Zarathustra, born at the lake Urmi, left his home when he was thirty years old, and went to the province of Aria and wrote there, during ten years of solitude in the mountains, the Zend-Avesta."[134] The central part of this text is taken from Hellwald, who wrote: "*Zarathustra,* the great prophet of the Iranians, [...] was born in the town of Urmi, by the lake of the same name. [...] At the age of thirty, he left his home, went eastwards to the province of Aria and spent there in the mountains ten years in solitude and occupied himself with composing the Zend-Avesta."[135] On the next three pages Hellwald referred to other aspects of Zarathustra's teaching, which Nietzsche made use of: "We thus for the first time encounter among the ancient Iranians the delusion of a *moral worldorder,* an idea to which only higher developed peoples reach, and which influence on the development of culture has been of incalcuable value."[136] Compare Nietzsche's explanation to why he chose Zarathustra as his spokesman in *Ecce Homo.*[137] In Hellwald's account of Zarathustra there are several further aspects that Nietzsche picked up and used in *Thus Spoke Zarathustra.*[138]

The Will to Power

The concept of the will to power is an explanatory one: everything wants to expand and to "control" its surroundings. Nietzsche used it mainly for human psychology but sometimes applied it to all life and perhaps even to inorganic matter. An important aspect of Nietzsche's view of psychology is thus his belief that the will to power is the most fundamental of all drives, motives or desires in all living beings. "All psychology has hitherto remained anchored to moral prejudices and timidities: it has not ventured into the depths. To conceive it as morphology and the *development-theory of the will to power,* as I conceive it—has never yet so much as entered the mind of anyone else."[139]

Nietzsche proposes the will to power in opposition to "the will to life," the Platonic eros, or more partial wills such as the will to truth.[140] The desired state is the feeling of increased power.[141] This power includes power over others as well as over oneself but also over more sublimated forms, such as the power to interpret one's surroundings: "it will have to be the will to power incarnate, it will want to grow, expand, draw to itself, gain ascendancy—not out of any morality or immorality, but because it *lives,* and because life *is* will to power."[142]

Will to power is for Nietzsche a motivating force, not a criterion of the value of an action or feeling. Will to power lies behind all actions and feelings, good ones (for example, exuberance) as well as bad ones (for example, resentment).

Nietzsche first publicly presented the will to power in the chapter "Of Self-Overcoming" in the second book of *Thus Spoke Zarathustra* (1883), but he had discovered it long before then. His very first use of the expression "Wille zur Macht" was in a note from 1876–77, almost certainly inspired by his reading of Rée's *Der Ursprung der moralischen Empfindungen* (1877), whose longest chapter is about vanity and related concepts, "Der Ursprung der Eitelkeit" ("The Origin of Vanity," 69–119).[143]

> The main element of ambition is to realize the *feeling* of one's own *power*. The enjoyment of power is not to be reduced to our enjoyment of being admired by others. Praise and reproach, love and hate, are of no consequence for the ambitious who want power.
>
> Fear (negative) and will to power (positive) explain our strong concern with the opinion of people.
>
> *Pleasure of power.*—The pleasure of power can be explained by the oft-experienced aversions to dependence, to helplessness. If this experience is not present, then the pleasure [of power] is also lacking.[144]

Although in 1878 and 1879 Nietzsche continued to be concerned with power to explain psychological phenomena and motives, he did not use the expression "will to power" at that time. His real discovery of the idea of the will to power came in the summer of 1880, and the idea then exploded in importance in 1883.[145]

The context of the discovery clearly seems to be psychological and biological rather than political or social. I have not found any serious discussion of the origin and stimulus of the idea of the will to power, and no definite source for the idea has been proposed.[146] Since the discovery and development of Nietzsche's concept of will to power lasted for such a long time (1876–83), it may be unlikely that it had only one principal source. One obvious alternative is Schopenhauer, whose emphasis on will and the will to life constituted a proposition that Nietzsche argued against. However, Nietzsche seems not to have read Schopenhauer during the relevant period (1880–83). Another possible source is Darwinism, with its emphasis on struggle and the survival of the fittest ("*Kampf ums Dasein*"). Several of the books Nietzsche read when he became increasingly interested in the will to power were books related to biology and Darwinism, such as Georg Heinrich Schneider's *Der thierische Wille* (1880)[147] and Hellwald's *Culturgeschichte* (1874–75).[148] Another possible stimulus, in 1880 and 1883, was J. J. Baumann's *Handbuch der Moral nebst abriss der Rechtsphilosophie* (Leipzig,

1879), which extensively discusses the will. The first chapters are called "Die Natur des Willens und die Gesetze der Willensbildung" and "Gang der Entwickelung der Menschheit auf Grund der ermittelten Natur des Willens und der Gesetze seiner Ausbildung." Nietzsche annotated these chapters extensively, with many instances of "!," "NB," "gut," and other words. On the bottom of the very first page Nietzsche wrote "Will[e] zur . . . ," but I have been unable with certainty to decipher the third and fourth words, and subsequent words are completely illegible, as the page was cut when the book was bound, and only the tops of a few letters are visible. The annotation probably reads: "Will[e] zur Macht als [-]." Baumann emphasizes on page one that the will must will *something*: "Der Wille muss *etwas* wollen, er muss einen Inhalt oder Gegenstand haben, welcher gewollt wird." In his annotation, Nietzsche is probably indentifying that "something" as power![149] Léon Dumont's *Vergnügen und Schmerz: Zur Lehre von den Gefühlen* (Leipzig, 1876), which Nietzsche read and excerpted in 1883 (but possibly also once or twice earlier, in the late 1870s and in 1881), is another possible source. Dumont has a similar view to Nietzsche's that matter is equivalent to force and that humans can be regarded as a system of forces (with pleasure and pain reflecting an increase or decrease of the amount of force). The book is one of the most heavily annotated in Nietzsche's library and, although consistently marked with a lead pencil, occasionally looks as if it has been annotated at different times (even on the same page), suggesting at least two readings. Nietzsche also frequently wrote comments in the margins, including the word "Rangordnung" twice and at the bottom of page 82 "Machtzuwachs und . . . ist . . ." ("Increase of power and . . . is . . ."), where unfortunately some words were completely cut away when the book was bound after 1889.[150] Especially if I am correct in assuming that Nietzsche read the book before 1883, in the late 1870s, and in 1881,[151] it is possible that the book was of pivotal importance for Nietzsche's idea of the will to power.

Further information about (and hints for the interpretation of) the will to power can be gained by examining the several places where Nietzsche wrote the expression "Wille zur Macht" in the margins of books he read, for example, in works by Drossbach, Liebmann, Höffding, and Rolph; three times in Guyau; and possibly, as discussed above, in Dumont and Baumann.[152]

Günter Abel has an extensive and interesting discussion of the will to power in his *Nietzsche: Die Dynamik der Willen zur Macht und die ewige Wiederkehr*, 2nd ed. (Berlin and New York: Walter de Gruyter, 1998). He emphasizes especially three sources: anti-Darwinism (especially Nietzsche's reading of Roux's *Der Organismus* and Rolph's *Biologische Probleme*, but Nietzsche only read these in 1881 and 1883 and in 1884–85, respectively); natural science, especially

Nietzsche's reading of or about *Robert Mayer* in 1881; and Spinoza, whom Nietzsche read about in Fischer's account in 1881. With the exception of Rolph, Nietzsche's reading of these works was probably important for the development of his concept of the will to power, but they all seem to have been read too late for them to be of importance for the origin of the idea.

Another possible source or stimulus for the idea of will to power is Nietzsche's reading of Alexander Bain's *Erziehung als Wissenschaft* (Leipzig, 1880), which Nietzsche probably read and annotated in its year of publication. In a short chapter called "Das Gefühl der Macht" ("The Feeling of Power"), Bain claims: "In the feeling of power lies one of the most important driving forces of the human spirit." And later in the book Nietzsche comments on and criticizes Bain's view of will and power. Still more important could be Nietzsche's reading of the section "Der Wille" in Bain's *Geist und Körper: Die Theorien über ihre gegenseitige Beziehungen* (*Mind and Body: The Theories of Their Relationship*) (Leipzig, 1874), in which he argues that the will is like a form of energy that releases itself spontaneously without particular goals or reasons. This view corresponds well with Schopenhauer's (and Nietzsche's) view of the will, which Nietzsche here encountered without an associated metaphysics.[153] In 1881 and 1882 Nietzsche read Robert Mayer's *Dynamik des Himmels* and *Die organische Bewegung*, in which a similar thesis is argued.

Other less likely suggested sources or stimuli are Emerson, who wrote "life is a search after power" in *The Conduct of Life* (while Nietzsche claimed that "Life is will to power"),[154] and Mainländer.[155]

Übermensch

Nietzsche used the word *Übermensch* almost exclusively in *Thus Spoke Zarathustra* (1883–85) and in later references to that work. This fact in itself shows that the word *Übermensch* was a metaphor for Nietzsche, not a realistic description of something that would one day happen. Nietzsche only used the word twice before he wrote *Thus Spoke Zarathustra* (and notes belonging to that work). The first time was in an essay that he handed in to Germania in 1861 while still at Schulpforta, with the title "Ueber die dramatische Dichtung Byrons." He there refers to Manfred as "this *Übermensch* who masters spirits."[156] His second use of the word was in *Die fröhliche Wissenschaft*, section 143 (1882).[157]

The word *Übermensch* occurs in several of the books Nietzsche read. It is present in at least three of the books in his library, in one of which he marked the word.[158] Apart from Goethe's *Faust*, it is also used in Otto Liebmann's *Zur Analysis der Wirklichkeit* (Strassburg, 1880) and Alfred Espinas's *Die Thierischen Gesellschaften*

(Braunschweig, 1879),[159] both of which he read between 1880 and 1883 and both of which contain annotations near the use of the word *Übermensch.*

Nihilism

The late Nietzsche was profoundly involved with the problem of nihilism. Although he sometimes discussed the concept in his published writings, from *Beyond Good and Evil* onward,[160] there is much more on this theme in his notebooks than in his published works, and he clearly intended to publish more on it.[161]

Nietzsche's first reference to nihilism dates from the summer of 1880 and was a direct response to his reading of Turgenev's *Fathers and Sons,* in a French translation with a preface by Mérimée, that—like the text of the book itself— discusses the concept of nihilism.[162] Nietzsche later made only a few rare references to nihilism until 1884, when he began to use the term more frequently, and then even more so from 1886 onward. His reading of other French literary critics during the middle of the 1880s, especially Paul Bourget (compare the discussion below in regard to *décadence*) and F. Brunetière,[163] gave him further information and stimulus for his continued use of the concept of nihilism.[164]

Décadence

Closely related to nihilism is Nietzsche's use of the concept of decadence, which he almost always used in the French form *décadence* because he picked it up from French literary critics. In his published works he began to use the term only in 1888, when it became a major leitmotif in the book *Der Fall Wagner.* Thereafter, he used it frequently in *Twilight of the Idols, The Antichrist,* and *Ecce Homo.* His very first use of the word decadence (without the accent on the first "e") occurred in 1876–77 in a note on the Spanish author Cervantes,[165] but he made more serious use of the concept after his reading of Paul Bourget's *Essais de psychologie contemporaine* (Paris, 1883), which he read in the winter of 1883–84.[166] Nietzsche subsequently used the word *décadence* only rarely until the autumn of 1887. Apart from Bourget, Nietzsche's frequent use of the concept of *décadence* may have derived from his extensive reading of French literary critics[167] and from his reading of contemporary medical literature, especially Herzen and Féré.[168]

Death of God

Nietzsche introduced the idea that God is dead publicly in section 125 of *Die fröhliche Wissenschaft* (1882) and then in *Thus Spoke Zarathustra* (1883). However, he hinted fairly clearly at the idea earlier, in *The Wanderer and His Shadow* (December 1879).[169] Nietzsche did not coin the phrase "God is dead," for it had been used by several authors before him. Nietzsche's use probably does not have a single obvious literary source.

Nietzsche's interest in Schulpforta in old Germanic and Scandinavian myths made him well aware of the *Götterdämmerung* and the mortality of gods. In an early version of his study of King Ermanarich (which he submitted to Germania) he had, for example, written: "That twilight of the gods, as the sun goes black, the earth sinks into the sea and whirlpools of fire uproot the all-nourishing cosmic tree, flames licking the heavens—it is the greatest idea human genius ever produced, unsurpassed in the literature of any period, infinitely bold and formidable, but melting into magical harmonies."[170] Another possible mythological source for the expression comes from Plutach and from Greek mythology. In late 1870 or early 1871, Nietzsche twice copied down into his notebook the expression "The great Pan is dead."[171] Later he read a fairly large number of books that may have been the stimulus for his own use of the phrase "God is dead." Among the suggested candidates are H. Heine's *Zur Geschichte der Religion und Philosophie in Deutschland*[172] and Max Stirner's *Der Einzige und sein Eigenthum* (although we have no definite knowledge that Nietzsche read either of these two works), the French moralist Charron,[173] Pascal, Max Müller's *Vergleichende Religionswissenschaft* (which Nietzsche read in 1870 and 1875), and Philipp Mainländer's *Philosophie der Erlösung* (1876) (which Nietzsche read in 1876–77 and later in 1883). Mainländer wrote: "God has died, and his death was the life of the world."[174]

6

The Late Nietzsche
1883–89

During the Zarathustra period (1883–85), when Nietzsche developed much of his new philosophy, he continued a relatively broad philosophical reading. This reading, as always, also consisted of much rereading of philosophical texts he had read earlier, such as Schopenhauer, Emerson, Dühring, Mainländer, and Lange.

Nietzsche's thinking is often divided into three periods: early, middle, and late. Nietzsche himself divided it in that way. The break between the middle, more positivistic period and the late period occurred in 1881–82, with the discovery of the idea of eternal recurrence (in August 1881) and came to be publicly expressed in the last sections of the fourth book of *Die fröhliche Wissenschaft* (1882) and then much more intensively in *Thus Spoke Zarathustra* (1883–85).[1] The possible influences and reasons behind Nietzsche's break with this period are less visible than the ones applicable to his earlier break in 1875–76. However, we can see a clear break with Rée's more positivistic and empiricist thinking, and Nietzsche's philosophical discoveries discussed at the end of chapter 5 were of paramount importance.

There is no single obvious major positive philosophical influence on Nietzsche in the period 1883–85, but Nietzsche seems to have read and reread Emerson and Montaigne with much enthusiasm. Within the field of ethics, he critically read and heavily annotated Eduard von Hartmann's massive 872-page *Phänomenologie des sittlichen Bewusstseins: Prolegomena zu jeder künftigen Ethik* (1879) in the spring and summer of 1883. During 1884–85 he read with appreciation both Rolph's *Biologische Probleme zugleich als Versuch zur Entwicklung einer rationellen Ethik,* 2nd ed. (Leipzig, 1884) and J.-M. Guyau's *Esquisse d'une morale sans obligation ni sanction* (Paris, 1885). Nietzsche is also likely to have reread several of Paul Rée's works during the period 1883–86, and they then played a pivotal role as stimuli and counterpoints to his *On the Genealogy of Morals.*

The extent to which the reading of these works may have influenced Nietzsche's view of morality (and immorality) seems not to have been examined.

The first of these books that he read or reread, Hartmann's *Phänomenologie des sittlichen Bewusstseins,* contains extensive accounts about almost all fields of ethics. Nietzsche read and annotated this work intensively and copied many short passages from it into his notebooks, where he also entered into a critical dialogue with the book.[2] The reading of the book probably taught him a great deal and was no small part of the background to what he later said with respect to different ethical traditions.

Nietzsche's reading of Rolph's *Biologische Probleme* in 1884–85 is likely to have been important both for his view of Darwinism and biology[3] and for his view of morality.[4] Nietzsche is likely to have read the book twice, for some pages are annotated with both blue and lead pencil next to one another. Rolph's critique of Spencer in the third chapter probably reinforced Nietzsche's critique of him (Nietzsche frequently wrote "gut" by places where Rolph criticized Spencer), and the more general last two chapters, heavily annotated, are relevant for Nietzsche's view of ethics (and its relation to biology).[5] Nietzsche also praised this work by Rolph, the one by Guyau, and Rée's magnum opus as the three best contemporary books on morality.[6]

Nietzsche's reading of the philosopher of life Guyau's *Esquisse* in 1885 is likely to have been of major importance for his views on ethics.[7] Nietzsche referred to it with appreciation as a fine book and to Guyau as the best and most courageous of thinkers.[8] However, although Nietzsche approved of many of its details, he actually disapproved of its general view and conclusions.[9] Nietzsche's copy of the book was very heavily annotated. It is one of the supreme examples of his entering into a dialogue with a book. On the front page, he summarized his views:

> This book has a *funny* fault: in the effort to prove that the moral instincts have their seat in life itself, Guyau has overlooked that he has proved the opposite—that is, that *all* fundamental instincts of life are *immoral,* including the so-called moral ones. The highest intensity of life, it is true, stands in a necessary relation to sa plus large expansion: only that this is the opposite of all "altruistic" facts,—this expansion is expressed as unrestrained *will to power.* Just as little is *breeding* the symptom of an altruistic character: it emerges from division and battle within an organism, excessively overloaded with booty, which does not have enough power to incorporate everything conquered.[10]

There has been almost no awareness and discussion of Nietzsche's reading of three of the most significant contemporary philosophers of science: Emil Du Bois-Reymond (1818–96), Richard Avenarius (1843–96), and Ernst Mach

(1838–1916). Nietzsche's response to this reading is relevant for his relation to science,[11] positivism, and a number of other philosophical topics.

Nietzsche possessed a copy of two of Du Bois-Reymond's essays, *Über eine Akademie der deutschen Sprache.—über Geschichte der Wissenschaft: 2 Festreden* (Berlin, 1874), bound together and constituting forty-nine pages. It seems to be the first of these essays that interested the early Nietzsche. He must have read it, and thereafter he discussed it with the Wagners and mildly criticized Du Bois-Reymond in two notes and in his published *Schopenhauer As Educator* (1874).[12]

We have no knowledge of his reading of the second essay, although it is not unlikely that he read it also. By 1881 Nietzsche seems to have become more interested in the physiologist and philosopher of nature Emil Du Bois-Reymond and asked Overbeck if there existed any complete collection of his essays (*Reden*).[13] Overbeck's answer has been lost, but no such collection was then available.[14] Later, probably between 1884 and 1887, Nietzsche bought two of Du Bois-Reymond's most well-known essays bound together, *Über die Grenzen des Naturerkennens, Die sieben Welträtsel: 2 Vorträge* (Leipzig, 1884), 110 pages.[15] In the first essay Du Bois-Reymond argues the case for a complete determinism (based on atoms in motion) but also discusses the limits of our ability to know, which led to a great debate over many years, called the *ignorabimus* debate. In the second essay, Du Bois-Reymond discusses seven questions, such as the origin of matter, motion, life and consciousness, and argues that some of them can eventually be solved, while others can never be solved. It is likely that Nietzsche read both essays, but no examination of this probable reading and its possible relevance for Nietzsche has been published. Some sort of response is likely, for Nietzsche sent his *On the Genealogy of Morals* to Du Bois-Reymond in November 1887,[16] and he seems to have been influenced by the *ignorabimus* debate.

Nietzsche's relation to critical positivism (empirio-criticism) has received no attention at all by historians of philosophy in spite of the fact that he had read books by the two founders of critical positivism, Richard Avenarius and Ernst Mach (although he never mentions or discusses any of them explicitly).[17] An understanding of this historical context and its influence on Nietzsche can help us to understand his often paradoxical statements regarding positivism, empiricism, truth, and science. Nietzsche's reading of Avenarius and Mach shows— counter to previous views—that Nietzsche encountered and was influenced by some of the principal ideas of what was to become logical positivism: the philosophy of the Vienna Circle and analytical philosophy.[18]

The founder and one of the two great representatives of empirio-criticism, or critical positivism, was the philosopher Richard Avenarius. He began to argue his empirio-critical views—that it is the task of philosophy to develop a natural concept of the world based on "pure experience" and the principle of "economy of thought"—in his *Philosophie als Denken der Welt gemäss dem Princip des kleinsten Kraftmasses: Prolegomena zu einer Kritik der reinen Erfahrung* (*Philosophy as Thinking of the World in Accordance With the Principle of the Least Amount of Energy: Introduction to a Critique of Pure Experience*) (Leipzig, 1876).[19] Nietzsche's bookseller sent him the book already in 1876,[20] and we know that he read it for the first or second time in the winter of 1883–84.[21] Nietzsche then excerpted and discussed this reading in several longer notes,[22] and shortly thereafter he wrote to Overbeck on April 7, 1884, stating that he needed to revise his views on epistemology and metaphysics.[23] It is thus possible that this reading was of great importance for his thinking at this time.

The excerpts from and the discussions of Avenarius's *Philosophie als Denken der Welt* that Nietzsche made during the winter 1883–84 concern important questions such as power (relevant for Nietzsche's thinking about power and will to power) and the critique of causality, will, purpose, and the concept of substance and thing. It seems likely, for example, that sections 14 and 15 of *Beyond Good and Evil*, with their critique of positivism and physiologists who emphasize the "smallest possible effort" (mit ihrem Princip der "kleinstmöglichen Kraft"), were written in response to Nietzsche's reading of Avenarius.

Apart from reading and excerpting Avenarius's *Philosophie als Denken der Welt* (1876), Nietzsche had two further connections to him.[24] He knew and corresponded with Richard Avenarius' brother, Ferdinand, who in 1887 founded the cultural journal *Kunstwart* to which Nietzsche contributed. More important is that Richard Avenarius in 1877 founded and thereafter edited, with the assistance of Max Heinze and Wilhelm Wundt, the quarterly journal *Vierteljahrsschrift für wissenschaftliche Philosophie,* at least until 1889. Later E. Mach was editor for a period. Avenarius wrote a number of articles in the first volumes of the journal, which Nietzsche may have read.[25] The journal had a strong antispeculative and antimetaphysical tendency and published articles about scientific philosophy, including many about epistemology and about the relation among psychology, natural science, and philosophy.[26] I have been unable so far to find any definite evidence that Nietzsche read this journal with its emphasis on critical positivism.[27] However, there are several reasons that make such reading probable and further investigation therefore worthwhile. Nietzsche twice in his writings refers to "wissenschaftliche Philosophie" in a manner that suggests that it could have been a response to the reading of this journal and its content, but this is far from certain.[28] The content of the journal was listed in several other journals, and it is almost certain that Nietzsche would know the content of the journal, even in the event that he did not read it, and Heinze had not told him.

A possible incentive for Nietzsche to know about the journal and perhaps to read it was Max Heinze's role in it. Heinze, the other editor of the journal, had not only been Nietzsche's teacher and private tutor at Pforta but had also remained a friend of Nietzsche's and an acquaintance of his family thereafter. Heinze was called, as professor of philosophy, to Basel in early 1874 and thus became a colleague of Nietzsche's. Nietzsche appreciated him, and they met frequently during 1874 and even celebrated Christmas together and continued in close contact later. If Nietzsche sometimes read *Vierteljahrsschrift für wissenschaftliche Philosophie,* as seems likely, he could have acquired a reasonably detailed knowledge of critical positivism.

Ernst Mach, the other great representative of critical positivism, or Empiriokritizismus, argued, from a positivistic and empiristic worldview, that all empirical knowledge was the result of simple sense experience (*Empfindungen*). His views became very influential and an important starting point for the logical positivists in the early twentieth century. Mach was especially influenced by Fechner's *Psychophysik* (1860) and worked extensively as a researcher on sense perception.

Nietzsche may have read several works by Mach. In 1882 Nietzsche wrote down the title of Mach's *Die Geschichte und die Wurzel des Satzes von der Erhaltung des Arbeit* (1872), presumably as intended reading relating to his thinking about eternal recurrence, but we have no certain evidence that he actually read it (or the other titles on the list).[29] In this essay of about fifty pages, Mach discusses some of the views he will later present in his *Beiträge zur Analyse der Empfindungen,* including his views about causality, space, and time. According to Max Oehler, Nietzsche read texts by Ernst Mach in a public reading room in Zürich in 1884.[30] It is also possible that Nietzsche would have read contributions by Mach or reviews and discussions of him in philosophical journals.[31] Later, probably in 1886 or 1887, Nietzsche bought and read one of Mach's most important works, *Beiträge zur Analyse der Empfindungen* (Jena, 1886), iv+168 pages.[32] We know that he read it, for two pages contain annotations.[33] In this work Mach argues that all sense experience finally consists of simple elements (such as color, sound, pressure, heat, etc.) and severely criticizes the concept of substance and the belief in a priori concepts. The concepts of objects and of the self, the I, is only a stopgap, Mach argues, for the purpose of acquiring a preliminary sense of orientation. The I is nothing but a complex of memories, impulses, sense perceptions, etc. Mach thus, through his disintegration of the concept of matter and soul, suggests a solution to the body-soul problem and thereby makes the connection between physiology and psychology more probable. The goal of science is not explanations through determining causes but rather the description of the simple elements.

Nietzsche never explicitly discusses Mach and his work; therefore, further examination is required to determine his response to this work.[34] He is likely to have approved of and shared Mach's critique of concepts, including of the concept of the self. *Twilight of the Idols* and, to a lesser extent, *On the Genealogy of Morals* and *Beyond Good and Evil* contain a number of aspects, which are likely to have Nietzsche's reading of Mach and Avenarius as a source or stimulus. This is true, for example, for Nietzsche's strong emphasis on empiricism and sense perception in *Twilight of the Idols*,[35] his constructivist view of how we conceive the world (with an emphasis on biological evolutionism), his view that fundamental concepts and science are useful and necessary fictions, his strong antimetaphysical emphasis, his belief in a connection between physiology (and physics) and psychology, and his pragmatic view of truth. Another similarity between Nietzsche's thinking and that of empirio-criticism is the strong emphasis on psychology as a way to solve epistemological and scientific problems.[36] It is also not impossible that Nietzsche was inspired by Mach and Avenarius in his belief in the possibility of developing a physiology of aesthetics and when he claims that atoms with extension do not exist but that they are useful fictions.[37]

However, as the conventional view states, the late Nietzsche was not a supporter of positivism. He criticizes it explicitly, denies the possibility of pure facts (they always involve interpretation), and emphasizes the importance of values, which is something the positivists more or less ignored. Nietzsche seems even possibly to directly criticize the critical positivists in section 10 of *Beyond Good and Evil*.[38]

An indication that Nietzsche found Mach interesting and relevant is that he sent Mach a copy of his *On the Genealogy of Morals* in November 1887. Nietzsche's library also contains a reprint of an article in *Repertorium der Physik* by Mach (and P. Salcher), "Photographische Fixierung der durch Projectile in der Luft eingeleiteten Vorgänge," with a dedication by Mach: "Herrn Prof. Dr. Nietzsche hochachtungsvoll E. M." This article was published in the summer of 1887, and Mach must have sent it to Nietzsche in return for his *On the Genealogy of Morals*.[39]

The philosophical reading and influence on Nietzsche during the late period seems to have been more negative than positive; that is, he primarily read and criticized counterpositions and influences, such as Schopenhauer, Kant, Rousseau, English philosophy, Hartmann, and Mainländer, and determined his own position in relation to these. Expressed differently, by this time Nietzsche had more or less worked out the fundamentals of his own philosophy, and therefore we no longer see any important positive philosophical influences on his thinking. What we instead see is primarily his discussion of and attack on other positions.

One epistemological and metaphysical problem that seems to have interested Nietzsche in these years and may have played an important role in the changes of his philosophy that took him from his middle to his late period is that of truth and appearance and their relation to one another. This was a question already much discussed in Greek philosophy and by Plato—as the relation between *episteme* and *doxa*—but it was also discussed at great length during the second half of the nineteenth century. Nietzsche attentively read a large number of studies and discussions relating to this question: Teichmüller, Drossbach,[40] Mainländer, Spir, Liebmann, and Widemann (for titles of these works, see table 1). Nietzsche's interest in, and discussion of, this problem—especially in relation to his extensive reading about it—has received surprisingly little attention.[41] Possibly under the influence of this reading, he came to reject a belief in truth in itself and a true world—a position he had been close to adopting during his middle positivistic period—and instead argued that we can never go beyond appearance.

Of special importance and interest is Nietzsche's reading of Gustav Teichmüller's *Die wirkliche und die scheinbare Welt: Neue Grundlegung der Metaphysik* (Breslau, 1882) in 1883 and 1885.[42] Although Nietzsche did not agree with the fundamental metaphysical and Christian tendency of this work, his reading of it seems to have inspired his own thinking on a number of different issues, such as his critique of metaphysics based on the I or the subjective and his perspectivism.

Teichmüller argues in the book that the I or the self is the only legitimate source for a metaphysics and claims. "For there exists, as shown above, no other source for the concept of 'substance' than the 'I.' According to the analogy of the 'I,' we correctly assume the existence of other beings external to us [...] When we recognize this situation, the illusion disappears, and thus, with that, we again are situated in the *real* [i.e., metaphysical] world."[43] Nietzsche's critique of and response to this position, of a metaphysics based on the subjective, is expressed on several occasions, including this passage from *Beyond Good and Evil*: "As for the superstitions of the logicians, I shall never tire of underlining a concise little fact which these superstitious people are loath to admit—namely, that a thought comes when 'it' wants, not when 'I' want; so that it is a *falsification* of the facts to say: the subject 'I' is the condition of the predicate 'think.' *It* thinks [...] we and the logicians as well will one day accustom ourselves to getting along without that little 'it' (which is what the honest old 'I' has evaporated into)."[44]

A still more important theme that seems to have its origin in the reading of Teichmüller is Nietzsche's perspectivism. It constitutes an important component of Nietzsche's epistemology and of his critique of dogmatism and belief in the absolute (including metaphysics). Nietzsche claims that "To be sure, to speak of spirit and the good as Plato did meant standing truth on her head and denying *perspective* itself, the basic condition of all life,"[45] and in *On the Genealogy of Morals* he wrote: "there is only a perspective seeing, *only* a perspective 'knowing.'"[46] Nietzsche's perspectivism becomes an explicit theme in his philosophy from about 1884–85 onward. It seems likely that this aspect of Nietzsche's thinking was profoundly influenced by his reading of and opposition to Teichmüller's study. In his work, Teichmüller extensively discussed "the perspectival," which he saw as inevitably associated with the apparent world, but which can be overcome in the real world (i.e., by a metaphysics based on the I).[47] Nietzsche, of course, opposed this view,[48] but Teichmüller's extended discussion of the dichotomy of the apparent (including the perspectival) contra the real is likely to have worked as a strong stimulus on Nietzsche. Teichmüller, for example, has a chapter titled "Eliminirung der sogennanten Gegenstände, d.h. der perspectivischen Anschauungsbilder," and later on page 183 he argues: "The world, as it appears to the eye, is always and everywhere ordered into perspectives, and neither microscope nor telescope can show us the order of things which we hold to be the real one. […] It requires that one recognizes the *cause* of the perspectival appearance." The argument recurs several times in the second half of the book, and the book ends with a chapter called "Die wirkliche und die scheinbare Welt" in which the apparent and perspectival world is rejected in favor of a real world.[49] However, Teichmüller was probably not the only inspiration for Nietzsche's perspectivism; A. Spir and F. A. Lange, whom he also reread during 1883–85, are further likely candidates.[50]

It may be worth reminding the reader here that many of the books Nietzsche read, even the late Nietzsche, he did not just read but worked through thoroughly, making extensive annotations and excerpts into his notebooks. For example, during the autumn of 1885, he reread Teichmüller's *Die wirkliche und die scheinbare Welt* and Spir's *Denken und Wirklichkeit* (Teichmüller for a second time and Spir, it appears, for a fourth time) very attentively, writing down arguments and quotations, with page references, from both books; comparing them to each other; and working out and putting forth his own position against them.[51]

Nietzsche's reading of Mainländer's *Philosophie der Erlösung* (Berlin, 1876; 2nd unchanged ed., 1879) in 1876 and 1883 is another example of a work he did not agree with but that stimulated his own thinking in important ways, as discussed above. Mainländer's pessimism was surely especially important during the 1880s, since pessimism was a philosophical position that Nietzsche examined and criticized during that period.

Philosophical pessimism (with respect to the value of life) was a problem that concerned Nietzsche from early on until his mental collapse. It was central to his worldview and was directly related to his concern with tragedy, nihilism, and life affirmation (Dionysos and eternal recurrence).[52] He first encountered this problem in the writings of Schopenhauer, and as he was philosophically educated in the Schopenhauerian tradition, the problem of pessimism became a major concern. In the early and middle 1870s Nietzsche encountered and read a fairly large number of texts and authors involved with it, including Hartmann, Bahnsen, Dühring, and Mainländer. Dühring was an optimist rather than a pessimist, but he took the problem seriously and argued against the Schopenhauerian position in *Der Werth des Lebens* (*The Value of Life*), which Nietzsche read carefully in 1875, and in other works. Mainländer was enough of a pessimist to take his own life as soon as the book where he argued in favor of pessimism was published. Another strong influence on Nietzsche was the Greek Weltanschauung and of the related problem of tragedy. As early as 1867–68 he formed an intention to write a work on Greek pessimism. In the early 1870s the center of gravity of Nietzsche's interest in relation to pessimism was on epistemological concerns, related to the idea that we can never know truth and reality. In the period 1875–79 Nietzsche showed less interest in pessimism, but thereafter his interest again increased, peaking in 1885 and continuing during the ensuing years. His emphasis then became more existential and value-oriented. He came to see pessimism as a preliminary form of, and as closely related to, nihilism. In a note from the summer of 1885, which might have been intended as part of the preface to *Beyond Good and Evil*, Nietzsche wrote:

> My friends, with what have I then occupied myself for so many years? I have attempted to explore pessimism in depth, for the purpose of salvaging it from the half Christian, half German narrowness and simplicity in the form in which I first encountered it in the metaphysics of Schopenhauer: so that man is mature enough for this sort of thinking by means of the highest form of pessimism. I have also sought a reverse ideal—a manner of thinking, which is the most high-spirited, lively and world-affirming possible: I found it by drawing the final conclusions of the mechanistic worldview: it is truly necessary to have the best temperament in the world to be able to stand a world of eternal recurrence, as I have proclaimed it through my son Zarathustra—that is, to include ourselves in the eternal da capo.[53]

When Nietzsche issued *The Birth of Tragedy* in a new edition in 1886, he also changed the title from *The Birth of Tragedy Out of the Spirit of Music* to *The Birth of Tragedy: Or, Hellenism and Pessimism*. During the 1880s he encountered a number of discussions of pessimism—apart from rereading the Schopenhauerian authors already mentioned—for example, in Martensen's study of Christian ethics, in Guyau's study of ethics and in several of the French literary critics he read, including Bourget. Most important, perhaps, was Nietzsche's intensive critical reading of Hartmann's *Phänomenologie des sittlichen Bewusstseins* (1879) in 1883. In it Hartmann argues that all previous efforts to provide a philosophical basis of ethics have failed but that pessimism could provide such a foundation.

Nietzsche also owned three other full works on pessimism, two of which he clearly read:

> F. A. v. Hartsen, *Die Moral des Pessimismus, nach Veranlassung v. Dr. Tauberts Schrift "Der Pessimismus und seine Gegner" geprüft* (Nordhausen, 1874). 50 pages. Contains no annotations. It is not certain that Nietzsche read it. Nietzsche also possessed two other works by Hartsen, at least one of which he read.
>
> O. Plümacher, *Der Pessimismus in Vergangenheit und Gegenwart* (Heidelberg, 1884). 355 pages. Annotated by Nietzsche throughout.[54]
>
> James Sully, *Le pessimisme (histoire et critique)* (Paris, 1882). 452 pages. Fairly heavily annotated. Several of Nietzsche's comments are written in French, implying a late reading, at least after 1884 but probably later.

As an example of the late Nietzsche's way of reading, we can examine his reading of St. Augustine's *Confessions* in 1885.[55] There are only four references to Augustine in Nietzsche's published writings.[56] From a conventional perspective these references seem to contain only highly hostile ad hominem statements and no discussion or analysis of views put forward by Augustine. However, what Nietzsche does is that he discusses and analyzes not so much Augustine's statements as his values and attitudes. In the first reference Nietzsche examines, as a sign of character, one's relation to and love of one's God. This theme is highly visible in Augustine's *Confessions*. Nietzsche finds his attitude too humble and self-abnegating and accuses him of using bad and false psychology to appear humbler than he was. In the second reference to Augustine, Nietzsche examines the type of personality that is characterized by containing or consisting of many contrary drives and values in conflict with one another. He shows that these traits can yield two very different kinds of characters: one searches for peace and has a purely negative definition of happiness, and another affirms the struggle and masters it through self-control, as did Caesar, Friedrich II, and Leonardo da Vinci. In the third reference, Nietzsche attributes the moralism of the *Confessions* to personal and psychological motives rather than to the will of God, as Augustine did. He treated moralism as a screen behind which the inferior character hid himself against spirit and spirituality. The fourth reference continues on the same theme, but this time emphasizing the physiological level—the lack of "*cleanly* instincts"—rather than the psychological. We know from a letter that Nietzsche had read *Confessions* shortly before he wrote the first published statements. In this letter he emphasized that he read the book in the manner of a "radical physician and physiologist," which is Nietzsche's way of saying that he attempted to reduce Augustine's statements, including the metaphysical ones, to psychological and physiological motives or causes.

> I have been reading, as relaxation, Augustine's *Confessions,* much regretting that you were not with me. O this old rhetorician! What falseness, what rolling of eyes! How I laughed! (for example, concerning the "theft" of his youth, basically an undergraduate story). What psychological falsity! (for example, when he talks about the death of his best friend, with whom he shared a *single soul,* he "resolved to go on living, so that in this way his friend would not wholly die." Such things are revoltingly dishonest). Philosophical value zero! *vulgarized* Platonism—that is to say, a way of thinking which was invented for the highest aristocracy of soul, and which he adjusted to suit slave natures. Moreover, one sees into the guts of Christianity in this book. I make my observations with the curiosity of a radical physician and physiologist.[57]

Apart from this reference (and one other) in Nietzsche's letters and the four in the published books, there are fourteen references to Augustine in Nietzsche's notebooks. Six of these, shorter and of less interest, were written before 1885 and hence before Nietzsche had read the *Confessions.* The other eight are similar to the published comments, with one interesting difference. Several of these references are more factual, and in them Nietzsche discusses or mentions themes such as bad conscience, grace, and sin, and they are thus closer to Augustine's text than are the references in his published books. This should not surprise us. Many of Nietzsche's notes in general are taken down as quotations from books or are his observations and thoughts while reading books, and as such they are more factual and are closer to the arguments of the thinker in question. When he later used these notes (analyzed them), he mostly did so in terms of seeing these statements, theories, and values as symptoms of a certain type of character, and this—the result of the analysis or diagnosis—is what he expressed in the published books. This means that Nietzsche reverses the practice of most other philosophers: they, too, experience persons, books, and events in a personal manner with their own personal preferences and prejudices, but when they write books they inhibit, hide, or transform these to more objective statements, that is, they hide the personal (and ad hominem) aspects of their view.

In yet another way, Nietzsche behaved unconventionally. Most philosophers, convinced of the justice of a negative value judgment of another philosopher or person, would nevertheless moderate the judgment before the public, expressing it less strongly in their published works than in private notebooks or letters. For Nietzsche, the reverse is true for the most part. In the case of Augustine, for example, his overall attitude in the notebooks is similar, that is, clearly hostile and contemptuous, but there are also references to him both as a philosopher and as one included in the group of "all more profound human beings."[58] As a consequence, it is often easier to understand the reasons for Nietzsche's ad hominem statements in his notebooks than in his published works. To take yet another example with regard to Augustine, we can compare the first published reference (*Jenseits von Gut und Böse,* sec. 50) with one of his notes, written during the early summer of 1885, that is, shortly after having read the *Confessions* and before writing *Jenseits von Gut und Böse.*[59]

The details and the basis of what is referred to in *Jenseits von Gut und Böse,* section 50, as Augustine's lack of nobility of bearing and desire, with special reference to his relation to his God, is spelled out more explicitly in the notebook section.[60] Praying, to which the *Confessions* is full of references, makes the one who prays unmanly and uncreative since it is depersonalizing and favors the lowest feelings and attitudes. Related to praying is begging or requesting, and Nietzsche finds that it is bad manners and in bad taste (ignoble) to ask for much instead of giving much. Nietzsche's interpretation of Augustine's view can be contrasted with his own, where the importance and nobility of giving (of being overfull and overflowing) is an important theme in all of his writings, but especially in *Also sprach Zarathustra.* Compare also Nietzsche's emphasis on the gift-giving virtue as the source of all virtues. Lastly, the lack of nobility in one's relation to one's God, referred to in *Jenseits von Gut und Böse,* section 50, is described in the notebook in more detail as "the mixture of humble servility with an often haughty plebeian obtrusiveness," which Nietzsche finds to be a doglike attitude.

During Nietzsche's last three active years, 1886 to 1888, he read fewer philosophical books than during the earlier parts of the 1880s. This was in part due to the fact that he was increasingly influenced by nonphilosophical sources, such as literature, literary criticism, studies of Christianity, and biographies, and in part due to the fact that he had found his own philosophical position and thus had less need for further philosophical reading and influences. It was also because much of Nietzsche's preoccupation during his last five years, and especially during 1887 and 1888, concerned his attempt to write a four-volume "Hauptwerk" or magnum opus.[61]

However, the first book Nietzsche published in these years, *Jenseits von Gut und Böse* (1886), is arguably his most philosophical work.[62] In it Nietzsche presented, in a much less poetical form than in *Also sprach Zarathustra,* his new philosophical position and his response to much reading during the preceding four or five years. Although not mentioned explicitly in *Beyond Good and Evil,* his reading and critique of Teichmüller, Spir, Liebmann (and other neo-Kantians), Hartmann, and others constitutes most of the background and motive for much of its philosophical content.

Nietzsche's main object of interest during the years 1886 to 1888 was an attempt to work out a revaluation of all values, and, related to that, an increasingly harsh critique of Christianity (Christianity in a broad sense, including much of philosophy and psychology). For his critique of Christianity and Christian values, his reading of Tolstoy, Dostoyevsky, Wellhausen, Lippert, Jacolliot, Strauss, Renan, Janssen, and the Bible was more relevant and influential than any reading of purely philosophical texts. He also became increasingly engaged in psychology (and physiology) and regarded it, rather than philosophy and metaphysical philosophy, as the road to the solution of the major philosophical problems.

However, even during these last three years he read a number of philosophical texts (especially in 1887), and perhaps still more important, he continued to reread texts and authors he had been reading for a long time, such as Schopenhauer, Mill, Hartmann, Montaigne, and Pascal. One new work he read, relating to epistemology and philosophy of nature, was C. v. Nägeli's *Mechanisch-physiologische Theorie der Abstammungslehre* (München and Leipzig, 1884). This is primarily a natural scientific work, important for its critique of Darwinism, but it also contains a lengthy appendix that includes several philosophical essays annotated by Nietzsche.[63]

The most important philosophical reading of this period, as expected, consisted of texts relating to Christianity: Guyau, Pascal, and Simplicius (together with a large number of historical, psychological, and other nonphilosophical texts on this theme).

Guyau's *L'irreligion de l'avenir: Étude sociologique,* 2nd ed. (Paris, 1887) is (together with Höffding) the most heavily annotated book of those Nietzsche read during this period.[64] Nietzsche read it in 1887 and filled it with both appreciative and critical comments including, for example, "Esel" (ass) on several occasions. Nietzsche at this point seems to have regarded Guyau as the sort of free thinker who rejects Christianity but holds on to Christian morality, in Guyau's case his belief in the triumph of love.[65] Much of this reading found its way into Nietzsche's *The Antichrist.*[66]

At approximately the same time, in 1887, Nietzsche also read the philosopher and sociologist Alfred Fouillée's *La science sociale contemporaine,* xiii+424 pages.[67] (Fouillée was Guyau's godfather.) In this work there are continual references to Spencer, Mill, contemporary French philosophy, and different theories about society, rights, and justice. In several notes from the autumn of 1887 Nietzsche criticized Fouillée (and Guyau),[68] and it seems likely that several of the late Nietzsche's statements about sociology and sociologists referred to Fouillée (and Guyau) and to what he learned from reading this book.[69]

Nietzsche's rereading of Pascal in 1887, when he was increasingly engaged with a battle against Christian values, caused him to regard Pascal more and more as an example of how Christianity can corrupt even the most supreme and honest of men.[70]

Nietzsche read and annotated Simplicius's *Commentar zu Epiktetos Handbuch* (Wien, 1867), translated by K. Enk, in January 1887. This reading would have supplemented Nietzsche's knowledge of Stoicism, but again, due to his preoccupation with Christianity, he mainly read it from the perspective of seeing the differences between a heathen and a Christian Weltanschauung. "I am at present reading, with such [*black*] thoughts, Simplicius's commentary to Epictetus: one has in him the complete *philosophical scheme* clearly before one, onto which Christianity has made its claim: so that this book by a 'heathen' philosopher makes the most Christian impression (except that the complete Christian emotional world and pathology is missing, 'love' as St. Paul speaks of it, 'fear of God,' etc). The *counterfeit* of everything factual by means of morality is everywhere to be seen; wretched psychology; the philosopher reduced to a 'country parson'— and of all this *Plato is the cause! he remains* the greatest misfortune of *Europe!*"[71]

Nietzsche read a number of books about psychology in the broad sense. To these books belong a number written by literary authors such as Stendhal, Dostoyevsky,[72] Tolstoy,[73] and Strindberg.[74] Biographical and cultural studies by the Goncourts, Galiani, Bourget, and Lefebvre were also of importance. Only one or two of these texts about psychology were of a philosophical nature (for example, Höffding and Joly), but others, such as Montaigne and Pascal, could also be included in this category.

The Danish philosopher Harald Höffding's *Psychologie in Umrissen auf Grundlage der Erfahrung* (Leipzig, 1887), 463 pages, is probably the most heavily annotated book Nietzsche read during this period, with annotations on almost every page.[75] The book contains discussions of psychology, including accounts of classical and contemporary philosophers' discussions of psychology. Höffding especially emphasized British and German views. The content of this book influenced Nietzsche and found its way into *Zur Genealogie der Moral* (1887) on several instances in terms of several smaller examples and the use of certain concepts and in larger themes such as the content of English philosophy and psychology, and the psychology of forgetting.[76] Nietzsche's reading of several works by Paul Rée was of paramount importance for the content of *On the Genealogy of Morals*, but his reading of Dühring, Renan, and others was also important.[77]

The book by Henri Joly, *Psychologie des grands hommes* (Paris, 1883), 280 pages, which Nietzsche read in 1887 (also annotated, but to a lesser degree), is less philosophical.[78] Joly discusses great men and geniuses and their dependence on the environment and heritage—themes Nietzsche discusses in *Twilight of the Idols*—including the theories of Darwin, Galton, and W. James.

In 1887 Nietzsche also read and heavily annotated Émile Gebhart's *Etudes méridionales* (1887), which contains a chapter on Machiavelli. It is probable that it was this reading, possibly together with a reading of *The Prince* in a French translation during the 1880s,[79] that led Nietzsche to praise Machiavelli highly in *Götzen-Dämmerung*.[80]

The most intensive purely philosophical reading Nietzsche seems to have done in these last three years was done in the library of Chur in May and early June 1887, followed by further reading shortly thereafter during the summer of 1887. In Chur Nietzsche read, apart from the British historian Buckle and other nonphilosophical texts, two volumes of Kuno Fischer's *Geschichte der neuern Philosophie*, the volumes about Spinoza and Kant. Nietzsche excerpted extensively from both these volumes.[81] Shortly thereafter he carefully read and annotated the neo-Kantian Otto Liebmann's *Gedanken und Tatsachen: Heft 1: Die Arten der Notwendigkeit—Die mechanische Naturerklärung—Idee und Entelechie* (Strassburg, 1882), v+121 pages. From this work Nietzsche excerpted a few remarks in relation to his continued thinking about the will to power, and he also wrote the expression "will to power" in the margin of a page in the book.[82]

During the autumn of 1887 or winter of 1887–88, Nietzsche read and annotated the Comtean E. de Roberty's account of the history of philosophy, *L'ancienne et la nouvelle philosophie: Essai sur les lois générales du développement de la philosophie* (Paris, 1887).

In 1888, Nietzsche's most productive year during which he wrote six books, he read of philosophical relevance in Victor Brochard's *Les sceptiques grecs* (Paris, 1887), which inspired Nietzsche's positive statements about the sophists in *Götzen-Dämmerung*,[83] and he reread Schopenhauer and Hartmann's *Philosophie des Unbewussten*. He also read or reread several books about religion, including Renan's *Vie de Jésus* (which this time he extensively excerpted), that helped to shape a number of Nietzsche's statements regarding the historical development of the concept of God, the Old Testament prophets, the psychology of Jesus, and the social psychology of the early Christian community in *The Antichrist*.[84]

Epilogue
On the Origin of, and Influences on, Nietzsche's Philosophy

An important approach to understanding a philosopher is to reconstruct his thinking, not in terms of a number of propositions but as answers to questions and implicit questions that he attempted to answer or to which he attempted to respond.[1] This can be done by using the philosopher's texts alone, but the result is greatly improved when his reading, and his response to this reading, also is taken into account. Doing so increases our factual knowledge of the thinker's interests and knowledge. But it can also help us to know and understand him better. If the philosopher annotated the books he read, as Nietzsche often did, then we are able to meet him not only in the omnipotent role of the author but also in the much humbler role of listener and commentator. This gives us the opportunity not merely to listen to the thinker proclaiming but also to listen in, so to speak, on his conversations with other thinkers. Many aspects of a philosopher's thinking become much clearer when we see his response to similar (or different) kinds of thinking in someone else's writings. Our knowledge of that sort of response can be an important contribution to the understanding of the origin of Nietzsche's ideas and to their interpretation. Almost all studies of Nietzsche's thinking so far have used his own statements (texts) as the starting point rather than the themes and questions to which his texts respond, which often came from his reading. One purpose of the present study has been to make possible the latter sort of approach.

The approach used so far is a bit like if one were to study Nietzsche's (or any other thinker's) correspondence and decided to use only what he says in his own letters, when, in fact, a large proportion of the letters to him are also available (which can illuminate not only many specific points and the general atmosphere and nature of the discussions but also the specific context and origin of many of the questions raised and to which Nietzsche responds). Anyone who has at first read only one side of a correspondence and thereafter read both sides realizes to what a large extent the latter approach improves and deepens the understanding.

Many Nietzschean terms, such as *ressentiment,* nihilism, Übermensch, *décadence* and *virtù,* occur in books Nietzsche read from which he presumably picked up most of them. Furthermore, he noted several of them in the margins of books he read. For example, the first time Nietzsche ever wrote the word *"ressentiment"* was in the margin of E. Dühring's *Der Werth des Lebens* (1865), which he read in 1875. He also wrote the expression "Wille zur Macht" in the margins of several books he read.[2] For the most part, this sort of information has previously been unavailable and unpublished. The fact that Nietzsche made such notations in the margins of books he read can give us further important information to help us illuminate the meaning of these concepts for him. Nietzsche's philosophy, as I have shown in this study, was profoundly colored by his reading of many other philosophers, both major and minor.

The fact that so little interest and research have been directed toward the implicit questions Nietzsche attempted to answer—and especially that so little use has been made of his reading and library—is surprising for several reasons. First, so much has been written about Nietzsche: more than forty-five hundred books and substantial articles by 1967, and more than another two thousand in English alone between 1968 and 1992. The recent five-volume *Weimarer Nietzsche-Bibliographie* (2000–2003), contains no less than 18,465 entries. It is astonishing that such an important source of information has been left untapped. Second, Nietzsche lived such an isolated life (at least during the last ten years of his productive life) that his reading seems very likely to have been important for him. Third, Nietzsche, like Plato and Rousseau, is easy to read but relatively difficult to understand and classify, and a knowledge of his reading and his response to this reading is likely to contribute significantly to the resolution of these problems. Fourth, Nietzsche's thinking has evoked interest in such diverse fields of knowledge (psychology, sociology, religion, and music among them) that one would have thought that people in these fields, more so perhaps than philosophers, would have been interested in what Nietzsche knew and how he came to know it as well as his response to reading books in their areas.

Finally, and most of all, we do not have to be satisfied with a mere list of titles of books Nietzsche read and then guess at his response, since his private library remains essentially intact. A large proportion of the books Nietzsche read he also owned (about half of them for the last four years of his active life, 1885–89), and these books have been microfilmed and are available for examination by researchers in Weimar. Nietzsche's private library consists today of about 1,000 titles—more than 1,500 volumes—of which about 600 contain his annotations or dog-ears and about 150 are heavily annotated.[3]

There are several reasons that this source of information has been used to such a limited extent. Nietzsche's own words in *Ecce Homo* and elsewhere implied that he read little and that this reading was not important. This view is often strengthened by a general Nietzscheanism shared by most writers on Nietzsche, that is, that one should concentrate on the overall or radical aspects of his philosophy and not on minor and scholarly details. Perhaps most important for the post–World War II period is that Nietzsche's library is situated in Weimar, which until recently was part of East Germany, where the authorities regarded Nietzsche as a nonperson and therefore kept the library closed to both visitors and researchers. The library has been open to researchers only since the early 1990s.[4]

Another rather mundane reason is that the existence of Nietzsche's library is not known to many scholars and philosophers. Although there exist three older published accounts and listings of the content of the library, these were all published in obscure journals and are not well known. The first two, published by Elisabeth Nietzsche, are incomplete and much less reliable and useful than the third.[5] Recently, a new and much more detailed, reliable, and extensive listing has been published by Giuliano Campioni, Paolo D'Iorio, Andrea Orsucci, Maria Cristina Fornari, and Francesco Fronterotta (with the assistance of Renate Müller-Buck), with the title *Nietzsches persönliche Bibliothek* (2003).

Nietzsche's reading and library were not used and are almost never even mentioned in the standard works about Nietzsche such as Kaufmann, Schacht, Clark, Danto, Heidegger, Deleuze, Löwith, Nehamas, Jaspers, and Lampert. Nor does it appear that the library (or its contents) is even mentioned in the two best-known English-language biographies of Nietzsche—R. J. Hollingdale, *Nietzsche: The Man and His Philosophy* (1965) and R. Hayman, *Nietzsche: A Critical Life* (1980)—or in the most recent one, Curtis Cate's *Friedrich Nietzsche* (2002). Also, as a further example, in none of the many books published in English about Nietzsche and politics during the last decades is there any discussion of Nietzsche's (limited) reading of political books and his response to this reading.

This means that the literature is lacking many studies that could shed light on Nietzsche's relation to, and knowledge of, thinkers and topics that were important to him. A few such specialist studies have been done but without knowledge of Nietzsche's library and reading. For example, G. C. Fidler has written an article about Guyau and Nietzsche without use of, or even reference to, Nietzsche's annotations in his two books by Guyau (which are two of the most heavily annotated books in Nietzsche's library).[6] Robin Small has written with insight about Nietzsche and Spir[7] and Nietzsche and Dühring[8] but without making use of, or reference to, Nietzsche's annotations of the relevant places in these heavily annotated books. More recently, Michael Green has written an interesting full monograph study of Nietzsche and Spir, *Nietzsche and the Transcendental Tradition* (2002), but likewise not making use of Nietzsche's annotations.

C. N. Stavrou's *Whitman and Nietzsche* claims that "no direct link between the two exists" and that they had no knowledge of each other's existence.[9] However, in fact, a book in Nietzsche's library by Karl Knortz, with whom Nietzsche corresponded, has the title *Walt Whitman: Vortrag* (New York, 1886), and Nietzsche also possessed the work *Amerikanische Gedichte der Neuzeit* (Leipzig, 1883), translated by Knortz.[10] George J. Stack has written two excellent full-size books, *Lange and Nietzsche* (1983) and *Nietzsche and Emerson* (1992), without using Nietzsche's limited annotations in his copy of Lange's *Geschichte der Materialismus* (the annotations in this work are so limited only because Nietzsche had given away or lost his copy of the first edition, which he had read intensively) and only very rarely mentioning Nietzsche's immense quantity of annotations in his Emerson books.

Even such simple questions as to what extent Nietzsche had read, say, John Stuart Mill, or when he read him, and what knowledge about Mill he possessed have until now remained essentially unanswered, and the name of Mill could be exchanged for almost any other name.[11] Without answers to such questions it is difficult to interpret, evaluate, or even to respond to most of Nietzsche's many statements—often ad hominem statements—in regard to other thinkers (except for the all too common simplistic response that Nietzsche was merely prejudiced). We have had a very limited knowledge of the persons, themes, and questions with which Nietzsche was acquainted and to which he responded.

There does not exist any previous book-size study, either in English or German, that deals with Nietzsche's reading and library to any significant extent. Nor do there seem to exist even any articles that deal more generally with these questions.[12] The one exception is the second essay (of three) in Ralph-Rainer Wuthenow's *Nietzsche als Leser: Drei Essays* (1994), which, however, consists of a rather short and general discussion of Nietzsche's reading—primarily of fiction—and view of reading, based only on his published statements (which, as we have seen above, are not always reliable).

What does exist is a rather small number of mostly recently published, specialized studies of Nietzsche's relation to one or a few books. Almost all of these seem to have been written in German,[13] and most of them have been published in *Nietzsche-Studien,* where one to two articles per year in recent years have dealt with Nietzsche's reading. *Nietzsche-Studien* also publishes yearly philological material relevant for Nietzsche's reading under the heading "Beiträge zur Quellenforschung."

In this book I have sought to remedy this situation. The interpretation and relevance of the information I have gathered will no doubt be matters of debate and controversy, but now that important debate can begin. It is my hope that the information and arguments presented here will lead to new and better-informed discussions of many topics and questions related to Nietzsche's thinking and about the context in which he thought and worked. This study can be regarded as a sort of skeleton consisting of a chronological listing and account of Nietzsche's philosophical reading and brief discussions of its relevance. Much more philosophical analysis and work on specific reading, periods, and topics ought now to be performed.

We have in this study encountered a new picture of Nietzsche not merely as a self-styled iconoclastic philosopher but also as a thinker who responds to, reads, and studies texts for the purpose of learning, testing, extending his thinking, and seeking stimuli. One ignores this context at one's peril.

Notes

Introduction

1. Nietzsche's borrowing, without citing sources, sometimes verged on plagiarism. The young Nietzsche, at Schulpforta, began this bad habit and directly plagiarized several times. Three essays written between 1861 and 1864 were, to a large extent, plagiarized: "Brief an meinen Freund," where Nietzsche strongly praised Hölderlin, BAW 2, 1–5; "Napoleon III als Praesident," BAW 2, 23–28; and "Primum Oedipodis regis carmen choricum," BAW 2, 364–94. Two of these essays were handed in as school assignments without the teachers noticing the plagiarism. Such copying from other sources is not easy to discover, and other early essays may well also be plagiarized. For further information, see my forthcoming study *The Young Nietzsche: An Intellectual Biography Based on Nietzsche's Reading and Private Library, 1850–68*. The cases mentioned here are early and extreme cases, but it was not uncommon for the mature Nietzsche to borrow significantly without naming his sources; see, for example, his use of Gustav Gerber in "About Truth and Lies in an Extra-Moral Sense" and Julius Wellhausen in *The Antichrist*.

2. Wilhelm Wundt, "Philosophy in Germany," *Mind* 2 (1877): 509. Nietzsche himself is likely to have read this article (or, rather, to have had it translated and read to him), for the editor of *Mind*, Robertson, told him about the article in a letter dated September 20, 1877.

3. Only in the last of these books, published in 1888, is he (although classified as a Schopenhauerian) seen as standing apart from the philosophy and sciences of his time.
The reviews of Nietzsche's books are listed in R. F. Krummel, *Nietzsche und der deutsche Geist* (Berlin and New York: Walter de Gruyter, 1974; 2nd enlarged ed., 1998).

4. The borderline between philosophical and nonphilosophical authors is clearly not easy to draw. Some of the authors mentioned here may not best be classified as philosophers, and, worse, some of the texts not mentioned may well be regarded as philosophical, at least in some senses. Such borderline cases can unfortunately not be avoided.

5. In the Oehler listing of Nietzsche's library from 1942, the philosophical titles ("Neuere Philosophie und Psychologie") constitute only about one-tenth of all the books in Nietzsche's library.

6. Sander L. Gilman, *Begegnungen mit Nietzsche* (Bonn: Bouvier Verlag, 1981). The second edition of this work is essentially identical but contains an index. A shortened version of the book has been published in English with the title *Conversations with Nietzsche* (New York and Oxford: Oxford University Press, 1987).

7. Two useful indices according to the place in Nietzsche's works and notebooks and according to the names of the authors read have been compiled by R. Ratsch-Heitmann and A. U. Sommer and have been published in "Quellenforschung," *Nietzsche-Studien* 30 (2001): 435–73.

8. For information, see Erdmann von Wilamowitz-Moellendorff, "Nietzsche-Bibliographie," *Nietzsche-Studien* 25 (1996): 392–93.

Chapter 1: Nietzsche As Reader

1. He made a similar claim in FW V, 366: "We do not belong to those who have ideas only among books, when stimulated by books. It is our habit to think outdoors.[...] We read rarely, but not worse on that account."

2. EH, "Why I Am So Clever," 3.

3. Ibid.

4. GM, III, 22.

5. This is a listing of the persons Nietzsche most often praised in his published works. For a fuller discussion, see my *Nietzsche's Ethics of Character* (Uppsala: Uppsala University Press, 1995).

6. KSA 14, 476–77. This earlier listing was written in October 1888 but was replaced by the printed version in December 1888.

7. A few of these may have been read to him by others, but the majority of them he certainly read himself.

8. During the period 1870–78, Elisabeth lived with Nietzsche in Basel for three and a half years in total. She often read to him during that time.

9. These are listed in KSA 15, 71.

10. Elisabeth Förster-Nietzsche, *Der Junge Nietzsche* (Leipzig, 1912).

11. In his first autobiography, titled "Aus meinem Leben" and written in 1858 at the age of thirteen, Nietzsche wrote: "I can still remember the reading-room [or study] on the top floor. The large number of books, among them some with many pictures, these works made this place to one of my favorite places." KGW I.1, 4[77], 283 (also in BAW 1, 2). The Nietzsche family moved from the house when Nietzsche was five and a half years old.

12. KGW I.1, 4[77], 301.

13. Letter from Franziska Nietzsche, August 10, 1857.

14. They themselves often referred to it as a scholarly, "*wissenschaftliche*," society.

15. A listing of these contributions is given in the history of the society written by Nietzsche in September 1862 in BAW 2, 88 and 90–99, and continued in June 1863, BAW 2, 214–20.

16. In the letter to Gersdorff, October 11, 1866, Nietzsche described having partaken in the auction of the Pforta-teacher Keil's library and his plans to acquire further books. An unpublished list of titles, dated October 11, 1866, in the Goethe-Schiller Archiv in Weimar, constitutes Nietzsche's selection from the Calvary's catalog. The day before, October 10, 1866, Nietzsche had written to his friend Hermann Mushacke in Berlin and asked him to give an accompanying letter to the Calvary bookshop. The list consists of forty-one titles, all either ancient authors or about ancient authors. Most likely, this was a list of some of the books Nietzsche wanted to acquire in 1866 but in the end did not buy at that time.

17. See my article "Nietzsche's Forgotten Book: The Index to the *Rheinisches Museum für Philologie*," *New Nietzsche Studies* 4 (Summer–Fall 2000): 157–61.

18. In a letter to Gersdorff, December 13, 1875, Nietzsche summarized his life and his hopes for the next year and the near future. In so doing he also indicated the importance that reading had for him (one of the tasks Elisabeth did, apart from organizing the household, was reading aloud for Nietzsche): "the possession of 40 good books from all times and peoples (and also further ones, not bad ones)."

19. Elisabeth Förster-Nietzsche, "Friedrich Nietzsches Bibliothek," in *Deutscher Bibliophilen-Kalender für das Jahr 1913,* ed. Hans Feigl (Vienna, n.d.), 107.

20. "With this clubfoot which I carry with me, I mean the 104 kilo books, I will not be able to flee far away from here." Letter to his mother, October 4, 1884, written in Zürich.

21. Compare Nietzsche's letter to his mother and sister, Genoa, April 28, 1881, and Elisabeth Förster-Nietzsche's preface to "Friedrich Nietzsches Bibliothek," 104.

22. Letter to his mother, Franziska Nietzsche, December 29, 1887.

23. Letters to his mother, December 11, 1888, and December 21, 1888.

24. Letter to Franz Overbeck, July 2, 1885.

25. Letter to Carl Fuchs, August 22, 1888.

26. For example, "The eyes, painful day and night, forbid reading and writing"; "the eye-morality calls to me 'do not read and write, my Herr Professor!'"; and "My eyes gives me great worry and still more discomfort and boredom. My condition is such that I only with effort can read because of the many veils which moves before my eyes: and the eyes weep continually."

27. Letter to Reinhart von Seydlitz in Munich, October 26, 1886.

28. "Obviously, we spoke much about books and authors. Nietzsche had the *le flair du livre* and read much in spite of his eye-problems. [...] Like almost all good readers he annotated [or marked] specific places in the text. Thus, a part of his intellectual life remains in the books he possessed." Meta von Salis-Marschlins, *Philosoph und Edelmensch: Ein Beitrag zur Charakteristik Friedrich Nietzsches* (Leipzig, 1897), 51.

29. Twice in Nietzsche's notebooks from 1885 he wrote that he needed to have someone read to him. KSA 11, 29[4] and 34[40].

30. See, for example, Nietzsche's letter to his mother, ca. August 10, 1885.

31. Nietzsche mentioned the desire to have a "reading-machine" in a letter to Franziska and Elisabeth, December 21, 1881, and in a letter to Overbeck, March 17, 1882: "Now

my friends must also invent a 'reading-machine': otherwise I will remain below what I can achieve and will be unable to acquire sufficient intellectual nourishment."

32. For example, Nietzsche's letter to his sister, May 20, 1885.

33. GD, "Maxims and Arrows," 34.

34. Nietzsche referred to the Leihbibliothek (the lending library, part of a bookshop) in letters from 1862, 1864, and 1865. A still extant bill from the Domrich dated "1/3 1868" (unpublished papers from the Goethe-Schiller Archiv in Weimar, GSA 71/219) lists "Fee for borrowing from the lending library 29/1-67 to 5/6-67," "Subscription to the lending library 26/9-67 to 26/3-68" and "Subscription to the musical lending library 7/2 to 7/7 67 and from 28/7 67 to 19/3 68."

35. Letter to mother and sister, October 31, 1866. It is not known what books Nietzsche borrowed in Leipzig, with the exception of a very few titles.

36. For example, to Mushacke, October 10, 1866, and to Ritschl, September 9, 1868.

37. To Deussen, April 4, 1867; to Gersdorff, April 6, 1867; and to Rohde, April 3, 1868, and January 16, 1869.

38. In letters to his friend Seydlitz, May 13, 1888, and to his sister, September 14, 1888.

39. Letter to Elisabeth Förster, November 3, 1886. Nietzsche continued in the letter: "Between us, my dear sister, the way I stand toward life and the task I have to perform, Europe is for me necessary, since it is the seat of science on Earth." In an earlier letter, from November 23, 1885, Nietzsche had written in regard to Paraguay: "The lack of larger libraries is perhaps not sufficiently emphasized [in the advertisement for Elisabeth and Bernhardt Förster's planned new colony in Paraguay]. Please forgive me, my dear Lama [Elisabeth's pet name], when the sickly cultural animal, your brother, allows himself a joke."

Nietzsche also quoted Cicero in a short note written between November 1887 and March 1888, KSA 13, 11[18], that just consists of the words "si hortum cum bibliotheca habes, nihil deerit. Cicero" (he who has a garden with a library lacks nothing).

In a letter from Chur, May 20, 1887, Nietzsche wrote: "The library in Chur, ca 20 000 volumes, gives me for education this and that." He then went on to discuss three books he had been reading there.

40. Letter to Franz Overbeck, April 14, 1887: "I need a place with a large library for my next work: I have considered Stuttgart. They have sent me the very liberal rules of the Stuttgart Library."

41. Elisabeth Förster-Nietzsche wrote in *Der Junge Nietzsche*, 40, that they early spent a summer with relatives near Leipzig: "From there, Fritz undertook many expeditions to the bookshops in Leipzig, in which he was immensely interested." Nietzsche also mentioned this in his first autobiography, KGW I.1, 4[77], 303.

42. Three book bills from Domrich from 1868 are still extant and cover a total of twenty-seven titles but many more volumes since several are complete works, such as Goethe in forty volumes and Aristotle in nine volumes.

43. Letter to Franziska Nietzsche, Turin, May 27, 1888: "Yesterday the local philosopher, Professor Pasquale D'Ercole, made a very polite visit. He, now dean of the philosophical faculty in the local University, had heard in the bookshop Löscher that I was here." Compare also the letter to Peter Gast, April 20, 1888.

In a letter to Nietzsche from his sister, March 14, 1880, she wrote that an employee in the Detloffschen Bookshop (probably in Basel) had told her that when he saw Nietzsche in the bookshop he always wanted to mention a cure for his headaches and dizziness but had been too reticent, implying not infrequent visits by Nietzsche.

44. In 1880 Nietzsche subscribed to a weekly list of new books and asked for other book catalogs. At this time Nietzsche also wrote to his sister, April 1880, and asked her to keep her eyes open for new interesting books: "If, my dear sister, when you read 'Revue des deux mondes' [you] see a book which is strongly recommended (historical or philosophical), you would write it to me, I would be very grateful."

45. This is to a large extent due to Nietzsche's interest in books and their content and to the fact that he often made lists of books and discussed them in his letters. This habit, in turn, may be attributed to his relatively isolated life, which led him to write many letters. Most of these have been preserved, because his sister, Elisabeth, kept a list of the works in his library and kept his papers, including book bills. She also took good care of Nietzsche's library so that most of the books are still extant.

46. The listing written by the young Elisabeth has not been published but will be included in my forthcoming study *The Young Nietzsche*.

47. I have discussed this tendency in regard to morality in my study *Nietzsche's Ethics of Character: A Study of Nietzsche's Ethics and Its Place in the History of Moral Thinking* (Uppsala: Uppsala University Press, 1995), especially in the chapter titled "The Place and Status of Persons in Nietzsche's Philosophy," 105–29.

48. VM, 408 (the last section). The names mentioned here are Epicurus, Montaigne, Goethe, Spinoza, Plato, Rousseau, Pascal, and Schopenhauer.

49. In a letter to his mother in late April 1885, Nietzsche wrote that since there were so few spiritual Germans, he "almost exclusively communicate[s] with dead men." In another letter to his sister and mother, March 14, 1885, he wrote: "Anyway, there is no one alive today in whom I would place *much* value: the persons whom I value have been dead a long long time, e.g. Galiani or Henri Beyle or Montaigne."

50. EH, "Why I Am So Clever," 8. Compare also FW V, 366, and KSA 13, 11[412].

51. GD, "Maxims and Arrows," 34.

52. KSA 11, 34[65].

53. JGB, 192.

54. Ibid., 246.

55. See, for example, his notes about future *Untimely Meditations*, KSA 7, 29[163 and 164], "12 Lesen Schrieben Presse."

56. AC, 59. In the last section of FW, 383, he expressed his willingness "to remind my readers of the virtues of the right reader—what forgotten and unknown virtues they are!" However, he did not actually do it there.

57. MA, 270.

58. In the preface to *Dawn,* sec. 5, written and added in 1886, Nietzsche wrote: "I just as much as my book, are friends of *lento.* It is not for nothing that I have been a philologist, perhaps I am a philologist still, that is to say, a teacher of slow reading: [...] For philology is that venerable art which demands of its votaries one thing above all: to go aside, to take time, to become still, to become slow—it is a goldsmith's art and connoisseurship of the *word* which has nothing but delicate, cautious work to do and achieves nothing if it does not achieve it *lento.* [...] [T]his art does not so easily get anything done, it teaches to read *well,* that is to say, to read slowly, deeply, looking cautiously before and aft, with reservations, with doors left open, with delicate eyes and fingers . . . My patient friends, this book desires for itself only perfect readers and philologists: *learn to read me well!*—."

Other places where Nietzsche discussed reading and emphasized that one needs to read slowly and carefully are GM, Preface, 8; GD, "What the Germans Lack," 6; AC, 52 (compare KSA 13, 14[60] and 15[90]) and EH, "Books," 5.

59. In EH, "Wise," 2, Nietzsche described the opposite of a decadent with the words: "He is always in his own company, whether he traffics with books, people or landscapes." The importance of personal involvement permeates Nietzsche's whole philosophy but is perhaps most visible in his rejection of philosophies that depersonalize.

60. EH, "Books," 3: "When I picture a perfect reader, I always picture a monster of courage and curiosity, also something supple, cunning, cautious, a born adventurer and discoverer."

EH, Foreword, 3: "How much truth can a spirit *bear,* how much truth can a spirit *dare?* that became for me more and more the real measure of value. Error (—belief in the ideal—) is not blindness, error is *cowardice* . . . Every acquisition, every step forward in knowledge is the *result* of courage, of severity toward oneself, of cleanliness with respect to oneself."

61. Compare, for example, his contrast of Plato with Thucydides in GD, "What I Owe to the Ancients," 2, describing Plato as an idealist and "a coward in face of reality" and Thucydides as a realist, as "the grand summation, the last manifestation of that strong, stern, hard matter-of-factness instinctive to the older Hellenes."

62. "The conditions under which one understands me and then *necessarily* understands—I know them all too well. One must be honest in intellectual matters.[...] Strength which prefers questions for which no one today is sufficiently daring; courage for the *forbidden.*[...] Reverence for oneself; love for oneself; unconditional freedom with respect to oneself . . . Very well! These alone are my readers." AC, Preface (Hollingdale's translation).

63. Although Nietzsche repeatedly stated how he wanted to be read—slowly, carefully, with rumination—in, for example, *Ecce Homo,* the preface to *Dawn,* and other prefaces, the *Zur Genealogie der Moral* is the only book in which he gave an explicit example and thus *showed* how he wanted to be read.

64. GM, Preface, 8. This is the last part of the preface, which Nietzsche added later, probably at the same time as he added a new first section (summary) to the third essay.

65. See John T. Wilcox, "What Aphorism Does Nietzsche Explicate in *Genealogy of Morals,* Essay III?" *Journal of the History of Philosophy* 35 (1997): 593–610; Maudemarie Clarke, "From the Nietzsche Archive: Concerning the Aphorism Explicated in *Genealogy* III," *Journal of the History of Philosophy* 35 (1997): 611–14; and Christopher Janaway, "Nietzsche's Illustration of the Art of Exegesis," *European Journal of Philosophy* 5 (1997): 251–68. See also Wilcox's later summary and discussion of the case in "That Exegesis of an Aphorism in *Genealogy* III: Reflection on the Scholarship," *Nietzsche-Studien* 27 (1998): 448–62.

The widespread acceptance of the earlier "standard view" of this problem, as Wilcox and Janaway point out, shows that many important Anglo-Saxon interpreters of Nietzsche have not only misread the third essay in *On the Genealogy of Morals* but, more importantly and problematically, have misread Nietzsche's example and account of how one is to read his writings.

66. This is an aspect of what I call Nietzsche's ethics of character. See my study *Nietzsche's Ethics of Character.* In chapter 5, "The Place and Status of Persons in Nietzsche's Philosophy," I discuss this aspect of Nietzsche as reader, exemplified by his reading of St. Augustine, Aristotle, Mill, and Kant.

Chapter 2: The Major Philosophical Influences on Nietzsche's Thinking

1. During the winter term of 1864–65, Nietzsche attended Otto Jahn's "Platos *Symposium*" (but no notes remain from this course, and it is possible that he only attended the beginning of it), and during the summer term of 1865 he attended two courses by Schaarschmidt, "Allgemeine Geschichte der Philosophie" and "Platos Leben und Lehre." Nietzsche's unpublished notes from these two courses are kept at the Goethe-Schiller Archive (GSA) in Weimar.

2. KSA 9, 12[151], autumn 1881.

3. BAW 2, 100. Nietzsche here misspelled his name as "Emmerson."

4. KGW I.2, 13[6] and 13[7], 431–40, also published in BAW 2, 54–62. Once in each of the essays Nietzsche referred explicitly to Emerson, but even a superficial reading of Emerson's essay "Fate" in *The Conduct of Life* (*Die Führung des Lebens*) shows another eleven places that are restatements from this essay, not including the titles that also reflect the essay by Emerson, which, in the translation Nietzsche read, was called "Das Fatum."

Compare George Stack's "Nietzsche's Earliest Essays: Translation of and Commentary on 'Fate and History' and 'Freedom of Will and Fate,'" *Philosophy Today* 37 (1993): 153–69.

5. Karl Jaspers quotes and briefly discusses these essays and finds it amazing to what degree Nietzsche expressed "even as a boy, impulses and thoughts belonging to his later philosophy." He mentions several specific themes and beliefs, which he sees as characteristic of the mature Nietzsche but which are already visible here. Karl Jaspers,

Nietzsche: An Introduction to the Understanding of His Philosophical Activity (New York and London: University Press of America, 1965), 56 and 367. Curt Paul Janz's standard biography of Nietzsche, *Friedrich Nietzsche,* 3 vols., 2nd ed. (München, Wien: Carl Hanser Verlag, 1993), Part 1, 98–104, quotes and discusses these essays in detail. (The first part of this biography was written by Richard Blunck but has been incorporated in Janz's continuation and is therefore hereafter referred to as Janz's.) Janz claims that almost all of Nietzsche's more important themes are "already visible here" (98), and they "already show all the impulses of Nietzsche's thinking and because they already circumscribe all the crucial problems.[...] He who reads them attentively will find everything on display here" (103). Janz makes strong claims for nineteen different themes, including atheism, the revaluation of all values, the relativity of morality, the philosophy of becoming, the innocence of becoming, that man is something to be overcome, the thought of the Übermensch, the eternal recurrence, the philosopher as prophet and law giver, *amor fati,* and the "positivistic ideas" of the middle Nietzsche. Janz even states that the essays are "wie ein Programm seines ganzen Leben und Denkens" (like a guide to his entire life and thought) (98). These claims are perhaps overstated but still appear to contain a large amount of truth. Surprisingly, neither Jaspers nor Janz observed, or mentioned, that both essays are profoundly indebted to Nietzsche's reading of Emerson. Ronald Hayman in his *Nietzsche: A Critical Life* (London: Quartet Books, 1980) discusses these two essays but also does not call attention to the debt to Emerson, and Carl Pletsch in his *Young Nietzsche: Becoming a Genius* (New York: Free Press, 1991) surprisingly fails to mention the essays at all. Others, such as George J. Stack in his *Nietzsche and Emerson: An Elective Affinity* (Athens: Ohio University Press, 1992), noted and emphasized Emerson's importance for these first philosophical attempts by Nietzsche but without going into any detail or discussing what in them specifically comes from Emerson.

The statements by Jaspers and Janz, even if somewhat exaggerated, when combined with an awareness of the essay's profound debt to Emerson illustrate the immense importance of Emerson not only for the young Nietzsche but also for his later philosophy.

6. BAW 3, 334. Eleven authors and their works are listed.

7. In Gersdorff's letter to Nietzsche, December 18, 1864, he wrote: "I immediately followed your friendly advice that I should acquire Emerson's Essays."

Eduard Baumgarten claims that Nietzsche read *Versuche* parallel to *Die Führung des Lebens* and that both works influenced the two Germania essays. This may be correct, but the evidence for it is slim, and it is unlikely that Nietzsche would have taken part of his title from Emerson's essay "Geschichte" in *Versuche* and written a general parallel to a place in the essay "Kreise" in the same work.

8. Letter to Gersdorff, April 7, 1866, and BAW 3, 370.

9. The work thus both begins and ends with references to Emerson, that is, in sections 1 and 8.

10. Nietzsche appears to have read him especially intensively in 1862 and 1863 (*Die Führung des Lebens*); in 1874 (*Versuche,* which was used for *Schopenhauer As Educator*); in

1876, when he bought and read Emerson's *Neue Essays* (1876) but was less enthusiastic about it and brought with him three works by Emerson during his spring holidays; in 1878, when he possibly bought and certainly read *Über Goethe und Shakespeare* (1857) and again intensively read and excerpted *Versuche;* in 1880 (*Versuche*); in 1881 (*Versuche*); in 1882 (*Versuche*); in 1883 (*Versuche*); in 1884, when he had Emerson's essay "Historic Notes of Life and Letters in Massachusetts" translated into German and again read *Versuche;* and in 1885 and 1887–88, when he seems to have reread *Versuche* yet again.

11. The books and texts by Emerson that we know Nietzsche possessed and read are:

Die Führung des Lebens: Gedanken und Studien. A translation of *The Conduct of Life* by E. S. v. Mühlberg (Leipzig, 1862). (Bound together with Emerson, *Über Goethe und Shakespeare.*) This work has now been lost from the library, but according to Oehler's list from 1942 it was much annotated. Probably bought in 1862 or 1863.

Versuche (Essays). Translated by G. Fabricius (Hannover, 1858). Very intensively annotated and excerpted. This work is a translation of both the first and second series of essays published in English for the first time in 1841 and 1844, respectively. All essays, with the exception of *Liebe,* have been heavily annotated by Nietzsche. He also excerpted much from this work into his notebooks. Note that the annotations we have knowledge about were done in 1874 or later, for Nietzsche's copy was stolen in 1874, and he then bought a new copy that is the copy now in his library. Bought in 1862–64 (?) and again in 1874.

Über Goethe und Shakespeare. A translation of two essays from *Representative Men,* with a critique of Emerson's works, by Hermann Grimm (Hannover, 1857). (Bound together with Emerson, *Die Führung des Lebens.*) This work has now been lost from the library, but according to Oehler's list from 1942 it was much annotated. The work contains *Goethe,* 1–46; *Shakespeare, der Dichter,* 47–90; and *Emerson,* by Grimm, 91–115. It is not known when Nietzsche acquired this work. His first known reference to it is from 1876 or 1878.

Neue Essays (Letters and Social Aims). Authorized translation, with an introduction by Julian Schmidt (Stuttgart, 1876). This work is lightly annotated by Nietzsche. The first and the last two essays are annotated by Nietzsche. Bought 1876.

The Atlantic Monthly: Devoted to Literature, Science, Art and Politics 52(312) (October 1883): 433–576. Pages 529–43 contain Emerson's "Historic Notes of Life and Letters in Massachusetts." This essay contains three marginal lines made by pencil on pages 538, 542, and 543. More importantly, Nietzsche had the essay translated, in writing, into German in 1884 and thus read it in German. Nietzsche acquired this issue of the journal in 1884. The translated version of it is still in GSA with the signum 71-0317-4.

We know that Nietzsche read the *Neue Essays* for the first time in 1876 and the essay in *The Atlantic Monthly* in 1884. We have no knowledge that Nietzsche read any other works by Emerson, but that possibility cannot be excluded, and further research may well be able to identify such reading.

12. Such a comparison and argument has been most extensively performed by George J. Stack in *Nietzsche and Emerson: An Elective Affinity* (Athens: Ohio University Press, 1992).

Stack's work is valuable and contains many insights and parallels between Nietzsche's and Emerson's works, but it also contains many minor errors and false assumptions often based on an overenthusiastic approach. This often makes it difficult to determine the certainty or the reliability of any specific assumed influence on Nietzsche. Stack repeatedly makes such claims as "The case for my view that virtually all of the significant aspects of Nietzsche's philosophy of existence are influenced by Emerson's proto-existential conception of self-becoming is overdetermined" (54).

Stack, for example, claims that "without exception, he was enthusiastic about what Emerson wrote. He expressed no critical comments, remarks, or asides" (3–4). However, Nietzsche in fact was critical—or at least unenthusiastic—about the *Neue Essays*. Furthermore, Stack restricts his discussion almost entirely to Nietzsche's relation to the work *Versuche,* even with respect to the young Nietzsche, for whom *The Conduct of Life* probably was much more important.

Stack often claims that Emerson was the first to imprint a general theme on Nietzsche or the first author Nietzsche read who argued for a general theme. Since Emerson appears to have been the first philosopher Nietzsche read extensively, this is often true and relevant, but it does not conclusively prove that Emerson actually inspired Nietzsche, for example, in his "perspectivism" or about the importance of danger (51).

A more recent valuable discussion of many aspects of the relationship between Nietzsche and Emerson is *ESQ: A Journal of the American Renaissance* 43 (1997–98), the special issue dealing with these two thinkers' relationship.

13. Eduard Baumgarten and Stanley Hubbard have given detailed information about Nietzsche's annotations in his copy of *Versuche.* Baumgarten and Max Oehler have both also published a few pictures of the much annotated pages of Emerson's book.

14. Its content is published in KSA 9, 13[1–22].

15. Letter from Gersdorff to Nietzsche, December 18, 1864.

16. Letter to Gersdorff, September 24, 1874.

17. KSA 8, 41[30], July 1879.

18. KSA 9, 12[68], autumn 1881.

19. KSA 9, 12[151].

20. FW, 92. "Four very strange and truly poetic human beings in this century have attained mastery in prose, for which this century was not made otherwise—for lack of poetry, as I have suggested. Not including Goethe, who may fairly be claimed by the century that produced him, I regard only Giacomo Leopardi, Prosper Mérimée, Ralph

Waldo Emerson, and Walter Savage Landor, the author of *Imaginary Conversations,* as worthy of being called masters of prose."

21. Letter to Overbeck, December 24, 1883.

22. Letter to Overbeck, December 22, 1884.

23. GD, "Expeditions of an Untimely Man," 13.

24. KSA 14, 476ff.

25. Emerson wrote "life is a search after power" in *The Conduct of Life,* while Nietzsche claimed that "Leben ist Wille zur Macht." This example is taken from page 145 of Baumgarten, "Mitteilungen und Bemerkungen über den Einfluß Emerson auf Nietzsche," *Jahrbuch für Amerikastudien* 1 (1956): 93–152.

26. Emerson also used this expression, although it has not been established that he did so in any texts that we know Nietzsche read.

27. Only three weeks after Nietzsche's discovery of the idea of the eternal recurrence in August 1881 did he refer to Zarathustra for the first time in a manner that clearly foreshadowed the end of *The Joyful Science* and *Thus Spoke Zarathustra.* KSA 9, 11[195]; compare also the two following notes. Although Nietzsche used the word *Übermenschlich* (superhuman) several times before then, the words *Übermensch* and *Übermenschen* first occur in his notes from 1882 and the winter of 1882–83, KSA 10, 3[1], 4[25 and 75]. In the commentary volume, KSA 14, 279ff., Montinari has suggested a place in Emerson's essay "Sitte" in *Versuchen* in which human greatness and the figure of Zarathustra are mentioned as the source and origin of Nietzsche's figure of Zarathustra. (Nietzsche wrote "Das ist es!" ["That's it!" or "There it is!"] in the margin.) This conclusion has generally been accepted; see, for example, Rüdiger Schmidt's and Cord Spreckelsen's commentary *Nietzsche für Anfänger: Also sprach Zarathustra* (München: DTV, 1995), 46–49.

However, Nietzsche's first reference to Zarathustra is in fact a direct quotation from the cultural historian and anthropologist Friedrich von Hellwald's *Culturgeschichte in ihrer natürlichen Entstehung bis zur Gegenwart,* 2nd ed. (Augsburg: Lampart und Comp., 1875), which Nietzsche read and excerpted in 1875 and 1881 and again in 1883. The one who first discovered this source was Paolo D'Iorio, "Beiträge zur Quellenforschung," *Nietzsche-Studien* (1993): 395–97.

Nietzsche read, annotated, and excerpted Emerson's *Versuche* intensively during 1881–83, at the time of the conception of the fundamental ideas and the overall content of *Thus Spoke Zarathustra.* Baumgarten, "Mitteilungen und Bemerkungen über den Einfluß Emerson auf Nietzsche," 96–99, followed by Stack and others, argued that Nietzsche read *Versuche* at the time he made the "discovery" of the eternal recurrence (i.e., in early August 1881) and that it was inspired by Emerson's words in the essay "Geistige Gesetze" ("Spiritual Laws"): "It will certainly accept your own measure of your doing and being, whether you sneak about and deny your own name, or whether you see your work produced to the concave sphere of the heavens, one with the revolution of the stars." There are several other and probably better potential sources for Nietzsche's discovery of the eternal recurrence, but Emerson may well be one of the sources that enabled Nietzsche to make the discovery.

Stack argues that Nietzsche's idea of the *Übermensch* "owes more to Emerson's poetic-philosophical sketches of 'transcendent' human beings than it does to any other single cultural or intellectual source with which Nietzsche was familiar" (Stack, *Nietzsche and Emerson*, 8). Compare also page 9, where the same claim is repeated, and pages 309–56, where Stack discusses this in more detail. It is possible that Nietzsche was not only inspired to the idea of an aristocratic and self-reliant "beyond-man" by Emerson but may even have taken the term *Übermensch* from the title of Emerson's essay "Oversoul." On the other hand, the word *Übermensch* was used in the German language long before Nietzsche, and it occurs explicitly at least in four of the books in Nietzsche's library. Nietzsche used it once in his youth, so it seems more likely that he picked it up from this tradition. See the discussion of Nietzsche's discovery of eternal recurrence and use of the word *Übermensch* at the end of chapter 5 in this volume.

28. BAW 2, 420–24, "'The Relation of Alcibiades' Speech to the Other Speeches of Plato's *Symposium*."

29. BAW 3, 68.

30. KGB, I.4, 338.

31. No notes by Nietzsche are extant from Jahn's course "Plato's *Symposium*," and only a few pages from Schaarschmidt's course "Plato's Life and Teaching" are extant.

32. The longest and most extensive direct discussion of Plato is in BAW 4, 93–97, where Nietzsche elaborated on Thrasyllus's edition of Plato's dialogues in the form of tetralogies, all done as part of his study of Democritus.

33. The most interesting notes are a few where Nietzsche asserted the contrast between Plato and Democritus and claimed that Plato wanted to burn Democritus's books. It is likely that Nietzsche here sided against Plato, although that is not stated explicitly. Once Nietzsche claimed that Plato did not burn them, although he wanted to since it was already too late, but that later Christianity had the texts destroyed. "This was the worst malice of supranaturalism," BAW 3, 363. This is also discussed at greater length on page 347. We can see that Nietzsche already at this early stage connected Plato and Platonism with Christianity, something that he later strongly emphasized, for example, in the preface to *Beyond Good and Evil* (1886).

34. The other names mentioned are Hesiod, Theognis, the elegiac poets, Democritus, Epicurus, Diogenes Laertius, Stobaeus, Suida [Suda], and Athenaeus.

35. KSA 7, 3[93 and 94].

36. KSA 7, 5[46]. This is repeated, for example, in KSA 7, 19[138], 23[16], and 28[6].

37. KSA 7, 7[70]. This is essentially the same argument as the one above, where he referred to them as theoretical men.

38. KSA 7, 7[156], written 1870–71: "*umgedrehter Platonismus*."

39. KGW II.4, 1–188. *Einführung in das Studium der platonischen Dialoge*, of which the second part is called *Platos Philosophie als Hauptzeugniß für der Menschen Plato*.

40. Nietzsche's knowledge of Plato, at least after 1871, was so detailed and extensive that when he refers to Plato it is often difficult to determine whether it comes from

current reading or from his previous knowledge. My statements here come from a very conservative estimate of Nietzsche's continued reading of Plato, based mainly on what Nietzsche said in his letters.

41. The last word, *platonizei*, is written in Greek and with Greek letters. Teichmüller's book contained continual discussions of Plato.

42. KSA 11, 25[257], early 1884.

43. KSA 11, 26[387]: "Kampf gegen Plato und Aristoteles."

44. CD, "What I Owe to the Ancients," 2.

45. Letter to Paul Deussen, November 6, 1887: "vielleicht ist dieser alte Plato mein eigentlicher großer Gegner? Aber wie stolz bin ich, einen solchen Gegner zu haben!"

46. Nietzsche was later to explain that the main reason Schopenhauer was so important for him was that he was an atheist. Nietzsche seems to have broken with the Christian faith shortly before he found Schopenhauer, between 1862 and 1865, but it was more than another decade before Nietzsche became hostile toward it.

47. Nietzsche described his discovery of Schopenhauer as sudden and unexpected (BAW 3, 297–99, and KGW I.4, 60[1], 506–30): "One day I found in the old Rohn's secondhand bookshop this book by Schopenhauer, took it in my hand, although it was completely unknown to me, and leafed through it" ("nahm es als mir völlig fremd in die Hand und blätterte").

However, it seems that he in fact had encountered Schopenhauer's philosophy before then. Nietzsche may have heard a lecture about Schopenhauer's aesthetics, when one of Nietzsche's teachers at Pforta, Franz Kern, gave a lecture sometime between 1860 and 1866 (the exact date is not known) with the title "Die Grundzüge der Schopenhauer-schen Aesthetik" at the *Literaria* that was open to the citizens of Naumburg. Furthermore, the journal *Anregungen für Kunst, Leben und Wissenschaft*, which Nietzsche read and subscribed to (at least for a year in 1861–62, together with his friends Pinder and Krug) published a number of articles about Schopenhauer (especially relating to his view of music). It is more certain that Nietzsche listened and noted down references to Schopenhauer in the university course "Outline of the History of Philosophy" by Schaarschmidt, which he attended during the 1865 summer term in Bonn. Nietzsche's lecture notes from this course, not yet published, contain no German philosophy with the exception of Kant and a one-page summary of Schopenhauer's critique of Kant's philosophy. Nietzsche also read Karl Fortlage's *Genetische Geschichte der Philosophie seit Kant* (Leipzig, 1852) in 1864–65. In this work he is likely to have read the chapter on Schopenhauer, 407–23, that consists of a relatively neutral account of Schopenhauer's philosophy.

48. BAW 3, 298. I am using Janaway's translation into English in Christopher Janaway, ed., *Willing and Nothingness: Schopenhauer as Nietzsche's Educator* (Oxford, UK: Clarendon, 1998), 16. Compare also EH, "Why I Am So Clever," 1.

49. In *Ecce Homo* Nietzsche claimed that it was atheism that attracted him to Schopenhauer.

50. In a letter to Rohde, October 8, 1868, Nietzsche gave some of the reasons he valued Schopenhauer: "I like in Wagner, what I like in Schopenhauer, the ethical air, the

faustian smell, cross, death and tomb etc. [Mir behagt an Wagner, was mir an Schopenhauer behagt, die ethische Luft, der faustische Duft, Kreuz, Tod und Gruft etc.].''

The late Nietzsche was extremely critical of pity (*Mitleid*), but the young and early
Nietzsche affirmed, with Schopenhauer, the feeling and affect of pity.

51. KGW I.4, 57[51–55 and 61], 418–30. The same notes—but less complete and
reliable—were published previously in BAW 3, 352–62. Two translations of these notes
into English have been published, by Crawford and Janaway, both from the earlier BAW
version. Karl Schlechta discusses these notes in his short article "Der junge Nietzsche
und Schopenhauer," *Das Jahrbuch der Schopenhauer-Gesellschaft* 26 (1939): 289–300.

52. Schlechta, "Der junge Nietzsche und Schopenhauer," 298.

53. Nietzsche responded to Deussen in October 1867 and in October 1868, that is,
once before the writing of the notes critical of Schopenhauer and once afterward.

54. I find it surprising that no serious attempt seems to have been made to do a
thorough examination of this important question. Our view of these notes and our
understanding of Nietzsche's whole relation to Schopenhauer depend on whether this
is Nietzsche's own critique or a summary of other persons' critiques. It is in fact not
even altogether impossible that Nietzsche wrote these notes for the purpose of writing
a defense of Schopenhauer—as Deussen had challenged him to do—although in that
case it would be surprising that he did not cite sources to show against whose attack he
was defending Schopenhauer.

However, in the notes Nietzsche did refer to Überweg's critique of Schopenhauer,
presumably in his *Grundriss,* in which his critique was fairly harsh (but not sufficiently
similar to Nietzsche's to explain the fundamental drive behind Nietzsche's critique). In
the letter Nietzsche wrote to Deussen in October 1868, that is, after he had written the
notes, he criticized two critics of Schopenhauer, Überweg, and Haym.

There are significant similarities between R. Haym's severe critique of Schopenhauer's
philosophy in his *Arthur Schopenhauer* (Berlin, 1864), 113 pages (no table of contents
or chapter divisions), which Nietzsche read in 1866 (and possibly again in 1868), and
Nietzsche's critique in these notes, but I have nevertheless been unable to conclude,
after a superficial examination, that Nietzsche's critique is directly based on Haym's or
inspired by it.

Many other possible sources also ought to be examined—many are mentioned in
Überweg's account of Schopenhauer in his *Grundriss*—especially Victor Kiy's *Der Pessimismus und die Ethik Schopenhauers* (1866), which Nietzsche seems to have read in
1866 (but Kiy's approach and critique is rather different from Nietzsche's), and Rudolf
Seydel, *Schopenhauers System dargestellt und beurtheilt* (Leipzig, 1857), which Überweg
refers to as one of the most critical of Schopenhauer. (We have no certain knowledge
that Nietzsche read Seydel's work.) Furthermore, Otto Liebmann's severe critique of
Schopenhauer in the chapter "Die transcendente Richtung: Schopenhauer," 157–203,
in his work *Kant und die Epigonen* (Stuttgart, 1865) may also be of importance, as suggested by the commentary in BAW 3, although Liebmann's critique is rather different
from Nietzsche's. Another source could be F. A. Lange, and at least one of Nietzsche's

comments seems to have its origin in his reading of his *Geschichte des Materialismus,* for his reference to Überweg and to "versteckte Kategorie" comes from Lange's work, 267–68, of the first edition, but Schopenhauer is not explicitly discussed on these pages. However, although Lange seems critical of Schopenhauer, he hardly ever mentions him at all in his *History of Materialism* (1866), so this cannot be a major source.

55. See, for example, KSA 8, 5[72–83] based on the second volume of Schopenhauer's *Die Welt als Wille und Vorstellung.*

56. BAW 3, 352–61, and letter to Cosima Wagner, December 19, 1876: "Will you be surprised if I admit a gradually developed difference of opinion with Schopenhauer's teaching, which I suddenly have become aware of? For almost all his general statements, I no longer stand on his side; already when I wrote Sch. [i.e., UB III, in 1875] I noticed that I had left all dogmatic aspects; all important for me was the *man*. Since then, my 'reason' has been very active—thus life has become in some ways more difficult, the burden heavier! How is one finally going to endure it?"

57. KSA 8, 8[4]. Compare also KSA 8, 8[3], and KSA 8, 9[1].

58. Three of these volumes contain annotations. The first volume of *Die Welt als Wille und Vorstellung* contains a few annotations in the fourth book, paragraph 54 (and one annotation in paragraph 55), while the second volume is fairly heavily annotated throughout. The second volume of *Parerga* contains a few annotations in the chapter "Ueber Schriftstellerei und Stil."

Nietzsche's annotations in the second volume of *Die Welt als Wille und Vorstellung* can profitably be used to better understand the reasons for Nietzsche's break from Schopenhauer's philosophy. Nietzsche's copy is full of underlinings, marginal lines, exclamation marks, and NBs but also has more direct comments that enable us to follow his response to the reading.

Here I will list some of Nietzsche's more informative comments and the page on which they are made to allow the reader to see what sort of response Nietzsche made while rereading this work in 1875: "aber das ist kein Einwand" (but that is no objection) (46), "ecce" (222), "folglich?" (therefore?) (260), "im gegentheil!" (on the contrary!) (278), "folglich!" (therefore!) (421), "falsch" (wrong) (438), "falsch" (wrong) (439), "*falsch*" (*wrong*) (440), "also umgekehrt"/"ist Unsinn"/"also" (thus the opposite/is nonsense/thus) (441), "ist Unsinn" (is nonsense) (444), "Unsinn" (nonsense) (450), "sehr gut" (very good) (452), "ja"/"falsch" (yes/wrong) (497), "ergo" (513), "warum" (why) (531), "Ist Unsinn" (is nonsense) (543), "Unsinn" (nonsense) (547), "als ob" (as if) (548), "also" (thus) (566), "falsch" (wrong) (583), "Hierbei ist immer die Hauptsache übersehn: dass das neue Indiv. nicht das alte, sondern das (alte+x) ist—dass in der Gewachen [uncertain reading] sich ein Gesamtwachsthumsprocess vollzieht" (Regarding this, the main point is always ignored: that the new individual, is not the old one, but the (old+x)—that in growth [uncertain reading] a general process of growth is performed) (586), "aber [-] nach Erhaltung der Gattung existiert gar nicht" [uncertain reading] (but [-] after survival of the species does not exist) (588), "falsch" (wrong) (592), "ja!" (671), "Unsinn" (nonsense) (678), "ist Sinnloß" (is meaningless) (688), "ist Unsinn" (is nonsense) (689), and "falsch" (wrong) (698).

59. For example, KSA 11, 25[351, 437, 441, 442], early 1884 and KSA 11, 26[78, 84, 85,96], summer–autumn 1884.

60. "Kritik des von Kant der Ethik gegebenen Fundaments."

61. In the preface, Schopenhauer writes about Kant: "Glücklicher weise hat er der Darstellung des *Fundaments* seines Ethik abgesondert von dieses selbst ein eigenes Werk gewidmet, der *Grundlegung zur Metaphysik der Sitten,* deren Thema also genau dasselbe ist mit dem Gegenstand unserer Preisfrage. [...] Aus allen diesen Gründen nehme ich in gegenwürdiges Kritik die zuerst gennante 'Grundlegung zur Metaphysik det Sitte' zu meinem Leitfaden, und auf diese beziehn sich alle ohne weitern Beisatz von mir angeführten Seitenzahlen, welches ich zu merken bitte." Arthur Schopenhauer, *Kleinere Schriften, Werke Band III* (Darmstadt: Wissenschafitliche Buchgesellschaft, 1980), 643–45.

62. Nietzsche's relations with bookshops were so close that they would send him books to look at, and he would keep the ones he wanted and return the rest. See, for example, letter to his sister, July 1, 1868.

63. Although Nietzsche interpreted Lange's thinking in a manner that made it similar to, or at least consistent with, Schopenhauer's philosophy, Lange himself hardly mentioned him at all in the book. In the preface he wrote: "Mit Befremden wird vielleicht mancher Leser in meiner Darstellung den Namen *Schopenhauer* vermissen, um so mehr, da manche Anhänger dieses Mannes in meiner Anschauungsweise viel Verwandtes finden dürften. Ich muss offen gestehen, dass mir viele Schüler dieses Philosophen lieber sind, als der Meister. Schopenhauer selbst konnte ich in meiner Arbeit deshalb keinen Platz einräumen, weil ich in seiner Philosophie einen entschiednen Rückschritt hinter Kant finde" (p. v in the 1866 edition).

64. Letter to Carl von Gersdorff, late August 1866. The other letters in which Lange is mentioned are one to Mushacke, November 1866—"NB. Das bedeutendste philosophische Werk, was in den letzten Jahrzehnten erschienen ist, ist unzweifelhaft Lange, Geschichte des Materialismus, über das ich eine bogenlange Lobrede schreiben könnte. Kant, Schopenhauer und dies Buch von Lange—mehr brauche ich nicht"—and a second later letter to Gersdorff, February 16, 1868. Nietzsche also alluded to the book and referred to some of its contents in his letter to Paul Deussen, end of April–early May 1868.

65. It is not clear why Nietzsche never publicly admitted the influence of Lange. I would like to suggest three possible reasons: (1) Lange's influence on Nietzsche was strongest in 1866–69 (and expressed in private notes and letters), and when it became relevant to refer to, or mention, this influence publicly in the mid-1870s, it simply was too long before to be relevant. (2) In 1875 Nietzsche bought (and presumably read) Lange's left-wing *Die Arbeiterfrage.* Nietzsche would have disagreed with most of its content, and it is likely to have lowered his estimation of Lange and therefore made him less willing to refer to him. (3) Nietzsche had a general tendency not to give credit to the "minor" figures who influenced him. Notwithstanding these possible explanations, one must ask whether Nietzsche nonetheless should have referred to Lange's influence. Given that almost all the claimed influence of Lange on Nietzsche was either on the

young Nietzsche or was very general in nature, it probably was not important for him to mention it.

66. See O. Crusius, *Erwin Rohde: Ein Biographischer Versuch* (Tübingen and Leipzig, 1902), 17: "Nietzsches Exemplar der Geschichte des Materialism begleitete Rohde nach Kiel." See also Rohde's letter to Nietzsche, November 4, 1868 (KGB I:3, 299): "Nicht wenig hat mich darin das Langesche Buch (das Du allernächstens wiederbekommst) bestärkt."

67. According to page 241 in Jörg Salaquarda, "Nietzsche und Lange," *Nietzsche-Studien* 7 (1978): 236–60.

68. Nietzsche's copy of this edition of Lange's *Geschichte des Materialismus* (1887) in one volume, 852 pages, has been sparsely annotated throughout, with both a lead and a blue pencil. The annotations are all in the form of marginal lines and underlinings (no words). Early in the book, the pages dealing with Epicurus and Lucretius are annotated; in the second half of the book, the two chapters "Individualism" and "Falsche und richtige Teleologie," both under the main heading "Darwinismus und Teleologie" contain annotations and finally at the end of the book; and the chapter "Die Physiologie des Sinnesorgan und die Welt als Vorstellung" also contains annotations.

69. Published in *Nietzsche-Studien* 31 (2002): 298–313. Nietzsche also bought and read Lange's second philosophical work, *Logische Studien: Ein Beitrag zur Neubegründung der formalen Logik und der Erkenntnistheorie* (1877), which was published posthumously. This work is significantly more technical than *Geschichte des Materialismus*. Nietzsche's copy of this work is still in his library in Weimar and contains a dog-ear on pages 26–27 but otherwise shows no other signs of having been read, which may indicate that Nietzsche only read it to this page. Nietzsche often used dog-ears to mark important pages or to indicate the extent of his reading. For a discussion of Nietzsche's reading of *Die Arbeiterfrage* (which contains little or no philosophy), see my article "Nietzsche's Knowledge of Marx and Marxism," *Nietzsche-Studien* 31 (2002): 298–313.

70. Friedrich Albert Lange's *Geschichte des Materialismus und Kritik seiner Bedeutung in der Gegenwart* (Iserlohn, 1866), which Nietzsche read and excerpted intensively several times between 1866 and 1869, has the following content:

Vorwort, i–xiv
Erstes Buch: Geschichte des Materialismus bis auf Kant
Zweites Buch: Geschichte der Materialismus seit Kant und Kritik seiner
    Bedeutung in der Gegenwart
    I. Die neuere Philosophie
        1. Kant und der Materialismus, 233
        2. Der philosophische Materialismus seit Kant, 278
    II. Die neueren Naturwissenschaften
        1. Der Materialismus und die exakte Forschung, 322
        2. Kosmische Fragen, 357
        3. Anthropologische Fragen, 410
    III. Der ethische Materialismus und die Religion, 501–563.

71. The two most important studies of Nietzsche's debt and dependence on Lange are by Salaquarda and Stack, and their works have given rise to a number of comments: J. Salaquarda, "Nietzsche und Lange," *Nietzsche-Studien* 7 (1978): 236–60; George J. Stack, *Lange and Nietzsche* (Berlin and New York: Walter de Gruyter, 1983); Daniel Breazeale, "Lange, Nietzsche, and Stack: The Question of 'Influence,'" *International Studies in Philosophy* 21(2) (1989): 91–103; George J. Stack, "From Lange to Nietzsche: A Response to a Troika of Critics," *International Studies in Philosophy* 21(2) (1989): 113–24; George J. Stack, "Kant, Lange, and Nietzsche: Critique of Knowledge," in Keith Ansell-Pearson, ed., *Nietzsche and Modern German Thought* (London: Routledge, 1991), 30–58; John T. Wilcos, "The Birth of Nietzsche Out of the Spirit of Lange," *International Studies in Philosophy* 21(2) (1989): 81–89; K. J. Ansell-Pearson, "The Question of F. A. Lange's Influence on Nietzsche: A Critique of Recent Research from the Standpoint of the Dionysian," *Nietzsche-Studien* 17 (1988): 539–54.

72. Letter to H. Mushacke, November 1866.

73. Several commentators have claimed that Lange was the cause of Nietzsche's interest in and reading of the natural scientists Boscovich and Zöllner. They were not mentioned in the first edition of Lange's work but were mentioned in the second enlarged edition from 1875, so Lange seems unlikely to have been the source in this case.

74. This critique of philology, but less strongly expressed, is also present in several other letters from this time, such as to Erwin Rohde (February 1–3, May 3 or 4, October 27, 1868, and January 16, 1869) and to Paul Deussen (June 2, 1868, and September 1868).

75. Letter to Paul Deussen, end of April–early May 1868. In this letter Nietzsche claimed that his dissertation would be half philosophical and half natural scientific and that the preliminary work was almost finished. Compare also the letter to Rohde, May 3 or 4, 1868, and BAW 3, 371–94.

76. This evidence for Nietzsche's reading of Lange can be found in KSA 7, 29[223]; KSA 9, 11[119]; KSA 10, 17[73] (which contains a reference that Nietzsche may have taken from Lange); KSA 11, 25[318 and 424]; and KSA 11, 34[99].

77. Curt Paul Janz, *Friedrich Nietzsche,* 3 vols., 2nd ed. (München, Wien: Carl Hanser Verlag, 1993), Part 1, 199.

78. Ibid., 504.

79. Letter to Mushacke, November 1866.

80. Letter to W. Vischer(-Bilfinger), Basel, probably January 1871.

81. BAW 3, 393–94. It seems as though all but a very few of these titles are taken from Überweg.

82. KGW II.4, 7. This is the very first page of the lecture notes. A similar statement was made about the relation between Plato and Kant, but in regard to morality and a moral "beyond," in a footnote on p. 88.

83. KGW II.4, 213–14.

84. Ibid., 294–95.

85. Ibid., 301.

86. A long quotation from *Allgemeine Naturgeschichte und Theorie des Himmels* in 1872 and several short quotations, with page references, to *Kritik der reinen Vernunft* in 1886 possibly imply at least a partial reading of these works. A more detailed study is required to confirm this. The quotation from *Allgemeine Naturgeschichte und Theorie des Himmels* could perhaps come from Zöllner, whom Nietzsche read at this time and who deals with Kant's relevance and importance for the natural sciences. The quotations from *Kritik der reinen Vernunft* could possibly come from Romundt's *Grundlegung zur Reform der Philosophie: Vereinfachte und erweiterte Darstellung von Immanuel Kants Kritik der reinen Vernunft* (1885).

87. KSA 12, 7[4]. *Kritik der praktischen Vernunft, Kritik der Urteilskraft, Der Streit der Fakultäten, Grundlegung zur Metaphysik der Sitten* and *Die Religion innerhalb der Grenze der bloßen Vernunft.* Four of these sources have been determined and published by the editors of KSA 14. I have been able to identify that the single section, of about thirteen lines (268–69), that was not identified in KSA comes from Kant's *Grundlegung zur Metaphysik der Sitten.* See "Beiträge zur Quellenforschung mitgeteilt von Thomas H. Brobjer," *Nietzsche-Studien* 30 (2001): 418–21.

88. Kant is mentioned in thirteen letters during the period 1864 to January 1871, and then there are only six mentions (actually only four original ones since two are duplicates sent to different recipients) for the period 1872–87. During the last year and a half there are five references to Kant.

89. The increase in references to Kant began as early as 1883, became most frequent during 1884–85, and was somewhat reduced thereafter. (There are about fifty references to Kant in the notebooks covering the period 1884–85.) Whether this was a mere coincidence, reflected either an independent increase of interest in Kantian (or rather anti-Kantian) problems, or was a response to reading Kant or some book about Kant remains to be determined. I would like to suggest that Nietzsche's reading is the main reasons for his increased references to Kant during this period. In 1883 he read and profusely annotated Hartmann's *Phänomenologie des sittlichen Bewußtseins* (1879), which contains much about Kant. That year Nietzsche also read and extensively annotated L. Dumont's *Vergnügen und Schmerz* (1876), which contains less about but mentions Kant, and several of Nietzsche's notes in his notebooks, including some concerning Kant, came from this work (see KSA 10, 7[233 and 234] and probably others nearby). He also probably read two Kantian works by his friend Romundt that year (see the discussions in chapters 3–6 below). I believe that Nietzsche's most important reading at this time, in or near 1884, was his detailed reading of Schopenhauer's *Preisschrift über die Grundlage der Moral,* with its detailed discussion of Kant, that gave rise to many excerpts in his notebooks: for example, KSA 11, 25[351, 437, 441, 442] (early 1884) and KSA 11, 26[78, 84, 85, 96] (summer–autumn 1884). This book (of less than two hundred pages) contains four parts. Part two, covering about seventy-five pages, is called "Critique of Kant's Foundation of Ethics" ("Kritik des von Kant der Ethik gegebenen Fundaments") and is a detailed discussion and critique, including many quotations, of Kant's ethics, especially his *Grundlegung der Metaphysik der Sitten.* The next year Nietzsche also read

several books containing much on Kant, especially Spir and Widemann and probably one by Romundt.

90. It should be noted that Nietzsche's reading of Kant may have been much more extensive. Most reading would not have resulted in specific comments or quotations. We can, for example, compare the evidence from Nietzsche's reading of Mill. The five volumes that Nietzsche possessed contain twenty-seven separate texts. From Nietzsche's annotations in his copy of these we know that he read at least nineteen of them (and there are strong reasons to believe that he read more). We also know that he read some of these twice. However, from only five or six of these texts do we have explicit traces in Nietzsche's written material. On the other hand, we have no indication that Nietzsche ever owned any work by Kant.

91. Nietzsche also possessed three other books by Romundt, and it seems likely that he read them the same year that they appeared: *Antäus. Neuer Aufbau der Lehre Kants über Seele, Freiheit und Gott* (1882), *Die Herstellung der Lehre Jesu durch Kants Reform der Philosophie* (1883) and *Grundlegung zur Reform der Philosophie. Vereinfachte und erweiterte Darstellung von Immanuel Kants Kritik der reinen Vernunft* (1885). Nietzsche owned three books by Paul Deussen, his friend and a specialist on Schopenhauer and oriental philosophy. Deussen's first book, *Die Elemente der Metaphysik* (1877), deals extensively with Kant, and its Kantian and Schopenhauerian stance is reflected in the preface: "Diesen *Standpunkt der Versöhnung aller Gegensätze* hat, wie wir glauben, die Menschheit der Hauptsache nach erreicht in dem von Kant begründeten, von Schopenhauer zu Ende gedachten Idealismus."

92. This list, however, is far from exhaustive. Some other books in Nietzsche's library may have been important, and books not in his library (with a few exceptions) have not been discussed. Kant is also mentioned or discussed briefly in many other books in Nietzsche's library, some of them important for covering more specialized aspects of his thinking.

93. Letter to professor Wilhelm Vischer-Bilfinger, probably January 1871.

94. See the discussion of Wundt's article "Philosophy in Germany" in *Mind* in my introduction above.

95. Nietzsche had even wanted to publish the book anonymously to make the break less obvious to his friends and to the Wagners, but his publisher would not allow it.

96. For an excellent account of the relation between Nietzsche and Rée, see B. Donnellan, "Friedrich Nietzsche and Paul Rée: Cooperation and Conflict," *The Journal of the History of Ideas* 43 (1982): 595–612. For more information about Rée, see also Hubert Treiber's "Zur Genealogie einer 'Science positive de la morale en Allemagne,'" *Nietzsche-Studien* 22 (1993): 165–221, and his "Nachträge zu Paul Rée," *Nietzsche-Studien* 27 (1998): 515–16. A recent discussion of Rée, with many references to earlier work, is Hans-Walter Ruckenbauer's *Moralität zwischen Evolution und Normen* (Würzburg, 2002). Of great value is also Robin Small's recent edition and translation of Paul Rée's *Basic Writings* (Urbana and Chicago: University of Illinois Press, 2003) and his study *Nietzsche and Rée: A Star Friendship* (Oxford, UK: Clarendon, 2005).

97. Nietzsche wrote, probably not completely accurately, in a letter to Rohde, shortly after June 16, 1878, that he and Rée had found each other on the same level: "Wir fanden einander auf gleicher Stufe vor: der Genuss unserer Gespräche war grenzenlos, der Vortheil gewiss sehr gross, auf beiden Seiten."

98. "Dem Vater dieser Schrift dankbarst deren Mutter." See the copy in Nietzsche's private library in Weimar.

99. MA, 37.

In the preface to his book, Rée had claimed: "Freilich, bevor die Entwicklungstheorie auftrat, konnten manche dieser Phänomene durch immanente Ursachen nicht erklärt werden, und gewiss ist eine transcendente Erkärung weit befriedigender,—als gar keine. Jetzt aber, seit *La Marck* und *Darwin* geschrieben haben, können die moralischen Phänomene eben so gut auf natürliche Ursachen zurückgeführt werden, wie die physischen: der moralische Mensch steht der intelligiblen Welt nicht näher, als der physische Mensch. Diese natürliche Erklärung fusst hauptsächlich auf dem satz: Die höheren Thiere haben sich durch natürliche Zuchtwahl aus den niederen, die Mensch sich aus den Affen entwickelt.

Auf eine Begründung dieses Satzes gehe ich nicht ein. Denn ich halte ihn durch die Schriften Darwins und zum Theil schon durch die La marck's für bewiesen. Wer anderer Meinung ist, mag auch diese Abhandlung ungelesen lassen: da er die Voraussetzung läugnet, kann er die Folgerung nicht zugeben." Paul Rée, *Der Ursprung der moralischen Empfindungen* (Chemnitz, 1877), vii.

The book contains the following chapters:

1. Der Ursprung der Begriffe gut und böse. 1
2. Der Ursprung des Gewissen. 21
3. Die Verantwortlichkeit und die Willensfreiheit. 28
4. Der Ursprung der Strafe und des Gerechtigkeitsgefühls; über Abschreckung und Vergeltung. 45
5. Der Ursprung der Eitelkeit. 69
6. Der moralische Fortschritt. 120
7. Das Verhältniss der Güte zur Glückseligkeit. 129
Rückblick und Schluss. 134–142

100. Rée wanted to dedicate this work to Nietzsche, but Nietzsche declined.

The table of contents of Rée's *Entstehung des Gewissen* (1885) lists the following chapters:

Einleitung 1–6
Uebernatürliche Erklärungen
Natürliche Erklärungen
Kampf der natürlichen Erklärungen mit den übernatürlichen
Uebernatürliche Erklärungen in der Philosophie
Natürliche Erklärungen in der Philosophie

101. Nietzsche's discussion and critique of Rée in *Zur Genealogie der Moral* was explicit in sections 4 to 7 of his preface. The observant reader who knows Rée's works will find much more, and there are many positive influences that Nietzsche did not mention. In notes from 1883 to 1885, Nietzsche was much more detailed in his discussions of Rée. See KSA 10, 7[17, 24, 48, 137], 15[47], 16[15 and 18], and 17[49] and KSA 11, 25[259], 26[202 and 218], 35[34], and 38[18].

102. Nietzsche's relation to the ancient Greeks generally and to the pre-Socratics (especially Heraclitus) did not change either, but he does not appear to have returned frequently to reread the pre-Socratics, by whom only fragments remain.

103. I discuss the influence of French philosophy on Nietzsche in my forthcoming study *Nietzsche's Knowledge of Philosophy: A Study and Survey of Nietzsche's Reading of and Relation to German, British, and French Philosophy*.

Chapter 3: The Young Nietzsche

1. To a large extent, this was probably the result of his reading (and the reading to him) of *Gedächtnis-Übungen zur Nahrung für Verstand und Herz für Kinder von 6 bis 9 Jahren* (Neustadt, 1845), which is in his library and consists of quotations from the Bible to be memorized.

2. BAW 1, 147.

3. GM, Preface, 3. "My curiosity as well as my suspicions were bound to halt quite soon at the question of where our good and evil really *originated*. In fact, the problem of the origin of evil pursued me even as a boy of thirteen: at an age in which you have 'half childish trifles, half God in your heart,' I devoted to it my first childish literary trifle, my first philosophical effort—and as for the 'solution' of the problem I posed at that time, well, I gave the honor to God, as was only fair, and made him the *father* of evil."

4. For a more detailed account of Nietzsche's early relation to Christianity and his relevant reading, see my "Nietzsche's Changing Relation to Christianity: Nietzsche As Christian, Atheist and Antichrist," in Donna Santaniello, ed., *Nietzsche and the Gods* (New York: State University of New York Press, 2001), 137–57.

5. For a more detailed discussion of Nietzsche's reading of this journal, which before now it was not known that he read, see the chapter "Nietzsche's Reading of Journals of Philosophy" in my forthcoming study *Nietzsche's Knowledge of Philosophy*.

6. For Christmas 1861, Nietzsche planned to ask for an unidentified book that Gustav Krug referred to in a letter to Nietzsche as "that dangerous book." This may have been Feuerbach's *Das Wesen der Christenthum*.

7. The essay "Fatum und Geschichte" begins with the words: "If we could, with a fine and unhindered eye, view the Christian teaching and the history of the Church, we would have to express some views that go counter to the common ideas." Further on he continues: "An endless confusion of thought in the people is the bleak result. There will be great revolutions once the masses finally realize that the totality of Christianity is grounded in presuppositions; the existence of God, immortality, Biblical authority, inspiration and other doctrines will always remain problems. I have attempted to deny everything: Oh, pulling down is easy; but rebuilding! [...] The question whether mankind hasn't been deceived for two thousand years by a phantom." BAW 2, 54–55.

In the letter, Nietzsche wrote: "First when we recognize that we are only responsible to ourselves, that a reproach over a failed direction in life only relates to us, not to any higher power.[...] Christianity is essentially a question of the heart.[...] The main teachings of Christianity only relates the fundamental truths of the human heart; they are symbols.[…] To become blessed through faith means nothing other than the old truth, that only the heart, not knowledge, can make one happy. That God became human only shows that humans should not seek their blessedness in eternity, but instead found their paradise on the earth; the delusion of an otherworldly world has brought the human spirit into a false relation to this world: it was the product of a people's childhood. […] It [humanity] recognizes in it 'the beginning, the middle, the end of religion.'"

8. In a letter from 1865, Elisabeth complained to Nietzsche that he had told her so much about "that unfortunate Strauss" during the Easter holiday.

9. In the third section of the preface to *On the Genealogy of Morals,* Nietzsche seems to suggest this (while speaking about his views on religion at the age of twelve): "Fortunately, I have since learned to separate theology from morality and ceased looking for the origin of evil *behind* the world. Some schooling in history and philology, together with an innate sense of discrimination with respect to questions of psychology, quickly transformed my problem into another one."

10. The apparent absence of influences of Cicero on Nietzsche is noteworthy. A thorough examination of Nietzsche's relation to Cicero seems not to have been carried out but ought to be.

11. Letter to Raimund Granier, July 28, 1862, and BAW 2, 100.
Nietzsche's claim to have read about materialism probably refers to his reading of articles in the journal *Anregungen für Kunst, Leben und Wissenschaft* (especially by the well-known German materialist Ludwig Büchner, who frequently wrote for the journal) and Feuerbach. However, Nietzsche returned Hobbes to Pinder in 1864 and possibly had borrowed and read him critically already at this time. Such an early reading and rejection of Hobbes could possibly explain why Nietzsche never later managed to show a positive interest in him, in spite of potential similarities and affinities between their philosophies.

12. BAW 2, 54–59, and 59–62. Also recently published in KGW I.2, 13[6] and 13[7], 431–40.

13. "Über das Verhältniss der Rede des Alcibiades zu den übrigen Reden des platonischen Symposium," BAW 2, 420–24.

14. In a short autobiography titled "Mein Leben" that he wrote on the occasion of leaving Pforta after six years, he stated: "I remember with the greatest pleasure the first impressions of Sophocles, Aeschylus, Plato, especially in my favorite piece, the Symposium, and then the Greek lyricists" (BAW 3, 68). In a letter dated October 31, 1864, to his former teacher Hermann Kletschke, Nietzsche made a similar claim: "At 12 o'clock I heard Jahn, who today began his lectures about the Platonic Symposium. I am sure that you can imagine how pleased I must be to hear one of the foremost classicists speak about one of my special favorites among the works of antiquity [ein mir besonders liebes Werk des Alterthums]" (KGB I.4, 15).

15. Nietzsche began to teach Plato at the Gymnasium in 1869 and gave a more ambitious university course, "Einführung in das Studien der platonischen Dialogue," during the winter term of 1871–72. He taught variants of this course under different names an

additional three times, during the winter term of 1873–74, the summer term of 1876, and the winter term of 1878–79. He also seems to have taught a course on Plato's *Apology* during the summer term of 1878.

For a more extensive discussion of Nietzsche's reading of and relation to Plato, see my "Nietzsche's Wrestling with Plato" in Paul Bishop, ed., *Nietzsche and Antiquity: His Reaction and Response to the Classical Tradition* (Rochester, NY: Camden House, 2004), 241–59.

16. Apparently, these volumes contained no annotations, but there is a single dog-ear in one of the volumes of Lessing's letters.

17. At this time, at the end of 1880, Nietzsche also rhetorically asked in one of his notes (KSA 9, 7[136]) who today can stand Lessing's *Die Erziehung des Menschengeschlechts* and thus implied that he had read it earlier.

18. David Strauss often referred to Lessing with great admiration, and thus Nietzsche frequently referred to Lessing in his study *David Strauss, the Confessor and the Writer* and in the notes relating to it.

19. KGB, I.4, 15. This letter of Nietzsche's was published for the first time in 1993 in the commentary volume to his letters. "Letztere [meine wissenschaftliche Thätigkeit] will ich in diesem Semester besonders auf Hebräisch richten, sodann auf Kunstgeschichte und Geschichte der Philosophie seit Kant, die ich mit Hülfe einiger Werke privatim treibe."

20. I believe that I am the first to identify that Nietzsche read this work by Fortlage. We have no evidence that Nietzsche read anything else by Fortlage—and I hold that to be unlikely—but he wrote a number of books about philosophy and also about music in antiquity that possibly could have been of interest to Nietzsche.

21. In the preface, Fortlage wrote: "so lange wir *Kant* und *Fichte* nicht vergessen, so lange sind wir noch nicht verloren" (vii). In the introduction he further adds: "daß wir sammt und sonders doch weiter nichts als verschieden gestaltete kantianer sind. [...] Diese höhe ist eine durch Kant gegründedte neue Anschauungsweise der Dinge, aus welcher alles Folgende hervorgewachsen ist" (2). "Der größte Philosoph der modernen Welt war der entschlossenste Mann der reinen Ueberzeugung, Kant. [...] Er ist daher das Munster des Philosophen, an ihm mehr, als an irgend sonst jemandem kann man sich zum überzeugungstreuen Selbstdenker heranbilden" (4). And on page 9 he claimed to place the center of gravity of the newer philosophical systems on Kant.

22. These papers are in the Goethe-Schiller-Archiv in Weimar with the classification number GSA 71-41.

23. In "Nietzsches frühe Begegnung mit dem Denken Indiens," *Nietzsche-Studien* 18 (1989): 455–71, Johann Figl gives a short outline of the content on pages 458–59, but the account here comes from my own examination of these notes. In these notes Nietzsche misspelled Buckle as "Bukle" and sense as "sens."

24. Compare the discussion in chapter 2 above.

25. Nietzsche was referring to David Friedrich Strauss's book *Die Halben und die Ganzen* (1865). It seems likely that Nietzsche read a work by Hegel at this time, but it is

not known which work (and it cannot be completely excluded that he refers to his reading of Fortlage's discussion of Hegel's philosophy). I examine the extent of Nietzsche's knowledge and reading of Hegel (and other classic German philosophers) in my forthcoming study *Nietzsche's Knowledge of Philosophy*.

26. Letter to Gersdorff, February 20, 1867.

27. The copy in Nietzsche's library contains no annotations, but there are several dog-ears in each of the two volumes.

28. Nietzsche mentioned in a letter dated February 16, 1868, to Gersdorff that he wanted to learn to personally know Lange, Spielhagen, Bahnsen, Dühring, and Frauenstädt. The latter four are all Schopenhauerians.

29. Nietzsche's library contains only the second volume of this work, of 503 pages. It contains no annotations or dog-ears.

30. It has not previously been known that Nietzsche with high probability read this work. A book bill shows that he bought it in 1868. Further examination of the work and its possible influence on Nietzsche ought to be carried out. The work could constitute an early naturalistic influence on Nietzsche, foreshadowing the influence of Rée in 1875–76. Lange speaks well of the work in *Geschichte des Materialismus,* and that may have been how Nietzsche discovered the work.

31. These titles are given in the footnotes to table 1. They point to an interest in physiology and in the philosophy of science, an interest to which Nietzsche returned in his middle period.

32. He seems to have read it several times in the first three years, 1866 to 1868; possibly returned to it in 1873, 1881, 1883, 1884, and 1885 (seen by long quotations and page references to the book made during these years); and returned to it again at least once in 1887 or 1888, for the copy in his library, which contains a few annotations throughout the book, was published in 1887.

33. Probably Windelband's *Über den gegenwärtigen Stand der psychologischen Forschung* (Leipzig, 1876), 24 pages.

Chapter 4: The Early Nietzsche

1. See my "Nietzsche's Forgotten Book: The Index to the *Rheinisches Museum für Philologie,*" *New Nietzsche Studies* 4 (Summer–Fall 2000): 157–61. The making of this index required Nietzsche to read many hundreds of articles and many additional shorter contributions. A not insignificant number of these articles and contributions discussed philosophical themes including different interpretations of tragedy, so important for Nietzsche at this time. The importance of this reading for Nietzsche's view of tragedy, and antiquity in general, appears not to have been examined.

2. In my article "Sources and Influences on Nietzsche's *The Birth of Tragedy,*" *Nietzsche-Studien* 34 (2005): 277–98, I discuss a number of previously unknown influences on *The Birth of Tragedy*.

3. Teichmüller is not mentioned at all in Nietzsche's letters from this time, except to say that he was leaving the university in late 1870 or early 1871. Likewise, Nietzsche hardly

ever refers to Teichmüller's successor Rudolf Eucken, but unlike the case with Teichmüller, we have no evidence that Nietzsche read anything by Eucken. While at Basel, Eucken worked intensively with different aspects of Aristotle's philosophy. Eucken's successor was Max Heinze, Nietzsche's teacher at Schulpforta. Nietzsche associated closely with him during the year he was in Basel and read several of the books that Heinze wrote.

Teichmüller was the second philosophy professor at Basel. Karl Steffensen (1816–88), the first and more influential and established professor (head of department), was metaphysically and theologically oriented and was critical toward Schopenhauer. He heard Nietzsche's two lectures on Socrates and objected to them and seems to have also objected to the possibility that Nietzsche would acquire the professorship after Teichmüller in 1871 (and to Nietzsche's Schopenhauerian friend Romundt's acquiring it the next two times it became vacant). Nietzsche's only reference to Steffensen was a brief negative comment in a letter to Rohde, March 29, 1871.

4. Nietzsche, however, did not mention this contribution in the letter to Rohde, November 3, 1867, where he told about his experience at the conference.

5. We know that Nietzsche read at least five or six books by Teichmüller:

> *Beiträge zur Erklärung der Poetik des Aristoteles* (Halle, 1866), possibly read by Nietzsche.
> *Aristoteles' Philosophie der Kunst* (Halle, 1869), read by Nietzsche.
> *Geschichte des Begriffs der Parusie* (Halle, 1873), read by Nietzsche.
> *Neuen Studien zur Geschichte der Begriffe* (Gotha, 1876), probably read by Nietzsche.
> *Darwinism und Philosophie,* of which Nietzsche read a long detailed review.
> *Ueber die Reihenfolge der Platonischen Dialoge* (1879), read by Nietzsche.
> *Studien zur Geschichte der Begriffe* (Leipzig, 1879), probably read by Nietzsche.
> *Aristotelische Forschungen, Neue Studien: Die praktische Vernunft Aristoteles,* read by Nietzsche.
> *Die wirkliche und die scheinbare Welt* (Breslau, 1882), read by Nietzsche.

6. Franz Overbeck's library contains only two works by Teichmüller, and it seems likely that they are the two books Nietzsche had borrowed from him: *Die wirkliche und die scheinbare Welt* (Belin, 1882) and *Litterarische Fehden im 4. Jahrhundert vor Christus* (Breslau, 1881). However, Paolo D'Iorio assumes that the second book is *Neue Studien zur Geschichte der Begriffe,* but it is not clear on what grounds; see his article "La superstition des philosophes critiques: Nietzsche et Afrikan Spir," *Nietzsche-Studien* 22 (1993): 257–94. I wish to thank Andreas Urs Sommer for helping me with information about Overbeck's library.

7. See footnote in Kaufmann's translation of *Ecce Homo,* 277.

8. He also read and heavily annotated Hartmann's *Phänomenologie des sittlichen Bewusstseins* (1879) in 1883 (and possibly as early as 1879).

9. F. Gerratana, "Der Wahn jenseits des Menschen: Zur frühen E. v. Hartmann-Rezeption Nietzsches (1869–1874)," *Nietzsche-Studien* 17 (1988): 391–433.

10. The three contemporary philosophers who influenced Nietzsche most are discussed in an essay by Otto Caspari, "Hartmann, Dühring and Lange, die Philosophen der Gegenwart," published in *Der Zusammenhang der Dinge* (Breslau, 1881), 279–98, which Nietzsche had read. In the text Caspari places Lange above the other two.

In 1876, Nietzsche had also bought and probably read Hans Vaihinger's study *Hartmann, Dühring and Lange: Zur Geschichte der deutschen Philosophie in XIX Jahrhundert: Ein Kritischer Essay* (Iserlohn, 1876), 235 pages.

11. Hartmann's *Philosophie des Unbewussten* (1869) was, despite the given publication year, published by the end of 1868. This edition does not contain an index, but the only slightly enlarged second edition, from 1870, contains a detailed index.

12. Nietzsche's copy of the work contains a few annotations in the early parts of the book, the last one on page 30.

This work, together with his *Wahrheit und Irrthum im Darwinismus* and a third text (*Die naturwissenschaftlichen Grundlagen der Philosophie des Unbewussten und die darwinistische Kritik*, first published separately in 1877) were later put together by Hartmann to constitute the third volume of *Philosophie des Unbewussten* with the title *Das Unbewusste und der Darwinismus*. (*Die naturwissenschaftlichen Grundlagen* was written partly in response to criticism from the biologist Oskar Schmidt, whom Nietzsche also had read.)

13. The work *Wahrheit und Irrthum im Darwinismus: Eine kritische Darstellung der organischen Entwicklungstheorie*, which Nietzsche bought in 1875, contains a detailed account and critique of Darwinism. For Nietzsche's relation to and reading about Darwinism, see the last chapter in my book *Nietzsche and the "English": British and American Influences on Nietzsche* (Amherst, NY: Prometheus, 2007).

14. KGB II.2, 7–10.

15. In a letter to Gersdorff, August 4, 1869, Nietzsche recommended Hartmann to him: "Ein wichtiges Buch für Dich ist 'Hartmann's Philosophie des Unbewußten,' trotz der Unredlichkeit des Verfassers." Later that year on November 11, 1869, Nietzsche responds to Rohde's critique and appreciation of Hartmann as expressed in a letter from Rohde to Nietzsche, November 5, 1869 (KGB II.2, 70–74) with the words: "Über Hartmann mit Dir einmündig und einmüthig. Doch lese ich ihn viel, weil er die schönsten Kenntnisse hat und mitunter in das uralte Nornenlied vom fluchwürdigen Dasein kräftig einzustimmen weiß. Er ist ein ganz gebrechlicher contrakter Mann—mit etwas Bosheit, scheint mir, hier und da auch kleinlich und jedenfalls *undankbar*. Und das ist für mich ein Halt in der Ethik und der ethischen Beurtheilung von Menschen und Thieren." A year later Nietzsche was pleased to see that a second edition of Hartmann's book had been published (letter to Gersdorff, December 12, 1870).

16. Letter to Fritzsch, second half of April 1872.

17. "[W]e shall for once let it cheer us by looking at it in the glittering magic mirror of a *philosophical parodist* in whose head the age has come to an ironical awareness of itself, and has done so with a clarity which (to speak Goethean) 'amounts to infamy.' Hegel once taught us: 'when the spirit changes direction, we philosophers too are there': our

age changed direction, to self-irony, and behold! E. von Hartmann too was there and indicated his celebrated philosophy of the unconscious, or,—to speak more clearly—his philosophy of unconscious irony. We have seldom read a merrier invention or a more philosophical piece of roguery than this of Hartmann; [...] as though it were a genuine serious philosophy and not only a joke philosophy—such a production marks its creator as one of the first philosophical parodists of all time [...] For what the unconscious parodist demands of each individual is 'the total surrender of the personality to the world-process for the sake of its goal, world-redemption': [...] but we are still far from that perhaps even more ideal condition in which mankind can read Hartmann's book with full conscious awareness. If they ever do so, no man will ever again utter the words 'world-process' without smiling; for they will call to mind the time when Hartmann's parodistic gospel was listened to [...] Our comedian has, of course, a different point of view." *Von Nutzen und Nachtheil der Historie für das Leben,* 9. The whole of section 9, several pages long, contains an extended critique of Hartmann. For an excellent and detailed discussion of Hartmann's importance for Nietzsche's *On the Uses and Disadvantages of History for Life,* see Jörg Salaquarda's "Studien zur Zweiten Unzeitgemäßen Betrachtung," *Nietzsche-Studien* 13 (1984): 1–45.

Nietzsche's later published references to Hartmann are to be found in JGB, 204; FW V, 357 (published in 1887); and GD, "Expeditions of an Untimely Man," 16. In the first of these, Nietzsche wrote: "such representatives of philosophy as are, thanks to fashion, at present as completely on top as they are completely abysmal (in Germany, for example, the two lions of Berlin, the anarchist Eugen Dühring and the amalgamist Eduard von Hartmann)."

18. Compare also Nietzsche's letter to Gersdorff, May 8, 1874, and his letter to Rohde, May 25, 1874.

19. Letter to Wagner, May 24, 1875: "On your travels through Germany I feel sure that you heard much, e.g., about the completely general, 'Hartmannian' illness [der ganz allgemeinen Krankheit 'des Hartmannianismus']." Later in the year, in a letter to Paul Rée, October 22, 1875, Nietzsche objected to the fact that there was an advertisement about Hartmann at the back of Rée's first book and recommended that he switch over to his own publisher. *Scheindenker* can be translated as "a merely apparent thinker" or as "a superficial thinker."

20. Letter to Schmeitzner, November 22, 1879.

21. This work has only eighty-six pages long and had no chapter divisions.

The book was very positively reviewed by Dr. Johannes Volkelt in *Philosophische Monatshefte* VIII (1872), 282–96. It is likely that Nietzsche read this review, for we know that he read several articles from this journal at this time, and he even sent in a short account of his own philosophical education and activities that was published in the journal this year. See my article "An Undiscovered Short Published Autobiographical Presentation by Nietzsche from 1872," *Nietzsche-Studien* 27 (1998): 446–47.

Nietzsche previously, in 1867, had read Bahnsen's *Beiträge zur Characterologie.*

22. FW V, 357 (published in 1887).

23. In 1878, after Nietzsche had broken with Schopenhauer, the very old Bahnsen read Nietzsche and sent him a letter, dated February 22, 1878, claiming that in spite of differences, their general approach to philosophy was similar. If Nietzsche wrote an answer, as is likely, it has unfortunately been lost.

R. Grimm discusses some limited aspects of Nietzsche's relation to Bahnsen in "Embracing Two Horses: Tragedy, Humor, and Inwardness; or, Nietzsche, Vischer, and Julius Bahnsen," *Nietzsche-Studien* 18 (1989): 203–20.

24. Walter Kaufmann's translation, *The Portable Nietzsche*, 46–47.

25. See, for example, JGB, secs. 16, 17, and 54.

26. GD, "Reason," 5.

27. To mention but two examples. Nietzsche listed and read (or intended to read) an article by Alberti titled "Sprachphilosophie vor Plato," published in *Philologus* (1856), KGW I.4, 57[29]. During the period 1867–71, Nietzsche worked on a detailed index to the classical journal *Rheinisches Museum,* which meant that he read through several articles relevant for the philosophy of language (particularly relevant to antiquity) during this time.

28. C. Crawford, *The Beginnings of Nietzsche's Theory of Language* (Berlin and New York: Walter de Gruyter, 1988).

29. After probably having read a long review of the book in *Philosophische Monatshefte,* as discussed in the chapter on Nietzsche's reading of philosophical journals in my forthcoming study *Nietzsche's Knowledge of Philosophy.*

30. There is some uncertainty as to when Nietzsche held this series of lectures for the first time, the winter term of 1872–73 or the summer term of 1874. Nietzsche's lecture notes have been published in KGW II.4, 413–520. The influence of Gerber is especially extensive in sections 3 and 7.

31. Nietzsche's dependence on Gerber was first pointed out by Ph. Lacoue-Labarthe and J.-L. Nancy in "Friedrich Nietzsche: Rhétorique et langage," *Poétique* 5 (1971): 98–143, and has thereafter been more extensively examined especially by A. Meijers and M. Stingelin, "Kondordanz," *Nietzsche-Studien* 17 (1988): 350–68 (and several articles published nearby this concordance), and T. Borsche's contribution "Natur-Sprache" in *'Centauren-Geburten,'* edited by T. Borsche, F. Gerratana, and A. Venturelli (Berlin and New York: Walter de Gruyter, 1994), 112–30. (This book contains several interesting and informative papers on Nietzsche's relation to language.) For further references, see the *Nietzsche Handbuch,* edited by Henning Ottmann (Stuttgart and Weimar: Verlag J. B. Metzler, 2000), 315 and 426, and the many references in H. G. Hödl's *Nietzsches frühe Sprachkritik: Lektüren zu 'Über Wahrheit und Lüge im aussermoralischen Sinne'* (Wien: WUV-Universitätsverlag, 1997).

32. As I show in my forthcoming study *Nietzsche's Knowledge of Philosophy: A Study and Survey of Nietzsche's Reading of and Relation to German, British, and French Philosophy.*

33. To give an idea of Nietzsche's relative interest of the individual pre-Socratics, I will here list the number of sections or notes in which their names occur in his collected works (KSA). However, since the early Nietzsche so frequently refers to antiquity

in general and to the pre-Socratics, I also list, as the second number, the number of occurrences after 1875 (i.e., approximately after Nietzsche had stopped working more intensively as a classical philologist).

Thales, 42, 1; Anaximander, 43, 4; Heraclitus, 119, 23; Xenophanes, 7, 0; Parmenides, 48, 4; Anaxagoras, 56, 5; Empedocles, 96, 10; Democritus, 62, 12; Pythagoras and Pythagorian, 76, 13.

These numbers can be compared with the total number of references he makes to Socrates, 372; Plato, 382; and Epicurus, 118.

34. KGW II.4, 328–40. It is not known for certain whether Nietzsche gave these lectures for the first time in the winter term of 1869–70 or in the summer term of 1872. He thereafter gave them in the winter term of 1875–76 and for the last time in the summer term of 1876.

Considering our knowledge of when Nietzsche read about the pre-Socratics, 1872 seems the more likely alternative.

35. For Nietzsche's relation to and reading about the sophists, see my "Nietzsche's Relation to the Greek Sophists," *Nietzsche-Studien* 34 (2005): 255–76.

36. In 1873 Nietzsche published *David Strauss: der Bekenner und der Schriftsteller,* the first of four essays (originally he had planned for thirteen essays). In 1874 he published the second and third, *Von Nutzen und Nachtheil der Historie für das Leben* and *Schopenhauer als Erzieher.* The last essay, *Richard Wagner in Bayreuth,* was published in 1876, but he had written most of it during the summer of 1875. During the spring of 1875 he also worked on, and almost finished, a planned *Unzeitgemäße Betrachtungen* with the title *Wir Philologen* (*We Classicists*).

37. We know that Nietzsche read both Strauss's *Voltaire* and *Lessing* in 1873; at least there are references to these works and their contents in UB I, secs. 9 and 10 (*Voltaire*) and sec. 4 (*Lessing*). Nietzsche had earlier read several other works by Strauss.

Strauss's book contains the following chapters:

Introduction
   I. Are We Still Christians?
   II. Have We Still a Religion?
   III. What Is Our Conception of the Universe?
   IV. What Is Our Rule of Life?

38. An additional psychological motive may have come from the fact that Wilamowitz, in his harsh attack on Nietzsche (and Rohde) explicitly used Strauss's critique of Schopenhauer and applied it to Nietzsche. Nietzsche wrote to Gersdorff on April 5, 1873 (just a few days before he began working on the first *Untimely Meditation*): "Do you know that the joker has published a second booklet with the same title, full of squabble and sophisms, not worthy of a refutation. Especially directed at Rohde, towards the end the text becomes more general, away from the two 'rotten brains'; David Strauss' words against Schopenhauer are used against me, word for word, and thus it appears as if I was a Herostratus, a desecrator of temples etc."

At the very end of chapter 2, titled "Have We Still a Religion," Strauss referred to Schopenhauer and stated: "But this was a digression; for we wished to discover whether our standpoint, whose highest idea is the law-governed Cosmos, full of life and reason, can still be called a religious one; and to this end we opened Schopenhauer, who takes every occasion to scoff at this idea. Sallies of this kind, as we remarked, impress our intelligence as absurd, but our feeling as blasphemous. We consider it arrogant and profane on the part of a single individual to oppose himself with such audacious levity to the Cosmos, whence he springs, from which, also, he derives that spark of reason which he misuses. We recognize in this a repudiation of the sentiment of dependence which we expect from every man. We demand the same piety for our Cosmos that the devout man of old demanded for his God. If wounded, our feeling for the Cosmos simply reacts in a religious manner." G. A. Wells, trans., *The Old Faith and the New* (1873; reprint, Amherst, NY: Prometheus, 1997), 167–68.

39. See my article "Nietzsche's View of the Value of Historical Studies and Methods," *Journal of the History of Ideas* 65 (2004): 301–22, and the related article "Nietzsche's Relation to Historical Methods and Nineteenth Century German Historiography," *History and Theory* 46 (May 2007): 155–79.

In the former article, I show that not only does Nietzsche have a different view of history and historical scholarship after 1875–76 but also that on many occasions he explicitly rejected the view he proposed in *Vom Nutzen und Nachtheil der Historie für das Leben.* For example, in 1877 he writes: "I want expressly to inform the readers of my earlier writings [i.e., *The Birth of Tragedy* and the *Untimely Meditations*] that I have abandoned the metaphysical-artistic views that fundamentally govern them: they are pleasant but untenable." And in 1883 he writes: "Behind my *first period* grins the face of *Jesuitism:* I mean the deliberate holding on to illusion and the forcible annexation of illusion as the *foundation of culture.*" Furthermore, Nietzsche very rarely discusses or praises his essay on history after 1875, in stark contrast to all of his other books, and after 1874 he never used the several concepts and expressions such as monumental, antiquarian, and critical history, or overhistorical that he coined and used in that book. In the latter article, I show that Nietzsche was profoundly influenced by and explicitly approved of the new historical methods that become current during the early nineteenth century, especially through the works of Wolff, Niebuhr, Ranke, and Mommsen.

40. Carl Fuchs, a composer and writer of music, was a Schopenhauerian and a personal friend of Nietzsche's. Nietzsche received long letters from him and had read several of his articles, most of them published in *Musikalisches Wochenblatt.* In a letter to Fuchs, April 28, 1874, Nietzsche suggested that he collect his essays and publish them together and then referred to some of his articles about Lotze, for and against Schopenhauer, about Renan, and about Grillparzer.

41. The neo-Kantians constituted the dominant philosophical school or tradition in Germany during the 1870s and 1880s, and as such it is remarkable that no study of Nietzsche's relation to them as a group seems to have been published. One short excep-

tion is the recently published article by Steven Galt Crowell, "Nietzsche among the Neo-Kantians," in B. Babich, ed., *Nietzsche, Theories of Knowledge, and Critical Theory: Nietzsche and the Sciences I* (Dordrecht: Kluwer, 1999), 77–86.

42. The table of contents of the second edition of this work is given below in connection with the discussion of Nietzsche's reading of this work in 1877.

43. The table of contents of Zöllner's *Über die Natur der Kometen* consists of more than twenty-four pages. Its main divisions are:

1. Zwei Abhandlungen über die physische Beschaffenheit der Cometen von Olbers und Bessel, 1

2. Ueber die Stabilität kosmischer Massen und die physische Beschaffenheit der Cometen, 77

3. John Tyndall's Cometen-Theorie.—Studien im Gebiete der Psychologie und Erkenntnisstheorie, 165

4. Aphorismen zur Geschichte und Theorie der Erkenntniss, 251 (this long chapter contains extensive sections dealing with "unbewussten Schlüsse" and Schopenhauer's philosophy)

5. Immanuel Kant und seine Verdienste um die Naturwissenschaft, 426

6. Nachträge, 485–524.

44. UB II, 6, and KSA 7, 29[34].

45. G. Abel, *Die Dynamik der Willen zur Macht und die ewige Wiederkehr* (Berlin and New York: Walter de Gruyter, 1984, 1999). Abel argues that eventually this even influenced Nietzsche's idea of the eternal recurrence.

46. See A. Orsucci, "Beiträge zur Quellenforschung mitgeteilt von Andreas Orsucci," *Nietzsche-Studien* 22 (1993): 371–75, and his "Unbewusste Schlüsse, Anticipation, Übertragung: Über Nietzsches Verhälnis zu Karl Friedrich Zöllner und Gustav Gerber," *'Centauren-Geburten'* (1994): 193–207. See also Robin Small's "Nietzsche, Zöllner, and the Fourth Dimension," *Archive für Geschichte der Philosophie* 76 (1994): 278–301.

47. In the note KSA 11, 25[307], Nietzsche claims that Zöllner does not belong "to us." This might suggest a rereading of Zöllner sometime after 1874.

48. Nietzsche and Romundt also visited each other several times during the intervening years.

49. Apart from having lived close to one another in Leipzig and shared a house in Basel, Romundt and Nietzsche also frequently corresponded with one another. Unfortunately, all but three of Nietzsche's letters have been lost, but sixty-five letters from Romundt to Nietzsche are extant.

50. Nietzsche's library contains four books by Romundt:
Die menschliche Erkenntnis und das Wesen der Dinge Habilitationsschrift (Basel, 1872), 96 pages
Antäus. Neuer Aufbau der Lehre Kants über Seele, Freiheit und Gott (Leipzig, 1882), 146 pages, with a personal dedication from the author to Nietzsche

Die Herstellung der Lehre Jesu durch Kants Reform der Philosophie, Sonderdruck
aus dem deutschen Protestantenblatt (Bremen, 1883), 34 pages, with a per-
sonal dedication from the author to Nietzsche
Grundlegung zur Reform der Philosophie. Vereinfachte und erweiterte Darstellung
von Immanuel Kants Kritik der reinen Vernunft (Berlin, 1885), 264 pages
Only the last one contains signs of having been read, in the form of a few dog-ears.
Apart from these, Romundt also (before 1889) published the following books that
Nietzsche may well have read:

Die Wurzel LEG [written in Greek] *im Griechischen* (diss., 1869), 32 pages
Vernunft als Christentum (Leipzig, 1882), 134 pages
Die Vollendung d. Sokrates: Immanuel Kant's Grundlegung zur Reform der Sitten-
lehre (Leipzig, 1885), 304 pages
Ein neuer Paulus: Immanuel Kants Grundleggung zu e. sicheren Lehre v. der Reli-
gion (Berlin, 1886), 309 pages
Die drei Fragen Kant's (Berlin, 1887), 64 pages

51. On the title page of his *Neuer Aufbau der Lehre Kants* (1882) Romundt had written: "Dem Physiker der Metaphysiker als Zeichen seiner Ergebenheit" ("To the physi-
cist [i.e., Nietzsche] from the metaphysician [i.e., Romundt] as sign of his devotion").

52. Nietzsche also gave a course on Aristotle's *Rhetoric* during both the summer and
winter terms that year.

53. Compare KSA 7, 509, and letter to Rohde, January 31, 1873.

54. KGW II.2, 437.

55. KSA 7, 19[292]. Written between the summer of 1872 and early 1873: "Das
schlechte Buch von *Lotze,* in dem der Raum mit besprechung eines ganz unaesthe-
tischen Menschen: *Ritter* [...] oder des verdrehten Leipziger Philosophen Weisse ver-
braucht wird."

56. "Anzugreifen." KSA 7, 19[259].

57. Letter to Rohde, February 21, 1873. Letter to Fuchs, September 30, 1873: "the
absurd gentlemen Lotze and Gervinus." And another letter to Fuchs, August 11, 1875:
"Your rebuff of Lotze [...] could as an *addition* show that you are good at duelling with
swords."

Chapter 5: The Middle Nietzsche

1. In the preface to *Human, All Too Human* (added in 1886), Nietzsche called the
change then a "great liberation," and in *Ecce Homo* he wrote: "*Human, All Too Human* is
a memorial of a crisis. [...] [W]ith this book I liberated myself from that in my nature
which *did not belong to me.* Idealism does not belong to me [...] [R]ealities were altogether lacking in my knowledge, and the 'idealities' were worth damn all! A downright
burning thirst seized hold of me: thenceforward I pursued in fact nothing other than
physiology, medicine and natural science" (EH, "Human, All Too Human," 1 and 3).

The change was in some ways rather sudden and fundamental, but it is also possible to see several premonitions of it earlier, such as in his desire to read natural science and philosophy of science in 1868 and then borrowing a fairly large number of books in these fields in 1873. Furthermore, the change was not a simple gradual one or a revolutionary one but rather was one in which Nietzsche several times during 1875 and 1876 seems to have switched back and forth between the old and the new way of thinking. Other figures toward whom his attitude changed at this time from positive to negative were Luther and Schiller.

2. That this relates to Nietzsche's own development is still clearer in an early draft, KSA 14, 140–41. In this earlier draft Nietzsche wrote in the form of "we" instead of "they," that is, the note then began: "We at present begin . . . our . . . [etc.]."

We thus see here a perfect example of how Nietzsche, as he does so often, draws conclusions from his own experience and applies them generally. Compare the next note for a similar example, again from *Menschliches, Allzumenschliches.*

3. KSA 8, 23[159], written between the end of 1876 and the summer of 1877. Several similar notes can be found from this period.

Compare MA, 599, in which an echo of this note reverberates. In it he claims that a "first maturity, with a strong residue of acidulousness," occurs between the age of twenty-six and thirty (i.e., in Nietzsche's case, ca. 1870–74) in which everything one writes is reactive and is a form of revenge for not receiving recognition.

4. KSA 10, 16[23], autumn 1883.

5. I examine and argue for the importance of British influences for this change in 1875–76 in the chapter "Nietzsche's Positivism and His Pro-British Period" of my study *Nietzsche and the "English": British and American Influences on Nietzsche* (Amherst, NY: Prometheus, 2007).

6. Conventionally, the two most common explanations for the change of Nietzsche's style at this time have been his illness, which, it is claimed, would not have allowed him to write long continuous texts, and the influence of the French moralists, who mostly wrote in the form of aphorisms. While his illness may have been a cause, I doubt that it was a determining factor. As to the French moralists, Nietzsche was induced to read them by Rée, so this influence, to a large extent, is part of Rée's influence.

7. Nietzsche seems to have read Helvetius in 1878 and Fontenelle in 1879. Rousseau's *Bekenntnisse* (*The Confessions*) (1870) is in Nietzsche's library, but it is not known if or when he read it. It contains fairly many dog-ears and two small penciled lines, clearly placed there by mistake. Nietzsche was already at this time critical of Rousseau. For a more detailed discussion of this, see my forthcoming study *Nietzsche's Knowledge of Philosophy: A Study and Survey of Nietzsche's Reading of and Relation to German, British, and French Philosophy.*

8. WS, 214. Published in December 1879 but with the publication year given as 1880.

9. Considering this, it is surprising how little attention has been given to Nietzsche's relation to Voltaire.

10. See letter to Elisabeth Nietzsche, April 8, 1876. "Meine erste Verehrung galt Voltaire, dessen Haus in Fernex ich aufsuchte" and letter to Carl von Gersdorff, April 15, 1876. "Wenn wir uns wiedersehn, will ich Dir von Ferney dem Sitze Voltaires (dem ich meine echten Huldigungen brachte) erzählen."

11. Letter to Franz Overbeck, December 6, 1876. "We have read much Voltaire."

12. In *Ecce Homo* he wrote: "'Human, All Too Human' is the memorial of a crisis. It calls itself a book for *free* spirits: almost every sentence in it is the expression of a victory—with this book I liberated myself from that in my nature which *did not belong to me*. Idealism does not belong to me [...] The expression 'free spirit' should here be understood in no other sense: a spirit that has *become free,* that has again seized possession of itself. The tone, the sound of voice has completely changed [...] For Voltaire is, in contrast to all who have written after him, above all a *grandseigneur* of the spirit: precisely what I am too.—The name of Voltaire on a writing by me—that really was progress—*toward myself.*" EH, "Why I Write Such Excellent Books"; EH, "Human, All Too Human," 1 (Hollingdale's translation).

13. For a discussion of Nietzsche's reading of and relation to Voltaire, see my forthcoming study *Nietzsche's Knowledge of Philosophy.*

14. A detailed examination and discussion of Nietzsche's reading of Lichtenberg has been published by Martin Stingelin, *'Unsere ganze Philosophie ist Berichtigung des Sprachgebrauchs': Friedrich Nietzsches Lichtenberg-Rezeption im Spannungsfeld zwischen Sprachkritik (Rhetorik) und historischer Kritik (Genealogie)* (München, 1996). In a long appendix, Nietzsche's many annotations in his Lichtenberg volumes are reproduced.

15. This is also true for Goethe and Heine, but Nietzsche's relation to them is not dealt with here, for they are not primarily philosophers.

16. Letter to Gersdorff, April 6, 1867.

17. It is not clear what sources Nietzsche was referring to with regard to Lessing and Lichtenberg. In the case of Schopenhauer, it almost certainly referred to a study of three sections of *Parerga und Paralipomena:* "Über Schriftstellerei und Stil," "Über Lesen und Bücher," and "Über Sprache und Worte." One can note that these sections of *Parerga und Paralipomena* seem to have been especially important to Nietzsche. In his copy of the book (which he bought in 1875), these are the only sections he annotated.

18. I have discussed Nietzsche's reading of natural scientific books, including many books in this series, in "Nietzsche's Reading and Knowledge of Natural Science: An Overview," in Gregory Moore and Thomas H. Brobjer, eds., *Nietzsche and Science* (Aldershot, Burlington, UK: Ashgate, 2004), 21–50.

19. This is also a theme in the first book of *Beyond Good and Evil.*

20. See my articles "Nietzsche's View of the Value of Historical Studies and Methods," *Journal of the History of Ideas* 65 (2004): 301–22, and "Nietzsche's Relation to Historical Methods and Nineteenth Century German Historiography," *History and Theory* 46 (May 2007): 155–79.

21. For Nietzsche's relation to Buddhism and oriental thought, see, for example, Freny Mistry, *Nietzsche and Buddhism* (Berlin and New York: Walter de Gruyter, 1981);

Graham Parkes, ed., *Nietzsche and Asian Thought* (Chicago and London: University of Chicago Press, 1991, 1996); Robert G. Morrison, *Nietzsche and Buddhism* (Oxford, UK: Clarendon, 1997); and my own articles "Nietzsche and the Laws of Manu," in A. L. Macfie, ed., *Eastern Influences on Western Philosophy: A Reader* (Edinburgh: Edinburgh University Press, 2003), 260–78 (previously published under the title "The Absence of Political Ideals in Nietzsche's Writings: The Case of the Laws of Manu and the Associated Caste-Society" in *Nietzsche-Studien* 27 [1998]); "Nietzsche's Reading about Indian Philosophy," *Journal of Nietzsche Studies* (Autumn 2004): 3–36, and "Nietzsche's Reading about China and Japan," *Nietzsche-Studien* 34 (2005): 329–36.

22. Deussen's letter to Nietzsche, January 17, 1875, is published in KGB II.6/1, 17–20, and Nietzsche's answer from a few days later is published in KSB 5, 10.

Deussen, who was a Kantian, wrote extensively about his plans and views. He wrote that he believed that all philosophers including the metaphysicians of religion (except the materialists, that is, the natural scientists) were essentially saying the same thing and were in agreement with Kant. Thereafter, Deussen described his plans to study Indian philosophy, which, he claimed, had close kinship with the thinking of Kant and Schopenhauer.

23. Letter to Gersdorff, December 13, 1875. Nietzsche wrote the epigram in German: "so wandle ich einsam wie das Rhinoceros." The work that Nietzsche borrowed appears to have been Coomaraswamy's abridged translation in English of the *Sutta-Nipata*.

24. In 1883 Nietzsche also copied down the title of H. Kern's *Der Buddhismus und seine Geschichte in Indien* (1882–84), but it is unlikely that he read it.

25. For the meaning of Nietzsche's discussions of Manu, see my "The Absence of Political Ideals in Nietzsche's Writings: The Case of the Laws of Manu and the Associated Caste-Society," *Nietzsche-Studien* 27 (1998): 300–318.

26. Nietzsche sent a book by Dühring to Cosima Wagner in 1869, probably his *Der Werth des Lebens* (1865); see KSA 15, 11.

27. The best account of Nietzsche's relation to Dühring is A. Venturelli's "Asketismus und Wille zur Macht: Nietzsches Auseinandersetzung mit Eugen Dühring," *Nietzsche-Studien* 15 (1986): 107–39. See also R. Small's "Nietzsche, Dühring and Time," *Journal of the History of Philosophy* 28 (1990): 229–50; and H. Reinhardt, ed., *Dühring und Nietzsche* (Leipzig, 1931).

28. Letter to Overbeck, October 22, 1879.

29. I discuss Nietzsche's reading of Dühring's more political works in my two articles "Nietzsche's Knowledge, Reading and Critique of Political Economy," *Journal of Nietzsche Studies* 18 (Fall 1999): 57–70; and "Nietzsche's Knowledge of Marx and Marxism," *Nietzsche-Studien* 31 (2002): 298–313.

30. KSA 8, 9[1], 131–81.

Surprisingly, no thorough examination of Nietzsche's long excerpt and discussion and no comparison with Dühring's *Der Werth des Lebens* (1865) seem to have been performed, with the exception of Venturelli's "Asketismus und Wille zur Macht," in spite of the fact that he wrote it at a pivotal period of his philosophical development.

31. The table of contents of Dühring's *Der Werth des Lebens: Eine philosophische Betrachtung* (Breslau, 1865) lists the following chapters:

Vorrede, i–vii
Einleitung, 1
    I. Das Leben als Inbegriff von Empfindungen und Gemüthsbewegungen, 13
    II. Der Unterschied als der eigentliche Gegenstand des Gefühls, 28
    III. Die Grundgestalt in der Abfolge der Lebenserregungen, 40
    IV. Der Verlauf eines Menschenlebens, 52
    V. Die Liebe, 87
    VI. Der Tod, 125
    VII. Das Gemeinleben, 148
    VIII. Die Erkenntniss, 163
    IX. Der Glaube an den Werth des Lebens, 181
Anhang:
    1. Der theoretische Idealismus und die Einheit des Systems der Dinge, 193
    2. Die transcendente Befriedigung der Rache, 219–234.

32. KSA 8, 8[4], summer 1875. "Pläne aller Art: [...] 3) Dühring, als den Versuch einer Beseitigung Schopenhauer's durchzustudiren und zu sehen, was ich an Schopenhauer habe, was nicht. Hinterdrein noch einmal Schopenhauer zu lesen."
Note that this was written during the summer of 1875, that is, after Nietzsche had written his third *Unzeitgemäße Betrachtungen,* with the title *Schopenhauer als Erzieher* (1874).

33. KSA 8, 8[1].

34. Nietzsche wrote the word *ressentiment* for the first time on the inside of the back cover, with two page references to where Dühring discussed it in the book, and also used it in his extensive excerpt from the book, KSA 8, 9[1], 176.

35. Nietzsche's first use of it in his published books is in *On the Genealogy of Morals.*

36. See, for example, the ambivalent section 92 in *Human, All Too Human.*

37. The table of contents of Dühring's *Cursus der Philosophie* (1875) consists of eight dense pages. Its main divisions are:

Einleitung: a. Bedeutung der Philosophie, 1
b. Bestandtheile und natürliches System, 8
    I. Grundgestalten des Seins, 16
    II. Principien des Naturwissens, 56
    III. Elemente des Bewusstseins, 128
    IV. Sitte, Gerechtigkeit und edlere Menschlichkeit, 192
    V. Gemeinwesen und Geschichte, 263
    VI. Individualiserung und Werthsteigerung des Lebens, 341
    VII. Socialisirung aller Gesammtthätigkeiten, 386
    VIII. Wissenschaft und Philosophie in der alten und in neuen Gesellschaft, 431
Schluss: Studium und Entwicklung der Wirklichkeitsphiluhie, 525–560

Nietzsche's copy of the book is fairly heavily annotated.

38. Although generally hostile to Dühring, Nietzsche could nonetheless write to Overbeck, as late as September 14, 1884, and express his pleasure to have met Heinrich von Stein, who regrettably was a Wagnerian, "but through the rational breeding that he has received in the vicinity of *Dühring,* he is well prepared for me!" (This was repeated with slightly different words in a letter to Peter Gast, September 20, 1884.) Nietzsche possibly recognized his own education through Dühring.

39. The table of contents of Mainländer's *Philosophie der Erlösung* (Berlin, 1876) lists the following content:

> Vorwort, v–viii; Analysis des Erkenntnißvermögens, 1; Physik, 47; Aesthetik, 113; Ethik, 167; Politik, 225; Metaphysik, 317 and Anhang: Kritik der Lehren Kant's und Schopenhauer's, 359–623.

40. KSA 8, 19[99]; KSA 8, 23[12]; and KSA 14, 124 (early version of MA, 27).

41. For a discussion of Nietzsche's reading of Mainländer and its importance, see W. H. Müller-Seyfarth, "Mainländer und Nietzsche: Ein Nachtrag zu Max Seilings Replik auf eine der 'unüberlegtesten Boutaden' Nietzsches," *Nietzsche-Studien* 28 (1999): 323–35; and F. Decher, "Der eine Wille und die vielen Willen. Schopenhauer—Mainländer—Nietzsche," *Nietzsche-Studien* 25 (1996): 221–38.

Decher emphasizes the importance of the fact that Mainländer reinterpreted Schopenhauer's metaphysical and single will to a less metaphysical multiplicity of wills (always in struggle) and the importance of this for Nietzsche's will to power.

42. It was in a letter to Cosima Wagner, December 19, 1876, that is, while reading Mainländer, that Nietzsche for the first time explicitly claimed to have parted ways with Schopenhauer.

It may be relevant that Mainländer's book ends with a long section (more than two hundred pages) consisting mainly of a critique of Schopenhauer's metaphysics.

43. "Gott is gestorben, und sein Tod war das Leben der Welt," *Philosophie der Erlösung,* 321.

44. KSA 10, 4[118], 7[134–36 and 140], and he is mentioned more generally in the summer–autumn of 1884, KSA 11, 26[383].

This time Nietzsche had probably borrowed Overbeck's copy, for Nietzsche gives a page reference to the second edition of the first volume, from 1879, and in a letter to Overbeck, July 2, 1885, he said he had just found Overbeck's Mainländer in his crate of books in Sils-Maria. I have attempted, but been unable, to establish that Nietzsche also had read the second volume, published in 1886, and thus conclude that it seems unlikely that he read that volume. The only indication that Nietzsche might have read Mainländer in 1886 or later is that he referred to him once in a note from early 1888 and that he discussed him with a bookshop keeper, whom Nietzsche liked, who was a follower of Mainländer.

45. See, for example, his letters to Meysenbug, April 14, 1876 (the complete letter consists of praise of the book); to Rohde, April 14, 1876; and to Gersdorff, April 15,

1876. In the letter to Rohde, Nietzsche wrote: "Und hast Du die jetzt eben erschienenen 3 Bände 'Memoiren einer Idealistin' gelesen? Ich bitte Dich sehr darum, es zu thun. Es ist das Leben unsrer herrlichen Freundin Frl v Meysenbug, ein Spiegel für jeden tüchtigen Menschen, in den man ebenso beschämt als ermuthigt blickt, ich las lange Zeit nichts, was mich so innerlich umdrehte und der Gesundheit näher brachte. Wir haben ja Verschiedenes diesen Winter zu tragen gehabt, aber was mir so wohlthat, wird auch Dir wohlthun, bei aller Verschiedenheit der Naturen und der Leiden. Overbeck hat es seiner Braut vorgelesen, nach jeder Sitzung, erzählte er, seien sie in neue Begeisterung und Ergriffenheit ausgebrochen. Es ist etwas von der höchsten caritas darin."

46. For a discussion of Meysenbug's importance for Nietzsche's view of women and feminism, see my forthcoming article "Literary Sources and Influences on Nietzsche's Views of Women and Feminism."

47. For a more extensive account of Nietzsche's knowledge of Marx, see my forthcoming *Nietzsche's Knowledge of Philosophy*, and for a fuller discussion, see my "Nietzsche's Knowledge of Marx and Marxism," *Nietzsche-Studien* 31 (2002): 298–313.

48. Later Nietzsche even hired people to read for him, and when visiting Naumburg his mother read to him extensively.

49. At least until February 1876, the manuscript was titled "Abrißeiner Moralphilosophie." See Hubert Treiber's "Zur Genealogie einer 'Science positive de la morale en Allemagne,'" *Nietzsche-Studien* 22 (1993): 165–221.

50. "*Fundamental questions of metaphysics.*—When one day the history of the genesis of thought comes to be written, the following sentence by a distinguished logician will also stand revealed in a new light: 'The primary universal law of the knowing subject consists in the inner necessity of recognizing every object in itself as being in its own essence something identical with itself, thus self-existent and at bottom always the same and unchanging, in short as a substance' [Quoted from Afrikan Spir's *Denken und Wirklichkeit* (*Thought and Reality*) (Leipzig, 1873, 1877)]. This law, too, which is here called 'primary,' evolved: one day it will be shown how gradually, in the lower organisms, this tendency comes into being: how the blind mole's eyes of this organization at first never see anything but the same thing; how then, when the various pleasurable and unpleasurable stimuli become more noticeable, various different substances are gradually distinguished, but each of them with one attribute, that is to say a single relationship with such an organism.—The first stage of the logical is judgment: and the essence of judgment consists, according to the best logicians, in belief. At the bottom of all belief lies the *sensation of the pleasurable or painful* in respect to the subject experiencing the sensation." MA, 18. "Scientific philosophy has to be very much on its guard against smuggling in errors on the basis of this need (a need that has come into existence and consequently also a transient one): even logicians speak of 'presentiments' of truth in morality and art (for example of the presentiment 'that the essence of things is one'): which is something that should be forbidden them." (MA, 131).

51. See the chapter "Nietzsche's Reading of Journals of Philosophy" in my forthcoming *Nietzsche's Knowledge of Philosophy*.

52. Nietzsche seems to have sold his copy of the book in 1875.

Much of the following account is based on Paolo D'Iorio's exemplary article "La superstition des philosophes critiques: Nietzsche et Afrikan Spir," *Nietzsche-Studien* 22 (1993): 257–94. This article contains much further important information for anyone interested in understanding Nietzsche's epistemology. An interesting and detailed study by Michael S. Green, *Nietzsche and the Transcendental Tradition* (Urbana and Chicago: University of Illinois Press, 2002), focuses on Nietzsche's relation and debt to Spir.

53. The full title is *Erkennen und Sein: Lösung des Problems des Idealen und Realen zugleich eine Erörterung des richtigen Ausgangspunktes und der Principien der Philosophie* (Karlsruhe and Leipzig, 1885), 239 pages.

54. Deussen's first book, *Die Elemente der Metaphysik* (1877), deals extensively with Kant and Schopenhauer. Deussen also attempts to show the kinship of their thinking with that of "insbesondere der Brahmavidja der Inder, der Ideenlehre des Platon und der Theologie des Christenthums."

The table of contents lists the following chapters:

A. Der empirische Standpunkt: System der Physik. 7–12, B. Der transscendentale Standpunkt: System der Metaphysik. Die Theorie des Erkennen, 13–41; Die Vernunft und ihr Inhalt, 42–55; Die Metaphysik der Natur, 56–94; Die Metaphysik des Schönen, 95–130; Die Metaphysik der Moral, 131–88.

55. Letter to Deussen, early August 1877. Compare letter to Meysenbug, August 4, 1877.

56. KSA 14, 487–88.

57. Nietzsche's possible reading of Locke is discussed in my study *Nietzsche and the "English."*

58. Nietzsche's reading of these and other French philosophers is discussed in my forthcoming *Nietzsche's Knowledge of Philosophy.*

59. This work, of about 550 pages, contains seventeen essays on different subjects, such as "De la physiologie; importance et progrès des études physiologiques," 245–305; "De quelques points de physiologie psychique," 306–30; "Origine de l'idée du justice," 331–47; and "De la condition essentielle qui sépare le sociologie de la biologie, 348–75. The only two essays annotated in Nietzsche's copy of the book are the ninth," "De la physiologie," and the sixteenth, "De l'histoire de la civilisation en Angleterre, par Buckle," 478–521, but it seems likely that he read the whole work.

60. I discuss Nietzsche's relation to British thinking, culture, and literature, including his relation to Darwin and Darwinism, in *Nietzsche and the "English"* (2007).

61. In 1877, in a letter to Rée from early August, Nietzsche referred to British philosophers and thinkers as "the only philosophically good company at present." In the same positive spirit he wrote another letter to Rée two years later, at the end of July 1879, saying: "Could you send me an informative book, if possible of English origin, but translated into German and with clear and large print?—I live here completely without

books, seven-eighths blind, but I would gladly accept the forbidden fruit from your hand." A few months later, in a letter to his publisher Schmeitzner, November 22, 1879, Nietzsche recommended to him that he have Spencer's *The Data of Ethics* translated into German and published. In the letter Nietzsche referred to Spencer with praise—"hochberümt," "höchst *lehrreich* für uns"—and further claimed that a translation would be the best alternative against Hartmann's latest impudence (i.e., latest book). When it turned out that the book had already been translated into German, Nietzsche asked his publisher to acquire it for him. Nietzsche then read *Die Thatsachen der Ethik* during 1880 and 1881 (i.e., at the same time as his reading of Mill).

62. The work is not mentioned in any of the listings of the holdings of Nietzsche's library, and it therefore seems likely that he no longer had the book in his possession at the time of his mental collapse in 1889.

63. "Sendet mir gleich den Koffer und legt folg<ende> Bücher hinein Spencer (Thats<achen> der Ethik); Baumann (Ethik), Martensen (Ethik) dann Stendhal, 2. Bd." Nietzsche to Franziska Nietzsche, March 27, 1880.

The fact that Nietzsche does not specify the number of volumes may indicate that he only possessed the first volume.

64. Nietzsche's reading of this book influenced sections 192, 210, and 339 of *Morgenröthe* and at least two notes from 1880, KSA 9, 3[67] and 5[37], as Andrea Orsucci has shown in *Orient-Okzident* (Berlin and New York: Walter de Gruyter, 1996), 174–77.

65. Höffding wrote: "Deshalb ist für S. Kierkegaard die Möglichkeit der Wiederholung das ethische Grundproblem" ("Therefore the possibility of repetition is the most fundamental ethical problem for S. Kierkegaard"). To this sentence a footnote is added in which a quotation from Kierkegaard has an astonishing similarity to Nietzsche's own psychology of the eternal recurrence. The beginning of the footnote reads as follows in English translation: "The one who only hopes, he is cowardly, the one who only wants to remember, he is voluptuous, the one who wants a repetition, he is a man . . . When one has travelled through existence, then it will be clear if one has the courage to understand that life is a repetition, and if one is willing to find joy in this." The underlining is Nietzsche's, and he also wrote an "NB" and drew a line in the margin.

66. For a fuller account, see my "Nietzsche's Knowledge of Kierkegaard," *Journal of the History of Philosophy* 41 (2003): 251–63.

67. Josef Popper (1838–1921), also called Popper-Lynkeus, contributed as a philosopher and thinker to three areas: social reform, critique of metaphysics and religion, and support for a radical ethical individualism. All three aspects are clearly visible in his *Das Recht zu leben und die Pflicht zu sterben: Socialphilosophische Betrachtungen, Anknüpfend an die Bedeutung Voltaire's für die neuere Zeit* (Leipzig, 1878; 2nd ed., 1879; 3rd ed., 1903). It is the second edition of this book that Nietzsche possessed and read with appreciation in 1879–80. Nietzsche never explicitly speaks of Popper but did possess this book, and we have a letter from Popper's publisher, Erich Koschny, obviously in response to an earlier letter from Nietzsche, who wrote to him on January 19, 1880: "Dear Herr Professor! Glad to hear that the views of the author of 'The Right to Live etc'

find your approval, and thus I feel honoured to give you the requested exact address of the same" (KGB III.2, 16–17). This address can also be found among Nietzsche's notes, although it is not included in KSA. Due to his radical ethical individualism—which can also be called a sort of humanitarian individualism—he in some ways reminds one of Max Stirner. But where Stirner is extreme and cynical, Popper is extreme and "idealistic." Every individual human life is the greatest event on Earth—not just for himself, as in the case of Stirner, but in a broader sense—and is much more valuable than any event, work, or discovery in politics, religion, aesthetics, or science. There can be little doubt that the late Nietzsche would have been highly skeptical of Popper's ideas, but in 1880 he seems to have been more sympathetic, as we have seen. Popper's book contains five chapters and a brief conclusion or summary. It is possible to establish or estimate how Nietzsche responded to this reading. For a full account and a general discussion of the approximately 150 books that Nietzsche read the two years prior to his writing *Morgenröthe* (i.e., 1879–81), see my forthcoming article "Nietzsche's Reading at the Time of *Morgenröthe*: An Overview and a Discussion of His Reading of J. Popper," presented at the conference "Philosophie de l'Aurore" in Nice/Tourtour, France, September 19–24, 2003, which will be published in the proceedings in 2007 or 2008, edited by Paolo D'Iorio. The table of contents of Popper's book is as follows:

1. "Würdigung Voltaire's," 1–51: This is a long chapter praising Voltaire, which Nietzsche had also done in 1878.
2. "Das Bedürfniss nach Religion und Metaphysik," 52–66: This chapter contains a harsh critique of Christianity and of our need for metaphysics. We can fight against this need, argues Popper, so that the role of Christianity and metaphysics will be significantly reduced in a hundred years. Popper expresses stronger critique of Christianity than Nietzsche does at this time.
3. "Das Recht zu leben," 67–96: In this chapter Popper argues for solving the social question by means of a guaranteed minimum level of sustenance, to be "paid" *in natura*. Nietzsche never expresses any interest in this or similar projects of social reform.
4. "Der Trieb zu Verbrechen und Strafen," 97–126: Here Popper argues against the contemporary view of crime and punishment. He is, like Nietzsche, against all punishment.
5. "Die Pflicht zu sterben," 127–37: Here Popper argues the "strange" case that each individual man should have the right to decide if he wants to join in a war or not, through a rather complicated registration procedure. There is no evidence that Nietzsche sympathized with or responded to this view.

68. Nietzsche wrote at least five notes referring to Epictetus in 1880 and discussed or quoted him three times in *Dawn*: KSA 9, 6[352, 395, 400]; KSA 9, 7[96 and 101]; and M, secs. 131, 195, and 546.

Nietzsche's reading of Epictetus's *Manual* at this time is also likely to have influenced many of his other notes, such as his discussion of Stoicism in *Dawn* (secs. 133, 139, and

251) and in FW (secs. 12, 99, 306, and 326) and the frequent discussions of Stoicism in the notes from this time (especially secs. 4 and 7 of KSA 9).

Two versions of the work exist in Nietzsche's library, one in German and one in French: *Handbuch: Aus dem Griechischen: Mit erläuternden Anmerkungen v. Gottl. Christian Karl Link* (Nürnberg, 1783) and *Maximes: Traduites par Dacier* (Paris, 1870). He seems not to be quoting from either of these two editions, and it seems likely that he read a third, different edition. The pages of the copy of the French edition in Nietzsche's library have not been completely cut open, which makes it less likely that Nietzsche used it. I learned this from Giuliano Campioni, Paolo D'Iorio, Andrea Orsucci, Maria Cristina Fornari, and Francesco Fronterotta (with the assistance of Renate Müller-Buck), *Nietzsches persönliche Bibliothek* (Berlin and New York: Walter de Gruyter, 2003).

69. Nietzsche briefly cited Marcus Aurelius in M, 450, and wrote in a note from the autumn of 1881 that he found him (and Grazian) astonishing: "Welches Erstaunen macht mir Marc Aurel und welches Grazian!" (KSA 9, 12[191]). And in a letter to Ferdinand Laban, July 19, 1881, he referred to their both holding Marcus Aurelius in high regard: "wie jener herrliche römische Kaiser, in dessen Verehrung wir Beide *einmüthig* sind."

70. Compare my article "Nietzsche's Reading of Epictetus," *Nietzsche-Studien* 32 (2003): 429–34.

71. Almost certainly Nietzsche's reading of Baumann, Lecky, Liebmann, and Caspari is of outmost importance for any discussion of Nietzsche's ethics and its relation to contemporary morality. Further studies are needed here.

72. I discuss Nietzsche's reading of Lecky in *Nietzsche and the "English,"* but much more needs to be done. Frank Cameron has written an article manuscript titled "The Influence of Lecky on Nietzsche's Moral Thought," which hopefully soon will be published.

73. Nietzsche's copy of the book is heavily annotated throughout, with many instances of "NB," "gut," and other comments in the margins.

The following is the table of contents of Liebmann's *Zur Analysis der Wirklichkeit* (1880):

Vorwort

Prolegomena, 1

I. Zur Erkenntnißkritik und Transcendentalphilosophie

  1. Idealismus und Realismus, 19

  2. Ueber die Phänomenalität des Raumes, 36

  3. Ueber die Phänomenalität des Raumes: Anhang, 69

  4. Raumcharakteristik und Raumdeduction, 72

  5. Ueber subjective, objective und absolute Zeit, 87

  6. Ueber relative und absolute Bewegung, 113

  7. Zur Theorie des Sehens: Erster Kapitel, 145

  8. Zur Theorie des Sehens: Zweiter Kapitel, 172

  9. Die Logik der Thatsachen oder Causalität und Zeitfolge, 187

  10. Die Metamorphosen des Apori, 208

II. Zur Naturphilosophie und Psychologie

III. Zur Aesthetik und Ethik

74. Letter to Overbeck, September 18, 1881, and KSA 9, 11[236].

75. KSA 12, 9[92].

76. The table of contents of Caspari's *Der Zusammenhang der Dinge* lists the following (the divisions within the different essays are not reproduced here): 1. Naturphilosophische Probleme; 2. Zur Erkenntnisskritik der transcendentalen Grundphänomene; 3. Zur Psychologie; and 4. Zur Ethik.

Paolo D'Iorio has some discussion of Nietzsche's reading of Caspari in "Cosmologie de l'éternel Retour," *Nietzsche-Studien* 24 (1995): 62–123, and I have briefly discussed his reading of *Die Urgeschichte der Menschheit* in "Women As Predatory Animals or Why Nietzsche Philosophized with a Whip," in Christa Davis Acampora and Ralph R. Acampora, eds., *A Nietzschean Bestiary: Becoming Animal beyond Docile and Brutal* (Lanham, MD: Rowman and Littlefield, 2004), 181–92.

77. *Die Urgeschichte der Menschheit. Mit Rücksicht auf die natürliche Entwicklung des frühesten Geisteslebens*, 2 vols. (Leipzig, 1877), and *Die Thomson'sche Hypothese von der endlichen Temperaturausgleichung im Weltall, beleuchtet vom philosophischen Gesichtspunkte* (Stuttgart, 1874).

78. Nietzsche made a reference to page 288 of Caspari's work (i.e., to an essay about Hartmann, Dühring, and Lange) in an early version of section 109 of FW; see KSA 14, 254. There is likely to exist further evidence of the reading of this work in Nietzsche's notebooks from this period.

79. William S. Wurzer, *Nietzsche und Spinoza* (Meisenheim am Glan: Verlag Anton Hain, 1975), 148, claims: "Von den modernen Philosophen war für den späten Nietzsche vielleicht keiner so bedeutend wie Spinoza. Man kann mit Recht sagen, daß

in der neuzeitlichen Philosophie Schopenhauer und Spinoza in entscheidender Weise die einflußreichsten Vorbilder für bestimmte Gedankengänge Nietzsches waren. Schopenhauers Denken sollte er schon früh in seinem Leben aufgeben. Spinozas Denken konnte Nietzsche nicht verlieren." To me this claim is exaggerated, although not without some justification.

80. The philosophers whom Nietzsche most frequently discusses and refers to in his published writings are Schopenhauer, Plato, Kant, and Socrates. These are followed by a group of philosophers of whom Spinoza is one: Epicurus, Hegel, Spinoza, Voltaire, Rousseau, Pascal, and Aristotle. I discuss Nietzsche's relation to other thinkers in my *Nietzsche's Ethics of Character* (Uppsala: Uppsala University Press, 1995).

81. The positive evaluations are referred to in the text below. The critical statements come from JGB, 5, 13, and 198.

82. It must be realized that it is almost impossible to prove or to be certain that someone has not read a certain book or author. My argument here is based not only on the fact that we have no evidence that Nietzsche ever read Spinoza but also on the fact that all of his important references to Spinoza can be traced to specific secondary literature. My discussion in this section is a shortened version of my article "Nietzsche's Knowledge of Spinoza" in *Spinoza in Nordic Countries,* edited by Vesa Oittinen (Helsinki: Department of Philosophy, University of Helsinki, 2004), 203–16.

83. It would be easy to give a large number of references to works where this has been done.

84. Many studies of Nietzsche and Spinoza have been published. An excellent and detailed examination is Wurzer's *Nietzsche und Spinoza.* Other relevant works are: Joan Stambaugh, "Amor dei and Amor fati: Spinoza and Nietzsche," in O'Flaherty, et al., eds., *Studies in Nietzsche and the Judaeo-Christian Tradition* (1985), 130–42; Yirmiyahu Yovel, "Nietzsche and Spinoza: Amor Fati and Amor Dei," in Y. Yovel, *Nietzsche As Affirmative Thinker* (1986), 183–203; and Greg Whitlock, "Roger Boscovich, Benedict de Spinoza and Friedrich Nietzsche: The Untold Story," *Nietzsche-Studien* 25 (1996): 200–20. Richard Schacht has in his *Making Sense of Nietzsche* (Urbana and Chicago: University of Illinois Press, 1995) an interesting chapter titled "The Nietzsche-Spinoza Problem: Spinoza as Precursor?" (167–86). Schacht emphasizes the kinship between the two thinkers and claims that most of Nietzsche's critique of Spinoza was due to the central role that self-preservation played for him. The title of the chapter notwithstanding, the discussion is carried out on a level where direct influence is not discussed.

85. Several both earlier and later editions exist, but this (or the edition from 1880) is the one that Nietzsche most likely read.

86. I have modified, according to KSB 6, 111, the translation by Christopher Middleton in *Selected Letters of Friedrich Nietzsche* (Indianapolis: Hackett, 1996).

87. These papers are in the Goethe-Schiller Archive in Weimar with the classification number GSA 71/41.

88. The longest continual discussion is to be found in *Über die vierfache Wurzel des Satzes vom zureichende Grunde,* sec. 8, titled "Spinoza" and covering about five and a half pages. To exemplify Schopenhauer's attitude, I quote from *Parerga und Paralipomena,* "Fragmente zur Geschichte der Philosophie," sec. 12: "Durch alles dieses ist denn Spinozas 'Ethica' durchweg ein Gemisch von Falschem und Wahrem, Bewunderungswürdigem und Schlechtem." At least one of Nietzsche's early quotations of Spinoza seems to come from Schopenhauer: the one in *Human, All Too Human,* 93, which is quoted in *Parerga und Paralipomena,* Vol. 2, 258.

89. This is true for the first edition of the work from 1866. In later enlarged editions, Spinoza is referred to much more frequently. Wurzer suggests that Lange's discussion of Spinoza was important to the early Nietzsche, but that seems unlikely to me, since Nietzsche seems not to have read much in the later editions of Lange.

90. There is a marginal line along the last thirteen lines of page 68, where the text discusses the seventh and last axiom of Spinoza's *Ethics.* Nietzsche made some excerpts from the book, and his copy contains, apart from the marginal line in the Spinoza section, a few dog-ears and spots distributed throughout the entire volume.

91. KSA 7, 19[47]. Nietzsche never mentioned Spinoza in his letters before 1875 (actually before 1877). The only mention of Spinoza in the letters to Nietzsche from this period is that Paul Deussen, June 29, 1866, told Nietzsche that he had read Spinoza.

92. An unpublished book bill in the Goethe-Schiller Archive shows that the book was sent to Nietzsche on July 13, 1875. See also Campioni et al., *Nietzsches persönliche Bibliothek.*

93. KSA 8, 9[1], 133 and 142. Nietzsche's excerpts are from pages 6 and 26, respectively, of Dühring's book. Wurzer, in his *Nietzsche und Spinoza,* 40–41, assumes (like many other readers) that the discussion is Nietzsche's own, and his analysis and conclusions are therefore mistaken.

94. There are only four or five mentions of Spinoza's name during these four years: one two-line quotation from the *Ethics* in Latin (KSA 8, 19[68]) from late 1876 and three highly complimentary remarks in his published books *Human, All Too Human,* 157 and 475, and *Assorted Opinions and Maxims,* 408. Nietzsche also, in *Human, All Too Human,* 93, quoted Spinoza's statement "Each man has as much right as he has power" in Latin. Nietzsche almost certainly took the quotation from Schopenhauer, who quoted the same words in *Parerga.*

95. See the discussion of this section in my forthcoming study *Nietzsche's Knowledge of Philosophy.* Spinoza was not the only of these thinkers whom, it seems, Nietzsche had not really read at this time. This is also true for Pascal and Rousseau.

96. In two letters from November 1877 and November 1879, the first to Rée and the second to Schmeitzner. The review was published in the *Jenaer Literaturzeitung,* October 13, 1877.

97. It is not known when he read it; early in the period 1875–80 seems most likely. I believe that Nietzsche annotated pages in the chapter on Spinoza in the book but have not confirmed this.

98. There is no index to the work in two volumes, but Spinoza is mentioned in the first volume on pages 45, 186, 281, and 344 and is discussed on pages 361–63. None of these pages are annotated by Nietzsche (in his otherwise heavily annotated copy), but the pages immediately preceding and following the longer discussion are annotated. Nietzsche read this work in the first edition in 1873 and 1874. He acquired the second edition from 1877 in that year and read it then and in 1881 and 1885.

Wurzer, *Nietzsche und Spinoza,* suggests that this work was important for Nietzsche's view of Spinoza, but that seems unlikely to me.

99. M, 481, 497, and 550.

100. Nietzsche's comments about Spinoza in *Dawn* were written before the summer of 1881 and thus before his intensive reading of Fischer.

101. Kuno Fischer's *Geschichte der neuern Philosophie: Zweiter Band: Descartes' Schule. Spinoza's Leben, Werke und Lehre* exists in a large number of editions, and Nietzsche seems to have used the second or third edition from 1865 or 1880.

These editions are at present not available to me, and I will therefore refer to the content of the fourth edition from 1898, but Fischer claims in the preface that the essence of his text and argument remains unchanged: "Er [der Geschichtspunkt] ist in allen vier Auflagen nach stets erneuter Prüfung unverändert geblieben, nur im Einzelnen, wie es der litterarische Stand der Sache mit sich gebracht hat, noch genauer und ausführlicher entwickelt worden." The edition from 1898 is about fifteen pages longer than the edition from 1880.

The first part of the volume (the first book) consists of only eighty-four pages discussing Geulinx and Malebranche. The lion's share of the volume, books two and three, deals with Spinoza, pages 87–574. Book two consists of twelve chapters discussing Spinoza's life and works, and book three consists of thirteen chapters dealing with his teaching. The account is thus detailed, and Fischer was a good historian of philosophy. The work contains no index.

Fischer's account of Spinoza and his philosophy was apparently translated into English by F. Schmidt as *Benedict Spinoza* (Edinburgh, 1882).

102. KSA 9, 11[132, 137, 193, 194, 307], 12[52], 14[20], and 15[17].

The page-and-a-half note 11[193] is especially important. It contains excerpts relating to Spinoza's rejection of altruism, free will, and teleology and ends with a critique of Spinoza's emphasis of "Selbsterhaltung" (self-preservation), which Nietzsche later will contrast with the more active will to power. But in this note he counters self-preservation by emphasizing that being a herd animal and being a function for others or for the group is older than the egoism implied by preservation of the individual.

Some of the statements and excerpts may possibly have worked as a stimulus for Nietzsche's thoughts about the will to power.

103. KSA 9, 11[307].

104. KSA 11, 12[52] and 15[17].

105. For example, William Hartpole Lecky's *Sittengeschichte Europas von Augustus bis auf Karl den Grossen* (1879) contains a few mentions of Spinoza, and so does Otto Liebmann's *Zur Analysis der Wirklichkeit* (Strassburg, 1880), in which Spinoza's rejection of free will is discussed on page 667, near which Nietzsche drew a marginal line and wrote "sehr gut."

106. The mild critique is done in sections 37 and 99; the first of these is connected with the more severe critique in section 333.

107. KSA 11, 25[454] and 26[432].

108. The quotation in the note KSA 10, 7[31] is taken from page 12 of Hartmann's book. I have not found the exact words of note 7[35], but Hartmann's said the same thing on pages 27, 37, and 173. The notes 7[20 and 108] are too general to be identified with any particular reading but are most probably also a response to his reading of Hartmann.

109. Spinoza is discussed on pages 6–23 and is thereafter mentioned on more than ten pages. The book contains an index, but this is very unreliable; most names are mentioned about twice as often as suggested by it.

Although Nietzsche's copy of the book is heavily annotated, none of Hartmann's discussions of Spinoza are annotated by Nietzsche.

Hartmann emphasized Spinoza's "pure intellectualism" and referred to and classified his morality as "individual-eudämonistisch" (where *eudämonistisch* means "maximazing the feeling of pleasure"), "raffinirte Egoismus," and "egoistische Pseudomoral."

110. For example, he wrote "Spinoza ist deshalb kaum ein grosses Philosoph zu nennen; da er wie die Scholastiker mit fertigen Dogmen anfängt" (6). Compare also pages xiii and 50.

111. KSA 11, 26[416].

112. KSA 11, 36[32].

113. KSA 12, 5[71], written between the summer of 1886 and the autumn of 1887.

114. In all his later published discussions and references to Spinoza, from *Beyond Good and Evil* onward, Nietzsche was almost exclusively critical of him. JGB, 5, 13, 25, and 198; FW V, 349 and 372; GM, Preface, 5, and II:6 and 15, III:7; GD, "Fabel," 1 (see KSA 14, 415); GD, "Reason," 4; GD, "Expeditions," 23, 49; and AC, 17.

115. KSA 12, 7[4]. The excerpts about Spinoza cover about three and a half pages. See "Beiträge zur Quellenforschung mitgeteilt von Thomas H. Brobjer," *Nietzsche-Studien* 30 (2001): 418–21.

116. On pages 308, 319, 327, 348, and 352.

117. GM, II, 6, from Höffding, 319. This "Lesefrucht" or source from Höffding has been identified by Marco Brusotti and published in his "Beiträge zur Quellenforschung," *Nietzsche-Studien* 21 (1992): 390–91. The long discussion in GM, II, 15, comes from Fischer (via KSA 12, 7[4]), 434–35 and 364, in the fourth edition from 1898.

118. Letter to Meta von Salis, June 17, 1888.

119. Nietzsche's project of a revaluation of all values also seems to have its explicit origin at this time as shown, for example, by his note KSA 9, 11[76], from shortly before

August 1881: "*Changing the setting of values* [*Veränderung der Werthschätzung*]—is my task." However, the roots of this project go back to the very beginning of Nietzsche's philosophizing.

For a discussion of the meaning of Nietzsche's revaluation of all values, see my article "On the Revaluation of Values," *Nietzsche-Studien* 25 (1996): 342–48.

120. There is still much debate over whether Nietzsche meant it to be a natural scientific hypothesis (or truth) or an existential one. I find the evidence much more convincing that the center of gravity for Nietzsche was on the existential sense, even if in his notebooks he also contemplated it as a scientific theory. However, it is true that Nietzsche's reading of natural scientific books is likely to have contributed importantly to, and been a stimulus for, his discovery of the idea.

121. At Schulpforta, Nietzsche had already encountered some Christian teachings similar to the idea of eternal recurrence. His personal tutor, professor Robert Buddensieg, published a scholarly work (published together with the Pforta *Jahresbericht* in 1856) with the title *Gottes Wort und die Wiederbringung aller Dinge*. Since Nietzsche had a warm friendship with Buddensieg and often discussed religion with him, it is not unlikely that Nietzsche read this work. Although the expression "Wiederbringung aller Dinge" does not have the same meaning as eternal recurrence, some of its meaning echoes in it, and Nietzsche himself used the expression a number of times in the early 1870s. Furthermore, the Old Testament states: "The Earth is forever the same. What has been will be again, what has happened will happen again. There is nothing new under the sun." One other later such distinctly religious stimulus to the idea of eternal recurrence could have been the lecture by the Basel philosopher Karl Steffensen that Nietzsche attended in October 1877. An eyewitness account of the occasion states: "I looked over at him out of the corner of my eye, while the other man at the rostrum celebrated the Christian rebirth of Plato in Origen and revelled in the *pochaastasix,* the eternal bringing back of all things, that boldest thought of the Greek church father." Edgar Steiger's account of the incident is published in Sander L. Gilman, *Begegnungen mit Nietzsche* (Bonn: Bouvier Verlag, 1981), 346–48; 95–99 in the English translation of this work.

An early religious inspiration to the thought of eternal recurrence is not unlikely. Nietzsche himself states: "I have found this idea in earlier thinkers: every time it was determined by other ulterior considerations (—mostly theological, in favor of the *creator spiritus*)" (KSA 13, 14[188]).

122. Stauss wrote, while discussing the modern conception of the universe in *The Old Faith and the New* (translated to the English by J. Fitzgerald): "He here [Kant in his *General History and Theory of the Heavens* (1755)] calls the world 'a phoenix, which but consumes itself in order to rise rejuvenated from its ashes.' [...] Neither, as already hinted, is any destruction final. Even as the order of Nature, such as it now exists, has evolved itself out of Chaos, so likewise can it again evolve itself out of the new Chaos occasioned by its destruction [...] If Kant, in so doing, speaks of the beginning of all things, we may take this quite seriously according to his theory; as, however, he admits that in the future also, after the destruction of our solar system, an exactly similar condi-

tion will result from the dissolution of its parts, he cannot determine whether in the first instance also this condition was not the result of a preceding destruction. Much less can we, who recognize a beginning of the Cosmos as little as an end, regard the matter in a different light.[...] At bottom this was the Cosmic conception of the Stoics; only they extended this view to the whole Cosmos, and conceived of it in harmony with their pantheism. The Primal Being secretes the world as its body, but gradually absorbs it again, so that at last this produces a universal conflagration, which reduces all things to their primal condition, i.e., resolves them in the divine primordial fire. But the great year of the world having thus elapsed, the formation of a new world begins, in which, according to a whimsical Stoic notion, the former one was exactly reproduced, down to particular events and persons (Socrates and Xanthippe). [...] According to Buddhism, also, there never has been a time when worlds and beings have not been evolved in endless revolutions of birth and decay: every world has arisen from a former ruined world.[...] These auguries of religion and philosophy have in recent times gained scientific probability, owing to two discoveries in physics. From the gradual diminution of the orbit of Encke's comet has been inferred the existence in space of matter, which [...] must gradually [...] narrow the orbits of the planets, and produce finally their collision with the sun. The other discovery is that of the conservation of energy" (174–81).

123. KSA 9, 11[163], written during the autumn of 1881.

124. In Hölderlin's writings there are statements that resemble Nietzsche's idea of eternal recurrence.

As early as 1900 Gustav Naumann, in his *Zarathustra-Commentar: Dritter Theil* (Leipzig, 1900), 9, emphasized that one can find the seed of Nietzsche's idea of eternal recurrence in "die Wiederkunftsidee des Hyperion" and gives eight page references to places in *Hyperion* where the idea is prominent. Apart from the references given by Naumann, the idea can also be found elsewhere in Hölderlin's texts, especially in *Empedokles*.

The importance of Hölderlin as an origin for this idea of Nietzsche's can be further strengthened not only by adding more examples and allusions to the idea in Hölderlin's texts but also by noting the existence of the idea in Neumann's text, biography, and selection of Hölderlin, *Moderne Klassiker: Deutsche Literaturgeschichte der neueren Zeit in Biographien, Kritiken und Proben: Friedrich Hölderlin* (Cassel, 1853, 1859), which Nietzsche possessed and had read intensively already in 1861. Neumann, in fact, explicitly claims that Hölderlin proclaimed a recurrence of all things: "The poet teaches a return of all things [Der Dichter lehrt eine Wiederkehr aller Dinge]" (167). Other, but less obvious, references to the idea of eternal recurrence can also be found in Neumann's text: "everything returns.—And what will happen, has already happened [es kehret alles wieder.—Und was geschehen soll, ist schon vollendet]" (44) and several similar statements at other places in the text.

For a more detailed discussion of Nietzsche's reading of Neumann's book on Hölderlin, see my "A Discussion and Source of Hölderlin's Influence on Nietzsche," *Nietzsche-Studien* 30 (2001): 397–412.

125. Nietzsche seems to have encountered and accepted the essential ingredients of the idea of eternal recurrence, including the existential affirmation of history and of a recurrence, by 1873 when reading David Hume. Compare the discussion of Nietzsche's reading of Hume in my study *Nietzsche and the "English."*

For a different, but similar, analysis of Hume's importance for Nietzsche's concept of eternal recurrence, see Margot Fleischer, "Hume—Auch eine Quelle für Nietzsches Lehre der ewigen Wiederkunft des Gleichen?" *Nietzsche-Studien* 25 (1996): 255–60. I did not find this article until after I had written my own account.

126. See, for example, the discussion in Wurzer, *Nietzsche und Spinoza.*

127. Nietzsche refers to Pythagoras's theory that everything returns in exactly the same manner in UB II, 2, and in KSA 7, 19[134], from 1872–73.

See also M. Djuric, "Die antiken Quellen der Wiederkunftslehre," *Nietzsche-Studien* 8 (1979): 1–16.

128. H. Lichtenberger has pointed out that A. Blanqui expressed ideas similar to Nietzsche's idea of eternal recurrence in his book *L'éternité par les astres* (Paris, 1872). Nietzsche listed the title of this work in his notebooks during the autumn of 1883. He may have had an interest in the work due to eternal recurrence (although it is not known whether he ever read it), but since the note was written two years after the discovery, Blanqui is unlikely to have been a source of Nietzsche's idea.

129. Dühring discussed the development of the universe in the second chapter of part 2 of his *Cursus der Philosophie als streng wissenschaftlicher Weltanschauung und Lebensgestaltung* (Leipzig, 1875) with the title "Grundgesetze des Universums: 1. Wesen des Naturgesetzes […] Die wiederholten und die einmaligen Entwicklung," especially on the pages 77–85, which are annotated in Nietzsche's copy of the book. Dühring, who was against the idea of repetition (and denied the possibility of the eternity of the world), wrote: "Nun versteht es sich von selbst, dass die Principien des Lebensreizes mit ewiger Wiederholung derselben Formen nicht verträglich sind. […] Aus dem, was zählbar ist, kann auch nur eine erschöpfbare Anzahl von Combinationen folgen. Aus dem aber, was seinem Wesen nach ohne Widerspruch gar nicht als etwas Zählbares concipirt werden darf, muss auch die unbeschränkte Mannichfaltigkeit der lagen und Beziehungen hervorgehen können" (84–85). This is part of a more extensive argument and discussion by Dühring. Nietzsche also later, in 1888 (KSA 13, 14[188]), referred to and criticized Dühring's views on this question.

Nietzshe read the book in 1881 (and possibly also in 1875, 1883, 1885, and 1888), that is, near the time of his own discovery of the idea.

130. Nietzsche wrote in a note from between the early part of 1881 to the autumn of the same year: "Wer nicht an einen *Kreisprozeß des Alls* glaubt, *muß* an den *willkürlichen* Gott glauben—so bedingt sich meine Betrachtung im Gegensatz zu allen bisherigen theistischen! (s. Vogt p. 90)" (KSA 9, 11[312]). Nietzsche was referring to J. G. Vogt's *Die Kraft: Eine real-monistische Weltanschauung* (1878). Nietzsche's copy of this work is annotated, including on page 90.

131. For an important contribution to the understanding of the eternal recurrence, see Paolo D'Iorio's detailed investigation and discussion of the natural scientific origin and component of this idea in "Cosmologie de l'éternel Retour," *Nietzsche-Studien* 24 (1995): 62–123, where he states: "le livre de Caspari, *Der Zusammenhang der Dinge*, [...] est la source principale de ce cours de reflexions" (78).

132. Nietzsche used the expression for the first time in two notes from the autumn of 1881, KSA 9, 15[20] and 16[22], and thereafter in FW, sec. 276 (1882). He also referred to it in a letter to Overbeck from June 5, 1882.

133. "Beiträge zur Quellenforschung mitgeteilt von Paolo D'Iorio," *Nietzsche-Studien* 22 (1993): 395–97.

134. KSA 9, 11[195]. The next note, on the same theme, under the title "Zum 'Entwurf einer neuen Art zu leben'" is at the end dated with the words "Sils-Maria 26. August 1881," that is, only a few weeks after his discovery of the idea of eternal recurrence.

135. Hellwald, *Culturgeschichte* (1874), 128: "*Zarathustra*, der grosse Prophet der Erânier, gewöhnlich nach der von den Griechen überlieferten Form Zoroaster [...] genannt, dessen Name im Zend übrigens eine schmucklose Bedeutung besitzt [footnote: Die noch von *Kolb, Culturgeschichte*. I. S 121 angeführte Bedeutung des Namens Zarathustra als 'Goldstern' ist längst widerlegt und von Prof. *Fried. Müller* erklärt als 'muthige Kameele besitzend' [...] stammte aus Azerbeidschan und war geboren in der Stadt Urmi am gleichnamigen See zwischen Kaspi- und Van-See. Im dreissigsten Lebenjahre verliess er die Heimat, zog östlich in die Provinz Aria und verbrachte dort zehn Jahre in Einsamkeit des Gebirges mit der Abfassung des Zend-Avesta beschäftigt. Nach Verfluss dieser Zeit wandte er sich nach Balkh, verkündete seine neue Lehre."

136. Hellwald, *Culturgeschichte* (1874), 129: "So begegnen wir bei den alten Erâniern zum ersten Male dem Wahngebilde von einer *sittlichen Weltordning*, eine Vorstellung, zu welcher nur höher gestiegene Völker gelangen und deren Einfluss auf die Culturentfaltung von unberechenbarem Werthe ist."

137. EH, "Why I Am a Destiny," 3.

138. "Das Feuer und die Sonne gelten in ihrer Reinheit nur als Symbole Gottes; deshalb soll der Betende sein Geschicht dem Feuer oder der Sonne zuwenden" (130). Compare the first book of *Thus Spoke Zarathustra*, where Zarathustra holds his speech to the sun.

"Während die Brahmanenlehre zur geistigen und körperlichen Unthätigkeit führte, zeigten Zarathustra und sein Parismus in der Welt einen grossen Kampfplatz, auf dem Jeder mitzukämpfen berufen ist—den Kampf um's Dasein!" (130–35). Compare the will to power, which Nietzsche lets Zarathustra introduce in the section "Of Self-overcoming."

"Wie schon erwähnt, ging es den Erâniern über Alles die Wahrheit zu sprechen [...] Wohlanständigkeit im Reden, Wahrheitsliebe und Rechtlichkeit mit strengem Worthalten seien hervorstechende Züge des persischen Nationalcharakters gewesen" (131). Compare "Von tausend und Einem Ziele," *Thus Spoke Zarathustra:* "'Wahrheit reden und gut mit Bogen und Pfeil verkehren'—so dünkte es jenem Volke zugleich lieb und schwer, aus dem mein Name kommt—der Name, welcher mir zugleich lieb und schwer ist." Nietzsche also restated this slightly differently in EH, "Schicksal," 3.

139. JGB, 23.

140. Ibid., 6.

141. "What is good?—All that heightens the feeling of power, the will to power, power itself in man. What is bad?—All that proceeds from weakness. What is happiness?—The feeling that power *increases*—that a resistance is overcome. *Not* contentment, but more power." AC, 2.

142. JGB, 259.

143. Rée, strongly influenced by Darwin and Schopenhauer, emphasized evolution and utility but also a more general feeling of pleasure and displeasure as the cause of vanity. Power is not prominent in his discussion of vanity and honor (and he never used the expression "will to power"), but occasionally he referred to power and somewhat more often to the feeling of superiority (*"das Gefühl der Superiorität"*). Rée, for example, wrote: "Wenn Jemand uns Leid zufügt, so beweist er hierdurch seine Macht, seine Superiorität über uns. [...] Das Vergnügen, Jemanden wieder zu ärgern hat denselben Ursprung. [...] Der Urspung der Rachelust ist die Eitelkeit (das Vergnügen, sich ausgezeichnet, superior über dem zu fühlen, der seine Superiorität über uns beweisen wollte) [...] Die Intensität der Rache erhöht man gern durch *Grausamkeit*. Denn jede Qual, die wir unserem Feinde zufügen, ist ein Beweisstück unserer Macht über ihn" (105-7). Surprisingly, no one seems to have pointed earlier to Rée as the first stimulus for Nietzsche's concept of the will to power.

144. KSA 8, 23[63], from the end of 1876 to the summer of 1877.

145. Nietzsche used the expression "will to power" once in the summer of 1880, KSA 9, 4[239]; once at the end of 1880, KSA 9, 7[206]; once during the winter of 1880–81, KSA 9, 9[14]; once in the summer of 1881, KSA 9, 11[346]; once or twice in 1882, FW, 249, and KSA 10, 5[1]; and then extensively during 1883 and thereafter.

However, at this time he also frequently used other similar expressions, such as "Gefühl der Macht" and "Gefühl von Macht" (feeling of power). Nietzsche used these expressions for the first time in KSA 8, 20[8] and in MA, 142, and thereafter about forty times in the notebooks from 1880 and 1881, starting in the summer of 1880, and these notes were then used for the writing of sections 23, 112, 113, 140, 184, 205, 348, 356, and 360 of *Dawn*, in which the expressions also are used. Nietzsche continued to use these expressions, as equivalent to will to power, after 1881 in, for example, *Twilight of the Idols* and in a fairly large number of notes from 1886 to 1888.

146. This does not mean that there do not exist several excellent studies of Nietzsche's concept of will to power. To mention but four examples, Walter Kaufmann has a long, detailed, and interesting chapter titled "The Discovery of the Will to Power," in his *Nietzsche: Philosopher, Psychologist, Antichrist* (Princeton, NJ: Princeton University Press, 1974), 178–210, but in those days not enough was known about Nietzsche's actual reading to connect it to direct sources. Volker Gerhardt, in his *Vom Willen zur Macht*

(Berlin and New York: Walter de Gruyter, 1996), argues that "Der 'Wille zur Macht' hat also einen werkästhetischen Ursprung; seine Konzeption stammt aus dem Erfahrungszusammenhang der kulturellen Selbstproduktion schöpferischer Individuen" and therefore says less about direct influences, although he discusses Schopenhauer's importance and several others. For Günter Abel's discussion of will to power in his *Nietzsche: Die Dynamik der Willen zur Macht und die ewige Wiederkehr*, 2nd ed. (Berlin and New York: Walter de Gruyter, 1998), see the discussion in the main text below. A recent interesting English-language study is Linda L. Williams's *Nietzsche's Mirror* (Lanham, MD: Rowman and Littlefield, 2001), but it contains no discussion of the sources of the idea and has no reference to German discussions of the question.

147. Nietzsche possessed, read, and annotated Georg Heinrich Schneider's *Der tierische Wille: Systematische Darstellung und Erklärung der tierischen Triebe und deren Entstehung, Entwickelung und Verbreitung im Thierreiche als Grundlage zu einer vergleichenden Willenslehre* (Leipzig, 1880), xx+447 pages, in 1883. The reading of this work is clearly relevant for Nietzsche's view of will and will to power.

Nietzsche also possessed and had read Schneider's *Der menschliche Wille vom Standpunkte der neueren Entwicklungstheorien. (Des "Darwinismus")* (Berlin, 1882), but it is not known when. Nietzsche annotated his copy sparingly in the following chapters: "Die Selection des grosse Weltgericht," "Die Vervollkommnung der Menschheit durch die Selection" in the first part and chapters 12 and 15 in the third part; "Das Verhältniss der Gefühle zu den Vorstellungen und zum Willen"; and "Gute und böse oder moralische und unmoralische Handlungen."

148. Nietzsche read this work by Hellwald in 1881 and 1883 (and perhaps also a little in 1875). Hellwald strongly emphasized the importance of power and of survival of the fittest, and the book was dedicated to the great German Darwinist Häckel.

149. If Nietzsche wrote the comment during his reading of the book in 1880, it would indicate that Baumann, perhaps together with Rée, should be regarded as the main source to Nietzsche's concept of power. However, we do not know when he wrote it down, and 1883 is at least as likely as 1880.

150. On page eighty-two Dumont wrote: "Es ist also nöthig, den Begriff der Kraft an die Stelle des Begriffs der Fähigkeiten zu setzen oder mindestens dies letzte Wort nur in einem ganz relativen Sinne zu nehmen. So würden wir heute, um die gleichen Ansichten Hamilton's auszudrücken, sagen, dass Vergnügen immer dann entsteht, wenn der Inbegriff der Kräfte, der das Ich constituirt, eine Vermehrung erfährt, ohne dass diese Vermehrung beträchtlich genug ist, um eine Aufhebung des Zusammenhangs dieser Kräfte herbeizuführen; Schmerz ist im Gegentheil vorhanden, wenn die Qualität der Kräfte eine Verminderung erfährt.

Nicht in der Verausgabung der Kraft erblicken wir die Bedingung des Vergnügens, sondern vielmehr in dem Empfange derselben. […] Ebenso verhält es sich mit Bain in seinen beiden Abhandlungen: 'Die Sinne und der Verstand' und 'Geist und Körper' [the latter Nietzsche possessed]. Er leitet dort das Vergnügen von einem Zuwachs und das Leiden von einer Verminderung irgendwelcher oder aller Lebensthätigkeiten ab. Nun, dies ist gewiss, dass die Steigerung der Thätigkeiten eine Verausgabung und Verminderng der Kraft herbeiführen muss und umgekehrt. Infolge einer leichten Ungenauigkeit des Ausdrucks würde diese Definitionen gerade das Gegentheil der unserigen besagung und Bain würde das Vergnügen dahin verlegen, wo sich nach unserer Auffassung vielmehr die Ermüdung und der Schmerz befinden." Nietzsche's underlinings. Near the first two underlings, Nietzsche also made five marginal lines (or it might possibly be an "NB").

151. We do not know when Nietzsche acquired the book, but it is volume 22 in the series Internationalle Wissenschaftliche Bibliothek, from which we know that he bought about twenty volumes in the mid-1870s, that is, directly as they were published. He seems to have subscribed to the series. This makes it likely that he acquired the book in 1876 or 1877. I am not aware of any examination of Nietzsche's reading of this important book.

152. With the exception of Nietzsche's annotations in Drossbach, discussed in Rüdiger Schmidt's "Nietzsches Drossbach-Lektüre. Bemerkungen zum Ursprung des literarischen Projekts 'Der Wille zur Macht,'" *Nietzsche-Studien* 17 (1988): 465–77, this information seems until now not to have been available and not to have been used.

153. I discuss Nietzsche's reading of and relation to Bain in more detail in my *Nietzsche and the "English."*

154. This was suggested by Baumgarten on page 145 of "Mitteilungen und Bemerkungen über den Einfluß Emerson auf Nietzsche," *Jahrbuch für Amerikastudien* 1 (1956): 93–152.

George J. Stack, in his *Nietzsche and Emerson: An Elective Affinity* (Athens: Ohio University Press, 1992), argues much more extensively for this claim in the chapter "Power in Nature and the Search after Power," 138–75.

Nietzsche read Emerson's *Essays* during the relevant period, but we have no evidence that he read *The Conduct of Life* then.

155. F. Decher, "Der eine Wille und die vielen Willen. Schopenhauer—Mainländer—Nietzsche," *Nietzsche-Studien* 25 (1996): 221–38, argues for the importance of Mainländer. However, since Nietzsche seems to have read Mainländer too early and too late, Decher does not explicitly claim that Mainländer was a direct source or stimulus.

156. "Das erste seiner Trauerspiele ist der in der Schweiz und am Rhein begonnene Manfred, in dramatischer Beziehung ein Ungethüm, man möchte sagen, der Monolog eines Sterbenden, in den tiefsten Fragen und Problemen wühlend, erschütternd durch die fruchtbare Erhabenheit dieses geisterbeherrschenden Uebermenschen, entzückend durch die prachtvolle, wunderbar schöne Diktion, aber undramatisch im höchsten Grad." KGW I.2, 12[4], 345.

It seems to me not improbable that Nietzsche's words may have been inspired by some secondary source.

157. For a discussion of the relatively frequent nineteenth-century use of the words *Übermensch* and *übermenschlich* and of other components than the "great men" idea of the Übermensch, such as its similarity to Nietzsche's conception of the Greek gods (as ideals), to Plato's and Aristotle's conception of the highest forms of human life, to its biological

evolutionary components, and to other authors' previous use of the term, see the chapter "The *Übermensch*" in my *Nietzsche's Ethics of Character: A Study of Nietzsche's Ethics and its Place in the History of Moral Thinking* (Uppsala: Uppsala University Press, 1995).

158. Nietzsche did not coin the word "*Übermensch*." According to *Duden Deutsches universalwörterbuch* (Mannheim: Dudenverlag, 1989), *Übermensch* means far superior to the ordinary man, transcending the limits of human nature or godlike man. The word existed in ancient Greek, although apparently not until after the classical era. Liddell and Scott's *Greek-English Lexicon* (Oxford, UK: Clarendon, 1991; impression of 1889 edition) lists two occurrences of the word "*hyperanthropos*," translated as superman, in Dionysius of Halicarnassos and Lucian. The *Thesaurus Linguae Graecae* confirms these and adds another twelve references to the words "*hyperanthropon*" and "*hyperanthropos*," of which one use in Plutarch and one each in the Scholia (i.e., later commentaries, to Aeschylus and Pindar, are the most interesting). It is likely that Nietzsche had read at least the Lucian reference to *hyperanthropos*. He possessed two copies of the complete works of Lucian in German translation, and he referred to Lucian (but not to his use of "*hyperanthropos*") in works, notes, and letters in his early philological period.

There also exist several Latin versions of the word. In German the oldest evidence for the use of the word "*Übermensch*" is in the theological literature from the sixteenth and seventeenth centuries. Herder used it on several occasions, and Goethe took it over from him. Goethe used it, in the sense of genius and a complete and strong human being, at least twice—in the poem "Zueignung" and in *Faust*, Part I, line 490. After Goethe it was used by Hippel, Jean Paul, and Hilpert. Jean Paul's use of it is particularly interesting since he, like Nietzsche later, associated it both with the Homeric gods and heroes and with Napoleon. Others who used it before Nietzsche are Daumer and Grabbe. Most of this information is taken from the gigantic *Deutsches Wörterbuch* (Leipzig, 1936), started by Jacob and Wilhelm Grimm and continued by Victor Dullmayr. Janz, without referring to most of the names I have mentioned above, claimed that according to Gustav Naumann's *Zarathustra-Kommentar* (Leipzig, 1899–1900), the word "*Übermensch*" was also used by Novalis and Heine, and Nietzsche had read at least Heine extensively.

Nietzsche came from a family of pastors and studied theology for one term at the university, so it is not impossible that he had come across the first theological German references to the word "*Übermensch*." He had only read a little of Herder, but Goethe, of course, Nietzsche knew well. The reference to "*Übermensch*" in *Faust* he would have read several times. Nietzsche had also read several of Jean Paul's books, but it is unclear which. In Nietzsche's library he had one work by Daumer (in which he had made annotations). He owned Grabbe's *Napoleon oder die hundert Tage* and two volumes from his collected works.

The word "*übermenschlich*" is common and has been in much greater use than the word "*Übermensch*." Among many others, it has been used by Luther, Herder, Goethe, Schopenhauer, Strauss, O. Jahn, Novalis, G. Freytag, Niebuhr, Lessing, Lichtenberg, Immermann, Mommsen, E. T. A. Hoffmann, and Dühring. In Nietzsche's copy of Dühring's *Der Werth des Lebens* (1865), he underlined the word *"Übermenschlich,"* and only that word, and drew a marginal line by it on page 6. All of these are authors Nietzsche had read, mostly extensively, and he had works by most of them in his library.

159. On page 618 in Liebmann and 510 in Espinas. This has been pointed out by Marie-Luise Haase, "Der Übermensch in '*Also sprach Zarathustra*' und im 'Zarathustra-Nachlaß 1882–1885,'" *Nietzsche-Studien* 13 (1984): 240.

160. Nihilism is discussed in sections 10 and 208 of *Jenseits von Gut und Böse* (1886) and became a major motif in *Zur Genealogie der Moral* (1887). Later it was also important in *Twilight of the Idols, The Antichrist,* and *Ecce Homo.*

161. One of the projected four books of his planned work "Will to Power"/ "Revaluation of All Values" was going to deal with the problem of nihilism.

162. Prosper Mérimée's "Lettre à l'éditeur" in Turgenev's *Pères et enfants* (1863).

163. Nietzsche possessed his *Le roman naturaliste* (Paris, 1884) and had fairly heavily annotated the chapter "Le roman du nihilisme," 29–50, in it. It is not known when Nietzsche read this work.

164. See Elisabeth Kuhn's excellent study *Friedrich Nietzsches Philosophie des europäischen Nihilismus* (Berlin and New York: Walter de Gruyter, 1992). I have taken the information about Nietzsche's reading of Turgenev's *Pères et enfants* from Kuhn's account. See also her articles "Nihilismus" and "Décadence" in *Nietzsche Handbuch,* edited by Henning Ottmann (Stuttgart and Weimar: Verlag J. B. Metzler, 2000).

165. KSA 8, 23[140].

166. Nietzsche only used the word *"décadence"* once at this time, in a note relating to his reading of the Goncourt brothers' novel *Manette Salomon* (1867), where he referred to Delacroix as related to Wagner and both of them as representing *décadence.* Shortly before, in a note with a page reference to the chapter on décadence in Bourget's book, he had discussed the "<u>style</u> of <u>decline</u> by Wagner" ["<u>Stil</u> des <u>Verfalls</u> bei Wagner"], KSA 11, 24[7], from the winter of 1883–84.

In his *Essais de psychologie contemporaine* (Paris, 1883) Bourget discusses Baudelaire, Renan, Flaubert, Taine, and Stendhal. Two of the chapters on Baudelaire are called "Le Pessimisme de Baudelaire," 9–17, and "Théorie de la décadence," 18–25. Two further chapters on Flaubert are also of special importance: "Du Romantisisme," 123–38, and "Du Nihilisme de Gustave Flaubert," 139–50.

This book is not in Nietzsche's library. He seems to have borrowed it from the public library in Nice. However, he also possessed, read, and annotated the second volume by Bourget, *Nouveaux essais de psychologie contemporaine* (Paris, 1885), in 1885. This work contained discussions of decadence and nihilism and a related emphasis on Schopenhauer's influence on French literature.

167. In the 1880s Nietzsche read, among others, French literary critical works by Sainte-Beuve, Taine, Renan, Brunetière, Bourget, d'Autrevilly, Paul Albert, Lois Desprez, Eugène Fromentin, Bérard Varagnac, Émile Gebhart, Jules Lemaître, Emil Montégut, Edmont Scherer, and the brothers Goncourt. For example, in Desprez's *L'évolution natu-raliste* (1884), which Nietzsche read probably in 1888, he would have encountered dis-

cussions of *décadence* in the chapter "Baudelaire et les Baudelairiens," 271–92. Nietzsche annotated the chapter sparingly.

168. See B. Wahrig-Schmidt, "'Irgendwie—jedenfalls physiologisch': Friedrich Nietzsche, Alexandre Herzen (fils) und Charles Féré 1888," *Nietzsche-Studien* 17 (1988): 434–64. Another recent work that emphasizes the biological influences on Nietzsche's view of decadence is Anette Horn, *Nietzsches Begriff der décadence: Kritik and Analyse der Moderne* (Frankfurt: Peter Lang, 2000).

169. In this beautiful parable, section 84 Nietzsche speaks of the death of the "prison-warden" (God). Thereafter the concept or expression occurs in several notes from the autumn of 1881 (KSA 9, 12[77 and 157] and 14[14, 25, 26]) and in several notes from 1885, which basically constitutes the background for his published use of it in sections 108 and 125 of FW, in several parts of *Thus Spoke Zarathustra*, and in section 343 of FW V, which was added to the book in 1887.

170. KGW I.2, 10[20], 281–82, that is, from Nietzsche's Ermanarich essay. I have used Hayman's translation, 40.

171. KSA 7, 5[116] and 7[8]. Olaf Pluta, "Zur Generse von Nietzsche's Parole 'Gott ist Todt!,'" in Renate Reschke, ed., *Zeitenwende-Werdewende* (2001), argues for the importance of Plutarch and a collection of stories from the Middle Ages, the *Gesta Romanorum*. However, he is unable to show that Nietzsche had read the latter.

172. Heine ended the book with reference to "a dying God": "Hört ihr das Glöck-chen klingeln? Kniet nieder—Man bringt die Sakramente einem sterbenden Gotte."

173. Karl Schlechta, *Nietzsches grosser Mittag* (Frankfurt, 1954), 26–27, argues that Charron may be the most likely candidate for Nietzsche's source for the phrase "God is dead" in 1881. However, Nietzsche referred to the concept of the death of God, without using the phrase, as early as 1879, that is, before he had read Charron, as discussed in the text.

174. See Eugen Biser, "Die Proklamation von Gottes Tod," *Das Hochland* 56 (1963): 137–52, for a brief general discussion.

Chapter 6: The Late Nietzsche

1. By the time he published *Die fröhliche Wissenschaft* in the summer of 1882, Nietzsche had moved into a new phase and was certain enough about it to write on the back of the book: "This book marks the conclusion of a series of writings by FRIED-RICH NIETZSCHE whose common goal it is to erect *a new image and ideal of the free spirit*. To this series belong [here he lists the title of the three volumes of *Human, All Too Human; Dawn;* and *The Joyful Science*]." In several letters to Lou Salomé, Nietzsche had stated that he was leaving the free-spirit phase. See letters to Salomé, June 27–28, July 3, and November 24, 1882 ("Do not let yourself be led stray about me—you do not believe, do you, that 'the free spirit' is my ideal?! I am—Forgive me! Dear Lou, be what you must be" ["Lassen Sie sich nicht über mich täuschen—Sie glauben doch nicht, daß 'der Freigeist' mein Ideal ist?! Ich bin—Verzeihung! Liebste Lou, seien Sie, was Sie sein müssen"]).

Later in the prefaces to *Human, All Too Human* and *Assorted Opinions and Maxims,* written in 1886, Nietzsche spoke extensively about his free-spirit period as an illness, as of him being "beside himself" and of him coming back to health in 1882–83: "And, to speak seriously: to become sick in the manner of these free spirits, to remain sick for a long time and then, slowly, slowly, to become healthy, by which I mean 'healthier,' is a fundamental *cure* for all pessimism."

2. This massive book is annotated by Nietzsche throughout, with many instances of "!," "NB," "gut," "ja," "nein," "?," and short comments such as "als ob!," "Esel," "Philister," "grundfalsch," "Falsch" but also with many longer comments.

3. Rolph was an opponent of Darwinism, and on page 114 he summarized some of the grounds for his opposition: "To briefly summarize, the aspect in which I differ from Darwin's theory are thus the following: The struggle for existence is in reality a striving for increased intake, for an increase of life, and <u>independent of the degree of availability of nourishment</u>; it occurs at all time, thus also <u>at times of surplus</u>" ["Die Punkte, in denen ich von der Darwin'schen Theorie abweiche, sind also, um es kurz zu recapituliren, folgende: Der Daseinskampf ist in Wirklichkeit ein Streben nach vermehrter Einnahme, nach Lebensmehrung, und <u>unabhängig von dem jedesmaligen Nahrungsangebot</u>; er findet jederzeit, also auch in <u>Ueberflusslage</u> statt"].

The underlinings are Nietzsche's.

4. The table of contents of Rolph's *Biologische Probleme* lists the following content:

Einleitung, 1
1. Evolutionslehre, 4
2. Subjective Systeme, 21
3. Herbert Spencer's Hedonismus, 32
4. Problem der Ernährung, 55
5. Problem der Vervollkommnung, 71 [Also called Beitrag zur Kritik des Darwinismus]
6. Problem der Fortpflanzung, 121
7. Animale oder natürliche Ethik, 170
8. Humane Ethik, 190–238

Nietzsche's copy of the book is heavily annotated and has many words and comments in the margins of pages.

5. For examples of Rolph's views on ethics and Nietzsche's response to his statements, let us look at a few of them: On pages 181–83 Rolph writes: "Ich stelle mich also mit der Behauptung, dass das <u>Rechthandeln</u> von dem Geschöpfe ein <u>Ueberschreiten der Normalen</u> verlangt, in directen Gegensatz zu *Spencer,* welcher die Einhaltung der Normalen als richtig und etisch hinstellt. Normal leben heisst stehen bleiben. Nicht aber <u>stehen bleiben,</u> sondern sich fortentwickeln ist das Gesetz der Natur und der Ethik: <u>nicht sich begnügen, sondern weiter streben.</u> Nicht bedürfnisslos bleiben, sondern <u>Bedürfnisse entwickeln</u> und befriedigen, ist die natürliche Lebensaufgabe der Geschöpfe. [In the margin to the first part of this text Nietzsche made a marginal line and wrote 'sehr sehr gut' and 'NB.']

Wenden wir die oben entwickelten Grundsätze auf die Thiere an, so gelangen wir zu der Anschauung, dass alle solitär lebenden Geschöpfe, das heisst solche, die mit ihresgleichen nicht in Berührung kommen, durchaus recht, gut und moralisch leben, wenn sie sich mit allem Kräften der <u>Verbesserung ihrer Lage</u> hingeben. Dass sie dabei andere Geschöpfe, Pflanzen und Thiere, die ihnen zur Beute fallen, schädigen, das darf uns nicht bekümmern, denn die sind zu ihrer Selbsterhaltung darauf angewiesen. [In the middle of this paragraph Nietzsche made three marginal lines and wrote 'ergo!' Along the last two lines he made one marginal line and wrote 'sehr gut.']

Das Grundprincip des thierischen Lebens ist demnach ein eminent egoistisches und erkennt kein anderes Recht an, als das der eigenen Person, als das Recht, <u>das die Macht verleiht.</u> *Spencer* freilich spricht schon auf der nierigsten Stufe organischen Lebens von einem Altruismus, auf welchen er das in der menschlichen Gesellschaft giltige Gebot der selbstlosigkeit stützt. Aber er begeht hiermit den fundamentalen und seine Ableitungen geradezu vernichtenden Fehler, dass er Egoismus und Altruismus nicht zuerst schaft und treffend zu definiren unternimmt. [Nietzsche drew a marginal line along this paragraph and wrote 'gut.']

Hätte *Spencer* das gethan, so würde er sicher gefunden haben, dass für Egoismus sowohl wie für Altruismus das einschränkende Kriterium des <u>Bewusstseins,</u> des Wollens unerlässlich ist."

On page 206 Nietzsche agreed with Rolph's view of altruism: "dass die <u>Billigkeit gegen Andere</u> nicht eine Einschränkung das Egoismus, sondern eine <u>Erweiterung des Egoismus</u> ist." (Nietzsche made a marginal line with blue pencil and wrote "NB" with a lead pencil.)

On page 207 Rolph emphasized the importance of equality for feelings of sympathy, and Nietzsche agreed with him: "In diesem Gefühl der <u>Gleichberechtigung, der Billigkeit</u> liegt die versteckte Quelle so mancher unerklärter Regungen. Hier liegt auch die Quelle der Sympathie oder des Wohlwollens, das sich nur da entwickeln kann, wo <u>das Gefühl von dem gleichen Rechte Anderer</u> stark ausgeprägt ist." (Nietzsche made two marginal lines with a blue pencil and wrote "gut" with a lead pencil in the margin at the beginning of this text. At the end is an "NB.")

The last sentence of the book, on page 238, states: "Ist er doch sicher, dass jeder <u>Fortschritt</u> in Cultur und Civilisation auch ein Uebel enthält, dass jedes Gute uns auch etwas Schlechtes bringt, jede neue Tugend den Keim zu einem Bösen in sich trägt. Die <u>moderne Humanität</u> hat uns mit einer gedankenlosen Weichherzigkeit und Weichmütigkeit, mit einer übertriebenen <u>Sucht zu vergeben</u> beschenkt, welche kein geringeres Zeichen von Sittenverfall ist als Immoralität selbst, denn sie untergräbt einerseits das öffentliche Urtheil, das <u>öffentliche Rechtgefühl</u>, während sie anderseits direct zur Unsittlichkeit anreizt." (From "Die Moderne Humanität" downward, Nietzsche drew two marginal lines.)

The underlinings are all Nietzsche's.

This book, so important for Nietzsche, ought to be carefully examined and studied. A preliminary examination has been carried out by Gregory Moore in his *Nietzsche, Biology and Metaphor* (Cambridge: Cambridge University Press, 2002).

6. See note 8 below.

7. The table of contents of *Sittlichkeit ohne "Pflicht"* (Leipzig, 1912), the German translation of Guyau's *Esquisse d'une morale sans obligation ni sanction* (Paris, 1885), lists the following content:

> Einleitung: Kritik des verschiedenen Versuch, die sittliche Verbindlichkeit metaphysisch zu rechtfertigen
>
> I. Die Triebfeder des Sittlichen vom Standpunkt der Wissenschaft aus. Erste Äquivalente für die Pflicht
>
> II. Letzte an der Aufrechterhaltung der Sittlichkeit beteilgte Äquivalente des Pflichtbegriffs
>
> III. Die Idee der Sanktion
>
> Schluss

Nietzsche's copy of the book (in French) was very heavily annotated and had many words and comments in the margins of pages. It was unfortunately lost sometime after 1942, but in the German edition from which I have quoted above, there is an appendix where all Nietzsche's marginal words and comments are reproduced (without underlines or marginal lines). See also H. E. Lampl, ed., *Zweistimmigkeit—Einstimmigkeit? Friedrich Nietzsche ind Jean-Marie Guyau* (*"Esquisse d'une morale sans obligation, ni sanction"*) (Cuxhaven, 1990). Just to reproduce Nietzsche's comments (and the corresponding text by Guyau) takes twenty-five full pages. Nietzsche had written many instances of "!," "NB," "ja," "gut," "bravo," "sehr gut," "warum?," and other words and names, including many longer comments. He also wrote "Wille zur Macht" twice and wrote several other comments relating to this, such as "das Machtgefühl" and "Macht auslassen." In addition, he wrote a number of comments relating to himself: several times "moi" and "oder meine eigene Existenz in Basel." A thorough examination of Nietzsche's debt and relation to Guyau goes beyond what is possible to do in this study but ought to be done. Compare also the brief discussion of Guyau in my forthcoming study *Nietzsche's Knowledge of Philosophy.*

8. In a long note from May or June 1885, KSA 11, 35[34], Nietzsche spoke of both of these latter works (by Guyua and Rolph) and of Paul Rée's *Der Ursprung der moralischen Empfindungen* (1877) as the three best contemporary books published about morality (and contrasted them with, among others, Hartmann's *Phänomenologie,* of which he was much more critical): "Nichts Kläglicheres als die moralistische Litteratur im jetzigen Europa. [...] Ich wüßte höchstens drei kleine Schriften herauszuheben (obwohl auch in diesen nichts Fundamentales gesagt ist): Einmal das Buch eines deutschen Juden, Paul Rée, das den Titel führt—Es verdient seiner *Form* wegen Auszeichnung und trägt etwas von jenem ächt-philosophischen habitus an sich.[...] Zweitens nenne ich das feine, schwermüthig-herzhafte Buch eines Franzosen — — — welches freilich, wie fast Alles, was jetzt aus Paris kommt, zum Übermaaß zu verstehen giebt, *wo* eigentlich heute der Pessimismus zu Hause ist: nämlich *nicht* in Deutschland. Und was hilft aller Positivismus und das entschlossene Kniebeugen vor den 'petits faits'! Man leidet in Paris wie an

kalten Herbstwinden, wie an einem Frost großer Enttäuschungen, als ob der Winter kommt, der letzte, endgültige Winter—und die Besten und Tapfersten, wie jener brave Guyau, zittern und schaudern dabei, auch wenn sie eine noch so gute Miene zu ihrem 'positivisme' machen: wer glaubt es ihnen, wozu sie uns mit Ironie überreden möchten, daß jenes Zittern und Schaudern noch zu den *Reizen* und Verführungskünsten des Lebens gehöre? Freilich: 'das Schaudern ist der Menschheit *schönster* Theil'—das hat Goethe gesagt, und Goethe—*durfte* es sagen! Aber ein Pariser?—Endlich zeichne ich die polemische Schrift eines deutschen Halb-Engländers aus, welche genug Geist, Säure und Wissenschaft enthält, um eine Vereinigung von bêtise und Darwinismus, welche Herbert Spencer unter dem Titel: 'Data of Ethics' in die Welt gesetzt hat, gründlich zu 'zersetzen': Rolph, Biologische Probleme 1881. Freilich, vom Polemischen abgesehen ist an dem Buche nichts zu loben; und im Grunde beleidigt hier, ebenso wie bei dem Buche, welches er bekämpft, das Mitreden-wollen unbedeutender Menschen auf Gebieten, wo nur eine ausgesuchte Art von Erkennenden und 'Erlebten' ohne Unbescheidenheit zu Worte kommt."

9. For discussions of Nietzsche relation to Guyau, but with little or no use of the annotations in his books, see D. Pécaud's "Ce brave Guyau," *Nietzsche-Studien* 25 (1996): 239–54; and G. C. Fidler's "On Jean-Marie Guyau, Immoraliste," *Journal of the History of Ideas* 55 (1994): 75–98.

10. "Dies Buch hat einen *komischen* Fehler: in dem Bemühen, zu beweisen, daß die moralischen Instinkte ihren Sitz im Leben selbst haben, hat Guyau übersehn, daß er das Gegenteil bewiesen hat—nämlich, daß *alle* Grundinstinkte des Lebens *unmoralisch* sind, eingerechnet die sogenannten moralischen. Die höchste Intensität des Lebens steht in der That im nothwendigen Verhältnis zu sa plus large expansion: nur ist diese der Gegensatz aller 'altruistichen' Thatsachen,—diese expansion drückt sich als unbändiger *Wille zur Macht* aus. Ebensowenig ist *Zeugung* das Symptom eines altruistischen Grundcharakters: sie entsteht aus Spaltung und Kampf in einem umäßig mit Beute überladenen Organismus, der nicht Macht genug hat, alles Eroberte einzuorganisieren."

11. I have examined and discussed Nietzsche's reading of scientific books in "Nietzsche's Reading and Knowledge of Natural Science: An Overview," in Gregory Moore and Thomas H. Brobjer, eds., *Nietzsche and Science* (Aldershot, Burlington: Ashgate, 2004), 21–50.

12. "[E]ven the German language is, through the foundation of an academy after the French model, to acquire 'sound taste' and rid itself of the questionable influence supposedly exerted upon it by Goethe—a view expressed quite recently by the Berlin academician Dubois-Reymond." UB III, 6.

Nietzsche's discussion with the Wagners is mentioned in Cosima's *Diaries* and is quoted in KSA 14, 78. Du Bois-Reymond is mentioned in the notes KSA 7, 32[83] and 35[12], 815.

13. Letter to Overbeck, August 20–21, 1881.

14. Such a collected volume appears to have been published in 1885–87 for the first time.

15. These essays were first published in 1872 and 1880, respectively.

16. Letter to Naumann, November 8, 1887.

17. However, two recent relevant papers are Dr. Nadeem Hussain's discussion of Nietzsche's reading of Mach, "Reading Nietzsche through Ernst Mach," in *Nietzsche and Science,* 111–29, and Dr. Vivette Vivarelli's work on Nietzsche and Mach, "Nietzsche e le 'spiegazioni rassicuranti' (tra Mach e Avenarius)," paper at a Nietzsche conference in Lecce, Italy, March 2003, that will be published in the proceedings.

18. For a brief discussion of how several members of the Vienna Circle regarded Nietzsche, see Kurt Rudolf Fischer's "Nietzsche and the Vienna Circle," in Babette Babich, ed., *Nietzsche, Theories of Knowledge and Critical Theory* (Dordrecht: Kluwer, 1999), 119–28.

19. This book is in fundamental ways similar to Mach's later and independently developed *Beiträge zur Analyse der Empfindungen* (1886).

20. A book bill in Weimar shows that Nietzsche received it from his bookshop in September 1876, but it seems as if he then returned it without buying it. There is no copy of the book in Nietzsche's library today. These books bills in Weimar have not been published, and therefore it has not previously been known that Nietzsche received this book by Avenarius.

21. Nietzsche frequently returned to and read books he had read before. We so far have no evidence that he read Avenarius's study before 1883–84, but a reading of it during his positivistic phase, 1875–76 to 1881–82, seems possible. For example, in three notes from between early 1880 and early 1881, KSA 9, 10[F97, F100, F101], he discusses sense perception and the relation between thinking and energy that may well have been inspired by Avenarius (or Mach).

22. KSA 10, 24[9+10+13]. That these notes are excerpts from Avenarius's book was first discovered and published in KGW VII.4/2, 665–70. Several other nearby notes also concern his reading of Avenarius.

23. KSB 6, 494ff. "Falls ich den Sommer nach Sils-Maria komme, so will ich eine Revision meiner Metaphysica und erkenntnißtheoretischen Ansichten vornehmen." Earlier in the letter, Nietzsche also criticizes Lipiner for influencing younger people toward mysticism and to feel contempt for scientific thinking.

24. It also seems as if Nietzsche and Avenarius studied in Leipzig at the same time, during 1865–68. Nietzsche studied classical philology but, in spite of his interest in Schopenhauer, Kant, and Lange, seems to have shown little interest in philosophy there. Avenarius studied philosophy and physiology. He became a professor in Zürich in 1877 and remained there until his death and was thus, like Nietzsche, a German professor in Switzerland. Nietzsche frequently visited Zürich and knew some of the students of philosophy (especially female ones) there.

25. In the first volume (1877) Avenarius wrote three contributions:

'Zur Einführung', 1
'Über die Stellung der Psychologie zur Philosophie: Eine Antrittsvorlesung', 471
'In Sachen der wissenschaftlichen Philosophie', 553.

The last article was continued in the second and third volumes from 1878 and 1879 (beginning on pages 468 and 53, respectively). Thereafter, he did not publish any articles in the journal until after Nietzsche's collapse in 1889. However, Avenarius's book *Philosophie als Denken der Welt gemäss dem Princip des kleinsten Kraftmasses* (Leipzig, 1876) was discussed in volumes 8 (1884) and 9 (1885).

26. An index for the first thirty years from 1908 exists.

27. See my forthcoming study *Nietzsche's Knowledge of Philosophy*, which contains a chapter about Nietzsche's reading of philosophical journals.

28. MA, 131, and JGB, 211.

29. KGW VII.4/2, 67 (which would be equivalent to KSA 10, 1[112], but this note has not been published in KSA).

30. This information is taken from Alwin Mittasch's *Friedrich Nietzsches Naturbefliessenheit* (Heidelberg, 1950), 21n: "Nach sicherer Überlieferung (Max Oehler) hat Nietzsche 1884 in Zürich in einem öffentlichen Lesezimmer Aufsätze von Mach gelesen." It is uncertain how reliable this information is.

31. I have not found any evidence that Nietzsche read such texts, but the statement by Oehler quoted above may suggest it, as does a statement by Mach's follower, Hans Kleinpeter, who in a letter to Mach, November, 1912, writes: "I received the news from Weimar, that Nietzsche read one of your essays in a scientific journal in 1885 and spoke very favourably about it." I have taken this information from Hussain, "Reading Nietzsche through Ernst Mach."

32. The table of contents of E. Mach's *Beiträge zur Analyse der Empfindungen* (Jena, 1886) lists the following chapters: "Preface [dated in Nov. 1885]; Antimetaphysische Vorbemerkungen, 1–24; Die Hauptgeschichtpunkte für die Untersuchung der Sinne, 25–39; Die Raumempfindung des Auges, 40–54; Weitere Untersuchung der Raumempfindungen, 55–78; Beziehung der Gesichtsempfindungen zu einander und zu andern psychischen Elementen, 79–102; Die Zeitempfindung, 103–112; Die Tonempfindung, 113–140; Einfluss der vorausgehenden Untersuchungen auf die Auffassung der Physik, 141–168."

33. On page 61 a correction is made from "auf" to "auch," not taken from the errata at the end of the book. There is also an underlining on page 85: "Das stärkere selbstständige Auftreten der Phantasmen [...] muss seiner biologischen Unzweckmässigkeit wegen als p a t h o l o g i s c h angesehen werden." There is also a marginal line here.

34. As an example of Nietzsche's possible use of this work, we can note that Mach on pages 107–8 writes:

> Wiederholt habe ich ein interessantes hierher gehöriges Phänomen beobachtet. Ich sass in die Arbeit vertieft in meinem Zimmer, während in einem Nebenzimmer Versuche über Explosionen angestellt wurden. Regelmässig geschah es nun, dass ich *zuerst* erschreckt zusammenzuckte, und *nachher* erst den knall hörte.
>
> Da im Traum die Aufmerksamkeit besonders träge ist, so kommen in diesem Fall die sonderbarsten Anachronismen vor, und jeder hat wohl solche Träume erlebt. Wir träumen z.B. von einem Mann, der auf uns losstürzt und schiesst,

erwachen plötzlich, und bemerken den Gegenstand, der durch seinen Fall den ganzen Traum erzeugt hat. Es hat nun nichts Widersinniges anzunehmen, dass der akustische Reiz verschiedene Nervenbahnen zugleich einschlägt, und hier in beliebiger verkehrer Ordnung von der Aufmerksamkeit angetroffen wird, so wie ich bei der obigen Beobachtung *zuerst* die allgemeine Erregung, und *dann* den Explosionsknall bemerkte. Freilich wird es in manchen Fällen zur Erklärung auch ausreichen, ein Verweben einer Sinnesempfindung in ein vorher schon vorhandenes Traumbild anzunehmen.

Nietzsche's reading of this is likely to have been a stimulus for his reflections in GD, "The Four Great Errors," 4: "The error of imaginary causes.—To start from the dream: on to a certain sensation, the result for example of a distant cannonshot, a cause is subsequently foisted (often a whole little novel in which precisely the dreamer is the chief character). The sensation, meanwhile, continues to persist, as a kind of resonance: it waits, as it were, until the cause-creating drive permits it to step into the foreground— now no longer as a chance occurrence but as 'meaning.' The cannonshot enters in a *causal* way, in an apparent inversion of time. That which comes later, the motivation, is experienced first, often with a hundred details which pass like lightning, the shot *follows*. . . . What has happened? The idea *engendered* by a certain condition have been misunderstood as the cause of that condition.—We do the same thing, in fact, when we are awake."

35. Nietzsche claims in GD, "'Reason' in Philosophy," 2: "The senses [. . .] they do not lie at all. It is what we *make* of their evidence that first introduces a lie into it, for example, the lie of unity, the lie of materiality, of substance, of duration."

36. Nietzsche writes in JGB, 23, that we should "demand in return that psychology shall again be recognized as the queen of the sciences, to serve and prepare for which the other sciences exist. For psychology is now once again the road to the fundamental problems."

37. See letter to Gast, end of August 1883: "dass die Annahme *erfüllter* Atompunkte *eine* für die strengste Wissenschaft der mechanik *unbrauchbare* Hypothese sei: ein Satz, der jetzt unter mathematisch geschulten Naturforschern als *kanonisch* gilt. Für die *Praxis der Forschung* ist er *gleichgültig*."

However, Nietzsche's and Mach's points are probably different. Nietzsche seems to reject filled atoms (i.e., with extension), while Mach rejects the existence of atoms as such since we have no sense experience of them.

38. Modern metaphysical philosophers "can no longer endure the bric-à-brac of concepts of the most various origin such as so-called positivism brings to the market today; the disgust of a more fastidious taste at the village-fair motleyness and patchiness of all these reality-philosophasters [Wirklichkeits-Philosophasters] in whom there is nothing new or genuine except this motleyness." Nietzsche is here discussing metaphysical philosophers' response to contemporary philosophy, most probably in response to his reading of Spir and Teichmüller.

39. *Repertorium der Physik* 23 (1887), 587–600. It seems to me unlikely that Nietzsche read the article.

The presence of this article (a reprint) confirms that Mach received Nietzsche's book. I am not aware of any examination of possible influences of Nietzsche on Mach.

40. The table of contents of M. Drossbach's *Ueber die scheinbaren und die wirklichen Ursachen des Geschehens in der Welt* (Halle, 1884) lists the following chapters:

Vorwort

1. Gegen die Causalität der Erscheinungen, 1
2. Gegen die auf der Causalität der Erscheinungen beruhende Erfahrung, 7
3. Sinnliche Wahrnehmung und Erfahrung, 11
4. Die Wechselwirkung oder das Verhältniss der Ursachen zu einander, 17
5. Die Nothwendigkeit des Geschehnens in der Natur und die menschlichen Handlungen, 30
6. Der Grund der Wechselwirkung, 44

Nachwort, 54

Anhang: Eine Untersuchung über die Wahrnehmbarkeit der Erscheinungen und die Unwahrnehmbarkeit der Wesen, 59–103

Nietzsche's copy of the book is heavily annotated throughout. He read it in 1885.

41. Two exceptions are Rüdiger Schmidt's "Nietzsches Drossbach-Lektüre. Bemerkungen zum Ursprung des literarischen Projekts 'Der Wille zur Macht,'" *Nietzsche-Studien* 17 (1988): 465–77; and Paolo D'Iorio, "La superstition des philosophes critiques. Nietzsche et African Spir," *Nietzsche-Studien* 22 (1993): 257–94.

See also Hans-Gerd von Seggern, *Nietzsches Philosophie des Scheins* (Weimar: VDG, 1999).

42. The table of contents of Gustav Teichmüller, *Die wirkliche und die scheinbare Welt: Neue Grundlegung der Metaphysik* (Breslau, 1882), lists the following chapters (the many subchapters are not listed here):

Erstes Buch: Die wirkliche Welt. Ontologie

1. Einleitung, 3
2. Topik der Idee des Seins, 17
3. Definition des Seins, 44
4. Umfang des Begriffs des Seins, 80
5. Die semiotische Erkenntniss, 91
6. Das Wesen und die Wesen, 120
7. Die Idee des Nichts, 142
8. Der allgemeine Begriff von Sein und Nichts, 169

Zweites Buch: Die scheinbare Welt. Phänomenologie

1. Die Zeit, 188
2. Der Raum, 247
3. Die Bewegung, 295

4. Die wirkliche und die scheinbare Welt, 332

Index, 351–57

Several of these chapters contain rather extensive discussions of earlier philosophers' views of being, time, etc. (e.g., those of Plato, Aristotle, Descartes, Spinoza, Kant, and Hegel).

43. Teichmüller, *Die wirkliche und die scheinbare Welt,* 347.

44. JGB, 17. See also JGB, 16; GD, "Reason," 5; and GD, "The Four Great Errors," 3.

However, as is so often the case, more than one author Nietzsche read also discussed similar questions. Paul Heinrich Widemann, a friend of Peter Gast's whom Nietzsche also knew, argued in his *Erkennen und Sein* (Karlsruhe and Leipzig, 1885) that the subjective was the adequate starting point of all philosophy and metaphysics. The second part (of three) is called "Beweis der absoluten Realität aller subjectiven Bedingungen a priori des Bewußseins," 121–202, and includes the chapter "Das Subject als Ding an sich." Widemann ended the book by referring to Dühring and Nietzsche (239), highly praising Nietzsche but in a manner and context of which Nietzsche did not approve. Nietzsche read this work in 1885 and annotated it.

45. JGB, Preface. Compare also sections 34 and 36 of the book.

46. GM, III, 12. Compare also, for example, FW V, 354 and 374; KSA 12, 7[21 and 60]; and KSA 13, 14[136].

47. In the index to the book there is even an entry called "Perspectivisch," followed by references to twenty-three pages where this is discussed.

48. See especially Nietzsche's discussions in GD, "'Reason' in Philosophy" and "How the 'Real World' at Last Became a Myth."

49. The first subchapter of this section is called "Die scheinbare Welt oder die perspectivische Auffassung," 345–46.

50. For further information about Nietzsche's relation to Teichmüller, see Karl-Heinz Dickopp, "Zum wandel von Nietzsches Seinsverständnis—Afrikan Spir und Gustav Teichmüller," *Zeitschrift für philosophische Forschung* 24 (1970): 50–71; and H. Nohl, "Eine historische Quelle zu Nietzsches Perspektivismus: G. Teichmüller: Die wirkliche und die scheinbare Welt," *Zeitschrift für Philosophie und philosophische Kritik* 149 (1913); and references in these.

51. This is obvious in the notes KSA 11, 35[56 and 61] and 40[12, 24, 30, 41], where he gives page references and mentions them by name, but many other notes nearby are also based on this intensive rereading and studying of these books.

52. Surprisingly, very little seems to have been written on Nietzsche and pessimism, and there is nothing at all relating to his reading of books and articles dealing with pessimism. Tobias Dahlkvist, Department of the History of Science and Ideas at Uppsala University, finishes a PhD dissertation during the autumn of 2007 on Nietzsche and pessimism, written in English and intended for publication.

53. KSA 11, 34[204 and 207], April–June 1885.

54. Nietzsche himself is mentioned in the book (176), and Paul Rée is discussed somewhat more extensively (175). Nietzsche did not annotate these two pages. Chapter 5, "Der philosophische Pessimismus," deals with Schopenhauer, Hartmann, Bahnsen, Mainländer, and "Pessimisten ohne selbständige Systeme" (175–79).

The fact that Nietzsche is mentioned in this work (which he even read) was not discussed in R. F. Krummel's otherwise excellent, useful, and massive *Nietzsche und der deutsche Geist* (Berlin and New York: Walter de Gruyter, 1998) where he lists and discusses all references to Nietzsche in the German language literature until 1900.

55. This book is not in Nietzsche's library. However, he did own Augustine's *De Civitate Dei,* two volumes (Leipzig, 1863), in Latin. It is not known if or when Nietzsche read this work.

56. "The passion for God: there is the peasant, true-hearted and importunate kind, like Luther's—the whole of Protestantism lacks southern *delicatezza.* There is an oriental ecstatic kind, like that of a slave who has been undeservedly pardoned and elevated, as for example in the case of Augustine, who lacks in an offensive manner all nobility of bearing and desire. There is the womanly tender and longing kind which presses bashfully and ignorantly for a *unio mystica et physica:* as in the case of Madame de Guyon." JGB, 50.

"The man of an era of dissolution [. . .] such a man of late cultures and broken lights will, on average, be a rather weak man: his fundamental desire is that the war which he *is* should come to an end; happiness appears to him, in accord with a sedative (for example Epicurean or Christian) medicine and mode of thought, pre-eminently as the happiness of repose, or tranquillity, of satiety, of unity at last attained, as a 'Sabbath of Sabbaths,' to quote the holy rhetorician Augustine, who was himself such a man." JGB, 200.

"*The revenge against the spirit and other ulterior motives of morality.* [. . .] It is from among men of this sort that those monsters of morality come who make noise, who make history—Augustine is one of them. Fear of the spirit, revenge against the spirit— how often these propelling vices have become the roots of virtues! Even nothing less than virtues." FW V, 359.

"Covert revengefulness, petty envy become *master!* Everything pitiful, everything suffering from itself, everything tormented by base feelings, the whole *ghetto-world* of the soul suddenly *on top!*—One has only to read any of the Christian agitators, Saint Augustine for example, to realize, to *smell,* what dirty fellows had therewith come out on top." AC, 59.

57. Letter to Franz Overbeck, March 31, 1885.

58. KSA 12, 1[55], autumn 1885 to early 1886.

59. KSA 11, 34[141], written during the period April–June 1885. This note, directly or indirectly, certainly constitutes the background to the statement in JGB, 50.

60. KSA 11, 34[141].

61. This intention, and the corresponding work, has been largely ignored among Nietzsche scholarship, as I discuss in my articles "Nietzsche's Magnum Opus," *History of European Ideas* 32 (September 2006): 278–94, and "*The Antichrist* As the First Volume of Nietzsche's Magnum Opus," under review for publication in *Ideas in History.*

62. A useful and insightful study of this work, including discussions of several of the books Nietzsche read at this time relating to morality, is Paul van Tongeren, *Die Moral von Nietzsches Moralkritik: Studie zu 'Jenseits von Gut und Böse'* (Bonn: Bouvier, 1989). Laurence Lampert, *Nietzsche's Task: An Interpretation of Beyond Good and Evil* (New Haven, CT, and London: Yale University Press, 2001), and Douglas Burnhan, *Reading Nietzsche: An Analysis of Beyond Good and Evil* (Montreal: McGill-Queen's University Press, 2007), provide philosophical interpretations to *Beyond Good and Evil* but on a different level with little discussion of Nietzsche's context, reading, and the origins of his thinking. A detailed philosophical and philological commentary, including discussions of Nietzsche's reading, to *Jenseits von Gut und Böse* would be a valuable contribution Nietzsche research. It is surprising and unfortunate that no such comprehensive study or commentary of his most philosophical work has been written.

63. The "Anhang," "Die Schranken der naturwissenschaflichen Erkenntniss," 555–682, contains the following chapters:

Vorwort, 555
Einleitung, 560
Beschaffung und Befähigung des erkennenden Ich, 565
Beschaffung und Zugänglichkeit der Natur, 570
Wesen des Erkennens, 578
Keine principielle Verschiedenheit zwischen unorganischer und organischer
    Natur, 585
Keine principielle Verschiedenheit zwischen unbeseelter und beseelter Natur,
    590–602

This is followed by nine added essays, for example, "Physische und metaphysische Atomistik," "Naturphilosophische Weltanschauungen: Entropie," and "Bedingungen für empirisches Wissen und Erkennen: Morphologische Wissenschaften."

Apart from the preface and introduction, Nietzsche has annotated all of these chapters and essays, many of them heavily, including with comments.

64. The table of contents of the English translation of Guyau's *L'irreligion de l'avenir,* 2nd ed. (Paris, 1887), lists the following parts and chapters:

First Part: The Genesis of Religion in Primitive Societies
1. Religious Physics
2. Religious Metaphysics
3. Religious Morals
Second Part: The Dissolution of Religions in Existing Societies
1. Dogmatic Faith
2. Symbolic and Moral Faith
3. Dissolution of Religious Morality
4. Religion and Non-Religion Among the People

5. Religion and Non-Religion and the Child
6. Religion and Non-Religion Among Women
7. The Effect of Religion and Non-Religion on Population and the Future of the Race
Third Part: Non-Religion of the Future
1. Religious Individualism
2. Association. The Permanent Element of Religions in Social Life
3. Theism
4. Pantheism
5. Idealism, Materialism, Monism

65. See KSA 12, 10[170 and 171], autumn 1887.

66. See Andreas Urs Sommer's *Friedrich Nietzsches "Der Antichrist": Ein philosophisch-historischer Kommentar* (Basel: Schwabe, 2000), for many examples of this.

However, no general discussion—taking Nietzsche's annotations into account—of the importance of Nietzsche's reading of Guyau's *L'irreligion* (and his *Esquisse*) seems to have been published.

67. The table of contents of Fouillée's *La science sociale contemporaine* lists the following content:

1. Le contrat social et l'ecole idéaliste, 1
2. L'organisme social et l'ecole naturaliste, 74
3. La conscience sociale, 192
4. La justice pénale et les collisions de droits dans le société, 259
5. La fraternité et la justice réparative, 323
Conclusion, 379–421

Nietzsche's copy of the book is heavily annotated with many instances of "!," "NB," "gut," "ja," and other comments in the margins of the pages.

68. KSA 12, 10[17], and KSA 13, 11[137 and 147].

69. However, Nietzsche also read a fair number of other books about sociology and society, most of them in the 1880s: H. Spencer, *Einleitung in das Studium der Sociologie* (Leipzig, 1875); A. Espinas, *Die tierischen Gesellschaften. Eine vergleichend-psychologische Untersuchung* (Braunschweig, 1879); A. Bordier, *La vie des sociétés* (Paris, 1887); J. Michelet, *Das Volk* (Mannheim, 1846); W. Bagehot, *Der Ursprung der Nationen Betrachtungen über den Einfluss der natürlichen Zuchtwahl und der Vererbung auf die Bildung politischer Gemeinwesen* (Leipzig, 1874); and E. Hermann, *Kultur und Natur: Studien im Gebiete der Wirtschaft* (Berlin, 1887).

70. There is a longer discussion of Nietzsche's reading of Pascal in my forthcoming *Nietzsche's Knowledge of Philosophy*.

71. Letter to Overbeck, January 9, 1887.

72. Nietzsche discovered Dostoyevsky in 1887 and read him intensively that year and in 1888.

73. Nietzsche had earlier read about Tolstoy in his reading of French literary critics and now read Tolstoy's *Ma religion* (Paris, 1885), 266 pages, in 1888.

74. Nietzsche corresponded with Strindberg in 1888 and during that year also read three of his works in French translations: *Les mariés, Père* (which Nietzsche read twice), and the short story *Remords*.

75. The table of contents of Höffding's *Psychologie in Umrissen auf Grundlage der Erfahrung* (Leipzig, 1887) lists the following main chapters:

1. Gegenstand und Methode der Psychologie, 1
2. Seele und Körper, 36
3. Das Bewusste und das Unbewusste, 88
4. Einteilung der psychologische Elemente, 107
5. Die Psychologie der Erkenntnis, 124
   A. Empfindung, 124
   B. Vorstellung, 150
   C. Auffassung des Zeit und des Raums, 231
   D. Die Auffassung des Wirklichen, 258
6. Die Psychologie des Gefühls, 278
   A. Gefühl und Sinnesempfindung, 278
   B. Gefühl und Vorstellung, 293
   C. Egoistisches und sympathisches Gefühl, 305
   D. Die Physiologie und Biologie des Gefühls, 338
   E. Die Gültigkeit des Gesetzes der Beziehung für die Gefühle, 348
   F. Einfluss des Gefühls auf die Erkenntnis, 377
7. Die Psychologie des Willens, 391
   A. Die Ursprünglichkeit des Willens, 391
   B. Der Wille und die andern Bewusstseinselemente, 408
   C. Der individuelle Charakter, 443–463

76. For three such examples, see "Beiträge zur Quellenforschung mitgeteilt von Marco Brusotti," *Nietzsche-Studien* 21 (1992): 390–91; and for another six examples see "Beiträge zur Quellenforschung mitgeteilt von Thomas H. Brobjer," *Nietzsche-Studien* 30 (2001): 418–21.

77. Werner Stegmaier's excellent study *Nietzsches "Genealogie der Moral"* (Darmstadt: Wissenschaftliche Buchgesellschaft, 1994) contains interesting material about books Nietzsche read at this time.

78. The table of contents of Joly's *Psychologie des grands hommes* (Paris, 1883) lists the following main chapters:

1. La préparation par la race
2. La préparation par l'hérédité dans la famille
3. Le grand homme et le milieu contemporain

4. Le génie et l'inspiration

79. A copy of *Le prince de Nicolaus Machiavel* (1873), 190 pages, is in Nietzsche's private library. Several of the pages of the preface have not been cut open, but those of the main text were cut with a pencil, which led to small penciled lines across some of the pages. The book contains no real annotations. It is not known when Nietzsche read this work.

80. "Thucydides, and perhaps the *Principe* of Machiavelli, are related to me closely by their unconditional will not to deceive themselves and to see reason in *reality*—not in 'reason,' still less in 'morality.'" GD, "What I Owe to the Ancients," 2.

81. KSA 12, 7[4], 259–70. See "Beiträge zur Quellenforschung mitgeteilt von Thomas H. Brobjer," *Nietzsche-Studien* 30 (2001): 421.

82. The table of contents of Liebmann's *Gedanken und Tatsachen* lists the following content:

Vorrede
Die Arten der Nothwendigkeit
Die mechanische Naturerklärung
Idee und Entelechie

Nietzsche's copy is fairly heavily annotated, with a number of comments written in the margins, including "Wille zur Macht" on page 11.

83. For Nietzsche's relation to and reading about the sophists, see my "Nietzsche's Relation to the Greek Sophists," *Nietzsche-Studien* 34 (2005): 255–76, and "Nietzsche's Disinterest and Ambivalence toward the Greek Sophists," *International Studies in Philosophy* 33 (Fall 2001): 5–23. For his reading of Brochard, see also my "Beiträge zur Quellenforschung," *Nietzsche-Studien* 26 (1997): 574–79. I have also discussed Nietzsche's relation to the sophists Trasymachos and Callicles in my article "Nietzsche's Wrestling with Plato," in Paul Bishop, ed., *Nietzsche and Antiquity: His Reaction and Response to the Classical Tradition* (Rochester, NY: Camden House, 2004), 241–59.

84. See Andreas Urs Sommer's *Friedrich Nietzsches "Der Antichrist": Ein philosophisch-historischer Kommentar* (Basel: Schwabe, 2000), for a detailed account of Nietzsche's reading of Renan and its relevance for *Der Antichrist*. This work contains much further useful information about Nietzsche's reading relevant for *Der Antichrist*.

Epilogue

1. R. G. Collingwood, *An Autobiography* (Oxford: Clarendon Press, 1939), has advocated this approach. See especially chapter 5, "Question and Answer," 29–43.

2. For example, he wrote "Wille zur Macht" in Drossbach, Liebmann, Höffding, and Schneider and twice in Guyau.

3. Apart from the information that can be gained from the annotations, the library shows us the extent, and the bias, of Nietzsche's knowledge of many fields, such as, evolution and cosmology. Still more obvious, Nietzsche's reading and library show us the extent, and the bias, of his knowledge about many individuals to whom he so often

refs with ad hominem statements in his published works. This includes not only such important figures as Mill, Kant, and Pascal but also such minor ones (for Nietzsche) as Max Stirner, Karl Marx, Kierkegaard, and William James, all of whom, as I have shown above, are discussed in books that Nietzsche read.

4. Until just a few years before the World War II, Nietzsche's library was guarded over by Elisabeth Förster-Nietzsche and thus was not available to researchers.

5. Elisabeth Förster-Nietzsche, "Friedrich Nietzsches Bibliothek," in Artur Berthold, ed., *Bücher und Wege zu Bücher* (1900), 427–56; Elisabeth Förster-Nietzsche, "Friedrich Nietzsches Bibliothek," in Hans Feigl, ed., *Deutscher Bibliophilen-Kalender für das Jahr 1913* (Vienna, n.d.), 103–23; and Max Oehler, "Nietzsches Bibliothek," in *Vierzehnte Jahresgabe der Gesellschaft der Freunde des Nietzsche-Archivs* (Weimar, 1942), 56 pages and 8 facsimile pages from books in the library. The third work also contains a listing of the books Nietzsche borrowed from the libraries at Pforta and Basel. A fuller account of this has been given by Luca Crescenti, "Verzeichnis der von Nietzsche aus der Universitätsbibliothek in Basel entliehenen Bücher (1869–1879)," *Nietzsche-Studien* 23 (1994): 388–442.

6. "On Jean-Marie Guyau, Immoraliste," *Journal of the History of Ideas* 55, (1994): 75–98.

7. "Nietzsche, Spir and Time," *Journal of the History of Philosophy* 32 (1994): 85–102.

8. "Nietzsche, Dühring and Time," *Journal of the History of Philosophy* 28 (1990): 229–50.

9. C. N. Stavrou, *Whitman and Nietzsche: A Comparative Study of Their Thought* (Chapel Hill, 1966, 1969).

10. Karl Knortz sent Nietzsche both of these books in June 1888. Only a few pages in the latter work have been cut. It is fairly likely that Nietzsche did not read these works or only read them very superficially. However, Nietzsche is also likely to have had some knowledge of Whitman from other secondary sources.

11. In regard to Mill, we now know that Nietzsche carefully read and studied him, including annotating almost every page of the five volumes of Mill's collected works that Nietzsche possessed, as I discuss in more detail in my study *Nietzsche and the "English."*

12. An exception is my own article "Nietzsche's Reading and Private Library, 1885–1889," *Journal of the History of Ideas* 58 (1997): 663–93.

13. Some work has also been published in Italian by, among others, Giuliano Campioni, Paolo D'Iorio, Andrea Orsucci, and Marco Brusotti.

TABLE 1

Chronological Listing of Nietzsche's Philosophical Reading

The first column lists the authors and titles. A dagger (†) signifies that Nietzsche may not have read the work (or not read it in the year listed). The second column (BN) lists whether the book is available in Nietzsche's private library with a "Y" for yes. Asterisks after the "Y" indicate light (*), medium (**), and heavy (***) annotations made by Nietzsche in his copy of the book. Some books present in his library, without asterisk indication, nonetheless contain some minor annotations or other signs of having been read. Parentheses around the "Y" means that the work has been lost from the library. The third column gives short comments about Nietzsche's reading of and response to the book. The term "p-ref" means that Nietzsche refers to specific page(s) of the work. The last column gives the reference where Nietzsche mentions, or discusses, the book (a two- or three-digit number for letters, as published in KSB and KGB, and a number containing brackets for his notebooks, as published in KSA and KGW). Letters to Nietzsche are identified by date. The young Nietzsche's writings are referred to as BAW (see note on references). GSA refers to unpublished papers in the Goethe and Schiller archive in Weimar.

Nietzsche read more philosophic works than are listed in this table (which only contains works for which one can determine the year he read them). Compare, for example, table 2.

Title	BN	Comment	Ref.
1857			
†Herder, *Der Cid*	—	N wrote long poems about Alfonso der Cid, probably based on reading Herder.	KGW I.1, 3[1+6]
Marcus Aurelius	—	School work.	KGW I.1, 3A[3]
1858			
†Herder, J. G., *Der Cid*	—	Probably list of books N wanted 1858. N only refers to the work as *Cid* or *Der Cid*, but it is very probably Herder's version of the story.	BAW 1, 400+ KGW, I.1, 4[4+5]
1859			
†Cicero's letters	Y	Pinder recommends N to read Cicero's letters. It is probable, but not certain, that N read them this year.	62+Pinder to N, April 1859
Novalis	—	N read Novalis ("whose philosophical thoughts interest me") in his uncle's library.	BAW 1, 147
1860			
Cicero's letters: K. F. Süpfle, *M. Tullii Ciceronis epistolae selectae temporum ordine compositae: Für den Schulgebrauch mit Einleitung und erklärenden Anmerkungen versehen*	(Y)	N writes a list of the books he will need and probably buy, for the coming school year (i.e., 1860–61).	173
1861			
Sallust [*Sallust und Ciceronis Opera, I,* vol. 1]	Y	Receipt. N bought this book in 1861.	KGB, I.4, p. 156+243+244
Cicero [*Sallust und Ciceronis Opera, I,* vol. 1]	Y	Receipt. N bought this book in 1861. N asked for money to have this work bound. At this time they read Cicero's *Oratio pro Murena* in the Latin class.	267+288+KGB, I.4, p. 156+243+244
Hölderlin, F., *Kurze Biographie und Proben*	(Y)[1]+Y	N was reading Hölderlin at this time. Listed title with	181+182+252+ 281+BAW 1,

TABLE 1   187

aus seinen Werken, 2 booklets from Verlag der modernen Klassiker		price and planned to work with during the holidays (1861 or 1862); wrote a school essay in 1861. "I need for a German work about Hölderlin [i.e., 'Brief an meinen Freund, in dem ich ihm meinen Lieblingsdichter zum Lesen empfehle'] necessarily his biography, it stands in my bookshelf."	251+253+BAW 2, 1–5
Voltaire, *Histoire de Charles XII*	—	N tells his sister of his studies at Pforta. N's library contains *Voltair's sämmtliche Schriften* (1786) in three volumes, but this work N read in French.	288
Herder, J. G., *Cid, Der*	—	Listed under the title "Bibliothek."	BAW 1, 250
†Feuerbach, *Das Wesen des Christenthums.*	—	List of books N wanted for his birthday in 1861.	BAW 1, 251
†Feuerbach, *Gedanken über Tod und Unsterblichkeit*	—	List of books N wanted for his birthday in 1861.	BAW 1, 251
†Cicero, 2 vols.	Y	Probably list of books N wanted to buy in 1861–62.	BAW 1, 263
†Unidentified book	—	G. Krug discusses an unidentified book N wanted for Christmas 1861 that aroused fear and anxiety in Krug.[2]	Krug to N, December 10, 1861
Anregung für Kunst, Leben und Wissenschaft	(Y)	N read this journal in 1861 and early 1862. The Germania had a subscription for 1861. N's library contains one issue from November 1859.	BAW 2, 100+BN
Cicero, *pro imp. Cu Pomp.*	—	School reading in Latin.	Jahresbericht 1861
Cicero, *pro Arch.*	—	School reading in Latin.	Jahresbericht 1861

1862

Machiavelli, *Il principe*	(Y)[3]	They read it in the Italian group.	293

Feuerbach, L., *Das Wesen des Christenthums*	—	N quotes a central theme from this work, and the whole letter is Feuerbachian in spirit.	301
Cicero	Y	N wrote an essay at Pforta on the theme "Aus welchen Gründen Cicero ins Exil gieng?" and received the highest grade. N claims in a letter to have taken sides against Cicero.	303+BAW 2, 43–53
Rousseau, *Emil*	—	N claims in this letter to having been occupied lately with refuting materialism and with Rousseau's *Emil*.	324
Schiller, *Aesthetische Erziehung*	Y	N began to read this work at Pforta.	BAW 2, 100
Emerson, *Die Führung des Lebens* (1862)[4]	Y**	Read in 1862. N paraphrases and uses.	BAW 2, 58–61+100
†Emerson, *Versuche* (1858)	Y***	N read this work in 1862 or 1863.	BAW 2, 100
Büchner, in *Anregungen für Kunst*	—	N read at least one article by Büchner in this journal in 1861 and 1862.	BAW 2, 100
Anregung für Kunst, Leben und Wissenschaft	(Y)	N read this journal in 1861 and early 1862. The Germania had a subscription for 1861. N's library contains one issue from November 1859.	BAW 2, 100+BN
Unidentified book(s) about materialism (?) or refers to his reading about materialism in the journal *Anregungen für Kunst, Leben und Wissenschaft* in 1861 and 1862? Or Feuerbach? Or Hobbes?	?	N claims to have read about materialism.	BAW 2, 100
Herder, J. G., *Der Cid*	—	Listed 1862 (probably as read).	BAW 2, 115

1863

Herder, *Cid*	—	"Meine Bücher," 1862 and 1863. One of 29 volumes N lists as his books.	GSA

TABLE 1   189

Plato, *Symposion*		"Gelesen am meisten," 1863.	BAW 2, 334
Hettners, H., *Literaturgeschichte des 18. Jahrh.:* Part II: *Geschichte der französischen Literatur im 18. Jahrh.*	—	Book bill. N bought and/or had this book bound. He made a 39-page excerpt/ summary of it. "Ich mache mir Auszüge aus Hettners Literaturgeschichte des 18. Jahrh., überhaupt treibe ich viel Literaturgeschichte." Most of the excerpt is about Voltaire.	349+353+366+ KGB I.1, 218+ BAW 2, 458+222
Dronke, G., *Die religiöse und sittlichen Vorstellungen des Aeschylus und Sophocles* (1861)	Y*	Birthday wish, and received.	382+Rosalie Nietzsche to N, shortly before October 15, 1863
Cicero, *Offic,* ed. Klotz	—	N asked for permission to acquire these at Pforta.	383+395
Platonis dialog. ex recog. Hermanni, Vol. II.[5]	Y	N asked for permission to acquire these at Pforta.	383+395
Emerson, *Die Führung des Lebens* and/or *Versuche*	Y***	Much read and excerpted this year. "Gelesen am meisten," 1863.	BAW 2, 58+ 61+100+221–2+ 257–61+334
†Machiavelli, Probably *The Prince* in Italian and/or German.	(Y)	N brings with him for his friend Pinder.	BAW 2, 222
Platon, *Apologie*	(Y***)	N planned to study after the summer holidays of 1863.	BAW 2, 223
Platon, *Kriton*	Y	N planned to study after the summer holidays of 1863.	BAW 2, 223
Platon, *Eutyphron*	Y	N planned to study after the summer holidays of 1863.	BAW 2, 223
Cicero, *Tusculanum*	—	School reading in Latin.	Jahresbericht 1863

1864

Cicero, *Opera,* 2 vols., Ludwig T.	—	N asked permission to buy and have bound at Pforta.	419+424
Hobbes	—	N had apparently borrowed this work from Pinder, who in two letters asked him to return it (and other books).	Pinder to N, April 12 and May 19, 1864

Cicero, *Scripta qui manserunt omnia,* ed. Klotz	—	N asks for permission to buy at Pforta.	427
Platon, *Dialogi ex rec. C. F. Hermanni,* in 6 vols. N asks for vol. 1 containing *Euthyphro, Apologia Socratis, Crito* and *Phaedo*	Y	N asked permission to buy and have bound at Pforta.	419+424+427
Plato, *Symposion*	Y	"One of the works of antiquity which I am especially fond of." N also wrote an essay, "Über das Verhältniss der Rede des Alcibiades zu den übrigen Reden des platonischen Symposion." N attended at least the beginning of O. Jahn's lectures on Plato's *Symposion* in Bonn 1864.	449a+BAW 2, 420–24
Lessing, G. E., *Nathan der Weise*	(Y)	N had in a lost letter discussed and recommended books to Gersdorff.	Gersdorff to N, December 18, 1864
Fischer, K., *Lessings Nathan der Weise* (Stuttgart, 1864)	—	N had in a lost letter discussed and recommended books to Gersdorff.	Gersdorff to N, December 18, 1864
Strauss, D. F., *Lessings Nathan der Weise* (Berlin, 1865)	—	N had in a lost letter discussed and recommended books to Gersdorff.	Gersdorff to N, December 18, 1864
†Beyschlag, W., *Lessings Nathan der Weise und das positive Christenthum* (Halle, 1863)	—	N had in a lost letter discussed and recommended books to Gersdorff.	Gersdorff to N, December 18, 1864
Schlegel, A. W. v., *Kritische Schriften 2* (1828)	—	Discussion or excerpts out of several works: *Über das Verhältniss der schönen Kunst zur Natur; Über Täuschung und Wahrscheinlichkeit; Über Stil und Manier* (1802)	BAW 2, 458
Herder	—	Excerpts.	BAW 2, 458
Cicero, *Brut.*	—	School reading in Latin.	Jahresbericht 1864
Cicero, *de off.*	—	School reading.	Jahresbericht 1864

TABLE I   191

| Plato, *Phaedo* | — | School reading. | Jahresbericht 1864 |
| Plato, *Symposion* | | N's "private" reading at Pforta 1864. Grade: gut. | GSA 71/361,2 |

1865

Strauss, D. F., *Das Leben Jesu*	—	N read this work this year.[6] Listed to bring along for the Easter holidays of 1865.	465 + BAW 3, 99
Hegel, unidentified work	—	N read an unidentified work by Hegel.	480
Strauss, D. F., *Die Halben und die Ganzen* (1865)	—	N read this work at this time.	480
Schopenhauer, A., *Die Welt als Wille und Vorstellung*	Y	N found Schopenhauer's magnum opus in a bookshop and read it in October or November 1865.	(486)+491
†Schopenhauer, A., *Parerga und Paralipomena*	Y	List of books N wanted for Christmas.	489
†Haym, R., *Arthur Schopenhauer* (Berlin, 1864)	—	List of books N wanted for Christmas.	489
Lessing, G. E., *Laokoon: oder über die Grenzen der Malerei und Poesie* (1766)	(Y)	Read and discussed at this time.	BAW 3, 116+119+207
Schopenhauer		Listed as the most important reading October 1865–Easter 1866.	BAW 3, 313
†Schopenhauer, *Über die vierfache Wurzel des Satzes von zureichenden Grunde*, 3rd ed. (Leipzig, 1864)	Y	List of three titles (which N wanted to acquire).	BAW 2, 406
†Schopenhauer, *Die beiden Grundprobleme der Ethik*, 2nd ed. 1860	Y	List of three titles (which N wanted to acquire).	BAW 2, 406
†Schopenhauer, *Über den Willen der Natur*, 2nd ed. (Frankfurt, 1854)	Y	List of three titles (which N wanted to acquire).	BAW 2, 406
Grote, *Geschichte Griechenlands*, übers. v. Meissner, 2 Bde.		Borrowed at Pforta between 1865 and 1869.	
Mullach, *Fragm. philos. Graecorum.*		Borrowed at Pforta between 1865 and 1869.	

Diogenes Laertius, ed. Hübner 2 Bde.		Borrowed at Pforta between 1865 and 1869.	

N's University Studies in Philosophy in Bonn

Jahn, O., "Platos Symposion"		Nietzsche attended at least the beginning of this course during the winter term of 1864–65.	KGB, I.4, 14–15
Schaarschmidt, C., "Allgemeine Geschichte der Philosophie"		N attended during the summer term in Bonn.	KGB, I.4, 357–58
Schaarschmidt, C., "Platos Leben und Lehre"		N attended during the summer term in Bonn.	KGB, I.4, 357–58

1866

Schopenhauer, A.	Y**	N read much Schopenhauer at this time and praises him.	491+493+500+ 504 passim
Emerson, R. W., *Versuche*	Y***	N refers to and paraphrases Emerson's essay "Nature" in his *Essays*.	500
Haym, R., *Arthur Schopenhauer* (Berlin, 1864)	—	Haym and Kiy "are not convincing: but they are, especially Haym, very mean-spirited."	504+517+ 576+595
Kiy, V., *Der Pessimismus und die Ethik Schopenhauers* (Berlin, 1866)	—	Haym and Kiy "are not convincing: but they are, especially Haym, very mean-spirited."	504
Lange, F. A., *Geschichte des Materialismus und Kritik seiner Bedeutung für die Gegenwart* (1866)	(Y)[7]	Very important reading for N at this time. "Kant, Schopenhauer and this book by Lange—I do not need anything more."	517+526+ 562+568
Many books borrowed from the university and city library in Leipzig		N borrows unidentified books "daily" from the university and city library in Leipzig. Mostly philological books.	524
Burley, W., *De vita philosophorum* (ca. 1486)	—	N borrowed from Leipzig Stadtbibliothek 1866 or 1867.	Oehler, Ns Bibliothek
Plutarch, *Moralia*, 5 vols.	—	N borrowed from Leipzig Stadtbibliothek 1866 or 1867.	Oehler, Ns Bibliothek
Gassendus, P., *De vita et moribus Epicuri* (1656)	—	N borrowed from Leipzig Stadtbibliothek 1866 or 1867.	Oehler, Ns Bibliothek
Diogenes Laertius	Y	N had worked with the sources to this work. A compe-	526

TABLE 1   193

tition on this theme was
announced in November.

1867

Diogenes Laertius	Y	N worked on his "De Laerti Diogenis Fontibus" over the Christmas holidays of 1866–67. In October 1867 he will win a university prize with it.	534+535+536+ 537+554 and others
Seneca, *Epistulae morales*	Y	N writes to Gersdorff: "If I may recommend you something to read which will hold you in antiquity and remind you of Schopenhauer, then take up Seneca's epistulae morales."	538
Democritus	?	N works on a study of "the false texts of Democritus." Later as "The Writings of Democritus."	548+552+561+ 562+BAW 3, 327–328+332– 335+345–50+ 362–68+BAW 4, 36–106
Schopenhauer, A., *Parerga und Paralipomena*	Y	N read here and there in *Parerga,* which was, to N, more sympathetic than ever before.	540+552
Bahnsen, J., *Beiträge zur Charakterologie,* 2 vols. (Leipzig, 1867)	Y	N read and praises the work full of "good thoughts and observations." The work is Schopenhauerian in intent. P-ref.	554+562+BAW 4, 125–26
Fischer, Kuno, *Immanuel Kant*	—	N read this work between October 1867 and April 1868. Quotations and p-refs.	BAW 3, 371+392+ 438+442
Prantl, K., *Übersicht der römisch-griechischen Philosophie* (Stuttgart, 1854)	Y	N uses for his Democritus study.	BAW 3, 327–35
†Liebmann, O., *Kant und die Epigonen* (1865)	Y	Paraphrase (somewhat uncertain).	BAW 3, 352
Meiners, Ch., *Geschichte des Ursprungs, Fortgangs*	—	N uses for his Democritus study.	BAW 3, 327

und Verfalls der Wissen-schaften in Griechenland und Rom (Lemgo, 1781)			
Zeller, E., *Die Philosophie der Griechen in ihrer geschichtlichen Entwicklung dargestellt* (Tübingen/Leipzig, 1859–68)	(Y)	N uses for his Democritus study.	BAW 3, 327
Cicero, *De fin*	Y	N uses for his Democritus study.	BAW 3, 327–28+385
Ueberweg, F., *Grundriss der Geschichte der Philoso-phie von Thales bis auf die Gegenwart,* 3 vols. (Berlin, 1866–67), Vol. 1: *Das Altertum*	Y	N bought this book in 1867 or 1868.	Bücherrechnungen

1868

Kohl, O., *I. Kants Ansicht von der Willenfreiheit,* diss. (Leipzig, 1868)	—	The dissertation was sent to N, who read it. Kohl was an acquaintance of N's in Leipzig.	565
Philosophical and scientific reading		In the spring of 1868 N planned to write, much inspired by Lange, his disserta-tion within a year on the theme "Der Begriff des Organischen seit Kant" or "*Zur Teleologie.*" N wrote: "half philosophic, half scientific. My preliminary work is almost finished." For this purpose he wrote down a number of notes, inspired from Lange, Fischer, Kant, Rosenkranz, and Ueberweg and many references for future reading (most of which comes from Ueberweg).[8]	565+568+569+ BAW 3, 371–94
Schopenhauer, General reading?	Y	N says that his philological reading cannot be compared with his reading of *Faust* or Schopenhauer.	575
Ueberweg, F., *Grundriß*	Y	N asked his sister to send him	577+BAW 3,

TABLE I   195

der Geschichte der Philosophie, 3 vols., (Berlin, 1866–67)		this book (and others) from Naumburg to Wittekind. N read and wrote down titles for future reading from vol. 3.	371–95
Schopenhauer, A., *Parerga und Paralipomena*	Y	N asked his sister to send him this book (and others) from Naumburg to Wittekind.	577
Mullach, *Fragmenta philosophorum graecorum*	—	N asked his sister to return this book to Pforta.	577+KGB, I.4, 505
Schleiermacher, F., "Über das Verzeichniß der Schriften des Demokritus bei Diogenes Laertius" (1835)	—	N has read and criticizes.	604
Lange, F. A., *Geschichte des Materialismus und Kritik seiner Bedeutung in der Gegenwart* (Iserlohn, 1866)	(Y)	Notes from the reading of Lange.	BAW 3, 332–35
Schopenhauer, *Welt* and *Parerga*	Y	Study, discussion, and p-refs.	BAW 3, 352–61
Emerson, *Versuche* (1858)	Y***	Quotation and p-ref.	BAW 3, 370
Kant, *Kritik der Urtheilskraft*	—	Several p-refs and quotations.	BAW 3, 376+ 384–95+391?+ 392–94
Rosenkranz, *Geschichte der Kantschen Philosophie*	—	Probably read.	BAW 3, 371+384+385
Fischer, K., *Immanuel Kant, Entwicklungsgeschichte und System der kritischen Philosophie*, 2 vols. (Mannheim, 1860)	—	P-refs and quotations. Much discussion is based on this reading.	BAW 3, 371+ 392+438+442
Lucretius, *Das Wesen der Dinge.* Metrisch übers. v. Gustaf Bossart-Oerden (Berlin, 1865).	Y	N bought this book in 1868.	Bücherrechnungen
Strauss, D., *Das Leben Jesu*	—	N bought this book in 1868.	Bücherrechnungen
Radenhausen, *Isis: Der Mensch und die Welt*, 4 vols. (Hamburg, 1863). Each volume of between 500 and 700 pages	—	N bought this book in 1868.	Bücherrechnungen

Bahnsen, J., *Beiträge zur Charakterologie mit besonderer Berücksichtigung pädagogischer Fragen,* 2 vols. (Leipzig, 1867).	Y	N paid for this book in 1868 but received it at the end of 1867.	Bücherrechnungen
Aristoteles, *Werke,* 9 vols. (Stuttgart, 1833–60)	Y	N bought this work in 1868.	Bücherrechnungen
Meiners, Ch., *Geschichte des Ursprungs, Fortgangs und Verfalls der Wissenschaften in Griechenland und Rom* (Lemgo, 1781)	—	N bought this work in 1868.	Bücherrechnungen

1869

Bahnsch, F., *Quaestionum de Diogenis Laertii fontibus initia,* Diss.	—	N says that it is not of much worth.	624
Schopenhauer, A., *Nachschriftlicher Nachlaß* (1844)	Y*	N quotes four lines in letter.	625
Deussen, P., *De Platonis Sophista,* diss. (Marburg, 1869)	Y	N thanks for the book.	633
Romundt, Grammatisch-philosophische dissertation about "logos."		N mentions it to Rohde. Probably read.	8
Hartmann, E. v., *Philosophie des Unbewußten* (1869)		N recommends the book to Gersdorff "in spite the dishonesty of the author." N responds and agrees with Rohde, who criticizes Hartmann sharply but is partly appreciative. N also adds: "However, I read him often for he has the most wonderful knowledge" and because he was a Schopenhauerian. Excerpt or paraphrase.	19+40+111 + KSA 7, 1[25]+ 5[32]
Teichmüller, G., *Aristotelische Forschung,* Vol. 2	—	Paraphrase.	KSA 7, 1[65]
Schlegel, A. W., *Vorlesungen über dramatische Kunst und Literatur*	—	Paraphrase and quotation.	KSA 7, 1 [ca. 85–105]

Table 1   197

Bernays, J., *Die Heraklitischen Briefe: Ein Beitrag zur philosophischen und religionsgeschichtlichen Litteratur* (Berlin, 1869)	N reviewed for the *Literarisches Centralblatt für Deutschland*.	
Plato, *Phaedo*	Paedagogium teaching summer term 1869.	
†Pre-Platonic philosophers	University teaching winter term of 1869–70.	
Plato, *Apologie*	Paedagogium teaching winter term of 1869–70.	
Plato, *Protagoras*	Paedagogium teaching winter term of 1869–70.	
Roth, E., *Geschichte unserer abendländischen Philosophie*, Bd. 2 (Mannheim, 1858)	Borrowed from the Basel University library 1869.	
Demokrit, *Operum fragmenta,* hrsg. von F. W. A. Mullach (Berlin, 1843)	Borrowed from the Basel University library 1869.	
Müller, E., *Geschichte der Theorie der Kunst bei den Alten,* 2 Bde. (Breslau, 1834–37)	Borrowed from the Basel University library 1869.	
Alberti, E., *Sokrates. Ein Versuch über ihn nach den Quellen* (Göttingen, 1869)	Borrowed from the Basel University library 1869.	
1870		
Byk, S. A., *Der Hellenismus und der Platonismus* (Leipzig, 1870)	N reviewed for the *Literarisches Centralblatt für Deutschland*. This was the last work he reviewed.	85+KGW, II.1
†Balche, A. de, *Renan et Schopenhauer: essai de critique* (Odessa, 1870)	— N thanks Gersdorff for having called his attention to this book, but it is unlikely that N read it.	111
Czermak, Article about Schopenhauer's color theory in *Berichten der Wiener Akademie der Wissenschaften*	N tells how this article confirms that Schopenhauer came to the same result as Young-Helmholz today.	111

Montaigne, *Versuche*, 3 vols. (1753–54)	Y*	"As Christmas gift I received . . . a magnificent edition of the complete Montaigne (whom I highly honour)."	116
Hartmann, E. v., *Philosophie des Unbewussten* (1869)	—	Paraphrase, quotations, and p-refs.	KSA 7, 3[3+5+ 10+11+17–20+ 23+55+95] + 5[32] + 7[104]
Bernays, J., *Grundzüge der verlorenen Abhandlung des Aristoteles über Wirkung der Tragödie*, Vol. 1 (Breslau, 1858)	—	Mentioned. Borrowed May 9, 1870.	KSA 7, 3[38]
Plato, *The Republic* and *Laws*	?	Discussion and p-ref.	KSA 7, 5[12+ 14+15]+121
†Voltaire, ?	?	Short French quotation.	KSA 7, 7[99]
Cicero, *Academica*		University teaching summer term of 1870 and winter term of 1870–71.	
Platon, *Phaedon*		Paedagogium teaching winter term of 1870–71.	
Volkmann, R., *Leben, Schriften und Philosophie des Plutarch von Chaeronea*, 2 Teile in einem Band (Berlin, 1869)		Borrowed from the Basel University library 1870.	
Voigt, G., *Die Wiederbelebung des classischen Alterthums oder das erste Jahrhundert des Humanismus* (Berlin, 1859)		Borrowed from the Basel University library 1870.	
Demokrit, *Operum fragmenta*, hrsg. von F. W. A. Mullach (Berlin, 1843)		Borrowed from the Basel University library 1870.	
Oncken, W., *Die Staatslehre des Aristoteles in historisch-politischen Umrissen. Ein Beitrag zur Geschichte der hellenischen Staatsidee und zur Einführung in die*		Borrowed from the Basel University library 1870.	

TABLE I   199

Aristotelische Politik, Teil I
(Leipzig, 1870)

Plato, *Opera omnia,* hrsg.   Borrowed from the Basel
von G. Stallbaum, Bd. 6   University library 1870.
(Gotha und Erfurt,
1827–60)

Plato, *Platonis philosophi*   Borrowed from the Basel
quae extant Graece, aus   University library 1870.
der Ausgabe von H.
Stephan mit Interpreta-
tionen von M. Ficino,
Bd. 3 (Biponto, 1781–87)

Plato, *Platonis dialogi*   Borrowed from the Basel
secundum Trasylli tetralogias   University library 1870.
dispositi, hrsg. von
K. F. Hermann, Bd. 3
(Leipzig, 1851–53)

Cicero, M. *Tulli Ciceronis*   Borrowed from the Basel
opera quae supersunt   University library 1870.
omnia, hrsg. von J. K.
Orelli, Bd. 4 (Zürich, 1861)

Yorck von Wartenburg,   Borrowed from the Basel
P., *Die Katharsis des*   University library 1870.
Aristoteles und der Oedipus
Coloneus des Sophokles
(Berlin, 1866)

Vischer, F. T., *Ästhetik oder*   Borrowed from the Basel
Wissenschaft des Schönen,   University library 1870.
Bd. 4 (Teil 3, Abschnitt 2)
(Leipzig, 1846)

Teichmüller, G., *Aristote-*   Borrowed from the Basel
lische Forschungen, Bd. 1   University library 1870.
(Halle, 1867)

Spengel, L., *Synagogè*   Borrowed from the Basel
teknon, sive artium   University library 1870.
scriptores ab initiis usque
ad editos Aristotelis de
rhetorica libros (Stuttgart,
1828)

Philosophische Monatshefte,   Borrowed from the Basel
hrsg. von I. Bergmann, 2   University library 1870.
(1869)

1871

Eucken, R., "Die Bedeutung des Aristoteles für die Gegenwart"	—	Inauguration speech at Basel.	168
Plato	Y	N prepares his course on Plato.	169+177
Rohde, E., Essay about Pythagoras	—	N read and appreciated.	177+229
Schiller, F., *Über naive und sentimentalische Dichtung*	Y	Paraphrase.	KSA 7, 9[142]
Schiller, F., *Sämtliche Werke,* 10 vols. (1844)	Y	Paraphrase and quotation.	
Schopenhauer, A., *Parerga,* Vol. 2	Y	Quotation and p-ref.	KSA 7, 12[1]
Grote, G., *Geschichte Griechenlands,* 6 vols. (Leipzig, 1850–56)	Y*	Paraphrase and p-ref to vol. 3.	KSA 7, 16[39]
Plato: Einführung in das Studium der platonischen Dialogue		University teaching winter term of 1871–72.	
Platon, *Phaedon*		Paedagogium teaching winter term of 1871–72.	
Lehrs, C., *Populäre Aufsätze aus dem Alterthum vorzugsweise zur Ethik und Religion der Griechen* (Leipig, 1856)		Borrowed from the Basel University library 1871.	
Cicero, *M. Tulli Ciceronis Opera quae supersunt omnia,* hrsg. von J. C. Orelli, Bd. 4 (Zürich, 1861)		Borrowed from the Basel University library 1871.	
York Von Wartenburg, P., *Die Katharsis des Aristoteles und der Oedipus Coloneus des Sophokles* (Berlin, 1866)		Borrowed from the Basel University library 1871.	
Bernays, J., *Grundzüge der verlorenen Abhandlung des Aristoteles über Wirkung der Tragödie* (Breslau, 1857)		Borrowed from the Basel University library 1871.	
Porphyrius, *De philosophia*		Borrowed from the Basel	

TABLE I   201

ex oraculis haurienda librorum reliquiae, hrsg. von G. Wolff (Berlin, 1856)	University library 1871.
Reinkens, J. H., *Aristoteles über Kunst, besonders über Tragödie. Exegetische und kritische Untersuchungen* (Wien, 1870)	Borrowed from the Basel University library 1871.
Susemihl, F., *Die genetische Entwicklung der Platonischen Philosophie, einleitend dargestellt,* Teil und 2 (Leipzig, 1855–60)	Borrowed from the Basel University library 1871.
Schaarschmidt, C., *Die Sammlung der Platonischen Schriften zur Scheidung der echten von unechten untersucht* (Bonn, 1866)	Borrowed from the Basel University library 1871.
Lewes, G. H., *Geschichte der Philosophie von Thales bis Comte,* Bd. 1, Deutsch nach der dritten Ausgabe von 1867 (Berlin, 1871)	Borrowed from the Basel University library 1871.
Karsten, H. T., *Commentatio critica de Platonis quae feruntur epistolis praecipue tertia septima et octava* (Utrecht, 1864)	Borrowed from the Basel University library 1871.
Stein, H. v., *Sieben Bücher zur Geschichte des Platonismus. Untersuchungen über das System des Plato und sein Verhältnis zur späten Theologie und Philosophie,* Teil I und 2 (Göttingen, 1862)	Borrowed from the Basel University library 1871.
Zeitschrift für Philosophie und philosophische Kritik, hrsg. von J. H. von Fichte, H. Ulrici und J. U. Wirth, N. F. 2 (1867)	Borrowed from the Basel University library 1871.
Plato, *Sämmtliche Werke,*	Borrowed from the Basel

übersetzt von H. Müller, mit Einleitungen von K. Steinhart, 8 Bde. (Leipzig, 1850–66)		University library 1871.	
Bahnsen, J., *Zur Philosophie der Geschichte. Eine kritische Besprechung des Hegel-Hartmannschen Evolutionis-mus aus Schopenhauerschen Principien* (Berlin, 1872)		Borrowed from the Basel University library 1871.	
Oncken, W., *Die Staatslehre des Aristoteles in historisch-politischen Umrissen. Ein Beitrag zur Geschichte der hellenischen Staatsidee und zur Einführung in die Aristotelische Politik,* Teil 1 (Leipzig, 1870)		Borrowed from the Basel University library 1871.	

1872

Zeller, E., *Die Philosophie der Griechen*	(Y)	N reads with mockery Zeller about Plato and about the pre-Socratics.	229
Romundt, *Die menschliche Erkenntnis und das Wesen der Dinge* (1872)	Y	N's friend R's habilitation-schrift, which was first called *Kant und Empedocles.*	233+248+264
Pre-Socratics	?	N read much about the pre-Socratics this summer and autumn.	252+258
Zöllner, J. C. F., *Über die Natur der Kometen: Beiträge zur Geschichte und Theorie der Erkenntnis* (1872)	Y	"there is enormously much for *us* in it." Discussion based on this reading.	272 + KSA 7, 19[93+142+159+ 161+164+165+ 173]
Grillparzer, Penultimate vol. of *Gesammtausgabe,* about aesthetics	—	"he is *almost* always one of us."	277
Strauss, D., *Der alte und der neue Glaube* (1872)	Y*	Paraphrase and discussion. The following year N writes UB I about Strauss.	KSA 7, 19[19+ 32+201+ 259+273]
Kant, I., *Kritik der reinen Vernunft*	—	Paraphrase, quotation, and reference to "second preface of	KSA 7, 19[34]

TABLE 1   203

		the critique." Possibly from Romundt or other secondary literature.	
Liebmann, O., "Über subjective, objective und absolute Zeit," in *Phil. Monadshefte VII,* 1871–72	—	Brief discussion based on this reading.	KSA 7, 19[140]
Schopenhauer, A.,	Y	Discussion with two p-refs.	KSA 7, 19[212]
Spir. A., *Forschung nach der Gewissheit in der Erkenntnis der Wirklichkeit* (Leipzig, 1869)	—	Discussion based on this reading.	KSA 7, 19[242]
Fischer, K.	—	Under the title *"Anzugreifen"* (i.e., to attack).	KSA 7, 19[259]
Lotze,	—	Under the title *"Anzugreifen"* (i.e., to attack).	KSA 7, 19[259+ 292]
Aristoteles, *De caelo*	Y	P-ref. N takes information about Empedocles from here.	KSA 7, 23[32]
Schopenhauer, A., *Die Welt als Wille und Vorstellung, II*	Y	P-ref.	KSA 7, 23[32]
Pre-Platonic philosophers: Die vorplatonischen Philosophen		University teaching summer term of 1872.	
Platon, *Protagoras*		Paedagogium teaching summer term of 1872 and winter term of 1872–73.	
Arnold, A., *Platons Werke einzeln erklärt und in ihrem Zusammenhange dargestellt,* Teil 1, Heft 1 und 2 (Berlin, 1835–36)		Borrowed from the Basel University library 1872.	
Bahnsen, J., *Zur Philosophie der Geschichte. Eine kritische Besprechung des Hegel-Hartmannschen Evolutionismus aus Schopenhauerschen Principien* (Berlin, 1872)		Borrowed from the Basel University library 1872.	
Karsten, H. T., *Commentatio critica de Platonis quae feruntur epistolis*		Borrowed from the Basel University library 1872.	

praecipue tertia septima et octava (Utrecht, 1864)	
Oncken, W., *Die Staatslehre des Aristoteles in historisch-politischen Umrissen. Ein Beitrag zur Geschichte der hellenischen Staatsidee und zur Einführung in die Aristotelische Politik,* Teil 1 (Leipzig, 1870)	Borrowed from the Basel University library 1872.
Plato, *Sämmtliche Werke,* übersetzt von H. Müller, mit Einleitungen von K. Steinhart, 8 Bde. (Leipzig, 1850–66)	Borrowed from the Basel University library 1872.
Schaarschmidt, C., *Die Sammlung der Platonischen Schriften zur Scheidung der echten von den unechten untersucht* (Bonn, 1866)	Borrowed from the Basel University library 1872.
Stein, H. v., *Sieben Bücher zur Geschichte des Platonismus. Untersuchungen über das System des Plato und sein Verhältnis zur späten Theologie und Philosophie,* Teil 1 und 2 (Göttingen, 1862)	Borrowed from the Basel University library 1872.
Susemihl, F., *Die genetische Entwicklung der Platonischen Philosophie, einleitend dargestellt,* Teil 1 und 2 (Leipig, 1855–60)	Borrowed from the Basel University library 1872.
Zeitschrift für Philosophie und philosophische Kritik, N. F. 2 (1867)	Borrowed from the Basel University library 1872.
Marcus Aurelius Antoninus, *Unterhaltungen mit sich selbst.* Übers. und hrsg. von J. M. Schultz (Schleswig, 1799)	Borrowed from the Basel University library 1872

TABLE I   205

Empedokles, *Carminum reliquiae,* hrsg. von S. Karsten (Amsterdam, 1838)		Borrowed from the Basel University library 1872.	
Parmenides, *Carminis reliquiae,* hrsg. von S. Karsten (Amsterdam, 1835)		Borrowed from the Basel University library 1872.	
Fragmenta philosophorum Graecorum, hrsg. von A. Mullach, Bd. 1 und 2 (Paris, 1860–67)		Borrowed from the Basel University library 1872.	
Zöllner, J. C. F., *Ueber die Natur der Cometen. Beiträge zur Geschichte und Theorie der Erkenntniss* (Leipzig, 1872)		Borrowed from the Basel University library 1872.	

1873

Hamann, ?	—	"I am reading Hamann . . . Very profound and sincere, but unworthy due to its inartistic manner."	294
Marcus Antoninus (Marcus Aurelius)	Y	N recommends him as a means of strength to Rohde: "it makes one so calm."	300
Strauss, D. F., *Der alte und der neue Glaube* (1872)	Y*	N reads it and is critical. Will write against it. Much, including many p-refs. Notes for N's *David Strauss: Writer and Confessor* (1873). N excerpts from both the first and the second edition.	304+306+307+ 309 + KSA 7, 26[24] + 27 passim
†Renan, E., *Paulus*	—	N sends as a gift to Cosima Wagner.	304
Spir, A., *Denken und Wirklichkeit,* Vol. 1 (Leipzig, 1873)	?	P-ref. Borrowed March 13, 1873.	KSA 7, 26[1]
Überweg, F., *Grundriss der Geschichte der Philosophie von Thales bis auf die Gegenwart,* Vol. 3 (Berlin, 1867)	Y	P-refs.	KSA 7, 26[1+ 4+5+7]

Magneni Democritus reviviscens Ticini (1646)	—	List of titles for information about Democritos.	KSA 7, 26[5]
Maignani cursus philosophicus (1652)	—	List of titles for information about Empedocles.	KSA 7, 26[5]
Lichtenberg, *Vermischte Schriften* (Göttingen, 1867)	Y	Several quotations, including p-ref.	KSA 7, 27[12+21] + KSA 7, 29[80+176] + KSA 7, 29[166] + KSA 8, 5[87]
Schopenhauer, *Parerga,* Vol. 2	Y	Quotation.	KSA 7, 27[27+31]
Strauss, D. F., *Der alte und der neue Glaube:* mit *Ein Nachwort als Vorwort zu den neuen Auflagen meiner Schrift* (Bonn, 1873)	—	Quotation. N here quotes from the second edition and its epilogue. He possessed the first edition.	KSA 7, 27[39]
†Zöllner, C. F., *Über die Natur der Kometen* (Leipzig, 1872)	Y	Discussion. Zöllner mentioned.	KSA 7, 29[24]
Hartmann, E. v., *Philosophie des Unbewussten* (Berlin, 1872)	—	Paraphrase, discussion, quotations, and p-refs.	KSA 7, 29[51–55+59+66+72]
Hegel, *Vorlesungen über die Philosophie der Geschichte*	—	Discussion and quotations.	KSA 7, 29[72–74]
Schiller, F., *Werke,* "Was heisst und zu welchen End studiert man Universalgeschichte"	Y	Discussion and quotation.	KSA 7, 29[75]
Hume, *Gespräche über natürliche Religion* (Leipzig, 1781)	Y	Discussion and quotation.	KSA 7, 29[86]+30[2]
Schiller, F., *Über naive und sentimentalische Dichtung*	Y	Discussion.	KSA 7, 29[116]
Hölderlin, *Sokrates und Alkibiades, Der Rhein*	?	Two quotations.	KSA 7, 29[202+203]
Lange, F. A., *Geschichte des Materialismus* (1866)	(Y)	Discussion based on this reading.	KSA 7, 29[223]
†Büchner, *Geist und Körper* (1860)	—	Two-line quotation and discussion.	KSA 7, 30[20]

TABLE I 207

†Smiles, S., ?	—	Discussion of Plutarch and Montaigne. Ref. to Smiles—possibly from secondary source.	KSA 7, 30[31]
Pre-Platonic philosophers (Die älteren griech. Philosophen bis Platon)		University teaching summer term of 1873.	
Platon, *Phaedon*		Paedagogium teaching summer term of 1873.	
Plato's life and writings (Über Platons Leben und Schriften)		University teaching winter term of 1873–74.	
Alberti, E., *Sokrates. Ein Versuch über ihn nach den Quellen* (Göttingen, 1869)		Borrowed from the Basel University library 1873.	
Spir, A., *Denken und Wirklichkeit. Versuch einer Erneuerung der kritischen Philosophie*, 2 Bde. (Leipzig, 1873)		Borrowed from the Basel University library 1873.	
Hamann, J. G., *Schriften und Briefe*, erläutert und hrsg. von M. Petri, Bd. 1 (Hannover, 1872)		Borrowed from the Basel University library 1873.	
Plato, *Opera omnia*, hrsg. von G. Stallbaum, Bd. 2 (Gotha und Erfurt, 1827–60)		Borrowed from the Basel University library 1873.	
Zöllner, J. C. F., *Ueber die Natur der Cometen. Beiträge zur Geschichte und Theorie der Erkenntniss* (Leipzig, 1872)		Borrowed from the Basel University library 1873.	
Plato, *Sämmtliche Werke*, übersetzt von H. Müller, mit Einleitungen von K. Steinhart, Bd. 1, 3, 6, 7, Leipzig, 1850–66		Borrowed from the Basel University library 1873.	
Steinhart, C., *Platons Leben* (Leipzig, 1873) [Plato, Sämmtliche Werke, übers. von H. Müller, Bd. 9]		Borrowed from the Basel University library 1873.	

Aristoteles, *Politik. Erstes, Zweites und Drittes Buch,* übers. von J. Bernays (Berlin, 1872)		Borrowed from the Basel University library 1873.	

1874

Fuchs, C., Several long articles in *Musikal. Wochenblatt.*	—	Fuchs praises N in one of them, but N regrets it. N suggests that Fuchs publishes his articles in the *Musikal. Wochenblattes* separately. N has read articles about Lotze, Schopenhauer, Renan, and Grillparzer.	353+356+360
Hartmann, E. v., *Romeo und Julia*	—	N is critical and sends the work to Gersdorff.	361+366+369
Strauss, D. F., *Der alte und der neue Glaube*	Y*	Romundt read aloud to N.	384
Emerson, *Versuche*	(Y)	This work, which N had with him to Bergün, was stolen.	390
Schopenhauer, A., *Parerga,* Vol. 2	Y*	Paraphrase and p-ref.	KSA 7, 34[11]
†Hausrath, A., *D. F. Strauss und die Theologie seiner Zeit* (1876–78)	—	Brief mention. Unclear if read or not.	KSA 7, 34[37]
Emerson, *Versuche*	Y***	N bought this book in 1874.	Bücherrechnungen
Plato,	Y?	N bought this work in 1874.	Bücherrechnungen
Cicero,	Y?	N bought this work in 1874.	Bücherrechnungen
Plutarchos,	Y?	N bought this work in 1874.	Bücherrechnungen
Logos, (probably Max Heinze, *Die Lehre vom Logos in der griechischen Philosophie.* Oldenburg, 1872)	Y	N bought this book in 1874.	Bücherrechnungen
Aristoteles	Y?	N bought this work in 1874.	Bücherrechnungen
Hercules, (possibly F. Buecheler, *Academicorum philosophorum index Herculanensis*)	Y	N bought this book in 1874.	Bücherrechnungen
Platon *Gorgias*		University teaching summer term of 1874.	
Aristoteles *Rhetorik*		University teaching summer term of 1874.	
Aristoteles *Rhetorik*		University teaching winter term of 1874–75.	

TABLE I 209

Aristoteles, *Ars rhetorica,* hrsg. von L. Spengel, 2 Bde. (Leipzig, 1867)	Borrowed from the Basel University library 1874.	
Aristoteles, *Politica,* hrsg. von F. Susemihl (Leipzig, 1872)	Borrowed from the Basel University library 1874.	
Spir, A., *Denken und Wirklichkeit. Versuch einer Erneuerung der kritischen Philosophie,* 2 Bde. (Leipzig, 1873)	Borrowed from the Basel University library 1874.	
Aristoteles, *Politik.* Erstes, Zweites und Drittes Buch, übers. von J. Bernays (Berlin, 1872)	Borrowed from the Basel University library 1874.	
11 Dissertationen Über Griechische Philosophie	Borrowed from the Basel University library 1874.	
Plato, *Sämmtliche Werke,* übersetzt von H. Müiler, mit Einleitungen von K. Steinhart, Bd. 1, 3, 6, 7 (Leipzig, 1850–66)	Borrowed from the Basel University library 1874.	
Steinhart, C., *Platon's Leben* (Leipzig, 1873) [Plato, *Sämmtliche Werke* übers. von H. Müller, Bd. 9]	Borrowed from the Basel University library 1874.	
Zöllner, J. C. F., *Ueber die Natur der Cometen. Beiträge zur Geschichte und Theorie der Erkenntniss* (Leipzig, 1872)	Borrowed from the Basel University library 1874.	

1875

Windisch, E., Indian philosophy	—	N and W had studied philology together in Leipzig. He had written a catalog of 300 Indian works.	418
Brockhaus, Rectoratsrede über indische Philologie	—	N now read or more probably had several years earlier. Attended Brockhaus's lecture	418

		"Overview of the Results of Indian Philology."	
Montaigne, *Essays*	Y+Y*	N searches and discusses a reference to Montaigne in *Schopenhauer als Erzieher* with his translator for the work into French.[9]	425+438
Draper, J. W., *Geschichte der geistigen Entwicklung Europas* (1871)	Y*	N bought this work. Gersdorff had been recommended the book by, or borrowed it from, N.[10] Paraphrase by N.	Bücherrechnungen. Gersdorff to N, April 25, 1875, and KSA 8, 5[198]
Translations of Indian Philosophy	?	Implies reading of Windisch and Deussen about Indian philosophy.[11]	448+494
†Hartmann, E. v., ?	?	N criticizes "des Hartmanni-anismus."[12]	449
†Grote, G., *Plato*	—	N discusses and discourages Baumgartner from translating this work from English to German, partly because it contains so much Greek. N seems to know the work but has probably not read it.[13]	475
Fuchs, Carl, Unpublished notes and essays	—	N recommends him to write and compile *Briefe über Musik,* which he also later does as *Die Zukunft des musikalische Vorträges* (1884).	479+640
Rée, Paul, *Psychologische Beobachtungen* (1875)	Y	N writes to Rée, October 22, 1875, and comments on the book. This marks the beginning of their friendship. N's copy of the book has a personal dedication from Rée.	492+554+613 + KSA 8, 10[3]+ 22[109]
Tripitaka der Buddhisten	—	N attempts to help to find publisher for the translation of this work (by Windisch?).	494+495
Senfft, Wolfgang, *Indischer Sprüche,* 3 vols.	—	Apparently an early Christmas present from Gersdorff. N thanks with appreciation.	495

TABLE 1   211

Sutta Nipáta (English translation)	—	N borrowed this book from Widemann, which contains "things from the sacred books of the Buddhists," and quotes from it.	495
Böhtlingk, O., *Indische Sprüche: Sanskrit und Deutsch,* 3 vols., (1870–73)	Y	Quotation and p-ref.	KSA 8, 2[1]+3[1]
Aristotle	Y	A note with the title "<u>Books</u> to buy and to exchange" after which follows a listing.	KSA 8, 4[1]
Schopenhauer	Y	A note with the title "<u>Books</u> to buy and to exchange" after which follows a listing. N bought Schopenhauer's *Werke* (1873–74) on June 25, 1875.	KSA 8, 4[1]
Schopenhauer, A., *Die Welt als Wille und Vorstellung*	Y	Paraphrase and quotations.	KSA 8, 5[73–84]
Xenophon, *Memorabilien*	—	Reference. N seems to have read this work this year and the following year.	KSA 8, 5[119+192]
Schopenhauer, A., *Parerga,* Vol. 1	Y	Quotations and p-ref.	KSA 8, 6[14+ 15+31+34]
Lichtenberg, G. C., *Einige Lebensumstände von Capt. James Cook, grösstentheils aus schriftlichen Nachrichten einiger seiner Bekannten gezogen* in *Vermischte Schriften*	Y**	Paraphrase and p-ref. N possessed *Vermischte Schriften,* 8 vols. (1867).	KSA 8, 5[87]+ 6[48]
†Voltaire, ?	Y	Short quotation in French.	KSA 8, 7[7]
Dühring, E., *Der Werth des Lebens: Eine philosophische Betrachtung* (Breslau, 1865)	Y*	N made a 63-page summary with comments. A list of books to buy. N acquired this book May 26, 1875.	Bücherrechnungen + KSA 8, 8[1+3]+9[1]
Dühring, E., *Cursus der Philosophie als streng wissenschaftlichen Weltan schaaung und Lebensgestaltung* (Leipzig, 1875)	Y**	A list of books to buy. N acquired this book on April 21, 1875, and read it in the summer of 1875. He later reread it in 1885.	Bücherrechnungen + KSA 8, 8[3]
Hillebrand, K., "Schopenhauer und das deutsche	Y	Brief mention. Implies having read.	KSA 8, 11[4]

Publikum," in *Zeiten,*
Völker und Menschen,
Vol. 2 (Berlin, 1875)

Schopenhauer, A., *Sämtliche Werke,* Frauenstädt, 6 vols. (Leipzig, 1873/4)	Y***	N bought this book in 1875.	Bücherrechnungen
Dühring, E., *Kritische Geschichte der Philosophie von ihren Anfängen bis zur Gegenwart* (Berlin, 1873)	Y	N bought this book in 1875.	Bücherrechnungen
Oncken, W., *Die Staatslehre des Aristoteles in historisch-politischen Umrissen,* 2 vols. (Leipzig, 1870)	Y	N bought this book in 1875.	Bücherrechnungen
Dühring, E., *Natürliche Dialektik* (Berlin, 1865)	Y	N bought this book in 1875.	Bücherrechnungen
Dühring, E., *Kritische Geschichte der allgemeinen Prinzipien der Mechanik* (Berlin, 1873)	Y	N bought this book in 1875.	Bücherrechnungen
Plato, many booklets	?	N bought these in 1875.	Bücherrechnungen
†Platonis, *Symposium* Rettig.	—	Sent to N by bookshop, but N returned it without buying.	Bücherrechnungen
†Spinoza, *Ethica*	—	Sent to N by bookshop, but N returned it without buying.	Bücherrechnungen
†Platoniis, *Opera*	—	Sent to N by bookshop, but N returned it without buying. (N possessed Plato in Greek and German in other editions.)	Bücherrechnungen
Confucius, *Ta-Hio*	—	N bought this book in 1875.	Bücherrechnungen
Confusius, *Lao-tse tao*	—	N bought this book in 1875.	Bücherrechnungen
Hillebrand, K., *Zeiten, Völker und Menschen* 2 vols. (Berlin, 1874–75)	Y**	N bought this book in 1875.	Bücherrechnungen
Dühring, E., *Kursus der National- und Sozialökonomie, einschliesslich der Hauptpunkte der Finanzpolitik* (Berlin, 1873)	Y	N bought this book in 1875.	Bücherrechnungen

TABLE I   213

Dühring, E., *Kritische Geschichte der Nationalökonomie und des Sozialismus* (Berlin, 1875)	Y*	N bought this book in 1875.	Bücherrechnungen
Draper, J. W., *Geschichte der Conflicte zwischen Religion und Wissenschaft* (1875), Int. wiss. Bibl. XIII	Y	N bought this book in 1875.	Bücherrechnungen
Spencer, H., *Einleitung in das Studium der Sociologie,* Vol. 1 (1875), Int. wiss. Bibl. XIV	Y*	N bought this book in 1875.	Bücherrechnungen
Spencer, H., *Einleitung in das Studium der Sociologie,* Vol. 2 (1875), Int. wiss. Bibl. XV	Y*	N bought this book in 1875.	Bücherrechnungen
Rée, P., *Psychologische Beobachtungen* (Berlin, 1875)	Y	N bought this book in 1875.	Bücherrechnungen
Aristoteles *Rhetorik*		University teaching summer term of 1875	
Diogenes Laertius *Demokritos*		University teaching winter term of 1875–76.	
Platon, *Phaedon, Protagoras, Symposion, Phaedrus und Politeia*		Paedagogium teaching winter term of 1875–76.	
Lewes, G. H., *Geschichte der Philosophie von Thales bis Comte,* Bd. 1 (Berlin, 1871)		Borrowed from the Basel University library 1875.	
Aristoteles, *Ars rhetorica,* hrsg. von L. Spengel, 2 Bde. (Leipzig, 1867)		Borrowed from the Basel University library 1875.	
Demokrit, *Operum fragmenta,* hrsg. von F. W. A. Mullach (Berlin, 1843)		Borrowed from the Basel University library 1875.	
Staphanus Byantinus, *Ethicorum quae supersunt,* hrsg. von A. Meineck, Bd. 1 (Berlin, 1849)		Borrowed from the Basel University library 1875.	

1876

Xenophon, *Memorabilien*	—	"I am reading Xenophon's Memorabilien with the greatest personal interest.—The classical philologists find it deadly boring, you see, how little of a philologist I am."	529 + KSA 8, 18[47]
Emerson, R. W., *Neue Essays* (1876). Original title: *Letters and Social Aims*	Y*	"The *new* Emerson has become a bit old, do you not also think so? The earlier essays are much richer, he now repeats himself, and finally he is all too much in love with life." Short quotation.	Bücherrechnungen + 529 + KSA 8, 16[19]
Emerson, Unidentified works. Probably two *Versuche, Die Führung des Lebens,* and *Über Goethe and Shakespeare*	Y?	N brought *Neue Essays* and two other volumes by Emerson with him for his holiday during March–April 1876.	KGW IV.4, 512
Emerson, Unidentified work. Probably two of *Versuche, Die Führung des Lebens,* and *Über Goethe and Shakespeare*	Y?	N brought *Neue Essays* and two other volumes by Emerson with him for his holiday during March–April 1876.	KGW IV.4, 512
Voltaire, Unknown work or works.	Y?	"We have read much Voltaire, now it is Mainländer's turn." Reading in Sorrento.	573+590
Mainländer, Philipp, *Die Philosophie der Erlösung* (1876)	—	"We have read much Voltaire, now it is Mainländer's turn." Reading in Sorrento and brief discussion. N bought this book in 1876.	Bücherrechnungen + 573 + KSA 8, 19[99] + 23[12]
Rée, P., *Der Ursprung der moralischen Empfindungen* (1877)	Y	Rée wrote it in Sorrento, where he lived together with N. N mentions that it is almost ready in December 1876. The personal dedication in N's copy reads: "From the book's mother to its father."	580+583+591
Strauss, D. F., *Der alte und der neue Glaube* (Leipzig, 1872)	Y	Discussion, quotation, and p-refs.	KSA 8, 15[5]

TABLE I   215

Lichtenberg, G. C., *Vermischte Schriften*	Y	Quotation.	KSA 8, 15[6]
†Chamfort		Short list of authors. To read?	KSA 8, 16[5]
†Coleridge, *Tischgespräche*		Short list of authors. To read?	KSA 8, 16[5]
†Vauvenargues	Y	Listed.	KSA 8, 16[5]
†Spinoza, *Ethica*	—	Two-line quotation in Latin from Spinoza, with Spinoza mentioned. Possibly from secondary source.	KSA 8, 19[68]
Voltaire, *Zadig*	Y	Two-line quotation in French from Voltaire, with Voltaire and the title given. Possibly from secondary source.	KSA 8, 19[81]
Larochefoucauld, de, *Réflexions, sentences et maximes morales.* (Paris, n.d.)	Y	N bought this book in 1876. Listed and discussed.	Bücherrechnungen + KSA 8, 16[5]+ 18[21]
Platonis *Phaedo* rec. Wohlrab	—	N bought this book in 1876.	Bücherrechnungen
Die vorplatonische Philosophen		University teaching summer term of 1876.	
Über Platons Leben und Lehre		University teaching summer term of 1876.	
Sokrates, Quellen zur Persönlichkeit des		Paedagogium teaching summer term of 1876.	
Platon, *Symposion, Phaedon,* and *Apology* N had no teaching during the winter term of 1876–77.		Paedagogium teaching summer term of 1876.	
Demokrit, *Operum fragmenta,* hrsg. von F. W. A. Mullach (Berlin, 1843)		Borrowed from the Basel University library 1876.	
Krohn, A., *Studien zur sokratisch-platonischen Literatur,* Bd. 1 (Halle, 1876)		Borrowed from the Basel University library 1876.	
Steinhart, C., *Platons Leben* (Leipzig, 1873) (Plato, *Sämmtliche Werke,* übers. von H. Müller, Bd. 9)		Borrowed from the Basel University library 1876.	

Krohn, A., *Sokrates und Xenophon* (Halle, 1875)		Borrowed from the Basel University library 1876.	
Xenophon, *Socratis apologia,* hrsg. von M. F. Bornemann (Leipig, 1824)		Borrowed from the Basel University library 1876.	

1877

Diderot	—	Group reading in Sorrento.	590
Spir, A., *Denken und Wirklichkeit: Versuch einer Erneuerung der kritischen Philosophie,* 2 vols. (2nd ed., 1877)	Y***	N orders this work through his publisher.	593+907
Plato, *Gesetze*		N brought with him three books to Rosenlauibad (Twain, Plato, Rée).	627
Rée, P., *Der Ursprung der moralischen Empfindungen* (1877)	Y	Short general discussion.	627 + KSA 8, 23[41+47]+MA, I, 37
Deussen, P., *Die Elemente der Metaphysik* (1877)	Y	N thanks for the book. "Your book serves me strangely enough as a happy collection of everything that I no longer hold for true. . . . Already when I wrote my small study about Schopenhauer I no longer held on to almost any of all the dogmatic aspects."	642+644
†La Rochefoucauld,	Y	Short general discussion.	KSA 8, 23[41+152]

N had no teaching during the summer term of 1877.

†Aristoteles, *Rhetorik*		University teaching winter term of 1877–78. Possibly not carried out this term.	

1878

Plato, *Verteidigungsrede des Sokrates* (1875)	Y***	N had ordered and now thanks his publisher for this work. Reads it.	713 + KSA 8, 28[11]+33[8]

TABLE I   217

Renan, *Philosophische Dialoge und Fragmente* (1877)	Y*	N orders from his publisher.	716
Dumont, E., *Der Fortschritt im Lichte der Lehren Schopenhauers und Darwins* (1876)	Y	Dumont sent to Nietzsche.	Dumont to N, December 22, 1878
Emerson, R. W., *Über Goethe und Shakespeare* (Hannover, 1857)	(Y)	Quotation/paraphrase and p-ref.	KSA 8, 27[12]
†Xenophon, *Memorabilia*	—	N has just read Plato's *Apology* and now has the wish to reread Xenophon's *Memorabilien*.	KSA 8, 28[11]
†Dühring	Y?	General statement.	KSA 8, 29[8]
Montaigne *Versuche*, 3 vols. (Leipzig, 1753–54)	Y*	N refers and quotes from vol. 3, with p-ref.	KSA 8, 29[25+26]+30[7]
†Gwinner, *Schopenhauer-biography*	—	N refers to it and to Schopenhauer as an entrance hall to Christianity. Possibly from earlier reading.	KSA 8, 30[9]
Emerson, *Versuche*	Y***	Quotations and p-refs. Including N's discussion of "Über-seele."	KSA 8, 30[94+98+103+104]+32[13+15+23]
Schopenhauer, *Parerga*, Vol. 2	Y	Quotations with p-ref.	KSA 8, 30[97+100]
†Augustinus,	?	N quotes two lines in Latin.	KSA 8, 36[1]
Pascal, B., *Gedanken Fragmente und Briefe* (Leipzig, 1865)	Y	Ten-line quotation.	KSA 8, 36[3]
Platon, *Apologie*		University teaching summer term of 1878.	
Einleitung in das Studium Platons		University teaching winter term of 1878–79.	
Locke, *Einige Gedanken über Erziehung* (Leipzig, Year of publication not given)	Y	N bought this book in 1878.	Bücherrechnungen
Lehrs, C., *Populäre Aufsätze aus dem Alterthum vorzugsweise zur Ethik und Religion der Griechen* (Leipzig, 1856)		Borrowed from the Basel University library 1878.	

Steinhart, C., *Platon's Leben* (Leipzig, 1873) (Plato, Sämmtliche Werke übers. von H. Müller, Bd. 9)		Borrowed from the Basel University library 1878.	
Plato, *Sämmtliche Werke,* übersetzt von H. Müller, mit Einleitungen von K. Steinhart, Bd. 8 (Leipzig, 1850–66)		Borrowed from the Basel University library 1878.	

1879

Fontenelle, B., *Dialogues des morts* (1876)	Y*	"Fontenelle's dialogues des morts are like blood-related to me."	831
Rée, P., Early versions of "Kritik des Gewissens"	—	Discusses it in letters with Rée. N probably read most of it in early versions.	844+857+ 869+899
Teichmüller, G., *Über die Reihenfolge der platonischen Dialoge* (1879)	Y	Overbeck sends to N.	August 2, 1879
Martha, B. C., *Les Moralistes sous l'empire romain, philosophes et poètes* (Paris, 1865)	—	"Oh, the eyes!! The first book that I took up is French (les Moralistes Romains, by Flotow) Sorry! von *Martha*."	872
Bilharz, A., *Der heliozentrische Standpunkt der Weltbetrachtung: Grundlegung zu einer wirklichen Naturphilosophie* (1879)	Y*	The author sends the book to N.	August 31, 1879
Spencer, H. *Die Tatsachen der Ethik* (1879)	Y**	N recommends his publisher to translate and publish this work. It was already published, and N orders it. N mentions that other earlier works already have been translated and published.[14] N then bought the book.	907+921+ Bücherrechnungen
Hartmann, E. v., *Phänomenologie des sittlichen Bewusstseins: Prologomena zu jeder*	Y***	"To translate Spencer's *The Data of Ethics* would be the best countermove against Hartmann's latest rudeness	907

TABLE 1   219

künftigen Ethik (1879)		'Prolegomena zu *jeder* zukünftigen Ethik'!!," N writes to his publisher.	
†Moore, T., *Utopia*	—	N explicitly says he has not read it: "it is unknown to me."	912
†Villari, P., *Machiavelli* (Rudolstadt, 1877–82)	—	List of books to read.	KSA 8, 39[8]
†Renan	Y?	List of books to read.	KSA 8, 39[8]
†Xenophon, *Memorabilia*	—	N praises highly.	KSA 8, 41[2]+ 42[48]+MA, III, 86
†Rivarol, *Fontenelle*	—	List of three "titles."	KSA 8, 41[73]

1880

Martensen, H. L., *Die christliche Ethik* (1871, 1873)	—	N wants book sent to him. This is also done.	18
Siebenlist, A., *Schopenhauer's Philosophie der Tragödie* (1880)	Y	Author sent it to N.	32 + May 28, 1880
Lüdemann, H., *Die Anthropologie des Apostels Paulus und ihre Stellung innerhalb seiner Heilslehre* (Kiel, 1872)	—	N wants to borrow the book from Overbeck. Paraphrase, quotation, and p-ref.	33+41 + KSA 9, 4[157–164+ 167+170–72+ 217–20+231+ 252–55+258]
Engelhardt, *Das Christenthum Justin*	—	N wants to borrow from Overbeck.	33+41
Wackernagel, *Buddhismus*	—	N wants to borrow from Overbeck.	33+41
Spencer, H., *Die Thatsachen der Ethik* (Stuttgart, 1879)	Y**	Discussion and p-ref.	18+195 + KSA 9, 1[11+105+106]+ 3[97]+10[B48]
Mill, J. S., *Auguste Comte und Positivismus*, Vol. 9 (Leipzig, 1869–80)	Y***	Paraphrase. Gast read Mill to N during the summer of 1880. N probably read five volumes of Mill.	KSA 9, 2[12]+4[68]
Mill, J. S., *Coleridge*, in *Gesammelte Werke*, Vol. 10	Y	Short quotation with explicit reference.	KSA 9, 4[86]
Mill, J. S., "Plato" in vol. 12 (Disc. of Grote's *Plato*)	Y**	Discussion with p-ref.	KSA 9, 4[301+ 302+304]

Baumann, J. J., *Handbuch der Moral nebst Abriss der Rechtsphilosophie* (Leipzig, 1879)	Y	Paraphrase, with p-ref.	18 + KSA 9, 4[52+53+57+ 121+130–33+ 274], 6[56+343]
Wackernagel, J., *Über den Ursprung des Brahmanismus* (Basel, 1877)	Y	Quotation with reference and paraphrase.	33+41 + KSA 9, 4[186+192+224]
Espinas, A., *Die thierischen Gesellschaften* (Braunschweig, 1879)	Y**	Paraphrase.	KSA 9, 4[201]
Littré, E., *La science au point de vue philosophique* (Paris, 1876)	Y*	Discussion and paraphrase. Reference.	KSA 9, 6[145+ 160+161]
Emerson, *Versuche*	Y***	Paraphrase with p-ref to the essay "Freundschaft."	KSA 9, 6[451]
Epiktet, *Handbuch*	Y	Quotation, paraphrase, and discussion.	KSA 9, 6[352]
Pascal, B., *Gedanken, Fragmente und Briefe* (Leipzig, 1865)	Y**	Discussions and quotations.	KSA 9, 7[29+144 +184+190+ 191+208+233+ 254+260+262+ 271+282], 8[31], 10[D68+D70]
Sainte-Beuve, *Port-Royal* (Paris, 1840–48)	—	Paraphrase and short quotation.	KSA 9, 7[228+260+ 261+278]
La Bruyère, *Die Charactere Theophrastos*	—	N bought this book in 1880.	Bücherrechnungen

1881

†Voltaire *Mahomet* (Goethe's translation)	Y	N recommends. Probably read earlier.	82
Lecky, W. E. H., *Sittengeschichte Europas von Augustus bis auf Karl den Grossen* (1879)	Y***	N orders.	93+105
Charron, *Drei Bücher von der Weisheit*	Y*	Read by N.	97+103
Caspari, O., *Der Zusammenhang der Dinge: Gesammelte philosophische Aufsätze* (Breslau, 1881)	Y***	N orders.	118

TABLE 1   221

Buckle, *Essays*	Y*	N orders.	118
Dühring, E., *Cursus der Philosophie als streng wissenschaftlicher Weltanschauung und Lebensgestaltung* (Leipzig, 1875)	Y**	N asks Elisabeth to send.	121+129
†Littré, E., *La science au point de vue philosophique* (Paris, 1876)	?	Apparently sent by Overbeck to N,[15] who claims that he will not read it. Possibly this is a different work by him than the *La science* that he read in 1880.	139
Caspari, O. *Die Thomson'sche Hypothese*	Y	N orders from Overbeck.	139
Fick, A. *Ursache und Wirkung*	—	N orders from Overbeck.	139+150
Liebmann, *Kant und die Epigonen*	Y	N orders from Overbeck.	139
Philosophische Monatshefte	—	N orders from Overbeck.	139+149
Kosmos (Journal)	—	N orders from Overbeck.	139+149
†Dubois-Reymond, *Reden*	—	N asks if it exists.[16]	139
Romundt, *Christenthum und Vernunft*	—	N discusses. Not read.	151+167+204
Pachnicke, H., *De philosophia Epicuri*	Y	N mentions with approval.	177
Emerson	Y?	Intensive reading, autumn–winter of 1881.	
Proctor, R. A., *Unser Standpunkt im Weltall* (Heilbronn, 1877)	Y*	Discussion and quotations.	KSA 9, 11[24]
Spencer, H., *Die Thatsachen der Ethik* (Stuttgart, 1879)	Y**	Critique, discussion, and p-ref.	KSA 9, 11[20+37+40+43+98+343], 12[185]
Lecky, W. E. H., *Geschichte des Ursprungs und Einflusses der Aufklärung in Europa* (Leipzig, 1873)	Y***	N orders. Discussions and quotations. Lecky mentioned.	93+105 + KSA 9, 11[85+86+92+94+95]
†Lange, F. A., *Geschichte des Materialismus* (1866)	(Y)	Quotation and discussion.	KSA 9, 11[119]
Fischer, K., *Geschichte der neuern Philosophie* I.2: *Descartes Schule, Geulinx,*	—	N orders from Overbeck. Paraphrase, quotation, and discussion.	123+135 + KSA 9, 11[193+194]

.

Malebrache, B. Spinoza (Heidelberg, 1865)			
Liebmann, O., *Zur Analysis der Wirklichkeit* (Strassburg, 1880)	Y***	N orders from Overbeck. Paraphrase.	139+149 + KSA 9, 11[236]
Vogt, J. C., *Die Kraft, Eine real-monistische Weltanschauung,* Vol. 1 (Leipzig, 1878)	Y*	N orders from Overbeck. Paraphrase. P-refs.	139 + KSA 9, 11[308+ 311+312]
Spir, A., *Denken und Wirklichkeit* Vol. 1 (1877).	Y***	N orders from Overbeck. Paraphrase.	139 + KSA 9, 11[321+329]
Chamfort, *Pensées-Maximes-Anecdotes-Dialogues*	Y*	Short praising comment and quotation.	KSA 9, 12[121] + 15[71]
Emerson, *Versuche* (1858)	Y***	N praises highly, but also criticizes. N writes much in the copy of the book. He had read it several times before, but his copy was stolen in 1876. He has now bought a new copy and reads and annotates it.	KSA 9, 12[68+ 151+227] + 13[1–22], 17[1–39]
†Voltaire	Y	N writes "Praise to Voltaire." Possibly reading now?	KSA 9, 12[190]
†Marcus Aurelius	Y	N praises M. Aurelius and Grazian. "What astonishment" they give him.	KSA 9, 12[191]
1882			
Emerson, *Versuche*	Y***	Excerpts from the first 57 pages of this work. P-ref.	KSA 9, 17[1–39] + 18[5] + FW (Motto to the first edition) + KSA 10, 5[1]228 + Za, I, Vorrede, 2
†Buckle, *Über Unsterblichkeit*	—	Short paraphrase? N discusses spiritism.	KSA 10, 1[31]
†Fechner, *Die physikalische und philosophische Atomlehre,* 2nd ed. (Leipzig, 1864)	—	List of titles to read (?).	KGW VII.4/2, 67 = KSA 10, 1[112]

TABLE 1   223

†Mach, E., *Die Geschichte und die Wurzel des Satzes von der Erhaltung der Arbeit*	—	List of titles to read (?).	KGW VII.4/2, 67 = KSA 10, 1[112]
†Lasswitz, *Atomistik und Kriticismus* (1878)	—	List of titles to read (?).	KGW VII.4/2, 67 = KSA 10, 1[112]
†Neumann, C., *Über die Principien der Galilei-Newtonschen Theorie*	—	List of titles to read (?).	KGW VII.4/2, 67 = KSA 10, 1[112]
†Moldenhauer, Th., *Die Axendrehung der Weltkörper* (Berlin, 1871), or *Das Weltall und seine Entwicklung* (Köln, 1882)	?	The name Moldenhauer listed.	KSA 10, 4[118], 9[57], 15[8+60]

1883

Teichmüller, G., Unidentified work that N had borrowed from Overbeck.	—	The book had been sent by Overbeck.	470
Hartmann, E. v., *Phänomenologie des sittlichen Bewusstseins. Prolegomena zu jeder künftigen Ethik* (Berlin, 1879)	Y***	N refers to many pages in this work. Paraphrases.	KSA 10, 7[2+ 10+25+31+176+ 206+208+213– 22+224+238+ 251+270+272]
Lecky, *Geschichte des Ursprungs und Einflusses der Aufklärung in Europa*, 2 vols. (Leipzig/Heidelberg, 1873)	Y	N refers to page in Lecky. Short discussion.	KSA 10, 7[8+49]
†La Rochefoucauld, *Maxime und Reflexionen* (Leipzig, 1875)	Y	Discussion.	KSA 10, 4[54]+ 7[40]
Baumann, J. J., *Handbuch der Moral nebst Abriss der Rechtsphilosophie* (Leipzig, 1879)	Y***	Discussion.	KSA 10, 7[69+96]
Dühring, E., *Cursus der Philosophie als streng*	Y**	P-ref and quotation.	KSA 10, 7[78]

wissenschaftlicher Weltanschauung und Lebensgestaltung (Leipzig, 1875)			
Mainländer, P., *Die Philosophie der Erlösung,* 2nd ed. (Berlin, 1879)	—	N had read this work in 1876 and now rereads (Overbeck's copy of) the second edition. P-refs.	KSA 10, 4[118], 7[134–36+140]
Emerson, *Versuche*	Y***	Quotations, paraphrases, and p-ref.	477 + KSA 10, 7[144+159+269]
Teichmüller, G., *Die wirkliche und die scheinbare Welt* (Breslau, 1882)	—	P-ref and discussion.	469 + KSA 10, 7[153+223]+ 20[4]
Schmidt, L., *Die Ethik der alten Griechen,* 2 vols. (Berlin, 1882)	Y*	Quotations, paraphrases, discussions, and p-refs.	KSA 10, 7[22+ 160–168+ca. 180–89], 8[15]
Espinas, A., *Die thierische Gesellschaften* (Braunschweig, 1879)	Y**	Paraphrase, discussion, and p-refs.	KSA 10, 7[173+ 244+245]
†Coleridge	—	Planned reading?	KSA 10, 15[8]
†Eckart, Meister, and Mystiker	—	Planned reading?	KSA 10, 15[8]
†Swedenborg	—	Planned reading?	KSA 10, 15[8]
Emerson, *Versuche*	Y***	Paraphrase and p-refs.	KSA 10, 15[27]+ 16[37]+17[39]+ 22[1]
†Hartmann, E. v., *Gesammelte Studien und Aufsätze gemeinverständlichen Inhalts* (Berlin, Naumburg, 1876)	—	List of planned reading?	KSA 10, 15[60]
†Bentham, J., *Grundsätze der Zivil- und Kriminalgesetzgebung,* 2 vols., deutsche Bearbeitung von Benecke	—	List of planned reading?	KSA 10, 15[60]
Rée, *Der Ursprung der moralischen Empfindungen* (1877)	Y	Quotations and discussion of Rée's work.	KSA 10, 16[15+18]
Spencer, H., *Die Thatsachen der Ethik* (Stuttgart, 1879)	Y**	Brief discussion and p-ref.	KSA 10, 17[34]

TABLE I   225

†Lange, A. F., *Geschichte des Materialismus*	(Y)	A. Blanqui, *L'éternité par les astres* (1872), listed.[17] Possibly from Lange who refers to the work, which contains discussions similar to N's eternal recurrence.	KSA 10, 17[73]
Spencer, H., *Einleitung in das Studium der Sociologie,* Vol. 2 (Leipzig, 1875)	Y*	Reference and p-ref.	KSA 10, 20[3]
Teichmüller, G., *Neue Studien zur Geschichte der Begriffe,* 3 vols., Vol. 3: *Die praktische Vernunft Aristoteles* (Dorpat, 1876–79)	—	Paraphrase and p-refs.	KSA 10, 20[4+7?]
Vogt, J. G., *Die Kraft: Eine real-monistische Weltanschauung* (1878)	Y*	P-ref and several quotations.	KSA 10, 24[36]

1884

Schopenhauer	Y	N looked through Schopenhauer.	498
Stein, H. v., *Über die Bedeutung des dichterisches Elements in der Philosophie des Giordano Bruno,* Habilitationschrift (1881)	Y	N thanks for this work, which Stein sent to him.	514
Montaigne, *Versuche,* 3 vols. (1753–54)	Y*	N asks mother to send Vol. 1.	537
Rolph, W. H., *Biologische Probleme zugleich als Versuch zur Entwicklung einer rationellen Ethik* (Leipzig, 1884)	Y***	Mention.	556
?	?	"Vielleicht habe ich auch im Sommer zu viel schlecht gedruckte Bücher gelesen (*deutsche* Bücher über Metaphysik!")	566
Emerson, "Historic Notes of Life and Letters in Massachusettes," *The Atlantic Monthly* (October 1883)	Y*	N had the essay translated.	566+504?
Emerson, *Versuche* (Hannover, 1858)	Y***	Short quotations and a paraphrase/quotation and p-ref.	KSA 11, 25[3]+31[42]

Schopenhauer, *Die Welt als Wille und Vorstellung.* Bd 2.	Y	P-ref. Two quotations.	KSA 11, 25[86]+26[159]
†Plato, *Theages*	Y	Reference, discussion, and two-line quotation.	KSA 11, 25[137]
Lange, F. A., *Geschichte des Materialismus* (1882)	(Y*)	Paraphrase, discussion, quotation, and p-ref. N's library contains the edition from 1887.	KSA 11, 25[318+424]
Schopenhauer, *Preisschrift über die Grundlage der Moral*	Y	Discussion, paraphrase, quotation, and p-refs.	KSA 11, 25[437+441–42] +26[78+84+ 85+96]
†Marcus Aurelius, *Selbstgespräche*	Y	"Marcus Aurelius Confessions are for me a comical book."	KSA 11, 25[511]
†Aristotle, *Nicomachian Ethics*	(Y)	Quotation from the section about *Megalopsychia*. Probably from secondary source.	KSA 11, 26[122+123]
†Comte, A., *Einleitung in die positive Philosophie* (1880)	Y	N criticizes Comte. Possibly from Dühring (*Sache, Leben und Feinde*), Mill, or other secondary source.	KSA 11, 26[232]
Dühring, E., *Sache, Leben und Feinde: Als Hauptwerk und Schlüssel zu seinen sämtlichen Schriften* (1882)	Y*	Reference and short discussion.	KSA 11, 26[233]
Montaigne, *Versuche,* 3 vols. (1853–54), Vol. 1	Y	Quotation and p-ref.	KSA 11, 26[291]
†Kant	—	N discusses and criticizes Kant's philosophy intensively at this time (1884 and 1885). It is not clear what reading, of or about Kant, this is based on.	For example, KSA 11, 26[371 +375+412+431+ 461+464]+ 34[37+79+82+ 116+185]+ 38[7] + JGB, 11
†Teichmüller, G., *Die wirkliche und die scheinbare Welt* (1882)	—	Paraphrase and discussion. Possibly from earlier reading.	KSA 11, 26[416]
Guyau, M., *Esquisse d'une morale sans obligation ni sanction* (Paris, 1885)	Y***	List of twelve books to buy and read. N bought this book in 1884.	Bücherrechnungen + KSA 11, 29[67]

TABLE I   227

1885

†Montaigne	Y*	General comment. N recommends the work.	578+581+584
†Renan	Y?	General comment.	578
Augustin, *Confession der heilige Augustin*	—	Reading, discussion, and critique.	589 + KSA 12, 1[65+70]
†Teichmüller (two books)	—	N returns two books to Overbeck in November 1885.	609+645
†Mainländer, P., *Die Philosophie der Erlösung*	—	N mentions that he has Overbeck's copy in Sils-Maria.	609
Widemann, P., *Erkennen und Sein. Lösung des Problems des Idealen und Realen* (Karlsruhe and Leipzig, 1885)	Y**	Mention, reading, and discussion.[18]	613+614+616+ 618 + KSA 12, 5[100]?
Dühring, E., *Cursus der Philosophie als streng wissenschaftliche Weltan- schauung und Lebensgestal- tung* (Leipzig, 1875)	Y**	Discussion and quotation.	613+624
Rée, P., *Entstehung des Gewissen*	—	Reading.	634+636+649
Emerson, R. W., ?	?	Quotation and p-ref (283).	KSA 11, 31[42]
†Kant, I., *Kritik der reinen Vernunft*	—	Discussion, paraphrase, and short quotations.[19] Possibly from secondary source. N discusses Kant intensively at this time.	KSA 11, 34[70+ 71+73+79+82]
Drossbach, M., *Über scheinbaren und wirklichen Ursachen des Geschehens in der Welt* (Halle, 1884)	Y***	Discussion and paraphrase.	KSA 11, 34[70+ 82+120+131+ 171+246–47] + 36[10+21+ 25+31]
Lange, F. A., *Geschichte des Materialismus und Kritik seiner Bedeutung*	(Y*)	Quotation and discussion.	KSA 11, 34[99]
†Spencer, H., *Die Thatsachen der Ethik* (Stuttgart, 1879)	Y**	Discussion.[20] Probably from earlier reading.	KSA 11, 35[34]
†Hartmann, E. v., *Phänomenologie des sittlichen Bewusstseins,*	Y***	Important discussion, probably based on the reading of this work in 1883.[21]	KSA 11, 35[34]

Prolegomena zu jeder künftigen Ethik (Berlin, 1879)

†Rée, P., *Der Ursprung der moralischen Empfindungen* (Chemnitz, 1877)	Y	Important discussion, probably based on earlier reading.	KSA 11, 35[34]
Guyau, J. M., *Esquisse d'une moral sans obligation ni sanction* (Paris, 1885)	(Y***)	Important discussion. Read in 1885.[22]	KSA 11, 35[34]
Rolph, W. H., *Biologische Probleme zugleich als Versuch zur Entwicklung einer rationellen Ethik* (Leipzig, 1884)	Y***	Important discussion. Read in 1884–85.[23]	KSA 11, 35[34]
Spir, A., *Denken und Wirklichkeit. Versuch einer Erneuerung der kritischen Philosophie*, 2 vols., (Leipzig, 1877)	Y***	N rereads this work now. Discussion and several quotations and p-refs.[24]	KSA 11, 35[56+61]+ 40[12+24+41]
†Leibniz	—	Six-line quotation of verse. N discusses Leibniz at this time. Could come from primary or secondary reading.	KSA 11, 37[10]
Teichmüller, G., *Die wirkliche und die scheinbare Welt: Neue Grundlegung der Metaphysik* (Breslav, 1882)	—	Discussion, quotations, and p-refs.[25]	KSA 11, 40[12+ 24+30+41]
Dühring, E., *Sache, Leben und Feinde. Als Hauptwerk und Schlüssel zu seinen sämtlichen Schriften* (Karlsruhe and Leipzig, 1882)	Y*	Critique.[26]	KSA 12, 1[226]+958
Montesquieu, *Persische Briefe*	—	N bought this book in 1885.	Bücherrechnun-gen

1886

†Lucretius, *De rerum naturae*	Y	Short quotation.[27]	KSA 12, 2[187]
†Ziegler, Th., *Geschichte der Ethik*, 2 vols. (1881, 1886)	—	Listed.[28] Probably intended reading but not carried out.	KSA 12, 5[1]

TABLE I   229

†Rée, P., *Ursprung der moralischen Empfindungen* (Chemnitz, 1877)	Y	Discussion. Possibly from earlier reading or rereading.	KSA 12, 5[5] + GM, Preface, 4+7

1887

Simplicius, *Kommentar zu Epiktetos Handbuch* (Wien, 1867)	Y***	Reading now. Discusses.[29]	790 + KSA 12, 10[150+151]
Montaigne, *Essays* (in German or French)	Y+Y*	Reading now.	940
†Stein, H. v., *Die Entstehung der neueren Äesthetik*	—	N praises it as "very learned" but also states: "it has been praised to me."	868
†Montesquieu, ?	?	Short French quotation.	KSA 12, 5[87]
†Gury, *Compendium theologiae Moralis Ratisbonae* (1862)	—	List of six titles. Probably not read.	KSA 12, 5[110]
Fischer, K., *Geschichte der neueren Philosophie I.2: Descartes Schule, Geulinx, Malebrache, B. Spinoza* (Heidelberg, 1865)	—	N read carefully and excerpted extensively about Spinoza, and also Leibniz, through this work. Paraphrases, quotations, and discussions.	KSA 12, 7[4+57?]
Fischer, K., *Geschichte der neuern Philosophie: Bd. 5: Immanuel Kant und seine Lehre*	—	N read carefully and excerpted extensively about Kant, and also Feuerbach, through this work. Paraphrases, quotations, and discussions.	KSA 12, 7[4]
Mill J. S., *August Comte und der Positivismus. Vermischte Schriften politischen, philosophies-chen und historischen Inhalts,* Vol. 9 (Leipzig, 1869)	Y***	Discussion and several quotations.[30]	KSA 12, 9[24+ 44+47+51+55] +10[147+170] +14[48]
Mill, J. S., *Über Aphorismen*	Y***	Discussion and quotation.	KSA 12, 9[67]
Joly, H., *Psychologie des grands hommes* (Paris, 1883)	Y*	Excerpts.	KSA 12, 9[67+ 68+69+70]
Schopenhauer, A., *Parerga,* Vol. 2	Y	Short abstract and p-ref.	KSA 12, 9[84]
Liebmann, O., *Gedanken und Tatsachen,* Vol. 1	Y**	Four short quotations and p-ref.[31]	KSA 12, 9[92]

(Strassburg, 1882)

Schopenhauer, A., *Welt2, Welt1, Parerga*	Y**	Several short quotations.	KSA 12, 10[98+99+101+166+173]
†Reuter, H., *Augustinische Studien* (Gotha, 1887)	—	Listed, possibly not read.	KSA 12, 10[120]
†Teichmüller, G., *Historia Philosophiae. Graecae et Ronmanae ex fontium locis contexta* (1875)	—	Listed, possibly not read.	KSA 12, 10[120]
Pascal, B., *Gedanken, Fragmente und Briefe* (Leipzig, 1865)	Y**	Quotation, discussion, and p-ref.	KSA 12, 10[128]
Guyau, M., *L'irréligion de l'avenir* (Paris, 1887)	Y***	Guyau mentioned in connection with religion.[32]	KSA 12, 10[170+171]
Höffding, H., *Psychologie in Umrissen* (1887)	Y***	Excerpts enter *Zur Genealogie der Moral.*	GM, Vorrede 2, I, 1–2, II, 1+6, III, 8+15+17, GD
Roberty, E. d., *L'ancienne et la nouvelle philosophie. Essai sur les lois générales du développement de la philosophie* (Paris, 1887)	Y***	Short discussion.[33]	969 + KSA 12, 9[57]

1888

Schopenhauer, A., *Die Welt als Wille und Vorstellung* II	Y**	Short discussion and p-ref.	975
Brandes, G., *Die romantische Schule in Deutschland,* Vol. 2 (1887)	Y	Reading now or recently.[34]	1009+1096
†Ercole, P. d., *Notizia degli scritti e del pensiere filosofico di Pietro Ceretti, accompagnata da un cenno autobiografico del medesimo, intitolato "La mia celebrita"* (Turin, 1886)	Y	N receives book and mentions it. Probably not read.	1039+1040+1043
†Carlyle, T., Unknown biography	—	Discusses Carlyle.[35] Possibly N refers to Taine's long account in *History of British Literature.*	KSA 13, 11[45] + GD, 12

TABLE I   231

Hartmann, E., *Philosophie des Unbewußten*	—	Discussion. Possibly from his reading of Sully.	KSA 13, 11[61+ 71+72+75+76+ 77+101]
Brochard, V., *Les sceptiques grecs* (Paris, 1887)	Y	Actualizes Pyrrho and the sophists.[36]	KSA 13, 14[85+ 100+129+135+ 137+141+142+ 149+150+162+ 191]+15[5+58]+ 21[1]+EH
†Teichmüller, G., *Die wirkliche und die scheinbare Welt. Neue Grundlegung der Metaphysik* (Breslav, 1882)	—	Listed, with three other titles. Read earlier.	KSA 13, 21[1]
†Spir, A., *Denken und Wirklichkeit. Versuch einer Erneuerung der kritischen Philosphie* (Leipzig, 1877)	Y***	Listed, with three other titles. Read earlier.	KSA 13, 21[1]

[1] Hölderlin, *Ausgewählte Werke,* from 1874 is present in Nietzsche's library.

[2] Gustav Krug writes to Nietzsche: "In betreff des Buches wirst Du wohl schon selbst einen Beschluß gefaßt haben, ich habe von dem Titel des Buches, das Du wünschest selbst etwas gehört, wobei es mir aber ganz Angst und Bange geworden ist, da ich so was von Problemen und anderen schrecklichen Dingen gehört habe. Doch glaube ich, daß Du erst nach reiflicher überlegung diesen Wunsch ausgedrückt hast. Ich kann Dir daher nicht meine Meinung über die Wahl aussprechen" (KGB I.1, 374). It is possible that the work referred to is one by Feuerbach.

[3] Nietzsche's library contains a French translation of this work from a later year (1873). It is most likely that Nietzsche read the work in Italian in 1862—but then with an emphasis on language (this was part of his study of Italian)—and then in French after 1880. (His French before ca. 1880 was such that he could only read it with difficulty.)

[4] Emerson's *The Conduct of Life* contains the following essays: "Fate," "Power," "Wealth," "Culture," "Behaviour," "Worship," "Considerations by the Way," "Beauty," and "Illusions."

[5] The full title of Plato's work is *Dialogi Secundum Thrasylli tetralogies dispositi. Ex recognitione Caroli Frederici Hermanni* (Leipzig, 1864), XXVI+382 pages. The volume contains the following dialogues: *Parmenides, Philebus, Symposion, Phaidros, Alkibiades, Alkibiades major, Hipparchos, Antirastai and Theageas.*

[6] That the reading of Strauss was important for Nietzsche at this time is reflected in a letter from Elisabeth to him, May 26, 1865: "Am allermeisten thut es mir aber leid, daß Du den unglücklichen Strauß mit in die Ferien gebracht hast, und daß ich so viel davon gehört durch Dich."

[7] Nietzsche had possessed Lange in the first edition (1866), but in his library is a copy of the fourth edition (Leipzig, 1887) containing a few annotations. Nietzsche also quotes from the second or third edition during the 1880s.

[8] The titles Nietzsche wrote down as future reading in the spring of 1868, in alphabetical order, were:

Bichat, *Recherches physiologiques sur la vie et la mort*
Carus, *Grundzüge der vergleichenden Anatomie und Physiologie*
Czolbe, *Die Grenzen und der Ursprung der menschlichen Erkenntniss* (Jena und Leipzig, 1865)
Czolbe, *Neue Darstellung des Sensualismus* (Leipzig, 1855)
Fries, *Mathematische Naturphilosophie* (Heidelberg, 1822)
Hamann, *Schriften*
Helmholtz, *Über die Erhaltung der Kraft* (Berlin, 1847)
Helmholtz, *Über die Wechselwirkung der Naturkräfte* (1854)
Herbart, *Analytische Beleuchtung des Naturrechts und der Moral*
Herder, *Ideen zur Philosophien der Geschichte der Menschheit*
Hettner, H., *Literaturgeschichte des achtzehnten Jahrhunderts,* Vol. 2: *Geschichte der französchichen Literatur im achtzehnten Jahrhundert* (1860)
Holbach, *Système de la nature*
Hume, *Dialogues concerning natural religion,* deutsch von Schreiter (Leipzig, 1781)
Kant, *Allgemeine Naturgeschichte und Theorie des Himmels* (1755)
Kant, *Kritik der reinen Vernunft*
Kant, *Kritik der Urtheilskraft* (1790)
Lotze, *Medicinische Psychologie* (1852)
Lotze, *Streitschriften* (Leipzig, 1857)
Maimon, Sal, "Über die Weltseele, entelechia univerens," in *Berliner Journal für Aufklärung,* von A. Riem, Vol. 8, 1790
Moleschott, *Die Einheit des Lebens* (Giessen, 1864)
Moleschott, *Kreislauf des Lebens* (1862)
Müller, J., *Über das organische Leben*
Müller, J., *Über die Physiologie der Sinne*
Oken, *Die Zeugung* (1805)
Oken, *Lehrbuch der Naturphilosophie* (1809, 1843)
Rosenkranz, C., *Schelling Vorles.* (Danzig, 1843)
Schelling, *Ideen zu einer Philosophie der Natur*
Schelling, *System des transscendenten Idealismus*
Schleiden, *Mechanischen Erklärbarkeit der Organismen*
Schleiden, *über den Materialismus in der neueren Naturwissenschaft* (Leipzig, 1863)
Schneider, G., *De Causa finali Aristotelea* (Berlin, 1865)
Schopenhauer, *Über den Willen in der Natur*
Strauss, D. F., *Kleine Schriften* (1862)
Trendelenburg, *Historische Beiträge zur Philosophie* (1855)
Trendelenburg, *Logische Untersuchungen,* Vol. 2 (Leipzig, 1862)
Trendelenburg, *Monatsbericht der Berliner Academie,* November 1854, February 1856
Treviranus, *Über die Erscheinungen und Gesetze des Organischen Lebens* (1832)
Überweg, *System der Logik*
Virchow, R., *4 Reden über Leben und Kranksein* (Berlin, 1862)
Virchow, R., *Gesammelte Abhandlung zur wissenschaftlichen Medizin* (Frankfurt, 1856)

Table 1   233

Wundt, *Vorlesungen über die Menschen- und Thierseele*
Zeller, *Die Philosophie der Griechen* (about the Stoics)

[9] Nietzsche admits that he has misquoted and probably misunderstood Montaigne's words. Nietzsche suggests a minor rewriting of the text for the French edition.

[10] Nietzsche's friend Gersdorff wrote to Nietzsche: "Finally *Draper* has also arrived and I will only by the way thank you for helping me to such good books." Gersdorff had also spoken of Mark Twain. It seems likely that Nietzsche has recommended Draper to him (but possibly he may also have sent him a copy). Nietzsche possessed in his library two copies of Draper, both containing annotations: *Geschichte der geistigen Entwicklung Europas* (Leipzig, 1871) iv+646 pages, and *Geschichte der Conflicte zwischen Religion und Wissenschaft* (Leipzig, 1875), xxiv+383.

[11] Nietzsche wants to write to his publisher Schmeitzner and suggest that he publish a series of good translation of Indian philosophy. Nietzsche has, for example, thought of Windisch and Deussen, who translated and worked with Indian philosophy.

[12] Possibly a reflection of Nietzsche's reading of Hartmann's *Das Unbewusste von Standpunkt der Physiologie und Descendenztheorie* (Berlin, 1872), published anonymously.

[13] Nietzsche's library contains Grote's *Geschichte Griechenlands* (1850, 1856) with a few annotations.

[14] Nietzsche's library contains two works by Spencer. An earlier work, *Einleitung in das Studium der Sociologie,* 2 vols., (1875), with some annotations, and *Die Tatsachen der Ethik* (Stuttgart, 1879), substantially annotated by Nietzsche.

[15] Nietzsche writes that he "will certainly not read it" due to the small print and his bad eyesight. Nietzsche's library contains one work by E. Littré, *La science au point de vue philosophique* (Paris, 1876).

[16] Nietzsche asks if there exists an edition of Dubois-Reymond's collected speeches or essays.

[17] H. Lichtenberger has pointed out in *Die Philosophie Fr. Nietzsches* (Leipzig, 1899), 204–9, that Blanqui expresses in this book ideas that are similar to Nietzsche's ideas of eternal recurrence.

[18] Paul Heinrich Widemann. Nietzsche knew Widemann personally. Nietzsche possessed two copies of *Erkennen und Sein: Lösung des Probleme des Idealen und Realen, zugleich eine Erörterung des richtigen Ausgangspunktes und des Principien der Philosophie* (1885). The bound copy contains no annotation, but in the paperback copy Nietzsche has made annotations in chapter 13: "Beweis des absoluten Daseins des Objecte" (203–14). The last page of Widemann's *Erkennen und Sein* contains a reference to Nietzsche's *Zarathustra* but also simultaneously places Nietzsche beside Dühring, which would not have been to Nietzsche's liking. Nietzsche also possessed another work by Widemann: *Über die Bedingungen der Übereinstimmung des diskursiven Erkennens mit dem intuitiven* (Schloss-Chemnitz, 1876).

[19] Immanuel Kant (1724–1804). During the spring or early summer of 1885, Nietzsche either read Kant or perhaps more likely a work that discusses Kant. There are many references to Kant near KSA 11, 34[70], including some short quotations from *Kritik der reinen Vernunft*. This could possibly come from a reading of his friend Heinrich Romundt's *Grundlegung* or from Drossbach.

[20] Herbert Spencer (1820–1903), English philosopher and thinker. Nietzsche read carefully and annotated Spencer's *Die Tatsachen der Ethik* (1879) in 1880 and 1881. What we see here in 1885 is a brief discussion of the work probably based on this earlier reading and possibly some secondary literature such as Rolph.

[21] In 1883 Nietzsche read carefully, heavily annotated, and discusses Hartmann's *Phänomenologie des sittlichen Bewußtseins: Prolegomena zu jeder künftigen Ethik* (1879), 872 pages. What we have here in 1885 is an important discussion of this work based on this earlier reading.

[22] Jean-Marie Guyau (1854–88), French philosopher. In 1885 Nietzsche read and heavily annotated his copy of *Esquisse d'une moral sans obligation ni sanction* (Paris, 1885), 254 pages. Nietzsche discusses the book for fifteen lines and regards it, together with those of Rée and Rolph, as one of the three least useless books on morality in present-day Europe ("even if also in these nothing fundamental is said"). Nietzsche's heavily annotated copy was in the library in 1942 but has since been lost. Nietzsche's annotations have, however, been published as an appendix to the German translation of the work by Elisabeth Schwarz, *Sittlichkeit ohne "Plicht": Anhang: Randbemerkungen Friedrich Nietzsches zu Guyaus "Esquisse d'une Morale"* (Leipzig, 1912), 279–303.

[23] William Henry Rolph (1847–83), British German biologist. In 1884 or 1885 Nietzsche read and heavily annotated his *Biologische Probleme zugleich als Versuch zur Entwicklung einer rationellen Ethik,* 2nd ed. (Leipzig, 1884), 238 pages. The ten-line discussion of this work here is Nietzsche's only mention of it. The whole of Nietzsche's copy is heavily annotated (except the first chapter), especially chapter 3, "Herbert Spencer's Hedonismus," 32–54, and the last two chapters, 7 and 8, "Animate oder natürliche Ethik," 170–90, and "Humane Ethik," 191–238.

[24] Afrikan Spir (1837–90), Russian German philosopher. Nietzsche read and borrowed the first edition of *Denken und Wirklichkeit: Versuch einer Erneuerung der kritischen Philosophie* (1873) three times from the university library at Basel between 1873 and 1875. In February 1877 he orders the second edition (1877), consisting of two volumes: volume 1, *Das Unbedingte,* and volume 2, *Die Welt der Erfahrung.* By November 1879 he has read it. He left the two volumes in Zürich with most of his other books when he left Basel. However, already in August 1881 he writes to Overbeck that he badly needs the two volumes by Spir. Nietzsche's copy is heavily annotated, and he seems to have read the work at least four times, in 1873, 1877–79, 1881, and 1885.

[25] Teichmüller. Nietzsche seems to have read Overbeck's copy of *Die wirkliche und die scheinbara Welt: Neue Grundlegung der Metaphysik* (Breslav, 1882), xxxvi+357 pages, which he returned in November 1885. It is likely that Nietzsche's reading of this work played an important role for his rejection of the distinction between a real and an apparent world and for his writing of the chapters "'Reason' in Philosophy" and "How the 'Real World' at Last Became a Myth" in *Götzen-Dämmerung.*

[26] Dühring. The note is probably a reference to Dühring's autobiography *Sache, Leben und Feinde: Als Hauptwerk und Schlüssel zu seinen sämmtlichen Schriften* (1882), x+431 pages. Nietzsche has annotated his copy sparsely from page 45 to page 318. In the note from the end of 1885 or early 1886, Nietzsche seems to be reading this work. In a letter from November 1887, Nietzsche refers to the content of the work.

[27] Lucretius, Roman epicurean philosopher. Nietzsche quotes five poetical words in Latin from his *De rerum naturae.* This could come from a reading of it, but it is much more probable that it is due to memory from earlier reading or possibly from reading a secondary source. Nietzsche possessed *De rerum naturae* in a German translation from 1865, but this copy is likely to have been in Naumburg with most of his other philological books.

[28] Theobald Ziegler (1846–1918), German philosopher and pedagogue. Ziegler was influenced by David Strauss and F. A. Lange. Ziegler wrote *Geschichte der Ethik* in two volumes:

TABLE I   235

volume I is titled *Die Ethik der Griechen und Römer* (1881), 342 pages, and volume 2 is titled *Geschichte der Christlichen Ethik* (1886), 607 pages. In a note from 1886 Nietzsche has written: "Th. Ziegler Geschichte der Ethik." There is no other reference to Ziegler by Nietzsche and hence yet no evidence of his reading either of the two volumes, although he might have done so.

[29] Simplicius, a sixth-century neo-Platonist pagan philosopher who wrote commentaries on Aristotle and one on Epictetus's *Enchiridion* (*Handbook of Ethics*). Nietzsche's copy of Simplicius is heavily annotated, including with words and sentences written in the margins. Several of Nietzsche's comments are critical. The book makes a Christian impression on him. There are a few references to Simplicius in Nietzsche's letters and notebooks.

[30] Nietzsche possessed five of the twelve volumes of the German translation of Mill's collected works and had read all or most of the twenty-nine works they contain in early 1880. During the autumn of 1887 Nietzsche returned to, and reread, the two studies on Comte: "August Comte und der Positivismus: 1. Der 'Cours de Philosophie positive'" and "2. Die späten Forschungen hrn Comtes" in volume 9 of the collected works. Nietzsche also read at least the short article "Ueber Aphorismen" in volume 10, 39–43, and heavily annotated it with marginal lines. The Comte texts are very heavily annotated by Nietzsche; most pages have more than ten pencil underlinings and marginal lines. More than ten pages per text contain words by Nietzsche, and there are more than ten NBs and thirty exclamation marks per essay. Nietzsche's reading about Mill was also extensive.

[31] Otto Liebmann (1840–1912), Neo-Kantian German philosopher. Nietzsche's copy of *Gedanken und Thatsachen: Philosophische Abhandlungen, Aphorismen und Studien* (1882) is extensively annotated. In KSA 12, 9[92], Nietzsche refers to page 11 of this work, which is part of a study titled "Die Arten der Nothwendigkeit," and quotes from this and nearby pages. On page 11 of Nietzsche's copy he has also written in the margin "Wille zur Macht." Nietzsche also possessed Liebmann's most well-known book, *Kant und die Epigonen* (Stuttgart, 1865), without annotations and *Zur Analysis der Wirklichkeit: Eine Erörterung der Grundprobleme der Philosophie,* 2nd ed. (Strassburg, 1880), which is very heavily annotated.

[32] Jean Marie Guyau (1854–88), French philosopher. Nietzsche read Guyau's *Esquisse* in 1885. In two notes from the autumn of 1887, Nietzsche twice refers to Guyau in general terms but related to religion. Nietzsche possessed Guyau's *L'irréligion de l'avenir: Étude sociologique,* 2nd ed. (Paris, 1887), 480 pages, and his copy is heavily annotated. Nietzsche must have read it in 1887 or 1888. These two references are the only ones we have, and it thus seems likely that he read it in, or shortly before, the autumn of 1887.

[33] Eugène de Roberty (1843–1915), Russian French sociologist. Nietzsche's copy of *L'ancienne et la nouvelle philosophie: Essai sur les lois générales du développement de la philosophie* (Paris, 1887) is heavily annotated. Roberty, a follower of Comte, sought general laws in the development of philosophy. Nietzsche expresses critique of this in the letter. There are no other references to Roberty in Nietzsche's works and letters.

[34] Georg Brandes (1842–1927). Nietzsche possessed *Die Literatur der 19. Jahrhunderts in ihren hauptströmungen. Band II. Die romatische Schule in Deutschland* (Leipzig, 1887). It had probably been sent to him by Brandes, but it is without a personal dedication. Nietzsche read it in 1888, but it does not contain any annotations. In a letter to Carl Fuchs, August 26, 1888, Nietzsche claims that "'die hauptströmungen der Literatur des neunzehnten Jahrhunderts' ist immer noch das beste deutsch geschriebene *Cultur-Buch* über dieses große Objekt," thus possibly implying that he had read more than volume 2.

[35] We have no certain evidence of Nietzsche's reading of any work by Carlyle. What we know is that Nietzsche claims in *Götzen-Dämmerung* to "have read the life of *Thomas Carlyle*," that is, a biography about him. However, Nietzsche's statements are so general that it would be difficult to determine which biography he read. One possibility is H. Taine's *L'idéalisme anglais: Étude sur Carlyle* (Paris, 1864), 187 pages, or more probably that he refers to the chapter about Carlyle in Taine's *History of British Literature,* which we know Nietzsche had read. Taine was a thinker whom Nietzsche read with pleasure, and his biography seems to be rather hostile.

[36] Victor Brochard (1848–1907), French philosopher. Nietzsche read his *Les sceptiques grecs* (Paris, 1887), 432 pages, in the spring of 1888. Nietzsche praises it in EH, "Warum ich so klug bin," 3. Nietzsche's copy contains no annotations, and he has not excerpted the work, but his reading of it can be shown to have influenced a rather large number of notes and probably some published texts. It actualizes the skeptic Pyrrho for Nietzsche, but it does not seem to have influenced his view of the skeptics, which was, already before this reading, that there exists two forms of skepticism: healthy and decadent. It does seem to be important for Nietzsche's high praise of the Sophists in 1888 (GD, "Alten," 3), as compared to his much more ambivalent view earlier.

TABLE 2

Philosophical Titles in Nietzsche's Library: Unknown If and When Read

A fairly large number of philosophical books in Nietzsche's library have not been listed in table 1 because either Nietzsche did not read them or we do not know in which year he read them. Many of these books are likely to be relevant (and a large number of them contain annotations), and for most of them Nietzsche's possible reading and response ought to be examined. Some of them I mention in my text. Note also that several of the books without any annotations nonetheless were carefully read by Nietzsche.

Bacon, Franz. *Neues Organ der Wissenschaften.* Aus dem Lateinischen übers. u. mit einer Einleitung u. Anmerkungen begleitet v. Anton Theobald Brück. Leipzig, Brockhaus, 1830. Contains a single annotation.

Bahnsen, Julius. *Der Widerspruch im Wissen und Wesen der Welt. Prinzip und Einzelbewährung der Realdialektik.* II. Bd. Leipzig, 1882. No annotations.

Bain, Alexander. *Erziehung als Wissenschaft.* Leipzig, Brockhaus, 1880. Annotated.

Barklai, Johann. *Gemälde der menschlichen Charaktere.* Aus dem Lateinischen übers. v. Anton Weddige. Münster, 1821. Contains a single annotation.

Bert, Paul. *La morale des Jesuites.* Paris, 1880. No annotations.

Comte, Auguste. *Einleitung in die positive Philosophie.* Deutsch v. G. H. Schneider. Leipzig, 1880. No annotations.

Delboeuf, J. *La matière brute et la matière vivante.* Paris, 1887. No annotations.

Drobisch, Moritz Wilh. *Neue Darstellung der Logik. Nach ihren einfachsten Verhältnissen mit Rücksicht auf Mathematik und Naturwissenschaft.* 4. Aufl. Leipzig, 1875. No annotations.

Ebeling, Ernst. *Darstellung und Beurteilung der religions-philosophischen Lehren J. G. Fichtes.* Hallenser dissertation. Halle, 1886. No annotations.

Engel, J. J. *Der Philosoph für die Welt.* Leipzig, Reclam, n.d. No annotations.

Erasmus von Rotterdam. *Das Lob der Narrheit.* Aus dem Lateinischen übers. u. mit erklärenden Anmerkungen versehen. St. Gallen, 1839. No longer in Nietzsche's library.

Fontenelle, Bernard de. *Histoires des oracles.* Paris, 1876. No annotations.

Fontenelle, Bernhard v. *Gespräche von mehr als einer Welt zwischen einem Frauenzimmer und einem Gelehrten.* Übers. u. mit Figuren u. Anmerkungen erläutert v. Joh. Chr. Gottsched. Leipzig, 1730. Contains a few annotations.

Fuchs, Carl. *Die Zukunft des musikalischen Vortrages und sein Ursprung. 2. Teile.* Danzig, 1884. With a personal dedication from the author. No annotations.

Gizycki, Georg v. *Grundzüge der Moral. Gekrönte Preisschrift.* Leipzig, 1883. No annotations.

Hartmann, Eduard v. *Das Unbewusste vom Standpunkt der Physiologie und Descendenztheorie. Eine kritische Beleuchtung des naturphilosophischen Teils der Philosophie des Unbewussten aus naturwissenschaftlichen Gesichtspunkten.* Berlin, 1872. A few annotations early in the text.

Hartsen, F. A. v. *Die Moral des Pessimismus, nach Veranlassung v. Dr. Tauberts Schrift "Der Pessimismus und seine Gegner" geprüft.* Nordhausen, 1874. No annotations.

Hartsen, F. A. v. *Grundzüge der Psychologie. 2. Aufl.* Halle, 1877. No annotations.

Hausegger, Friedrich v. *Richard Wagner und Schopenhauer. Eine Darlegung der philosophischen Anschauungen Wagners an der Hand seiner Werke.* Leipzig, 1878. No annotations.

Heinze, Max. *Der Eudämonismus in der griechischen Philosophie. 1. Abhandl. Vorsokratiker, Demokrit, Sokrates. Abhandlungen der königl. Sächs. Gesellschaft der Wissenschaften, VIII. Bd., Nr. VI.* 1883. No annotations.

Heinze, Max. *Die Lehre vom Logos in der griechischen Philosophie.* Oldenburg, 1872. No annotations.

Heinze, Max. *Gottfried Wilhelm Leibniz. Rede zur Feier der Denkmalsentfüllung am 25. October 1883 gehalten in der Aula der Universität zu Leipzig.* Leipzig, 1883. No annotations.

Heinze, Max. *Über den sittlichen Wert der Wissenschaft. Rede des antretenden Rektors.* Leipzig, 1883. No annotations.

Helvetius, C. A. *Diskurs über den Geist des Menschen.* Übers. v. J. G. Forkert. Mit Vorrede v. Joh. Chr. Gottsched. Leipzig u. Liegnitz, 1760. Annotated.

Hermann, Karl Friedrich. *Geschichte und System der platonischen Philosophie. Teil I: Historisch-kritische Grundlegung.* Heidelberg, 1839. Annotated.

Holsatius, Joannis Jonsius (Jonsius, Joh.). *De scriptoribus historiae philosophicae libri IV.* Frankfurt, 1659. Annotated on three pages.

Houssaye, Henry. *Les hommes et les idées.* Paris, 1886. No annotations.

Jacoby, Leopold. *Die Idee der Entwicklung. Eine sozial-philosophische Darstellung. 2. Aufl. 2 Bde. i. 1 gebd.* Zürich, 1886–87. Annotated on two pages.

Lange, Friedrich Albert. *Logische Studien. Ein Beitrag zur Neubegründung der formalen Logik und der Erkenntnistheorie.* Iserlohn, 1877. No annotations.

Larochefoucauld, François de. *Maximen und Reflexionen.* Deutsch v. Friedrich Hörlek. Leipzig, Reclam, year of publication not given. Lost from the library.

TABLE 2   239

Larochefoucauld, François de. *Sätze aus der höheren Welt- und Menschenkunde.* Deutsch hrsg. v. Friedrich Schulz. Breslau, 1793. Now lost from the library but apparently heavily annotated.

Lehmann, Rudolf. *Kants Lehre vom Ding an sich.* Göttinger dissertation. Berlin, 1878. No annotations.

Lewes, George Henry. *Geschichte der alten Philosophie.* Berlin, 1871. Contains annotations but probably not Nietzsche's.

Lotze, Hermann. *Grundzüge der ästhetik. Diktate aus den Vorlesungen.* Leipzig, 1884. No annotations.

Lotze, Hermann. *Grundzüge der Metaphysik. Diktate aus den Vorlesungen.* Leipzig, 1883. No annotations.

Mably, G. B. de. *Entretiens de Phocion sur le rapport de la morale et de la politique.* Paris, 1877. No annotations.

Macauly, T. B. *Kritische und historische Aufsätze.* Deutsch v. J. Moellenhoff. *I. Bd. John Milton.* Leipzig, Reclam, n.d. No annotations.

Mach, E. *Beiträge zur Analyse der Empfindungen.* Jena, 1886. Annotations on two pages.

Mach, E., and P. Salcher. "Photographische Fixierung der durch Projektile in der Luft eingeleiteten Vorgänge." Sonderdruck aus dem *Repertorium der Physik,* hrsg. v. F. Exner. With a personal dedication from the author. No annotations.

Machiavel, Nicolas. *Le prince.* Traduction précédé de quelques notes sur l'auteur par C. Ferrari. Paris, 1873. No annotations.

Montesquieu, Ch. de. *Considerations sur les causes de la grandeur dos Romains et de leur décadence.* Paris, 1836. Annotated.

Montesquieu, Ch. de. *Das Werk von den Gesetzen.* Aus dem Französischen übers. 3 Bde. Frankfurt u. Leipzig, 1753. No annotations.

Montesquieu, Ch. de. *Hinterlassene Schriften, nach seinem Tode als ein Nachtrag zu seinen Werken* hrsg. Übers. v. E . Gottlieb Küster. Altenburg, 1798. Lost from the library.

Müller, J. G. *Die Messianischen Erwartungen des Juden Philo.* (Programm für die Rektoratsfeier der Universität Basel.) Basel, 1870. No annotations.

Münter, Gustav Wilh. *Geschichtliche Grundlagen zur Geisteslehre des Menschen oder die Lebensäusserungen des menschlichen Geistes im gesunden und krankhaften Zustande.* Halle, 1850. Annotations on one page.

Oettingen, Alexander v. *Die Moralstatistik in ihrer Bedeutung für eine Sozialethik.* 3. Aufl. Erlangen 1882. Annotated.

Ölzelt-Newin, Anton. *Die Unlösbarkeit der ethischen Probleme.* Wien, 1883. Annotated.

Pachnicke, Hermann. *De philosophia Epicuri.* Hallenser dissertation. Halle, 1882. No annotations.

Platner, Ernst. *Ein Gespräch über den Atheismus.* Leipzig, 1781. Annotated.

Plümacher, O. *Der Pessimismus in Vergangenheit und Gegenwart.* Heidelberg, 1884. Annotated.

Popper, Josef. *Das Recht zu Leben und die Pflicht zu Sterben. Sozial-philosophische Betrach-tungen, anknüpfend an die Bedeutung Voltaires für die neuere Zeit.* 2. Aufl. Leipzig, 1879. No annotations.

Richet, Charles. *Essai de psychologie générale.* Paris, 1887. No annotations.

Richet, Charles. *L'homme et l'intelligence. Fragments de physiologie et de psychologie.* Paris, 1884. No annotations.

Ritter, H., and L. Preller. *Historia philosophiae graecae et romanaeex fontium locis con-texta.* 4. Aufl. Gotha, 1869. Annotated.

Romundt, Heinrich. *Antäus. Neuer Aufbau der Lehre Kants über Seele, Freiheit und Gott.* Leipzig, 1882. With a personal dedication from the author. No annotations.

Romundt, Heinrich. *Die Herstellung der Lehre Jesu durch Kants Reform der Philosophie.* Sonderdruck aus dem deutschen Protestantenblatt. Bremen, 1883. With a personal dedication from the author. No annotations.

Romundt, Heinrich. *Grundlegung zur Reform der Philosophie. Vereinfachte und erweit-erte Darstellung von Immanuel Kants Kritik der reinen Vernunft.* Berlin, 1885. No annotations.

Rousseau, J. J. *Bekenntnisse.* 3. Aufl. 9 Bde. i. 2 gebd. Leipzig, 1870. No annotations.

Schmitz-Dumont, O. *Die Einheit der Naturkräfte und die Deutung ihrer gemeinsamen Formel.* Berlin, 1881. Annotated.

Schmitz-Dumont, O. *Die mathematischen Elemente der Erkenntnistheorie. Grundriss einer Philosophie der mathematischen Wissenschaften.* Berlin, 1878. Contains a few annotations.

Schneider, Georg Heinr. *Der menschliche Wille vom Standpunkte der neueren Entwick-lungstheorien. (Des "Darwinismus").* Berlin, 1882. Contains a few annotations.

Seiling, Max. *Mainländer, ein neuer Messias.* München, 1888. Possibly a few annotations.

Stein, Heinrich v. *Über die Bedeutung des dichterischen Elementes in der Philosophie des Giordano Bruno.* Habilitationsschrift. Halle, 1881. No annotations.

Sully, James. *Le pessimisme (histoire et critique).* Traduit de l'anglais par Alexis Bertrand et Paul Gerard. Paris, 1882. Annotated.

Sully, James. *Les illusions des sens et de l'esprit.* Paris, 1883. Annotated.

Taine, H. *Philosophie der Kunst.* Übersetzung. Paris, 1866. Heavily annotated.

Tyndall, John. *Der Materialismus in England.* Vortrag. Übers. v. Emil Lehmann. Berlin, 1875. No annotations.

Vauvenargues, Marquis Luc de Clapiers. *Oeuvres choisies.* Paris, 1870. One page annotated.

Vauvenargues, Marquis Luc de Clapiers. *Oeuvres choisies. Avec les notes de Voltaire, Morel-let, Suard, Fortia etc. Precedees d'une notice sur la vie et les ouvrages de Vauvenargues par Suard.* Paris, n.d. Annotated.

Voltaire. *Geist aus Voltaires Schriften, sein Leben und Wirken.* Stuttgart, 1837. No annotations.

Voltaire. *Lettres choisies. Précédées d'une notice et accompagnées de notes explicatives sur les faites et sur les personnages du temps par Louis Moland.* 2 Bde. Paris, 1876. Annotated.

TABLE 2   241

Voltaire. *Sämtliche Schriften,* Bd. 1–3. Berlin, 1786. No annotations.

Voltaire. *Zaïre. Trauerspiel.* Übers. v. Malwine Maltzan. Leipzig, Reclam, n.d. No annotations.

Weygold, G. P. *Die Philosophie der Stoa nach ihrem Wesen und ihren Schicksalen.* Leipzig, 1883. No annotations.

Widemann, Paul Heinr. Über die Bedingungen der Übereinstimmung des diskursiven Erkennens mit dem intuitiven. Schloss-Chemnitz, 1876. No annotations.

TABLE 3

Alphabetical Listing of Nietzsche's Philosophical Reading

A dagger (†) signifies that Nietzsche probably did not read the work that year (although there is some reference to it). The year read can only be regarded as approximate. Nietzsche read more philosophic works than those identified here.

Title	Year Read
Alberti, E. *Sokrates. Ein Versuch über ihn nach den Quellen* (Göttingen, 1869)	1869
Alberti, E. *Sokrates. Ein Versuch über ihn nach den Quellen* (Göttingen, 1869)	1873
Anregung für Kunst, Leben und Wissenschaft	1861
Anregung für Kunst, Leben und Wissenschaft	1862
Aristoteles. *Werke* 9 vols. (Stuttgart, 1833–60)	1868
Aristoteles. *De caelo*	1872
Aristoteles. *Politik. Erstes, Zweites und Drittes Buch*, übers. von J. Bernays (Berlin, 1872)	1873
Aristoteles. *Ars rhetorica*, hrsg. von L. Spengel, 2 Bde. (Leipzig, 1867)	1874
Aristoteles. *Politica*, hrsg. von F. Susemihl (Leipzig, 1872)	1874
Aristoteles. *Politik. Erstes, Zweites und Drittes Buch*, übers. von J. Bernays (Berlin, 1872)	1874
Aristoteles. *Ars rhetorica*, hrsg. von L. Spengel, 2 Bde. (Leipzig, 1867)	1875
Aristotle	1875
†Aristotle. *Nicomachian Ethics*	1884
Arnold, A. *Platons Werke einzeln erklärt und in ihrem Zusammenhange dargestellt*, Teil 1, Heft 1 und 2 (Berlin, 1835–36)	1872
Augustin. *Confession der heilige Augustin*	1885
†Augustinus	1878
Bahnsch, F. *Quaestionum de Diogenis Laertii fontibus initia*, Diss.	1869

Bahnsen, J. *Beiträge zur Charakterologie,* 2 vols. (Leipzig, 1867)   1867

Bahnsen, J. *Beiträge zur Charakterologie mit besonderer Berücksichtigung pädagogischer Fragen,* 2 vols. (Leipzig, 1867).   1868

Bahnsen, J. *Zur Philosophie der Geschichte. Eine kritische Besprechung des Hegel-Hartmannschen Evolutionismus aus Schopenhauerschen Principien* (Berlin, 1872)   1871

Bahnsen, J. *Zur Philosophie der Geschichte. Eine kritische Besprechung des Hegel-Hartmannschen Evolutionismus aus Schopenhauerschen Principien* (Berlin, 1872)   1872

†Balche, A. de. *Renan et Schopenhauer: essai de critique* (Odessa, 1870)   1870

Baumann, J. J. *Handbuch der Moral nebst Abriss der Rechtsphilosophie* (Leipzig, 1879)   1880

Baumann, J. J. *Handbuch der Moral nebst Abriss der Rechtsphilosophie* (Leipzig, 1879)   1883

†Bentham, J. *Grundsätze der Zivil- und Kriminalgesetzgebung,* 2 vols., deutsche Bearbeitung von Benecke   1883

Bernays, J. *Die Heraklitischen Briefe: Ein Beitrag zur philosophischen und religionsgeschichtlichen Litteratur* (Berlin, 1869)   1869

Bernays, J. *Grundzüge der verlorenen Abhandlung des Aristoteles über Wirkung der Tragödie* (Breslau, 1858)   1870

Bernays, J. *Grundzüge der verlorenen Abhandlung des Aristoteles über Wirkung der Tragödie* (Breslau, 1857)   1871

†Beyschlag, W. *Lessings Nathan der Weise und das positive Christenthum* (Halle, 1863)   1864

Bilharz, A. *Der heliozentrische Standpunkt der Weltbetrachtung: Grundlegung zu einer wirklichen Naturphilosophie (1879)*   1879

Brandes, G. *Die romantische Schule in Deutschland,* Vol. 2 (1887)   1888

Brochard, V. *Les sceptiques grecs* (Paris, 1887)   1888

Brockhaus. *Rectoratsrede über indische Philologie*   1875

Büchner, L. In *Anregungen für Kunst*   1862

†Büchner, L. *Geist und Körper* (1860)   1873

Buckle, H. T. *Essays*   1881

†Buckle, H. T. *Über Unsterblichkeit*   1882

Burley, W. *De vita philosophorum* (ca. 1486)   1866

Byk, S. A. *Der Hellenismus und der Platonismus* (Leipzig, 1870)   1870

Böhtlingk, O. *Indische Sprüche: Sanskrit und Deutsch,* 3 vols. (1870–73)   1875

Carlyle, T. Unknown biography   1888

Caspari, O. *Die Thomson'sche Hypothese*   1881

Caspari, O. *Zusammenhang der Dinge*   1881

†Chamfort, S. R. N.   1876

Chamfort, S. R. N. *Pensées-Maximes-Anecdotes-Dialogues*   1881

Charron, P. *Drei Bücher von der Weisheit*   1881

TABLE 3   245

†Cicero   1859
Cicero's letters: K. F. Süpfle, *M. Tullii Ciceronis epistolae selectae temporum
ordine compositae: Für den Schulgebrauch mit Einleitung und erklärenden
Anmerkungen versehen*   1860
†Cicero. 2 vols.   1861
Cicero. *pro Arch.*   1861
Cicero. *pro imp. Cu Pomp.*   1861
Ciceron. *Opera,* 1 vol.   1861
Cicero   1862
Cicero. *Offic,* ed. Klotz   1863
Cicero. *Tusculanum*   1863
Cicero. *Brut.*   1864
Cicero. *de off.*   1864
Cicero. *Opera,* 2 vols., Ludwig T.   1864
Cicero. *Scripta qui manserunt omnia,* ed. Klotz   1864
Cicero. *De fin*   1867
Cicero. *Academica*   1870
Cicero. *M. Tulli Ciceronis opera quae supersunt omnia,* hrsg.
     von J. K. Orelli, Bd. 4 (Zürich, 1861)   1870
Cicero. *M. Tulli Ciceronis Opera quae supersunt omnia,* hrsg.
     von J. C. Orelli, Bd. 4 (Zürich, 1861)   1871
Cicero   1874
†Coleridge. *Tischgespräche*   1876
†Coleridge   1883
†Comte, A. *Einleitung in die positive Philosophie* (1880)   1884
Confucius. *Ta-Hio*   1875
Confusius. *Lao-tse tao*   1875
Czermak. Article about Schopenhauer's color theory in *Berichten der
     Wiener Akademie der Wissenschaften*   1870
Democritus   1867
Democritus. *Operum fragmenta,* hrsg. von F. W. A. Mullach (Berlin, 1843)   1869
Democritus. *Operum fragmenta,* hrsg. von F. W. A. Mullach (Berlin, 1843)   1870
Democritus. *Magneni Democritus reviviscens Ticini* (1646)   1873
Democritus. *Operum fragmenta,* hrsg. von F. W. A. Mullach (Berlin, 1843)   1875
Democritus. *Operum fragmenta,* hrsg. von F. W. A. Mullach (Berlin, 1843)   1876
Deussen, P. *De Platonis Sophista,* Diss. (Marburg, 1869)   1869
Deussen, P. *Die Elemente der Metaphysik* (1877)   1877
Diderot   1877
Diogenes Laertius. Hübner, ed., 2 Bde.   1865
Diogenes Laertius   1866
Diogenes Laertius   1867
Draper, J. W. *Geschichte der geistigen Entwickelung Europas* (Leipzig, 1871)   1875

Draper, J. W. *Geschichte der Conflicte zwischen Religion und Wissenschaft*
(1875) Int. wiss. Bibl. XIII   1875

Dronke, G. *Die religiöse und sittlichen Vorstellungen des Aeschylus und
Sophocles* (1861)   1863

Drossbach, M. *Über scheinbaren und wirklichen Ursachen des Geschehens
in der Welt* (Halle, 1884)   1885

Du Bois-Reymond, Emil. *Reden*   1881

Dühring, E. *Cursus der Philosophie als streng wissenschaftlichen
Weltanschaaung und Lebensgestaltung* (Leipzig, 1875)   1875

Dühring, E. *Der Wert des Lebens. Eine philosophische Betrachtung*
(Breslau, 1865)   1875

Dühring, E. *Kritische Geschichte der allgemeinen Prinzipien der Mechanik*
(Berlin, 1873)   1875

Dühring, E. *Kritische Geschichte der Nationalökonomie und des Sozialismus*
(Berlin, 1875)   1875

Dühring, E. *Kritische Geschichte der Philosophie von ihren Anfängen bis
zur Gegenwart* (Berlin, 1873)   1875

Dühring, E. *Kursus der National- und Sozialökonomie, einschliesslich
der Hauptpunkte der Finanzpolitik* (Berlin, 1873)   1875

Dühring, E. *Natürliche Dialektik* (Berlin, 1865)   1875

†Dühring, E.   1878

Dühring, E. *Cursus der Philosophie*   1881

Dühring, E. *Cursus der Philosophie als streng wissenschaftlicher
Weltanschauung und Lebensgestaltung* (Leipzig, 1875)   1883

Dühring, E. *Sache, Leben und Feinde: Als Hauptwerk und Schlüssel zu
seinensämtlichen Schriften* (1882)   1884

Dühring, E. *Sache, Leben und Feinde. Als Hauptwerk und Schlüssel zu
seinen sämtlichen Schriften* (Karlsruhe and Leipzig, 1882)   1885

Dühring, E. *Cursus der Philosophie als streng wissenschaftliche
Weltanschauung und Lebensgestaltung* (Leipzig, 1875)   1885

Dumont, E. *Der Fortschritt im Lichte der Lehren Schopenhauers
und Darwins* (1876)   1878

†Eckart, Meister, and Mystiker   1883

Emerson, R. W. *Die Führung des Lebens* (1862)   1862

Emerson, R. W. *Versuche* (1858)   1862

Emerson, R. W.   1863

Emerson, R. W. *Versuche* (1858)   1863

Emerson, R. W. *Versuche*   1866

Emerson, R. W. *Versuche* (1858)   1868

Emerson, R. W.   1874

Emerson, R. W. *Versuche*   1874

Emerson, R. W. *Neue Essays,* "Letters and Social Aims," Übers.
u. Einl. v. Julian Schmidt (Stuttgart, 1876)   1876

TABLE 3   247

Emerson, R. W. Unidentified work. Probably two of *Versuche,* *Die Führung des Lebens,* and *Über Goethe and Shakespeare*	1876
Emerson, R. W.	1878
Emerson, R. W. *Über Goethe und Shakespeare* (Hannover, 1857)	1878
Emerson, R. W. *Versuche*	1878
Emerson, R. W. *Versuche*	1880
Emerson, R. W.	1881
Emerson, R. W. *Versuche* (1858)	1881
Emerson, R. W. *Versuche*	1882
Emerson, R. W. ?	1883
Emerson, R. W. *Versuche*	1883
Emerson, R. W. "Historic Notes of Life and Letters in Massachusettes," *The Atlantic Monthly* (October 1883)	1884
Emerson, R. W. *Versuche* (Hannover, 1858)	1884
Emerson, R. W. ?	1885
Empedokles. *Carminum reliquiae,* hrsg. von S. Karsten (Amsterdam, 1838)	1872
Engelhardt. *Das Christenthum Justin*	1880
Epictetus. *Handbuch*	1880
†Ercole, P. d. *Notizia degli scritti e del pensiere filosofico di Pietro Ceretti,* *accompagnata da un cenno autobiografico del medesimo, intitolato* *"La mia celebrita"* (Turin, 1886)	1888
Espinas, A. *Die thierische Gesellschaften* (Braunschweig, 1879)	1883
Espinas, A. *Die thierischen Gesellschaften* (Braunschweig, 1879)	1880
†Fechner, G. Th. *Die physikalische und philosophische Atomlehre,* 2nd ed. (Leipzig, 1864)	1882
†Feuerbach, L. *Das Wesen des Christenthums.*	1861
†Feuerbach, L. *Gedanken über Tod und Unsterblichkeit*	1861
Feuerbach, L. *Das Wesen des Christenthums*	1862
Fick, A. *Ursache und Wirkung*	1881
Fischer, Kuno. *Lessings Nathan der Weise* (Stuttgart, 1864)	1864
Fischer, Kuno. *Immanuel Kant*	1867
Fischer, Kuno. *Immanuel Kant, Entwicklungsgeschichte und System* *der kritischen Philosophie,* 2 vols. (Mannheim, 1860)	1868
Fischer, Kuno	1872
Fischer, Kuno. *Geschichte der neuern Philosophie I.2: Descartes Schule,* *Geulinx, Malebrache, B. Spinoza* (Heidelberg, 1865)	1881
Fischer, Kuno. *Immanuel Kant, Entwicklungsgeschichte und System der* *kritischen Philosophie,* 2 vols. (Mannheim, 1860)	1887
Fischer, Kuno. *Geschichte der neuern Philosophie I.2: Descartes Schule,* *Geulinx, Malebrache, B. Spinoza* (Heidelberg, 1865)	1887
Fontenelle, B. *Dialogues des morts* (1876)	1879
Fragmenta philosophorum Graecorum, hrsg. von A. Mullach, Bd. I und 2 (Paris, 1860–67)	1872

Frauenstädt, J. *Schopenhauer [...]*	1873
Fuchs, Carl. Articles in *Musikal. Wochenblatt.*	1874
Fuchs, Carl. Unpublished notes and essays	1875
Gassendus, P. *De vita et moribus Epicuri* (1656)	1866
Grillparzer, F. Penultimate vol. of *Gesammtausgabe*, about aesthetics	1872
Grote, G. *Geschichte Griechenlands*, Vol. 2.	1865
Grote, G. *Geschichte Griechenlands*, 6 vols. (Leipzig, 1850–56)	1871
Grote, G. *Plato*	1875
†Gury. *Compendium theologiae Moralis Ratisbonae* (1862)	1887
Guyau, J. M. *Esquisse d'une morale sans obligation ni sanction* (Paris, 1885)	1884
Guyau, J. M. *Esquisse d'une morale sans obligation ni sanction* (Paris, 1885)	1884
Guyau, J. M. *Esquisse d'une moral sans obligation ni sanction* (Paris, 1885)	1885
Guyau, J. M. *L'irréligion de l'avenir* (Paris, 1887)	1887
†Gwinner. *Schopenhauer-biography*	1878
Hamann, J. G. *Schriften und Briefe*, erläutert und hrsg. von M. Petri, Bd. 1 (Hannover, 1872)	1873
Hartmann, E. v. *Philosophie des Unbewussten* (1869)	1869
Hartmann, E. v. *Philosophie des Unbewussten* (1869)	1870
Hartmann, E. v. *Philosophie des Unbewussten* (Berlin, 1872)	1873
Hartmann, E. v. *Romeo und Julia*	1874
Hartmann, E. v. ?	1875
Hartmann, E. v. *Phänomenologie des sittlichen Bewusstseins: Prologomena zu jeder künftigen Ethik* (1879)	1879
†Hartmann, E. v. *Gesammelte Studien und Aufsätze gemeinverständlichen Inhalts* (Berlin, Naumburg, 1876)	1883
Hartmann, E. v. *Phänomenologie des sittlichen Bewusstseins. Prolegomena zu jeder künftigen Ethik* (Berlin, 1879)	1883
†Hartmann, E. v. *Phänomenologie des sittlichen Bewusstseins, Prolegomena zu jeder künftigen Ethik* (Berlin, 1879)	1885
Hartmann, E. *Philosophie des Unbewußten*	1888
†Hausrath, A. *D. F. Strauss und die Theologie seiner Zeit* (1876–78)	1874
†Haym, R. *Arthur Schopenhauer* (Berlin, 1864)	1865
Haym, R. *Arthur Schopenhauer* (Berlin, 1864)	1866
Hegel, G. W. F. ?	1865
Hegel, G. W. F. *Vorlesungen über die Philosophie der Geschichte*	1873
Heinze, Max. Listed as "Logos"; probably refers to *Die Lehre vom Logos in der griechischen Philosophie*. [Oldenburg, 1872]	1874
Hercules. (possibly F. Buecheler, *Academicorum philosophorum index Herculanensis*)	1874
†Herder, J. G. *Der Cid*	1857
†Herder, J. G. *Der Cid*	1858
Herder, J. G. *Cid, Der*	1861

Table 3   249

Herder, J. G. *Der Cid*	1862
Herder, J. G. *Cid*	1863
Herder, J. G.	1864
Hettner, H. *Literaturgeschichte des achtzehnten Jahrhunderts. Part II: Geschichte der französischen Literatur im XVIII Jahrhundert*	1863
Hettners, H. *Literaturgeschichte des 18. Jahrh.: Part II: Geschichte der französischen Literatur im 18. Jahrh.*	1863
Hillebrand, K. "Schopenhauer und das deutsche Publikum," in *Zeiten, Völker und Menschen,* Vol. 2 (Berlin, 1875)	1875
Hillebrand, K. *Zeiten, Völker und Menschen,* 2 vols. (Berlin, 1874–75)	1875
Hobbes, T.	1864
Hume, D. *Gespräche über natürliche Religion* (Leipzig, 1781)	1873
Höffding, H. *Psychologie in Umrissen* (1887)	1887
Hölderlin, F. *Kurze Biographie und Proben aus seinen Werken,* 2 booklets from Verlag der modernen Klassiker	1861
Hölderlin, F. *Sokrates und Alkibiades, Der Rhein*	1873
Joly, H. *Psychologie des grands hommes* (Paris, 1883)	1887
Kant, I. *Kritik der Urtheilskraft*	1868
Kant, I. *Kritik der reinen Vernunft*	1872
†Kant, I.	1884
†Kant, I. *Kritik der reinen Vernunft*	1885
Karsten, H. T. *Commentatio critica de Platonis quae feruntur epistolis praecipue tertia septima et octava* (Utrecht, 1864)	1871
Karsten, H. T. *Commentatio critica de Platonis quae feruntur epistolis praecipue tertia septima et octava* (Utrecht, 1864)	1872
Kiy, V. *Der Pessimismus und die Ethik Schopenhauers* (Berlin, 1866)	1866
Kohl, O. *I. Kants Ansicht von der Willenfreiheit,* Diss. (Leipzig, 1868)	1868
Kosmos (Journal)	1881
Krohn, A. *Sokrates und Xenophon* (Halle, 1875)	1876
Krohn, A. *Studien zur sokratisch-platonischen Literatur,* Bd. 1 (Halle, 1876)	1876
Labruyère, J. *Die Charactere Theophrastos*	1880
Labruyère, J. 1876	1876
Lange, F. A. *Geschichte des Materialismus und Kritik seiner Bedeutung für die Gegenwart* (1866)	1866
Lange, F. A. *Geschichte des Materialismus und Kritik seiner Bedeutung in der Gegenwart* (Iserlohn, 1866)	1868
Lange, F. A. *Geschichte des Materialismus* (1866)	1873
Lange, F. A. *Geschichte des Materialismus* (1866)	1881
Lange, A. F. *Geschichte des Materialismus*	1883
Lange, F. A. *Geschichte des Materialismus* (1882)	1884
Lange, F. A. *Geschichte des Materialismus*	1885
Lange, F. A. *Geschichte des Materialismus* (1887)	1887–88

†Larochefoucauld, F. de. *Maxime und Reflexionen* (Leipzig, 1875)   1883
†Larochefoucauld, F. de.   1877
Larochefoucauld, F. de. *Réflexions, sentences et maximes morales.* (Paris, n.d.)   1876
Lecky, W. E. H. *Geschichte des Ursprungs und Einflusses der Aufklärung
   in Europa* (Leipzig, 1873)   1881
Lecky, W. E. H. *Geschichte des Ursprungs und Einflusses der Aufklärung
   in Europa*, 2 vols. (Leipzig and Heidelberg, 1873)   1883
Lecky, W. E. H. *Sittengeschichte Europas*   1881
Lehrs, C. *Populäre Aufsätze aus dem Alterthum vorzugsweise zur Ethik
   und Religion der Griechen* (Leipzig, 1856)   1871
Lehrs, C. *Populäre Aufsätze aus dem Alterthum vorzugsweise zur Ethik
   und Religion der Griechen* (Leipzig, 1856)   1878
Leibniz, G. W.   1885
Lessing, G. E. *Laokoon: oder über die Grenzen der Malerei und Poesie* (1766)   1865
Lessing, G. E. *Nathan der Weise*   1864
Lewes, G. H. *Geschichte der Philosophie von Thales bis Comte*, Bd. 1
   (Berlin, 1871)   1871
Lewes, G. H. *Geschichte der Philosophie von Thales bis Comte*, Bd. 1
   (Berlin, 1871)   1875
Lichtenberg, G. C. *Vermischte Schriften* (Göttingen, 1867)   1873
Lichtenberg, G. C. *Einige Lebensumstände von Capt. James Cook,
   grösstentheils aus schriftlichen Nachrichten einiger seiner Bekannten
   gezogen* in *Vermischte Schriften*   1875
Lichtenberg, G. C. *Vermischte Schriften*   1876
†Liebmann, O. *Kant und die Epigonen* (1865)   1867
Liebmann, O. "Über subjective, objective und absolute Zeit," in *Phil.
   Monadshefte VII* (1871–72)   1872
Liebmann, O. *Kant und die Epigonen*   1881
Liebmann, O. *Zur Analysis der Wirklichkeit* (Strassburg, 1880)   1881
Liebmann, O. *Gedanken und Tatsachen*, Vol. 1 (Strassburg, 1882)   1887
Littré, E. *La science au point de vue philosophique* (Paris, 1876)   1880
Locke, J. *Einige Gedanken über Erziehung* (Leipzig, n.d.)   1878
Lotze, H.   1872
Lucretius. *Das Wesen der Dinge.* Metrisch übers. v. Gustaf Bossart-Oerden
   (Berlin, 1865)   1868
†Lucretius. *De rerum naturae*   1886
Lüdemann, H. *Die Anthropologie des Apostels Paulus und ihre Stellung
   innerhalb seiner Heilslehre* (Kiel, 1872)   1880
Machiavelli. *Il principe*   1862
†Machiavelli. Probably *The Prince* in Italian   1863
Maignani cursus philosophicus (1652)   1873
Mainländer, P. *Philosophie der Erlösung* (Berlin, 1876)   1876

TABLE 3   251

Mainländer, P. *Die Philosophie der Erlösung,* Vol. 1, 2nd ed. (Berlin, 1879)   1883
†Mainländer, P. *Die Philosophie der Erlösung,* Vol. 1, 2 vols. (1876, 1886)   1885
Marcus Aurelius.   1857
Marcus Aurelius Antoninus. *Unterhaltungen mit sich selbst.* Übers.
und hrsg. von J. M. Schultz (Schleswig, 1799)   1872
Marcus Antoninus (Marcus Aurelius)   1873
†Marcus Aurelius   1881
†Marcus Aurelius. *Selbstgespräche*   1884
Martensen, H. L. *Ethik*   1880
Martha, B. C. *Les Moralistes sous l'empire romain, philosophes et poètes*   1879
Meiners, Ch. *Geschichte des Ursprungs, Fortgangs und Verfalls der*
Wissenschaften in Griechenland und Rom (Lemgo, 1781)   1867
Meiners, Ch. *Geschichte des Ursprungs, Fortgangs und Verfalls der*
Wissenschaften in Griechenland und Rom (Lemgo, 1781)   1868
Mill, J. S. Different works of (Gast read to N), Summer 1880   1880
Mill, J. S. "Plato" in vol. 12 (Disc. of Grote's *Plato*)   1880
Mill, J. S. *Auguste Comte und Positivismus,* Vol. 9 (Leipzig, 1869–80)   1880
Mill, J. S. *Coleridge* in *Gesammelte Werke,* Vol. 10   1880
Mill, J. S. *August Comte und der Positivismus. Vermischte Schriften*
politischen, philosophieschen und historischen Inhalts, Vol. 9 (Leipzig, 1869)   1887
Mill, J. S. *Über Aphorismen*   1887
†Moldenhauer, Th. *Die Axendrehung der Weltkörper* (Berlin, 1871)
or *Das Weltall und seine Entwicklung* (Köln 1882)   1882
Montaigne, M. d. *The Complete Works*   1870
Montaigne, M. d. *Essays*   1875
Montaigne, M. d.   1876
Montaigne, M. d. *Versuche,* 3 vols. (Leipzig, 1753–54)   1878
Montaigne, M. d. *Versuche,* Vol. 1, 3 vols. (1853–54)   1884
†Montaigne, M. d.   1885
Montaigne, M. d. *Essais avec des notes de tous les commentateurs*
(Paris, 1864)   1887
Montesquieu. *Persische Briefe*   1885
†Montesquieu. ?   1887
†Moore, T. *Utopie*   1879
Mullach, E. *Fragm. philos. Graecorum.*   1865
Mullach, E. *Fragmenta philosophorum graecorum*   1868
Müller, E. *Geschichte der Theorie der Kunst bei den Alten,* 2 Bde.
(Breslau, 1834–37)   1869
Novalis   1859
Oncken, W. *Die Staatslehre des Aristoteles in historisch-politischen*
Umrissen. Ein Beitrag zur Geschichte der hellenischen Staatsidee
und zur Einführung in die Aristotelische Politik, Teil 1 (Leipzig, 1870)   1870

Oncken, W. *Die Staatslehre des Aristoteles in historisch-politischen Umrissen.*
Ein Beitrag zur Geschichte der hellenischen Staatsidee und zur Einführung
in die Aristotelische Politik, Teil 1 (Leipzig, 1870)   1871
Oncken, W. *Die Staatslehre des Aristoteles in historisch-politischen Umrissen.*
Ein Beitrag zur Geschichte der hellenischen Staatsidee und zur Einführung
in die Aristotelische Politik, Teil 1 (Leipzig, 1870)   1872
Oncken, W. *Die Staatslehre des Aristoteles in historisch-politischen Umrissen,*
Vol. 1, 2 vols. (Leipzig, 1870)   1875
Oncken, W. *Die Staatslehre des Aristoteles in historisch-politischen Umrissen,*
Vol. 2, 2 vols. (Leipzig, 1875)   1875
Pachnicke, H. *De philosophia Epicuri*   1881
Parmenides. *Carminis reliquiae,* hrsg. von S. Karsten (Amsterdam, 1835)   1872
Pascal, B. *Gedanken Fragmente und Briefe* (Leipzig, 1865)   1878
Pascal, B. *Gedanken, Fragmente und Briefe* (Leipzig, 1865)   1880
Pascal, B. *Gedanken, Fragmente und Briefe* (Leipzig, 1865)   1887
Philosophische Monatshefte, hrsg. von I. Bergmann, 2 (1869)   1870
Philosophische Monatshefte   1881
Plato. *Symposion*   1863
Plato. *Apologie*   1863
Plato. *Eutyphron*   1863
Plato. *Kriton*   1863
Plato. *Platonis dialog. ex recog. Hermanni,* Vol. II.   1863
Plato. *Phaedo*   1864
Plato. *Symposion*   1864
Platon. *Dialogi ex rec. C. F. Hermanni,* in 6 vols. N asks for heft or
vol. 1 containing *Euthyphro, Apologia Socratis, Crito,* and *Phaedo*   1864
Plato. *Apologie*   1869
Plato. *Phaedo*   1869
Plato. *Protagoras*   1869
Plato   1869
Plato. *Opera omnia,* hrsg. von G. Stallbaum, Bd. 6 (Gotha and Erfurt,
1827–60)   1870
Plato. *Platonis dialogi secundum Trasylli tetralogias dispositi,* hrsg.
von K. F. Hermann, Bd. 3 (Leipzig, 1851–53)   1870
Plato. *Platonis philosophi quae extant Graece,* aus der Ausgabe von H.
Stephan mit Interpretationen von M. Ficino, Bd. 3 (Biponto, 1781–87)   1870
Plato. *The Republic* and *Laws*   1870
Plato. *Phaedon*   1870
Plato   1871
Plato. *Sämmtliche Werke,* übersetzt von H. Müller, mit Einleitungen
von K. Steinhart, 8 Bde. (Leipzig, 1850–66)   1871
Platon. *Phaedon*   1871

TABLE 3   253

Plato. *Sämmtliche Werke,* übersetzt von H. Müller, mit Einleitungen
    von K. Steinhart, 8 Bde. (Leipzig, 1850–66)   1872

Plato. *Protagoras*   1872

Plato. *Opera omnia,* hrsg. von G. Stallbaum, Bd. 2 (Gotha und Erfurt,
    1827–60)   1873

Plato. *Sämmtliche Werke,* übersetzt von H. Müller, mit Einleitungen
    von K. Steinhart, Bd. 1, 3, 6, 7 (Leipzig, 1850–66)   1873

Plato. *Sämmtliche Werke,* übersetzt von H. Müller, mit Einleitungen
    von K. Steinhart, Bd. 1, 3, 6, 7 (Leipzig, 1850–66)   1874

Plato. Many booklets.   1875

†Plato. Platoniis *Opera*   1875

†Plato. *Symposium* Rettig.   1875

Plato. Platonis *Phaedo* rec. Wohlrab   1876

Plato. *Gesetze*   1877

Plato. *Sämmtliche Werke,* übersetzt von H. Müller, mit Einleitungen
    von K. Steinhart, Bd. 8 (Leipzig, 1850–66)   1878

Plato. *Verteidigungsrede des Sokrates* (1875)   1878

†Plato. *Theages*   1884

Plutarch. *Moralia,* 5 vols.   1866

Plutarcos   1874

Porphyrius. *De philosophia ex oraculis haurienda librorum reliquiae,* hrsg.
    von G. Wolff (Berlin, 1856)   1871

Prantl, K. *Übersicht der römisch-griechischen Philosophie* (Stuttgart, 1854)   1867

†Pre-Platonic philosophers   1869

Pre-Platonic philosophers   1872

Pre-Socratics   1872

Proctor, R. A. *Unser Standpunkt im Weltall* (Heilbronn, 1877)   1881

Radenhausen, J. *Isis: Der Mensch und die Welt,* 4 vols. (Hamburg, 1863).
    Each volume of between 500 and 700 pages   1868

Rée, P. *Psychologische Beobachtungen* (Berlin, 1875)   1875

Rée, P. *Der Ursprung der moralischen Empfindungen* (1877)   1876

†Rée, P.   1877

Rée, P. Early versions of *Entstehung des Gewissens*   1879

Rée, P. *Der Ursprung der moralischen Empfindungen* (1877)   1883

†Rée, P. *Der Ursprung der moralischen Empfindungen* (Chemnitz, 1877)   1885

Rée, P. *Entstehung des Gewissens* (1885)   1885

†Rée, P. *Ursprung der moralischen Empfindungen* (Chemnitz, 1877)   1886

Reinkens, J. H. *Aristoteles über Kunst, besonders über Tragödie. Exegetische
    und kritische Untersuchungen* (Wien, 1870)   1871

†Renan, E. *Paulus*   1873

Renan, E. *Philosophische Dialoge und Fragmente* (1877)   1878

Renan, E.   1879

†Renan, E.	1885
†Reuter, H. *Augustinische Studien* (Gotha, 1887)	1887
Rivarol. *Fontenelle*	1879
Roberty, E. d. *L'ancienne et la nouvelle philosophie. Essai sur les lois générales du développement de la philosophie* (Paris, 1887)	1888
Rohde, E. Essay about Pythagoras	1871
Rolph, W. H. *Biologische Probleme zugleich als Versuch zur Entwicklung einer rationellen Ethik* (Leipzig, 1884)	1884
Rolph, W. H. *Biologische Probleme zugleich als Versuch zur Entwicklung einer rationellen Ethik* (Leipzig, 1884)	1885
Romundt, H. Grammatisch-philosophische dissertation about "logos"	1869
Romundt, H. *Die menschliche Erkenntnis und das Wesen der Dinge* (1872)	1872
Romundt, H. *Christenthum und Vernunft*	1881
Rosenkranz. *Geschichte der Kantschen Philosophie*	1868
Roth, E. *Geschichte unserer abendländischen Philosophie*, Bd. 2 (Mannheim, 1858)	1869
Rousseau. *Emil*	1862
Sainte-Beuve. *Port-Royal* (Paris, 1840–48)	1880
Sallust und Ciceronis Opera, I, Vol. 1	1861
Schaarschmidt, C. *Die Sammlung der Platonischen Schriften zur Scheidung der echten von unechten untersucht* (Bonn, 1866)	1871
Schaarschmidt, C. *Die Sammlung der Platonischen Schriften zur Scheidung der echten von den unechten untersucht* (Bonn, 1866)	1872
Schiller, F. *Aesthetische Erziehung*	1862
Schiller, F. *Sämtliche Werke,* 10 vols. (1844)	1871
Schiller, F. *Über naive und sentimentalische Dichtung*	1871
Schiller, F. *Über naive und sentimentalische Dichtung*	1873
Schiller, F. *Werke,* "Was heisst und zu welchen End studiert man Universalgeschichte"	1873
Schlegel, A. W. v. *Kritische Schriften 2* (1828)	1864
Schlegel, A. W. v. *Vorlesungen über dramatische Kunst und Literatur*	1869
Schleiermacher, F. "Über das Verzeichniß der Schriften des Demokritus bei Diogenes Laertius" (1835)	1868
Schmidt, L. *Die Ethik der alten Griechen,* 2 vols. (Berlin, 1882)	1883
Schopenhauer, A. *Die Welt als Wille und Vorstellung*	1865
†Schopenhauer, A. *Parerga und Paralipomena*	1865
†Schopenhauer, A. *Die beiden Grundprobleme der Ethik,* 2nd ed. 1860	1865
†Schopenhauer, A. *Über den Willen der Natur,* 2nd ed. (Frankfurt, 1854)	1865
†Schopenhauer, A. *Über die vierfache Wurzel des Satzes von zureichenden Grunde,* 3rd ed. (Leipzig, 1864)	1865
Schopenhauer, A.	1866
Schopenhauer, A. *Parerga und Paralipomena*	1867

TABLE 3   255

Schopenhauer, A. *Parerga und Paralipomena*   1868
Schopenhauer, A. *Welt als Wille* and *Parerga*   1868
Schopenhauer, A. *Nachschriftlicher Nachlaß* (1844)   1869
Schopenhauer, A. *Parerga*, Vol. 2   1871
Schopenhauer, A.   1872
Schopenhauer, A. *Die Welt als Wille und Vorstellung*   1872
Schopenhauer, A. *Parerga*, Vol. 2   1873
Schopenhauer, A. *Parerga*, Vol. 2   1874
Schopenhauer, A. *Die Welt als Wille und Vorstellung*   1875
Schopenhauer, A. *Parerga*, Vol. 1   1875
Schopenhauer, A. *Sämtliche Werke*, Frauenstädt, 6 vols. (Leipzig, 1873–74) 1875
Schopenhauer, A. *Parerga*, Vol. 2   1878
Schopenhauer, A.   1884
†Schopenhauer, A. *Die Welt als Wille und Vorstellung, Band 2*   1884
Schopenhauer, A. *Preisschrift über die Grundlage der Moral*   1884
Schopenhauer, A. *Parerga*, Vol. 2   1887
Schopenhauer, A., *Welt2, Welt1, Parerga*, etc.   1887
Schopenhauer, A. *Die Welt als Wille und Vorstellung* II   1888
Seneca. *Epistulae morales*   1867
Senfft, Wolfgang. *Indischer Sprüche*, 3 vols.   1875
Siebenlist. *Schopenhauers Phil. Tragödie* 1880   1880
Simplicius. *Kommentar zu Epiktetos Handbuch* (Wien, 1867)   1887
†Smiles, S. ?   1873
Spencer, H. *Einleitung in das Studium der Sociologie*, Vol. 1 (1875)
    Int. wiss. Bibl. XIV   1875
Spencer, H. *Einleitung in das Studium der Sociologie*, Vol. 2 (1875)
    Int. wiss. Bibl. XV   1875
Spencer, H. *Die Tatsachen der Ethik* (Stuttgart, 1879)   1879
Spencer, H. *Die Thatsachen der Ethik* (Stuttgart, 1879)   1880
Spencer, H. *Die Thatsachen der Ethik* (Stuttgart, 1879)   1881
Spencer, H. *Die Thatsachen der Ethik* (Stuttgart, 1879)   1883
Spencer, H. *Einleitung in das Studium der Sociologie*, Vol. 2 (Leipzig, 1875) 1883
†Spencer, H. *Die Thatsachen der Ethik* (Stuttgart, 1879)   1885
Spengel, L. *Synagogè teknon, sive artium scriptores ab initiis usque ad
    editos Aristotelis de rhetorica libros* (Stuttgart, 1828)   1870
Spinoza. *Ethica*   1875
Spinoza. *Ethica*   1876
Spir, A. *Forschung nach der Gewissheit in der Erkenntnis der
    Wirklichkeit* (Leipzig, 1869)   1872
Spir, A. *Denken und Wirklichkeit*, Vol. 1 (Leipzig, 1873)   1873
Spir, A. *Denken und Wirklichkeit. Versuch einer Erneuerung der kritischen
    Philosophie*, 2 vols. (Leipzig, 1873)   1874

Spir, A. *Denken und Wirklichkeit: Versuch einer Erneuerung der kritischen*
    Philosophie, 2 vols., 2nd ed. (1877)   1877

Spir, A. *Denken und Wirklichkeit* (1877)   1881

Spir, A. *Denken und Wirklichkeit. Versuch einer Erneuerung der kritischen*
    Philosophie, 2 vols. (Leipzig, 1877)   1885

†Spir, A. *Denken und Wirklichkeit. Versuch einer Erneuerung der kritischen*
    Philosphie (Leipzig, 1877)   1888

Staphanus Byantinus. *Ethicorum quae supersunt,* hrsg. von A. Meineck,
    Bd. 1 (Berlin, 1849)   1875

Stein, H. v. *Sieben Bücher zur Geschichte des Platonismus. Untersuchungen*
    über das System des Plato und sein Verhältnis zur späten Theologie
    und Philosophie, Teil I und 2 (Göttingen, 1862)   1871

Stein, H. v. *Sieben Bücher zur Geschichte des Platonismus. Untersuchungen*
    über das System des Plato und sein Verhältnis zur späten Theologie
    und Philosophie, Teil 1 und 2 (Göttingen, 1862)   1872

Stein, H. v. *Über die Bedeutung des dichterisches Elements in der Philosophie*
    des Giordano Bruno, Habilitationschrift, 1881   1884

Stein, H. v. *Äesthetik*   1887

Steinhart, C. *Platon's Leben* (Leipzig, 1873) [Plato, *Sämmtliche Werke,*
    übers. von H. Müller, Bd. 9]   1873

Steinhart, C. *Platon's Leben* (Leipzig, 1873) [Plato, *Sämmtliche Werke,*
    übers. von H. Müller, Bd. 9]   1874

Steinhart, C. *Platon's Leben* (Leipzig, 1873) [Plato, *Sämmtliche Werke,*
    übers. von H. Müller, Bd. 9]   1876

Steinhart, C. *Platon's Leben* (Leipzig, 1873) [Plato, *Sämmtliche Werke,*
    übers. von H. Müller, Bd. 9]   1878

Stendhal   1876

Strauss, D. F. *Lessings Nathan der Weise* (Berlin, 1865)   1864

Strauss, D. F. *Das Leben Jesu*   1865

Strauss, D. F. *Die Halben und die Ganzen* (1865)   1865

Strauss, D. F. *Das Leben Jesu*   1868

Strauss, D. F. *Der alte und der neue Glaube* (1872)   1872

Strauss, D. F. *Der alte und der neue Glaube* (1872)   1873

Strauss, D. F. *Der alte und der neue Glaube: mit Ein Nachwort als Vorwort*
    zu den neuen Auflagen meiner Schrift (Bonn, 1873)   1873

Strauss, D. F. *Der alte und der neue Glaube*   1874

Strauss, D. F. *Der alte und der neue Glaube* (Leipzig, 1872)   1876

Susemihl, F. *Die genetische Entwicklung der Platonischen Philosophie,*
    einleitend dargestellt, Teil und 2 (Leipzig, 1855–60)   1871

Susemihl, F. *Die genetische Entwicklung der Platonischen Philosophie,*
    einleitend dargestellt, Teil 1 und 2 (Leipzig, 1855–60)   1872

Sutta Nipáta (English translation)   1875

TABLE 3   257

†Swedenborg	1883
Teichmüller, G. *Aristotelische Forschung,* Vol. 2	1869
Teichmüller, G. *Aristotelische Forschungen,* Vol. 1 (Halle, 1867)	1870
Teichmüller, G. *Über die Reihenfolge der platonischen Dialoge* (1879)	1879
Teichmüller, G. ?	1883
Teichmüller, G. II ?	1883
Teichmüller, G. *Die wirkliche und die scheinbare Welt* (Breslau, 1882)	1883
Teichmüller, G. *Neue Studien zur Geschichte der Begriffe,* 3 vols., Vol. 3: *Die praktische Vernunft Aristoteles* (Dorpat, 1876–79)	1883
†Teichmüller, G. *Die wirkliche und die scheinbare Welt* (1882)	1884
†Teichmüller, G. Two books.	1885
Teichmüller, G. *Die wirkliche und die scheinbare Welt: Neue Grundlegung der Metaphysik* (Breslav, 1882)	1885
†Teichmüller, G. *Historia Philosophiae. Graecae et Ronmanae ex fontium locis contexta* (1875)	1887
†Teichmüller, G. *Die wirkliche und die scheinbare Welt. Neue Grundlegung der Metaphysik* (Breslav, 1882)	1888
Tripitaka der Buddhisten	1875
Ueberweg, F. *Grundriss der Geschichte der Philosophie von Thales bis auf die Gegenwart,* 3 vols. (Berlin, 1866–67), Vol. 1: *Das Altertum*	1865
Ueberweg, F., *Grundriß der Geschichte der Philosophie,* 3 vols., (Berlin, 1866–67)	1868
Ueberweg, F. *Grundriss der Geschichte der Philosophie von Thales bis auf die Gegenwart,* Vol. 3. (Berlin, 1867)	1873
†Unidentified book	1861
Unidentified book(s) about materialism (?) or refers to his reading about materialism in the journal *Anregungen für Kunst, Leben und Wissenschaft* in 1861 and 1862.	1862
University course: O. Jahn, "Platos Symposion"	1864–65
University course: C. Schaarschmidt, "Allgemeine Geschichte der Philosophie"	1864–65
University course: C. Schaarschmidt, "Platos Leben und Lehre"	1864–65
Vauvenargues	1876
Villari, P. *Machiavelli* (Rudolstadt, 1877–82)	1879
Vischer, F. T. *Ästhetik oder Wissenschaft des Schönen,* Bd. 4 (Teil 3, Abschnitt 2) (Leipzig, 1846)	1870
Vogt, J. G. *Die Kraft, Eine real-monistische Weltanschauung,* Vol. 1 (Leipzig, 1878)	1881
Vogt, J. G. *Die Kraft: Eine real-monistische Weltanschauung* (1878)	1883
Voigt, G. *Die Wiederbelebung des classischen Alterthums oder das erste Jahrhundert des Humanismus* (Berlin, 1859)	1870

Index

THOMAS H. BROBJER is an associate professor in the Department of the History of Science and Ideas at Uppsala University, Sweden. He has previously published *Nietzsche's Ethics of Character: A Study of Nietzsche's Ethics and Its Place in the History of Moral Thinking* (Uppsala: Uppsala University Press, 1995) and *Nietzsche and the "English": British and American Influences on Nietzsche* (Amherst, NY: Prometheus, 2007). Together with Gregory Moore, Brobjer edited *Nietzsche and Science* (Aldershot, UK: Ashgate, 2004). His essays have appeared in numerous journals, including *International Studies in Philosophy, Nietzsche-Studien,* and the *Journal of the History of Ideas,* and in many books of collected essays.

The University of Illinois Press
is a founding member of the
Association of American University Presses.

Composed in 10.5/13 Adobe Garamond
with Adobe Garamond display
by BookComp, Inc.
Manufactured by Sheridan Books, Inc.

University of Illinois Press
1325 South Oak Street
Champaign, IL 61820-6903
www.press.uillinois.edu